Neville Chamberlain and British Rearmament

Neville Chamberlain

Neville Chamberlain and British Rearmament

Pride, Prejudice, and Politics

John Ruggiero

Contributions to the Study of World History, Number 71

GREENWOOD PRESS
Westport, Connecticut • London

Library of Congress Cataloging-in-Publication Data

Ruggiero, John, 1933–
    Neville Chamberlain and British rearmament : pride, prejudice, and
politics / John Ruggiero.
       p. cm.—(Contributions to the study of world history, ISSN
0885–9159 ; no. 71)
    Includes bibliographical references and index.
    ISBN 0–313–31050–5 (alk. paper)
    1. Chamberlain, Neville, 1869–1940—Views on military policy.
2. Great Britain—Military policy—History—20th century. 3. Great
Britain—Politics and governnment—1936–1945. 4. Great Britain—
Defenses—History—20th century. 5. World War, 1939–1945—Causes.
I. Title. II. Series.
DA585.C5R62 1999
941.084′092—dc21   99–14841

British Library Cataloguing in Publication Data is available.

Library of Congress Catalog Card Number: 99–14841
ISBN: 0–313–31050–5
ISSN: 0885–9159

First published in 1999

Greenwood Press, 88 Post Road West, Westport, CT 06881
An imprint of Greenwood Publishing Group, Inc.
www.greenwood.com

Printed in the United States of America

Copyright Acknowledgments

The author and publisher gratefully acknowledge permission for use of the following material:

Excerpts from *The Chamberlain Papers: Diary and Letters* by Neville Chamberlain. Reprinted by
permission of Special Collections, University of Birmingham Library, Birmingham, UK.

Excerpts from Cabinet Records. Reprinted by permission of Record Office, The National
Archives.

Contents

A photo essay follows Chapter 5.

Acknowledgments

I would like to take this opportunity to thank those who have helped with this endeavor. First, I would like to express my gratitude to Saint Francis College for its generous support in providing me with the time, staff, and technical assistance necessary to bring this book to fruition. Special thanks are owed to my secretaries, Sandra Valeri, Terri Kirby, Alisha Jones and Linda A. Kline for their amazing skills on the word processor and for the patience and good humor with which they put up with my impossible demands.

I would also like to thank Drs. Robert Shay, Keith Eubank, and William Rock for their painstaking efforts and valuable comments in preparing the manuscript. Dr. Sidney Aster was also helpful in refining the title, and in providing general comments on the thesis. Of course, the views expressed are mine alone, and I take full responsibility for them.

I would also like to thank the Special Collections staff at the University of Birmingham for their kind cooperation in accessing the Chamberlain Papers and permitting me to quote from them. Likewise, the staffs at Cambridge University Library and the Public Records Office at Kew are to be commended for the courteous and efficient manner in which they assisted in my seemingly endless search for new materials.

Finally, I would like to acknowledge the unselfish sacrifice of my wife, Theresa, for her unconditional support spanning many years and involving long absences away from home for this project.

Abbreviations

AA	Antiaircraft
ADGB	Air Defense of Great Britain
AEU	Amalgamated Engineering Union
ARP	Air Raid Precautions
BBC	British Broadcasting Company
CAB	Cabinet Records
CID	Committee for Imperial Defense
COS	Chiefs of Staff
CP	Cabinet Paper
DCM	Ministerial Committee on Disarmament
DP(P)	Defense Plans (Policy) Committee
DPR	Defense Policy and Requirements Committee
DRC	Defense Requirements Committee
EEF	Engineering Employers' Federation
EEU	Electrical Employees Union
FBI	Federation of Business Industries
FPC	Foreign Policy Committee
GCTUC	General Council of the Trades Union Congress
MP	Member of Parliament
NDC	National Defense Contribution
NEC	National Executive Council
PLP	Parliamentary Labor Party
PSOC	Principal Supply Officers' Committee
RA	Regular Army
SBAC	Society of British Aircraft Constructors
TA	Territorial Army
TUC	Trades Union Congress

Chapter 1

Introduction

"Chamberlain" and "appeasement" have become the twin symbols of a failed diplomacy, signifying moral cowardice and national dishonor. To this day the Munich syndrome continues to haunt statesmen with its perceived lessons. One of its lessons is to recognize the importance of a strong defense program to give effect to diplomatic initiatives. Or, as Ambassador William Bullitt so aptly explained to President Roosevelt, "If you have enough planes, you do not have to go to Munich."

As early as 1933 the Foreign Office warned that German rearmament was of such magnitude that by 1938 it would be "an unequaled instrument of force with which to support its policy."[1] Consequently, the British Government resolved to repair its worst deficiencies in arms by 1939. Yet in 1936, Austen Chamberlain was forced to rise in the House of Commons to question the Government's rearmament program, which he characterized as "an unexplained mystery" that "makes us anxious" that the country should be subjected "to more dangerous circumstances that might well be fatal."[2] Two years later, as General Edmund Ironside was about to assume his duties as Chief of the Imperial General Staff, he complained, "The paper on rearmament . . . is the most appalling reading. How we can have come to this state is beyond believing. . . . No foreign nation would believe it."[3] And in 1939, President Roosevelt expressed his disbelief to a British journalist following the German march into Prague and the Polish guarantee that the British Government did not have conscription, or "why it hadn't built more bombers, or at least say it was building more bombers." Or why it did not "leak out more stories about the tremendous preparations on foot to bomb Germany."[4] An official in the U.S. State Department, George Messersmith, was even more blunt in his criticism of Britain's policy. He charged that "the stupidities being committed are so great that they are more than criminal," and he accused Neville Chamberlain of "criminal participation in Hitler's aggressive plans."[5]

The purpose of this book is to explain why, after five years of warning and four years of defensive preparations, the British Government abandoned centuries of its traditional foreign policy, but found itself virtually unprepared to defend its vital interests, and was forced time and again to capitulate to Hitler's blackmail tactics. It was not until 1939 that conscription and a Ministry of Supply were adopted (and then only on a limited basis), both too late to prevent Germany's inexorable drive to achieve hegemony on the European continent or even to assure Britain's independence. That Great Britain narrowly escaped total disaster on the beaches of Dunkirk and in the Battle of Britain, owed more to Providence than to Britain's military preparations and foreign policy.

As the chief architect of British policy, Neville Chamberlain has come under intense scrutiny by historians. Initially portrayed as the naive dupe of the dictators, he is now seen in more sympathetic, revisionist terms, as the embattled statesman who did his best to play out the bad hand dealt to him.[6] Revisionists have argued that his policy of appeasement was mandated by the lack of resources needed to deal with the potential threat to the Empire from three different quarters. Relying primarily on Cabinet papers and official Government documents released in 1967, the revisionists have succumbed to the same arguments that persuaded the Cabinet to adopt its policy in the first place. Using the same data as the Cabinet ministers invariably led the revisionists to the same conclusions, and though they did not necessarily accept those conclusions, they were nevertheless impressed with the logic of appeasement. Without adequate sources of finance, manpower, industrial capacity, and skilled labor, rearmament policy had to be tailored to the cloth. Thus, British Cabinet ministers were now perceived in more sympathetic terms and not in the sinister light of Cato's indictment nor under the cloud of naked appeasement studies.[7]

Another problem with the revisionists is their failure to understand the precise nature of Chamberlain's role in the National Government. Paul Kennedy, for example, criticizes the Chiefs of Staff for the "excessively pessimistic nature of their advice" to the politicians during the Czech crisis, but then concedes that it was Chamberlain's "personal net assessment" that was really important.[8] And while all historians have attested to Chamberlain's considerable influence in government, most have failed to appreciate the enormous power that he exerted. Influence is not the same as power. It only contributes to the final result. Power is the right to have the final say, the "yes"or "no" that decides the debate. Chamberlain's influence, while more than considerable as Chancellor of the Exchequer, became an overwhelming exercise in power as Prime Minister. Of the many books that have been written about British rearmament and appeasement in the 1930s, none have focused on Chamberlain's singular role in defining, coordinating, and directing the whole of defense policy.[9] The revisionists have simply assumed that his actions were motivated by noble, humanitarian, and patriotic reasons, or out of naivete; nor would he have acted on a prejudice. That whatever mistakes Chamberlain made were due to his sincere desire to maintain the peace, and not out of malevolence or stupidity. These are questionable assumptions that must be addressed.

The revisionists have tried to have it both ways. While expressing their disapproval of appeasement, they have been reluctant to place the major burden of responsibility for Britain's defense program on Chamberlain's shoulders, because they have generally assumed that the Chamberlain Cabinet was a traditionally functioning Cabinet, acting on the principle of collegiality and without adequate resources for imperial defense. Invariably reference is made to a Government policy, or a Cabinet decision, when in fact, the decision was made, or engineered, or in someway shaped by Chamberlain's personal actions. Thus, Wesley Wark is perplexed to explain the sudden failure of the British intelligence services from 1936–1939 "to incorporate a more balanced vision of German strengths and deficiencies."[10] But then again he is surprised to learn that the apparatus has "regained its confidence" after Prague. He attributes this failure to the various government committees, although he acknowledges the responsibility of those at the top who invariably chose to act on a "worst case"scenario in interpreting the data. It is not by accident that these years happen to coincide with Chamberlain's growing domination of the Cabinet in 1936 and the loosening of his grip in early 1939. By adopting a worst case scenario, despairing of Britain's inability to compete with the dictator states in an arms race, Chamberlain was able to build support for his policy of appeasement.[11] But after the Holland war scare, that argument no longer carried the same weight.

Other revisionists have argued that if any responsibility is to be accorded, it should be shared by all, not just by Chamberlain. Outward appearances certainly lent credibility to this perception. Unfortunately, the operation of the British Cabinet under Chamberlain belied its traditions. In his excellent study on the British Cabinet between 1938 and 1940, Christopher Hill[12] concluded that the Cabinet was effectively controlled by the Executive, which he described as a collaborative effort between the Prime Minister and his Foreign Secretary. The study is valid as far as it goes, but regrettably it is confined to the post-Munich period when Chamberlain's authority had been diminished and Lord Halifax's stature grew as a result of his opposition to the Godesberg terms. Had the study been rolled back to 1937, it would have yielded vastly different results: Anthony Eden's well-known differences with Chamberlain obviously refutes Hill's thesis. This lack of coordination resulted in Eden's forced resignation from the Cabinet. But the study does raise the question of defining executive leadership. If Eden did not share that power in 1937, who did?

The portrait that emerges is not a pretty one. Executive leadership was supplied by Chamberlain alone. He clearly dominated his Cabinet, though he preferred to have others "devil" for him, giving the appearance of collegiality.[13] What Chamberlain sought was approval for his policies, not participation. If one were simply to read the Cabinet minutes, one might gain the impression of a free and independently functioning directorate. David Margesson, who worked closely with Chamberlain as the Chief Government Whip, described Chamberlain as "an excellent Chairman of Committee and allows the freest expression of opinion, but once he has given his own there is no more to be said."[14]

But Cabinet and committee records can be misleading. Telephone calls, personal conversations, secret meetings, and posturing need to be factored into the record also along with Chamberlain's private thoughts. We do know that Chamberlain often circumvented the process or met with his ministers beforehand in order to control the agenda and to anticipate any differences likely to surface in the Cabinet or committee setting, so that he could prepare his ground, or perhaps dissuade or preempt a wavering member.[15] Gaines Post observed that Chamberlain, even as Chancellor, was more skillful and methodical than his ministerial colleagues in using the agenda and current policy as procedural devices to stop or steer discussion that might otherwise have led to decisions inconsistent with his comprehensive view of policy.[16] And, as Prime Minister, he had "a habit of prematurely summing up the sense of the Cabinet" making it difficult for dissident voices to engage in a meaningful debate.[17] Gustav Schmidt has concluded that foreign policy decisions (he might have added defense policy) were made according to decisions already taken within Government strictures, and that it was impossible for new information that arose to question the adopted positions.[18] Only within this context can one truly appreciate the enormous effect of Chamberlain's leadership abilities in the rearmament program.

This study has tried to provide a contemporaneous account of Chamberlain's thoughts and actions as revealed through his diary and his weekly correspondence with his sisters, as well as his official conduct in office as seen in the weekly Cabinet meetings and accompanying documents. Unlike Stanley Baldwin and Ramsay MacDonald, Britain's foremost politicians of the interwar years, Chamberlain's strong character and principled leadership evince a logical framework and a pattern of conduct that are remarkably consistent, enabling the historian to reconstruct the record with a fair degree of certitude.[19] The policies that Chamberlain carried out as Prime Minister conformed closely to those that he advocated as Chancellor of the Exchequer, and even though the international situation had steadily deteriorated since 1931, policy was not modified to meet the exigencies created by the new situation, owing largely, and certainly decisively, to the persistent efforts of Chamberlain to control the agenda. The determination that he displayed in trying to implement his policy, even after all bastions of his support had fallen around him after Munich is perhaps the most revealing aspect of his character and policy that had remained fixed ever since his days at the Exchequer.

Chamberlain always made his position abundantly clear either personally, or in writing, or through an intermediary such as Sir Horace Wilson, who served as *alter ego* for the busy Prime Minister. Ministers were expected to play up to Chamberlain's lead, and if they did not, they were isolated and eventually driven into resignation, as happened with Anthony Eden, Alfred Duff Cooper, Lord Swinton, and Thomas Inskip. Sir Eric Phipps, once a strong critic of Nazi Germany as Ambassador to Germany (1934–1937), became an "appeaser" when he was Ambassador to France in 1937. Sir Alexander Cadogan, the Permanent Undersecretary of State for Foreign Affairs, understood that he too "would have been let go" if he had not played up to Wilson, whom he "detested."[20] The same *modus operandi* applied to civil servants as well. Three legendary Permanent Undersecretaries, Sir Warren Fisher, Sir Maurice Hankey, and Sir Robert Vansittart were eased out of the Chamberlain Government as well as Sir Jonathan Reith of the BBC for failing to give unswerving support to Chamberlain's policies.

Control over the Cabinet and the bureaucracy was but one aspect of Chamberlain's personalized style of executive leadership. The same urgency that compelled him to assert his dominance over the Cabinet required that his Parliamentary position should be sustained as well. Strong pressure was applied through the Central Office of the Conservative Party and through the Chief Whip, David Margesson, to prevent backbenchers from defecting to a small camp of about thirty dissidents. Honors, favors, and privileges, as well as threats, were used to obtain their support. But Chamberlain's debating skills should not be overlooked as a source of his Parliamentary strength. Always prepared with the facts, articulate, and unflappable under fire, he won the respect and confidence of his party (half of whom were corporate directors), as it struggled against the Labor opposition.

Norman Gibbs' official monumental study, *Rearmament*, while excellent on the technical, military, and strategic aspects of British rearmament, is weak on critical analysis because it fails to deal with Chamberlain's dominant position in the Government. Paradoxically, while Gibbs acknowledged that Chamberlain was the most important member of the Government, he absolved him from personal responsibility, concluding that no one could have aroused enough public support in the country for a greater rearmament program.[21] This is a gratuitous assumption unsupported by accompanying data. But even if it were true, that does not excuse the fact that Chamberlain never tried to educate public opinion to the dangerous situation confronting the country. On the contrary, public opinion, the cornerstone of democracy, was seduced by Chamberlain's incomparable managerial skills.[22] R.A.C. Parker (*Chamberlain and Appeasement*), surprisingly, concurs in most respects with Gibbs, ignoring such studies as Richard Cockett's excellent monograph, *Twilight of Truth,* on the manipulation of the press by Chamberlain, and James Margach's, *The Abuse of Power*. He glosses over Chamberlain's rationale for continuing his policy after Munich and, more inexplicably, after Prague. Parker is right to argue that Chamberlain's policy had the support of the British people up to Godesberg, but he does not explain why Chamberlain chose to restrain the growth of the rearmament program thereafter, although he concedes that Chamberlain could have opted for a greater acceleration of the rearmament program, but did not.[23]

It was not until Munich that Chamberlain's control of the Government began to weaken. The emergency call-up lifted the mantle of ignorance from the British people. Public opinion manifested itself more vocally as it began to crystallize against further appeasement of Nazi Germany's territorial appetite. But still Chamberlain did not seize the opportunity to accelerate Britain's defenses, if indeed it had ever been his intention.[24] Instead, he persisted in his efforts to restrain the growth of the rearmament program, and he must therefore be held accountable for its deficiencies. Britain's foreign and defense policies were designed and controlled by Neville Chamberlain in conformity with his own strongly held (prejudicial) beliefs about British society and the future of the British Empire.

For those revisionists who have conceded Chamberlain's dominance over the Government but have absolved him of personal responsibility for the sad state of Britain's defenses, Chamberlain is portrayed as a conduit for outside pressures acting upon the Government. Most often cited are pressures from the Treasury, the Conservative Party, the business community, or public opinion.[25] If Chamberlain was a creature of the Conservative Party, one must explain his failure to rearm the country more completely after Munich, when many Conservatives and the Conservative press were advocating greater rearmament measures. He certainly could have carried the Party with him.[26] As for the Treasury, all Chamberlain needed to do was to replace those obstructionist officials with more compliant ones, as was his style. One has to read the Chamberlain papers with microscopic curiosity to uncover a single instance where Chamberlain ever acknowledged outside pressure as a convincing reason for abandoning his policy. Whatever actions were taken by Chamberlain were, indeed, his own. His secretive back-channel diplomacy underscores the lack of public support for his personal policy of appeasement and limited defensive measures. Any study of British rearmament that fails to recognize this essential relationship needs to be re-examined in the light of Chamberlain's personality, character, and power. For without Chamberlain, British policy would have taken an entirely different approach to Britain's formidable problems in the 1930s, and Hitler conceivably might have been more reluctant, or even unable, to have risked war as he did. Even Parker has been forced to admit that Chamberlain's powerful, obstinate personality and his skill in debate probably stifled serious chances of preventing World War II.[27]

While historians have been reluctant to appreciate Chamberlain's unique position in the British Government, Hitler was not. Hitler understood it only too well, and he relied on it. Unwittingly, Chamberlain became the linchpin of Hitler's foreign policy. Without Chamberlain, Hitler's risky policy could not succeed. Germany's military leaders had consistently refused to support Hitler's adventurism for sound military reasons. However, they did not know what Hitler intuitively understood.[28] Chamberlain was a "peace at any price" man, and as long as he was in firm control of the British Government, Germany could alter the status quo in Eastern Europe without fear of British (and consequently, French) intervention. Keeping his eye on Chamberlain's Cabinet appointments, on Britain's limited rearmament measures,[29] the "damped down" reporting by the British media of Germany's aggressive actions on the Continent, and mistakenly on the size of Chamberlain's parliamentary majorities, Hitler was able to carry out his policy without the risk of interference from Great Britain and her allies. Chamberlain's determined opposition to conscription, a Ministry of Supply, and a Continental army became the benchmark by which Hitler measured British intentions. Confidently the German Embassy in London reported that as long as Chamberlain remained in office, "a relatively moderate course of action could be assured."[30]

To allege, as Parker has, that Chamberlain "preferred conciliation whenever possible,"[31] is an understatement. Chamberlain played a much more active role than he is credited with. Chamberlain's numerous back-channel sources and personal contacts anxious to cut a deal with Hitler also confirmed Hitler's judgement that Britain could be discounted as a serious factor in European affairs,[32] at least until 1942, when the British rearmament program was expected to be completed.[33] And without Britain, France would be neutralized and the Soviet Union isolated. Only when Hitler failed to appreciate the change in Chamberlain's position after Munich and Prague did he overreach himself and stumble into war.

Chamberlain's persistent efforts to appease Hitler during the summer of 1939 only reinforced and misled Hitler into thinking that he could have a free hand in Eastern Europe. The Nazi-Soviet Non-Aggression Pact, signed on 23 August 1939, appeared to make a Continental war less likely for Hitler now that Poland was effectively isolated from her allies.[34] But Chamberlain could not contain the groundswell of opinion mounting against Hitler, and ultimately was forced into a declaration of war he did not want. Even after war had been declared, a "phony war" ensued as Chamberlain tried to minimize its effects and find a way out of it. That he expressed interest in peace offers right up to his removal from office demonstrates just how strongly felt was his desire for peace at any price, and throws retrospective light on his true policy. If Chamberlain had had his way, conceivably he might have found a pretext for abandoning Poland for the sake of peace just as he had rationalized Czechoslovakia's destruction.[35]

Some historians have mistakenly attributed Chamberlain's strong pacifist feelings to his humanitarian desire for peace.[36] There is little documentary evidence to support this conclusion. In fact, Chamberlain publicly denied that he was a "peace at any price man." To associate Chamberlain with the pacifist humanitarian views of Arthur Ponsonby or George Lansbury is hardly convincing. Nor does it appear that Chamberlain was moved to the point of decisive action by the horrors of the Great War that had claimed the life of his best and, probably, only real friend — his cousin Norman Chamberlain. Ordinarily, one would expect to find a plethora of evidence of his grief, or a determination to avoid a repetition of this tragedy among his considerable writings. But there is little to be found beyond the normal expressions of grief and remorse for the loss of a loved one. Fear of communism also strengthened Chamberlain's desire for peace, although one cannot rule out the possibility that his love of peace might conceivably have been inspired by his sympathy with Fascist ideals.[37]

More frequently cited by Chamberlain as a reason for avoiding a military confrontation was the public's inveterate desire for peace, born out of the disillusionment of World War I. But the only occasions on which Chamberlain is recorded as expressing a concern for the public's desire for peace were usually in the context of his on-going battle to defeat the Army's proposals to honor its Continental commitment. Such expressions of concern are more properly understood as politically inspired than as of his true feelings. To ascribe genuine pacifist feelings to a national leader who showed such little sensitivity to the plight of the Jews after Kristallnacht, or for the victims of Guernica, Nanking, Czechoslovakia, or Poland, strains one's sense of credulity. Chamberlain was a pragmatist, not an idealist or a moralist. So, aside from Chamberlain's alleged pacifism or moral aversion to war, the question of motive arises. Why was Chamberlain so locked into a policy of peace that he was willing to place the Empire at such great risk?

To a great extent, more than is usual for democratic states, the answer to that question lies within the man. Strong-willed, obstinate, and domineering by nature, Chamberlain presented carefully thought-out positions that assumed a prejudicial modality not uncommon in the authoritarian personality.[38] Sure that he was right on every question, he disdained advice that contradicted his own beliefs. Just how much weight these beliefs (many of them inherited from his famous father, including anti-Semitism)[39] carried into his decision-making process is difficult to assess. But they were unmistakably a part of Chamberlain's value system. Perhaps psychologists could offer more insight into this aspect of Chamberlain's behavior and character, but one need not see the snow fall at night to conclude upon waking in the morning that it had snowed last night. Chamberlain's actions need not be proved to have been motivated by prejudice if in fact the end result was prejudicial, whether intended as such or not. Chamberlain's consistent, prolonged and even visceral opposition to such commonsense defense measures as conscription, National Service, a Ministry of Supply, or alliances can be only explained by the existence of a prejudicial hidden agenda. And, because his policy lacked a moral imperative, he could not in the long run find adequate support for it in his party or in the country, which explains why he was forced to resort to chicanery and subterfuge in order to advance his perfidious policy.

Even after war had begun in September 1939, Chamberlain clung to his desperate hope of peace. He wrote to his sister that, "While war was still arrested, I felt I was indispensable, for no one could carry out my policy. Today that position has changed. Half a dozen people could take my place." Yet, he did not step aside and let Churchill, whom he recognized as a more able War Minister, take over, because he felt "[he] might still be needed when it came to discussing peace terms."[40] In this context the "Phony War" makes sense. Just as Chamberlain had limited the growth of the rearmament program to promote his policy of peace at any price in the prewar years, so the Phony War made it possible for Chamberlain to secure peace with a minimum of destruction to the British Empire and the social order dependent on it[41] by cutting a deal with Germany at the appropriate time.

NOTES

1. E. L. Woodward and Rohan Butler, eds., *Documents on British Foreign Policy* (London: HMSO, 1957), 2nd series, vol. 6, #103, 6 December 1933. Hereafter cited as DBFP. This concern was shared by the French Foreign Office as well, CP 151(33). The British Foreign Secretary, John Simon, had warned at an even earlier date, that a European war would break out in three to four years' time, CAB 24/239/52.

2. House of Commons *Debates* (London: HMSO) 5th series, vol. 308: 1360, 14 February 1936. Hereafter cited as *Debates*.

3. Roderick McLeod and Denis Kelly, eds., *The Ironside Diaries, 1937–1940* (London: Constable, 1962), 29 March 1938, 53–54.

4. Norman Graebner, *America as a World Power* (Wilmington, Del.: Scholarly Resources, 1984), 58.

5. C. A. MacDonald, *The United States, Britain, and Appeasement, 1936–1939* (New York: St. Martin's Press, 1981), 131.

6. Cf. John Charmley, *Chamberlain and the Lost Peace* (London: Hodder and Stoughton, 1989), for a defense of Chamberlain's policies. Also G. A. H. Gordon, *British Seapower and Procurement Between the Wars: A Reappraisal of Rearmament* (Annapolis, Md: Naval Institute Press, 1988); and Donald Cameron Watt, *How the War Came: The Immediate Origins of the Second World War, 1933–1938*, (London: Heinemann, 1989); to a lesser extent, Norman Gibbs, *Rearmament* (London: HMSO, 1976); and R.A.C. Parker, *Chamberlain and Appeasement* (New York: St. Martin's Press, 1993), have been more gentle in their treatment of Chamberlain, trying to separate him from the policy. J.P.D. Dunbabin, "British Rearmament in the 1930s: A Chronology and Review," *Historical Journal*, vol. 6 (1975): 587–609; David Dilks, "Appeasement Revisited," *University* of *Leeds Review*, vol. 15, 28–56, 1972; Larry Fuchser, *Neville Chamberlain and Appeasement* (New York: Norton, 1982); Robert Shay, *British Rearmament in the Thirties* (Princeton: Princeton University Press, 1977). This is just a representative list. Those more critical of Chamberlain personally are: William Rock, *Chamberlain and Roosevelt, 1937–1940* (Columbus: Ohio State University Press, 1988); and Sidney Aster, "The Guiltiest Man?," Robert Boyce and Esmonde Robertson, eds., *Paths to War* (New York: St. Martin's Press, 1989).

7. Cato was the pseudonym used by three British journalists, Michael Foot, Peter Howard, and Frank Owen, who, in the aftermath of Dunkirk, came close to accusing the National Government of treason for failing to rearm the country more adequately in the 1930s. Cato, *Guilty Men* (New York: Frederick Stokes, 1940). Also see Paul Kennedy, "Appeasement," 154–157, in Gordon Martel, ed., *The Origins of the Second World War Reconsidered* (London: Unwin Hyman, 1986).

8. Paul Kennedy, "British Net Assessment and the Coming of the Second World War," in Williamson Murray and Allan Millett, eds., *Calculations: Net Assessment and the Coming of World War II* (New York: Free Press, 1992), 48–49.

9. Shay, *British Rearmament in the Thirties*; George Peden, *British Rearmament and the Treasury* (Edinburgh: Scottish Academic Press, 1980); Gibbs, *Rearmament*; Brian Bond, *British Military Policy Between the Wars* (Oxford: Clarendon Press, 1980); Peter Dennis, *Decision by Default* (Durham, N.C: Duke University Press, 1972); Michael Howard, *The Continental Commitment* (London: Temple Smith, 1972); Dunbabin, "British Rearmament in the 1930s"; Uri Bialor, *The Shadow of the Bomber: Fear of Air Attack and British Politics, 1932–1939* (London: Royal Historical Society, 1980); Gaines Post,

Dilemmas of Appeasement: British Deterrence and Defence, 1934–1937 (Ithaca: Cornell University Press, 1993), 237. Post acknowledges Chamberlain's critical role, but his study is confined to 1934–1937. Bell, *Chamberlain, Germany and Japan*, is more argumentative than conclusive even for the limited time frame.

10. Wesley Wark, *The Ultimate Enemy: British Intelligence and Nazi Germany, 1933–1939* (London: Tauris, 1985), 236. Wark has implicitly affirmed Chamberlain's role by issuing the caveat that "his study has not attempted to investigate the social or intellectual" bases of the people involved in the interpretation and usage of the data. Ibid., 234–236.

11. Ibid., 234–235; Patrick Finney, ed., *The Origins of the Second World War* (New York: St. Martin's Press, 1997), 15.

12. Christopher Hill, *Cabinet Decisions on Foreign Policy: The British Experience, October 1938–June 1941* (New York: Cambridge University Press, 1991).

13. Eustace Percy, *Some Memories* (London: Eyre and Spotwood, 1958), 149; NC 18/1/929, 25 August 1935.

14. David Margesson, "A Candid Portrait" [of Neville Chamberlain], Margesson Papers 1/5, n.d., late 1939.

15. NC 2/24A, 7 February 1937; NC 18/1/1089, 12 March 1939. Also see Gustav Schmidt, *The Politics and Economics of Appeasement* (New York: St. Martin's Press, 1986), ch. 2, sec. 5, for an interesting analysis of how the committee system was used to advance a particular agenda. Also see Parker, *Chamberlain and Appeasement*, 157; Post, *Dilemmas of Appeasement*, 237, 313.

16. Post, 237.

17. Hill, 54.

18. Schmidt, 314.

19. Williamson Murray, *The Change in the European Balance of Power, 1938–1939* (Princeton University Press, 1984), 56.

20. David Dilks, ed., *The Diaries of Sir Alexander Cadogan* (New York: Putnam, 1972), 53. Hereafter cited as *Cadogan Diaries*. Also see James Margach, *The Abuse of Power* (London: W. Allen, 1978), 32, 103. Margach claimed that Chamberlain was "ruthless" in dismissing officials whose loyalty to him was suspect.

21. Gibbs, *Rearmament*, 319, 806–811. Gibbs says that the "guilty men" who joined in a conspiracy of silence and deception in order to hold onto power "represented a mood and spirit of the inter-war age, nothing more, nothing less."

22. See Richard Cockett, *Twilight of Truth* (New York: St. Martin's Press, 1989); W. J. West, *Truth Betrayed* (London: Duckworth, 1987); Margach, *Abuse of Power*, and J. W. Reith, *Into the Wind* (London: Hodder and Stoughton, 1948).

23. Parker, *Chamberlain and Appeasement*, 346–347.

24. NC 18/1/1086, 19 February 1939. Chamberlain told his sisters even at this late date, "If given 3 or 4 more years . . . ." He had said the same thing in 1936. NC 2/23, 9 February 1936. Even after war had been declared, his actions in the Phony War also throw some retrospective light on his true intentions as he continued to argue for a reduction in arms. See Scott Newton, *Profits of Peace: The Political Economy of Anglo-German Appeasement* (Oxford: Oxford University Press, 1996), 140. Lord Swinton later recalled that Chamberlain never whole-heartedly accepted that rearmament was necessary. J.A. Cross, *Lord Swinton* (Oxford: Oxford University Press, 1982), 600. Miss Maxse of the Central Office of the Conservative Party also questioned Chamberlain's commitment to prepare the country's defenses. John Harvey, ed., *The Diplomatic Diaries of Oliver*

Harvey (London: Collins, 1970), hereafter cited as *Harvey Diaries,* 12 October 1938, 213.

25. See Shay, *British Rearmament;* Peden, *British Rearmament and the Treasury;* Parker, *Chamberlain and Appeasement;* Gibbs, *Rearmament;* Stephen Roskill, *Hankey: Man of Secrets*, vol. 3 (London: Collins, 1974).

26. Parker, 344. Also, David Irving, ed., *Breach of Security* (London: William Kimber, 1968), 51. The Japanese Ambassador conceded that "No one in the country was opposed to rearmament after Munich." Also, Thomas Jones, *A Diary with Letters, 1931–1950* (Oxford: Oxford University Press, 1954), 30 October 1938, 140, 418. Hereafter cited as *Jones Diary*.

27. Parker, 347.

28. Williamson Murray, "Net Assessment and Nazi Germany," in Williamson Murray and Allan Millett, eds. *Calculations: Net Assessment and the Coming of World War II* (New York: Free Press, 1992), 60–96; Telford Taylor, *Munich: The Price of Peace* (New York: Vintage, 1980), 681–685; 693–699.

29. Nevile Henderson, *Failure of a Mission* (New York: Putnam, 1940), 156.

30. Raymond Sontag and James Beddie, eds., *Documents on German Foreign Policy* (Washington, D.C: U.S. Government Printing Office, 1949), hereafter cited as DGFP, series D, vol. 6, #35, 18 February 1939.

31. Parker, 345.

32. DGFP, series D, vol. 7, #192, 22 August 1939; T. Taylor, 684–685.

33. DGFP, series D, vol. 2, 671–673, 7 September 1938. Hitler told Mussolini that Britain was determined to get rid of one or the other of the two totalitarian states as soon as she had completed her rearmament.

34. Boyce and Robertson, eds., *Paths to War*, ch.10.

35. NC 18/1/1107, 15 July 1939; PREM 1/331; Richard Lamb, *The Ghosts of Peace* (London: Michael Russell, 1987), 119; *Harvey Diaries*, 27 August 1939, 307; Nicholas Bethell, *The War Hitler Won* (New York: Holt, 1972), 180.

36. Charmley, *Chamberlain and the Lost Peace;* Fuscher, *Neville Chamberlain and Appeasement;* Keith Feiling, *The Life of Chamberlain* (London: Macmillan, 1946).

37. *Jones Diary,* 20 March 1938, 397; John Ramsden, *The Making of Conservative Party Policy* (New York: Longmans, 1980), 90; Bethell, *The War Hitler Won*, 180. For an extreme claim, see Clement Leibowitz and Alvin Finkel, *In Our Time: The Chamberlain–Hitler Collusion* (New York: Monthly Review Press, 1997).

38. See Theodore W. Adorno et al., *The Authoritarian Personality* (New York: Harper, 1950), 57.

39. Chamberlain wrote to his sister in 1939, "the Jews weren't a loveable people; I don't care about them myself." NC 18/1/1110, 30 July 1939. (This single quote is not intended to prove that Chamberlain was anti-Semitic, but it does raise the question when placed against his other actions.)

40. NC 18/1/1116, 10 September 1939.

41. The desire to preserve Britain's trading position is presented as the "vital determinant" of Chamberlain's policy in Martin Thomas, *Britain, France, and Appeasement: Anglo-French Relations in the Popular Front Era* (New York: Oxford, 1996). Also see Schmidt, 13–14; and Newton, *Profits of Peace*, 140–141.

Chapter 2

Chamberlain

Neville Chamberlain's role in the defense program commenced with his tenure at the Exchequer (1931–1937), where he had been called upon to help resolve Britain's most serious economic crisis in its history. The Chancellor of the Exchequer occupies a unique position in the British Government. Not only is he responsible for the conduct and administration of fiscal policy, but he also supervises the standards and conduct of all civil servants. Ordinarily, most Chancellors, like most Cabinet ministers, are more concerned with policy and personnel matters than with detail, and are content to leave the administration of the department to the civil servants. But Neville Chamberlain was not an ordinary politician. He took a personal interest in the day-to-day operation of his department and developed a loyal following of lower-level employees. The consummate bureaucrat, he effectively stamped his imprimatur on government policy through the power of the purse, in keeping with Sir Warren Fisher's instructions to Treasury Department officials that they should not hesitate to concern themselves with policy.[1] Whenever policy matters were discussed by the Cabinet or its many subcommittees, the Treasury argument as defined by Chamberlain invariably prevailed.[2]

Though denied the advantages of a prestigious education, Chamberlain possessed a keen mind honed by decades of practical experience in the world of business before becoming a member of Parliament in 1918, at the age of forty-nine. Not given to bouts of idle speculation or academic jousting, Chamberlain never became acculturated to reconciling differing points of view, preferring to rely on the immediately observable and demonstrable facts. Once grasped, these observations became "truths," and when they were wedded to a strong sense of self-righteousness, they tended to take on a prejudicial character. Consequently, those who disagreed with Chamberlain's carefully thought-out programs must be either wrong or misguided, since his programs were based on irrefutable facts and grounded on sound logical principles. Sentimental arguments framed in terms of "fairness," as most Labor programs were, lacked objectivity and therefore had to be resisted before they gained widespread public acceptance.

As one of the founders of the Conservative Research Department and as Chairman of the Conservative Party, Chamberlain brought the party under his direct and personal control in the early 1930s. Self assured, confident of his ability to master the facts, analyze a problem and produce a solution, Chamberlain set up the appropriate committees, provided them with terms of reference, approved of their members, and reviewed their reports before they were submitted to the Government ministers for their recommendations.[3]   These unique circumstances provided   Chamberlain with a welcome opportunity to play a leadership role in the Cabinet.[4] Whatever economic proposals he submitted for consideration were routinely accepted by the Cabinet with little dissent. In foreign affairs, his views, though not compelling, were accorded weighty consideration. His views on rearmament, when articulated in financial terms, became more authoritative as the years wore on. And finally, as Prime Minister his was the only voice that mattered in defense or foreign policy.

Embracing the orthodox economic policies recommended by the May Committee for a balanced budget, Chamberlain prepared his first budget in 1932 by cutting Government spending programs (including defense), raising taxes, and restoring a favorable balance of trade. To achieve these goals, the country went off the gold standard, an Import Duties Bill was passed that increased imports by 10 percent, and the income tax was increased from 4s 6d to 5s in the pound. Later in the year a system of imperial protection was agreed upon by the Dominions in Ottawa. Despite these efforts the budget year 1932 closed with a deficit of £32 million but £37 million had been paid into the sinking fund and the £80 million loan reduced by nearly half. While the numbers were impressive, the social cost was formidable. At Chamberlain's urging, a rigid means test was imposed on welfare recipients in order to control welfare costs as unemployment rose to over 3 million in late 1932. Chamberlain's popularity among the working class, never very high, plummeted to a new low triggering numerous demonstrations against the means test.

Many historians have seen Chamberlain's well-publicized differences with Labor as ideologically inspired, but he also had little love for the Liberal Opposition.[5] Chamberlain was not as much an ideologue as he was a pragmatist. His official biographer called him a "very Radical sort of Conservative."[6] Chamberlain disliked being called a "Conservative."[7] He was not averse to socialistic ideas as shown by his founding of a municipal bank while Mayor of Birmingham, and in his subsidized public housing program while Minister of Health in the 1920s. Campaigning for Parliament for the first time in 1918, he advocated a social agenda that would have been resisted by Conservative diehards as fiercely as they had opposed Lloyd George's Budget Bill of 1909. Most of the opposition to his social programs came from the ultra-Right Federation of British Industries (FBI). But Chamberlain pressed on. Health, public housing assistance, ample pensions, shorter hours, and aid for widows with young children topped his list of his social reforms.   At first glance it might appear that his ideas were influenced by the fact that he was campaigning for a seat in a predominantly working-class district, but Chamberlain was too principled to stoop to political pandering to gain public office. More than likely he was moved, as was his father, by a sense of *noblesse oblige.*

Chamberlain's social policy led to his appointment as Minister of Health in 1920. The reason he gave for accepting the Ministry of Health was "to show [his] gratitude to those who fought and died for England by making it a better place to live in."[8] But he was not unmindful of the political ramifications of social reform. He told his private secretary that unless the Conservative Party made its mark as a social reformer, "The country will take it out on us thereafter."[9] As Minister of Health he submitted twenty-five programs to deal with Britain's festering post war social problems. It was a *tour de force* without precedent in British history, placing Chamberlain in the forefront of the hotly contested Parliamentary debates over a wide range of topics affecting housing, pensions, insurance, medical care and everyday bread-and-butter issues. The Labor Opposition, unhappy with the limited scope of these programs, charged that the Government's programs were "murdering babies" and were indifferent to the rights and interests of the working class.[10] Often Chamberlain had to bear the brunt of the debate alone because his reforms were never really popular among Conservatives. In this atmosphere "was dug deep the gulf" between Chamberlain and the Parliamentary Labor Party (PLP) "which afterwards was to wreak so much evil," according to Chamberlain's biographer.[11] Once he was under attack, Chamberlain's hand went immediately to the sword. He returned Labor's attacks with biting sarcasm and displayed an undisguised contempt for those who argued without knowing all the facts. "Their gross exaggerations, their dishonesty in slurring over facts that tell against them, and their utter inability to appreciate a reasonable argument, do embitter my soul sometimes, and if I seem hard and unsympathetic to them, it is the reaction brought about by their own attitude."[12] He also tended to take their criticism personally. In a letter to his sister Chamberlain betrayed his emotions and confided that the bill that he had just proposed "gives one not the slightest satisfaction and has no redeeming feature from my point of view. . . . Meantime I get cursed for a thief, a cad, and a bully because I resist obstruction. . . . Even the least sensitive among us don't like to be treated as I was last night by the Labor men, and though I don't believe I showed it, I did feel the strain."[13]

Newspaper stories about his being heartless and evil were resented by the much-maligned Chamberlain who was convinced that he was only acting in the public good. His diary began to fill with exasperation and finally contempt toward his critics. Even those closest to him recognized his increasingly intolerant and hostile behavior toward his political opponents. His brother Austen was concerned enough to write to their sister that "Neville's manner freezes people. Can we help him?"[14] David Margesson, who worked closely and faithfully with Chamberlain as Chief Whip when Chamberlain was Prime Minister, has provided us with an up close, unblemished portrait. According to Margesson, Chamberlain "engendered a personal dislike among his opponents to an extent almost unbelievable . . . he beat them up in argument and debunked their catchphrases. Those of us who have lived in the country know how much a man they call 'sarcastic' is disliked. It's a form of mental inferiority which produces hate."[15] Stanley Baldwin had to take Chamberlain aside to remind him that when he spoke in the House of Commons, he was addressing a meeting of gentlemen who should not be treated like "dirt." But Chamberlain was unrelenting. He answered that the reason he treated them like that was because intellectually, with a few exceptions, "they are dirt."[16]

As Chancellor of the Exchequer, Chamberlain's smug and arrogant manner only served to embitter his relations with the Labor Party. And although he occasionally made favorable references to individual members of that party, such as Lord Snowden and Walter Citrine, he generally despised the rank-and-file members for their intellectual vacuity, their blind adherence to broad principle, and their apparent inability to deal with the hard facts at hand that did not fit into their program. Like his father, what he disliked most about the PLP was its class consciousness[17] because it appeared to be more concerned with selfish class interests than with the national welfare. For that reason, it must never be permitted to return to power as long as he had anything to say about it.

NOTES

1. George Peden, "Sir Warren Fisher and British Rearmament Against Germany," *English Historical Review* (January 1979), 94: 30.

2. Post, *Dilemmas of Appeasement*, 237.

3. Ramsden, *The Making of Conservative Party Policy*, 45–54.

4. Roskill, *Hankey*, 75. Chamberlain was even more important in the Cabinet than Baldwin according to Margesson. *Margesson Papers 1/5*, "A Candid Portrait;" Gibbs, Rearmament, 535.

5. NC 7/11/32/236, 6 February 1939. Chamberlain to Sinclair.

6. Feiling, 79–87.

7. David Dilks, *Neville Chamberlain, 1869–1929* (London: Macmillan, 1984), 410.

8. Ibid., 81.

9. P. J. Grigg, *Prejudice and Judgement* (London: Jonathan Cape, 1948), 24. Grigg was Chamberlain's private secretary at the time.

10. Alfred Havigurst, *Britain in Transition* (Chicago: University of Chicago Press, 1985), 206.

11. Feiling, 142.

12. Ibid.

13. Ibid., 134.

14. Robert Self, ed., *The Austen Chamberlain Diary Letters, 1916–1937* (London: Cambridge University Press, 1995), 2 November 1924.

15. *Margesson Papers 1/5*, "A Candid Portrait."

16. Dilks, *Chamberlain*, 519.

17. Elsie Guley, *Joseph Chamberlain and English Social Politics* (New York: Octagon Books, 1974), 291.

Chapter 3

Defense in the Light of Finance and Politics

While domestic concerns naturally occupied the front pages of the nation's dailies during the Great Depression, the foreign situation drew the attention of the Chiefs of Staff (COS) and the Foreign Office. Japan had invaded Manchuria in September 1931, and while the National Government was in a state of transition, France was struggling through one of its twelve governments between 1929 and 1933. Japan's timing in Manchuria was perfect. Great Britain and France were, for all practical purposes, the embodiment of the League of Nations, and in their present difficulties could not be expected to give a strong lead to any League initiatives to resist aggression.

The Manchurian incident presented the League of Nations with its most serious challenge to date. Following several minor successes in the 1920s the League had acquired a benign mystique as a panacea for maintaining world peace. But the Manchurian incident was unlike other international dispute in the 1920s. It was the first involving a major military power and a member of the Security Council. In addition, unique geopolitical factors combined to compromise the League's ability to deal effectively with Japanese aggression 10,000 miles from the League powers. Henceforth League members would have to be very careful in their reliance on the League to resolve international disputes and maintain world peace. Great Britain's failure to take the appropriate steps to place its foreign policy on a more realistic foundation caused it considerable difficulties in the years ahead.

The danger of a militant, unfriendly power in the Far East was doubly impressed on the Chiefs of Staff a few months later when Japanese troops landed in Shanghai, threatening considerable British interests there.[1] Moreover, the threat extended to the whole area from India to Australia to Hong Kong, and the vast trade conducted there. Helplessly the Chiefs of Staff acknowledged, and the

Cabinet agreed, that nothing, not even sanctions under the League Covenant, could be applied. Even if the Government was willing to act, British reinforcements could not be deployed there for at least six weeks, and then must be prepared to sustain their presence for an indefinite period. Painfully aware of their totally inadequate defense system, the COS seized the opportunity to recommend cancellation of the Ten Year Rule. The Ten Year Rule was a guideline laid down by the Cabinet after World War I for the service chiefs to assist them in preparation of their annual budgets. They were told to base their estimates on the assumption that no war was to be contemplated for at least ten years. Obviously unable to maintain that proposition under the circumstances of growing Japanese militancy in the Far East, the Cabinet reluctantly agreed to rescind the rule on 23 March 1932. Chamberlain cautioned the Cabinet that its acceptance of the COS recommendation should not be taken as a justification for increased defense expenditures without regard to the very serious financial and economic situation that still prevailed. He went on to note that in the light of the on-going Geneva Disarmament Conference, "further exploration" of the subject was required. Having been called into existence by the unprecedented severity of the economic crisis the National Government could hardly take exception to the Chancellor's well thought-out and articulate presentation. Without adequate time or data to challenge his argument the Cabinet deferred to Chamberlain's expertise and approved his recommendation without dissent. It was part of a pattern that was to become all too familiar.

Chamberlain's austere 1932 budget called for a reduction in defense spending from £110 million to £104 million — the lowest total in the inter-war period. In effect it meant that the Treasury considered it more important to repay half of an £80 million loan and place £37 million into the sinking fund for 1932 than it was to prepare its defenses in the Far East. Between 1932 and 1935 Chamberlain placed £87 million into debt reduction.[2] Labor complained that the economies being effected were at the expense of the working-class consumer and were undermining the physical and mental health of the people.[3] One of the factors encouraging the Cabinet in its decision to prioritize economic over defense considerations, aside from Chamberlain's personal influence, was the hope that the recently convened Geneva Disarmament Conference and a League conference on Manchuria might lead to an easing of international tensions, thereby precluding the necessity for vast military programs that would undermine economic recovery programs at home.

The Geneva Disarmament Conference began on 2 February 1933 under the chairmanship of Arthur Henderson, the former Foreign Secretary of the second Labor Government. Convinced that the arms race was one of the primary causes of World War I, Henderson worked tirelessly in the cause of disarmament through the League. But now he was only a private citizen, not an official of the British Government, having lost his seat in the 1931 election. His standing at the Geneva Conference was thereby diminished. Nevertheless, public opinion generally approved of the initiative.[4] Even the skeptics had to give their qualified support to disarmament, owing to its popular image. However, it had long been apparent to the National Government that the disarmament talks were in trouble because French demands for security could not be reconciled with German demands for equality. Acceptable definitions for such technical terms as "offensive weapons" and "defensive weapons" proved extremely frustrating. The British were not without fault either. They posed objections to supervision and inspection teams because they did not want to expose their weakness to the world.[5]

Many newspapers, especially those of the Opposition parties, became critical of the government's weak role in Geneva.[6] At last Ramsay MacDonald produced a plan in March 1933 that called for a reduction in French arms and a corresponding increase in German strength. By then it was a case of too little, too late. Hitler had come to power in Germany, and Japan had walked out of the League of Nations.

Warnings poured in from many quarters about the dangers from a rearmed Nazi Germany. The Foreign Office, led by Sir Robert Vansittart, Permanent Undersecretary of State, was appalled by the brutal character of the Nazi regime and was well aware of its clandestine efforts to rearm.[7] Maurice Hankey, Chairman of the Committee for Imperial Defense (CID) and spokesperson for the COS, urged Prime Minister MacDonald to act on the Cabinet decision to rescind the Ten Year Rule and rearm, but MacDonald was in the process of submitting his disarmament plan at Geneva and could not very well take the first steps toward rearmament. Hankey then turned to Chamberlain and pleaded with him that the international situation was so grave that he found it impossible to believe "that the greatly needed rehabilitation of our Services can be much longer delayed."[8] Echoing the views of the COS, Hankey campaigned for strengthening the Far East defenses, since they were the most vulnerable and in need of the most immediate attention. After all, what had happened in Shanghai could be repeated again in Hong Kong, or Singapore, or anywhere else on a moment's notice.

Adding his voice to those urging rearmament was Sir Warren Fisher, Permanent Secretary of the Treasury and head of the civil service. He agreed with Hankey's assessment on the need to rearm, although he advocated a Europe-first strategy. He cautioned the Government not to antagonize Japan in the process but to rush the completion of the Singapore naval base. Encouraged by an improvement in the economy, Chamberlain agreed that "common prudence would seem to indicate some strengthening of our defenses."[9] The rearmament program was about to begin.

While the British Government was moving cautiously toward rearmament, the Disarmament Conference was floundering. The Labor Party was quick to exploit the issue to rebuild its fortunes after its disastrous defeat in the 1931 election. By mid-1933 unemployment had dropped significantly, trade had picked up, and the economy was on the upswing. As the National Government's policies appeared to be working, Labor's prospects for electoral vindication diminished. But when Arthur Henderson returned from Geneva in the spring of 1933, he launched into an attack on the Government's ineffectual role at the Geneva

Conference. He struck a responsive chord with the public's inveterate desire for peace. Subsequently, Labor's attacks on the National Government increasingly emphasized disarmament as an issue with which to recover its electoral strength and demonstrate its legitimacy as an alternative government, while the Conservative Party took a position of strengthening its defense program. At the annual Labor Party conference on 5 October 1933, the National Executive Council (NEC) was instructed to

launch a vigorous propaganda campaign to counter in advance those tendencies in the present social system which predisposed large sections of the population to respond readily to war appeal; to work within the Socialist International for an uncompromising attitude against war preparations; and to pledge itself to take no part in war and to resist it with the whole force of the Labor movement; and to seek consultation forthwith with the trade union and cooperative movements with a view to deciding and announcing in the country what steps, including a general strike, are to be taken to organize the opposition of the organized workers in the event of war or its threat.[10]

The decision by the Labor candidate, John Wilmot, to contest the East Fulham by-election on the question of disarmament proved successful. He was able to turn a 14,000 Conservative majority into a 5,000 plurality for Labor. Thereafter, other Labor candidates campaigned on a peace through disarmament platform, though they were careful to tie it in with economic and social issues as well. In the five by-elections held in the month following East Fulham, all five Labor candidates managed to reduce the Government majorities by an average of 22.2 percent.[11] Nevertheless, Labor lost all five elections because of a steadily improving economy. Whereas Baldwin appeared to have been shaken by the results of the East Fulham election, Neville Chamberlain read it differently. He felt that the East Fulham defeat was to be attributed more to the means test than to disarmament.[12] Both were right.

On 12 October 1933, in preparation of its annual report on imperial defense policy for 1933, the Chiefs of Staff submitted a watered-down version of its defense requirements to its parent committee, the Committee for Imperial Defense. The CID recommended that a new committee be established to develop a defense program that would meet Britain's "worst deficiencies." The Defense Requirements Committee (DRC), as it was known, held its first meeting on 14 November. It consisted of the three Chiefs of Staff, a representative from the CID (Hankey), one from the Treasury (Fisher), and one from the Foreign Office (Vansittart). It was directed to prepare only a military analysis, which should then be forwarded to a ministerial committee, where its recommendations could be considered "in their political aspects."[13] The Cabinet also stipulated that its defense plans should be based on the assumption that no war with France, the United States, or Italy was to be contemplated.[14]

While the DRC met secretly to develop a program to correct the country's worst deficiencies in defense matters, the National Government continued with the disarmament talks in Geneva despite Germany's absence. The

National Government was torn between the contradictory programs of rearmament and disarmament, and could not make up its mind. The ambivalence was symptomatic of the malaise besetting the National Government in preparing its defense program during the early 1930s. Nearly two years had now lapsed since the COS recommended abolishing the Ten Year Rule, but not a single pound had been appropriated for upgrading the nation's defenses.

Arguably, financial problems might have justified the low priority assigned to the defense program in 1932. But when the economy showed definite signs of improvement in 1933, politics replaced finance as the chief concern of the government. The by-elections in late 1933 demonstrated the popular appeal of peace and disarmament, and although the Government generally prevailed in those elections, it did not feel comfortable or confident in its ability to stake out a clear position on the need for rearmament. It was one thing to admit the failure of the disarmament talks, but it was another matter to undertake a serious effort to rearm the country to the extent necessary to provide a defense adequate to its needs. Of the 21 by-elections held between 14 October 1933 and 31 July 1934, the Opposition parties prevailed in eight of them (six by Labor).[15] Thus, the National Government proceeded to repair only the "worst deficiencies" in its defense programs. By adopting this "worst deficiency" standard, the Government could, in truth, deny Labor's charge of secret rearmament plans. Under its terms of reference to the service departments, no new construction was to be authorized to repair the worst deficiencies in defense. Only replacement costs could be used by the COS in their budget estimates, not new construction.

The DRC completed its first deficiency report on 28 February 1934, and it was discussed in the Cabinet the following week. Predicated on fulfilling its existing obligations under the Locarno Agreement and the Nine Power Treaty, as well as its imperial obligations, the report recommended formation of an expeditionary force of four infantry divisions and several auxiliary units capable of being mobilized within one month of hostilities; modernization of its capital ships; completion of the Singapore naval base; and a metropolitan air force of 52 squadrons. The 52 squadrons had been authorized in 1923 but were still deficient by half at the time of the report, placing Great Britain fifth among the air powers.[16]

Torn between the need to rearm and a desire to appease the pro-disarmament sentiment in the country, the Government proceeded cautiously at Chamberlain's urging. Without taking action on the first DRC report, it adopted defense measures only to the extent that it could rebut Opposition charges of not pursuing disarmament seriously enough. Accordingly, the 1934 defense budget intended only to restore the cuts in the defense program effected since the onset of the Depression in 1929, from £104 million to £114 million. At the same time, however, Chamberlain's 1934 budget, reflecting a £29 million surplus with an eye toward the next general election, sought to redress some of the draconian measures imposed on the economy. The cuts in unemployment benefits and half the cuts in Government and teachers' salaries were restored, while the income tax was reduced from 5s to 4s 6d per pound, to redeem the Government's pledge to restore the taxes it had imposed in the austere 1932 budget.

Thus, as far as the British electorate could discern, British defense policy had not really changed much, and Opposition charges of rearmament leading to war could readily be dismissed as political hyperbole. A futile vote of censure against the 1934 estimates failed by a convincing margin of 404–60. The country and its representatives in Parliament were completely oblivious to the narrowing window of security offered by the Government's defense program. Solitary voices like those of Winston Churchill went unheeded when he warned the House of Commons on 7 November 1933 of the rapid rate of German rearmament and of the militant character of the Nazi regime. He repeated those warnings to the House in the debate on air force estimates in March 1934. As a result, Baldwin was forced to reassure the House that "this Government will see to it that in air strength and air power, this country shall no longer be in a position inferior to any country within striking distance of our shores."[17] In his memoirs Churchill criticized the National Government for failing to lead the country to greater rearmament with its overwhelming majority in the House of Commons. He claimed that the country would have followed its lead, had it been tendered.[18]

There is considerable merit in his assertion. While it is undoubtedly true that the country desired peace and disarmament, it is equally true that it was afraid of a "knockout blow" from the air, and thus could be expected to support a concept of more air rearmament at least, if the Government had chosen to make a case for it. After all, that was the virtue in having a truly National Government! But the Conservative-dominated National Government chose not to make the case, fearing a public reaction that would jeopardize its standing in the polls, and Chamberlain was more afraid of unleashing pent-up social forces. Foreign Secretary John Simon's lukewarm appeal for Chamberlain's support "to call our people to face the new situation" fell on deaf ears.[19]

It has become fashionable to criticize Labor opposition to the defense program as a reason for the government's policy of appeasement.[20] Much has been made of Labor's well-known opposition to rearmament at the time. One apologist for the Government wrote:

Not only was rearmament opposed by Attlee and the Parliamentary Labor Party right up to 1937, behind the PLP stood the powerful Trades Unions Congress which . . . was far from abandoning its opposition to rearmament. . . . Certainly the National Government bears heavy responsibility for slowness on rearmament; but it is a great deal less than fair to acquit the Opposition of all responsibility and find "guilty men" only in the Tory ranks.[21]

But this argument really begs the question of responsibility. Is the Labor Party really to be held accountable for fulfilling its constitutional duty to oppose the Government? It is even paid to do it. It is in the very nature of the democratic system of government to contend for political advantage. However, in cases of national security and dire emergency, party differences are traditionally minimized and political temperatures lowered to a point where a meaningful political dialogue can be held. Only the party in power can communicate that signal because of its unique position of receiving and controlling the dissemination of information. Without that signal from the party in power to indicate the existence of an emergency, "politics as usual" continues to set the agenda. This is where the Conservative-dominated National Government failed in its responsibility to the nation. Churchill's point was well taken.

In introducing a motion of censure in 1934, the Labor Party announced that it would not approve any expansion of our armaments unless it was made clear that the Disarmament Conference has failed and unless a definite case can be established.[22] Herbert Samuel echoed the same complaint for the Liberals. He asked, "What is the case in regard to Germany? Nothing we have seen so far or heard would suggest that our present force is not adequate to meet any peril at the present time from this quarter."[23] Clearly, opposition to the British rearmament proposals stemmed as much from political posturing as from the National Government's failure to make a case for them. Without that lead from the National Government, it is difficult to understand how any meaningful rearmament program could have been carried out. Yet the National Government tried to walk the fine line between rearmament and political expediency. It did not feel that it could afford to alienate the public's desire for peace by introducing a plan that could be called rearmament while the Geneva Disarmament Conference was still in session, even though the Conference had effectively been aborted in October when Germany left it. Only when it was announced in April that further discussions were fruitless did the British Government feel confident enough to get on with its rearmament plans, although it did not feel comfortable in sharing its dilemma with the Opposition parties while plans for a new election were being discussed.[24] Nevertheless, the British Government continued to express its interest in arms limitation agreements, hoping to head off a destructive arms race.

Acting on a COS report that recognized the immediate danger to the British Empire from Japan, but singled out Germany as the greater "menace in five or six years, maybe four,"[25] the Cabinet resolved that the country's military deficiencies should be eliminated in five years.[26] Well aware of the impact of a five-year rearmament program on the economy and of its political implications, the COS suggested that the Opposition parties be informed of the serious nature of the German threat so as to win their support for rearmament.[27] The Cabinet took the recommendation under consideration but generally agreed that it was premature to take such a step because of the "political difficulties" it would raise. The failure of the Cabinet to take the Opposition parties into its confidence was understandable under the circumstances.

The National Government had pledged to restore the budget cuts as soon as possible, but postponing tax cuts and rearming would open to charges that it was preparing for war at the expense of much-needed social programs. It could not take that chance with an election close at hand. And if perchance it should lose the election, the National Government could argue, as it did, that the rearmament program itself would be placed in jeopardy if Labor were to take over, because of Labor's past opposition to rearming. Chamberlain was well aware, and deeply concerned, that the failure of the disarmament talks must lead to an arms race with its "staggering costs."[28] Thereupon, in an effort to avoid a devastating arms race, he submitted a plan of limited liability to the Cabinet that he called "the best thing I have ever done in the Cabinet."[29] In his diary he revealed his thoughts: " Our greatest interest was peace, in the sense of a general pacification. If complete security reigned throughout Europe, that would be the greatest possible boon to us, with our world-wide trading and financial ramifications."[30] At this point Chamberlain's interest in peace was in line with prevailing opinion in the Cabinet, the Foreign Office, and the country, which enabled him to gain such widespread support for his policies. Only later did it become clear that he was prepared to go to extraordinary lengths to maintain the peace, peace at any price, which separated him from the rest of his colleagues and the country.

Chamberlain's plan envisioned the cooperation of the major European states, "of say, Germany, France, Italy, UK, Poland, and Czechoslovakia, under which, each of the other signatories undertakes to put a limited specified force at the disposal of the joint body. . . to aid the aggrieved party." Under such a scheme the harmful effects of a rearmament program on industry, finance, and, ultimately, social policy could be avoided under an affordable, limited defense force. Chamberlain's plan was then forwarded to the COS, where, he said, it was "shot to pieces"[31] because of its impracticality, and it filled him with a sense of foreboding for the future.[32] It was one of the few times that Chamberlain failed to have his way in defense matters. Despair soon gave way to optimism as his third budget received a good reception in the House. It strengthened his determination to bring the defense program under control. Prudence, indeed, dictated some strengthening of defenses, but how much was to be spent, and in what area was defense spending to be directed? These were the questions that Chamberlain focused on throughout this rearmament period.

After the Geneva talks finally fell through in April 1934, the Cabinet referred the 28 February DRC Report, ironically, to the Ministerial Committee on Disarmament (DCM) on 2 May, so it could be examined in its political aspects.[33] Chamberlain's influence in defense matters quickly became apparent in the DCM even though he had failed to obtain enough support for his scheme of limited liability from the COS. At his own suggestion he was asked to prepare a revised estimate of the DRC's program "in the light of politics and finance."[34] By 12 May he could write with some justification that he had "practically taken charge of the defense requirements of the country."[35] Whereas the DRC under Hankey's influence had recommended a rather balanced approach to repairing the worst deficiencies in the defense program, the DCM modified the DRC report by upgrading the air defenses at the expense of the other two services. Chamberlain had a great deal to do with its revised form. After describing the DRC's proposals as "impossible to carry out," he set down his own views with respect to meeting the defense requirements over the next five years, "which must be chiefly designed for the defense of these islands."[36] In retrospect, these words take on an added significance because the defense program proceeded along those very lines until the Inskip Memorandum gave it lawful effect in 1937.

And although the DCM concluded that it would be "unsafe to delay the initiation of steps to provide for the safety of the country," it made a concession to Chamberlain that he should not be bound to find the money for defense within five years.[37] From then on, defense matters and foreign affairs preoccupied his attention no less than Treasury concerns. To him, they became one and the same problem. As the military budget was expected to grow by £85 million over and above the normal expenditures for the next five years,[38] the responsibility for financing those programs fell largely on his shoulders. And in matters of finance his view always prevailed.

Since Germany had been singled out as the immediate threat to British security, the "worst deficiencies" to be repaired obviously required a response to meet Germany's expected threat from the air. Action to meet the Japanese threat, not considered to be as serious by the COS, could be postponed until the German threat abated or the British economy recovered sufficiently to provide simultaneously for both threats. But Chamberlain did not believe that Britain could "provide simultaneously for hostilities with Japan and Germany," and he proposed that the Government should get back on its old terms with Japan.[39] Serious discussion ensued about the desirability of renewing the Anglo-Japanese alliance or of negotiating a non-aggression pact with Japan. Only Prime Minister MacDonald's strong opposition prevented the initiative from going forward. He feared its impact on Anglo-American ties, not only because it conflicted with the Nine Power Treaty,[40] but also because he wanted to reassure Britain's Asian Dominions of British support in the region.[41] This rare setback was Chamberlain's last until 1937, when he gave way on his National Defense Contribution Bill. He did, however, succeed in enlarging the size of the air force.

Hankey opposed the Japanese initiative as well as a greater air force because they conflicted with the desire of the COS for a better balanced imperial defense strategy. He wanted a strategy that could meet the threat at home and also protect the Dominions and trade routes abroad. Although no attempt was made by the COS to prioritize defense needs, it hoped to beef up the defenses in the Far East rather quickly, in order to impress the Japanese and make it easier to deal with Germany later. The COS took the strategic view that what affected one part of the Empire affected another. This dilemma created innumerable difficulties for the Government with respect to strategy, planning, and execution of its defense policy. For example, the decision of the DCM to prioritize air defense over the other two services necessitated cuts and postponements in the Army's Continental role in defending the Low Countries as long as finances were limited, as well as delay of the completion of the Singapore naval base. One of the reasons for assuming the Continental role was to fulfill Great Britain's obligation to guarantee the Locarno Agreement. Another, more self-interested motive was to prevent Germany from acquiring air and naval bases within easy striking range of Great Britain, and at the same time to provide Great Britain with convenient bases from which to retaliate deep inside the German heartland.[42] Any defense program worthy of the name could not ignore this essential interrelationship among the services.

What was needed was a Continental commitment to defend the Low Countries, which had been a strategic British interest for centuries, and an air force capable of retaliating on German soil with sufficient power to act as a credible deterrent to the German threat. Although Chamberlain professed to accept this assessment,[43] he raised objections to a larger Continental army because, he argued, "We could not tell Belgium, if we do this will you do this?" Nor would public opinion support such a commitment after the carnage suffered in World War I.[44] Chamberlain's revision of the DRC report was crafted more for its political and financial advantage than for the real security that it afforded the nation in terms of its ability to protect vital interests. In place of a Continental commitment Chamberlain supported an increase to 38 air squadrons, mostly for home defense, instead of the 10 proposed by the DRC, but the Navy was not allowed to have any replacement ships. Chamberlain thus managed to reduce the projected DRC recommendation from £76,800,000 to £50,300,000.[45] And although the Air Ministry was the chief beneficiary of this proposal, Secretary of Air Lord Londonderry protested that the new plan was merely "window dressing," since it did not make adequate provision for reserves.[46]

In the light of politics, Chamberlain's revised plan with its emphasis on air power was designed to satisfy the concerns of the public for adequate protection from Germany's emerging air program. Yet it was crafted in such a way as not to cause undue alarm in the country.[47] For that reason the Cabinet decided to postpone action on air raid precautions (ARP). By presenting the plan in this manner, the Government lost a great opportunity to educate public opinion to the dangers on the horizon. And of course, its cost-saving features were not lost on the Chancellor of the Exchequer, who had taken a consistent stand against uncontrolled defense spending during these discussions in the DCM and the Cabinet. He opposed all spending that could possibly be deferred to a later date, so that currently approved programs could be financed out of existing revenues. Hitler's abortive attempt at Anschluss in July 1934 cast doubts upon Germany's ability to wage war in five years.[48] As a result, Chamberlain was able to gain wider acceptance for his policy of limited liability among his colleagues.

Actually, with a £31 million surplus in the budget it would have been possible to finance most of the DRC proposals for a more balanced defense program than it did. But Chamberlain and the National Government were committed to restoring the domestic cuts made in the aftermath of the 1931 crisis, and to reducing the income tax. The Government was extremely sensitive to Labor's charge that the surplus had been achieved at the expense of the working classes because it showed that many of the social programs that had been gutted were either unnecessary or could have been restored earlier.[49] Baldwin's suggestion to borrow for defense, supported by Fisher, met with disapproval from the Chancellor of the Exchequer, who thought it was premature to talk about deficit financing.[50] It would send the wrong signal to the City, he told them.

The Parliamentary debates on the revised air estimates (Scheme A) in July transformed the parameters of the debate. Public opinion, though supportive of the disarmament initiative, preferred security first, and the Cabinet agreed.[51] It was no longer a question of whether the country should rearm, but to what extent. The Labor Party got the same message. At its annual conference it changed its position from unequivocal opposition to rearmament, to a qualified rearmament program necessary to fulfill Britain's obligations under the League of Nations.[52] On the other hand, the Conservative Party conference went on record as supporting defense preparations adequate to the needs for imperial defense much more confidently than it had in the past.[53]

No sooner had the controversy over the July air estimates subsided when another debate erupted in November over a Government announcement of a new proposal for its air program. This latest revision became necessary when the CID learned in October that earlier intelligence estimates of German air strength had been too low. The plan agreed upon in July was no longer sufficient to keep pace with German developments in the air. This new information indicated that Germany would have 576 front-line planes by October 1935, instead of 500, and by October 1936, they would have 1,368 instead of 1,000.[54] In other words, Germany would have surpassed Great Britain's figure of 1,200 front-line planes within a year. Clearly, Germany's industrial capacity had been vastly understated. The political implications weighed heavily with the Cabinet as it faced the most crucial decision to date in its rearmament program.

A decision to expand the rearmament program beyond its present limits meant a certain dislocation of the export trade, tax increases, and/or borrowing, all politically undesirable. And finally, depending on the extent of the rearmament program as the demand for more industrial capacity, skilled labor, and manpower grew, there was the lurking danger of social revolution because of the social programs inherent in any scheme to ensure industrial peace. World War I had given rise to socialist ideas, and another war would strengthen them. For these reasons Chamberlain believed that an arms race with Germany had to be avoided and the political opposition kept out of office in order to make sure that these developments did not materialize. Chamberlain, therefore, opposed those in the Cabinet who advocated a rearmament program, narrowly conceived on security grounds alone, without regard for its long-term social and political effects.

Despite the alarming news of Germany's progress in air rearmament, Chamberlain persisted in financing the rearmament program out of existing revenue for as long as possible, because "he still saw nothing that would justify an expensive rearmament program at this time."[55] However, in November, when faced with Churchill's announced intention of confronting the Government in Parliament with his own figures on the German air threat the Government was forced to take action it would have preferred to deal with more quietly.[56] It decided on an acceleration of Scheme A rather than on a new program.[57] The date for completion of Scheme A was advanced from 1939 to 1937, to allay the public's concern for security, and at the same time to deflect the expected Labor attacks on a rapidly developing arms race that it feared would lead to war.

Churchill's information about Germany's none-too-secret air force closely paralleled the Government's own intelligence estimates. He predicted that Germany would have an air force equal to Great Britain's in one year and would double it in two years. But Baldwin effectively rebutted Churchill's figures in the House on 28 November. Whether by design, or out of ignorance as Churchill has suggested, Baldwin answered that although their numbers for 1935 and 1936 were substantially in agreement, Churchill's estimates of overall German air power were grossly exaggerated. Their numbers, he argued, did not reflect actual "first-line strength," whereas the British figures were of the first-line variety with a "considerably larger reserve at our disposal." He put Germany's strength at "not fifty percent of our strength in Europe today." Moreover, he could not "look farther than the next two years," at which time Churchill predicted Germany would surpass Great Britain. At any rate, Baldwin repeated his pledge on behalf of the Government, not to accept any position of inferiority with regard to Germany's air force.[58] Thus reassured, the back-benchers fell into line with their leadership and Churchill's efforts to awaken the country to the dangers of delay failed, again reflecting the low state to which his political fortunes had sunk. He had lost a great deal of credibility by his determined opposition to the India Bill.

Nor did the criticisms of the Labor Party amount to much, given its weak representation in the House. All it could do was revive claims of Government insincerity in matters of disarmament and of excess profiteering. The Labor Party would have preferred that the Government work within a framework of collective security through the League of Nations and a strengthening of ties with countries willing to resist the aggressor states. Such arguments were easily dismissed as political posturing and carried little weight with the public.

As Chancellor of Exchequer, Chamberlain was faced with the responsibility for financing the accelerated air program, which was not really much of a problem in itself.[59] The trick was to finance it out of the revenue without running up a deficit or increasing taxes. Aided by a recovering economy, a raid on the Road Fund, and suspending payment on debt reduction, he managed to find the means to provide for additional defense spending in 1934, although it was still considerably less than what the services considered necessary to fulfill their responsibilities. Chamberlain realized that this budgetary process could not be expected to continue indefinitely, and sooner, rather than later, hard choices would have to be made between budgetary restraint and rearmament.

For Chamberlain, diplomacy was the key to the situation. Japan's rebuff of recent British overtures for a *modus vivendi* in the Far East did not discourage him from reviving his earlier proposal for an international peace-keeping force as the Saar plebiscite drew near. In December he recorded his thoughts in his diary:

We had a heaven-sent opportunity to put ourselves right with the world, take the lead, and incidentally stage an example of an international peace force. . . . I strongly urge that we ourselves should propose, not an Anglo-Italian, but truly international force. . . backed by very strong representations in the same sense from Eden in Geneva.[60]

The virtue of his plan lay in its ability to cap military spending by reducing its international obligations. Also, he hoped that a truly international force might act as a restraint on German or Japanese adventurism. Nor was Chamberlain unmindful of the political advantage to be gained from such a scheme. By placing reliance on collective security, the Opposition parties would be preempted in their expected attack on the 1935 defense budget, because they, too, had been in favor of collective security. The international peace-keeping force was a great idea from a moral, financial, and political standpoint, but its obvious impracticality failed to win support from the service chiefs.[61] Who would command such a force? Where would it be stationed? Against whom should it be used? And under what conditions? Chamberlain was not so naive as to fail to anticipate these problems, but they became inconsequential to his way of thinking. He believed that the mere existence of an international force would obviate the need to address these vexing questions, since the would-be aggressor states would not dare to act when confronted with such a force. Hence, the answers to these questions were largely academic to him. What was important, was to create the international force, which would somehow act as a deterrent, much as the scarecrow in the field wards off the birds.

While Japanese bullying tactics in the Far East could safely be ignored, Germany's rearmament in the air could not. Any British Government, even a Labor Government, would have been criminally negligent for failing to upgrade Britain's defenses under the circumstances. Sir Arnold Wilson, a staunch Conservative and an apologist for Nazi Germany, did not detect any serious opposition in the country to Britain's rearmament as long as other countries were doing the same.[62] Surely Chamberlain could not have been restrained from rearming for fear of weakening his party base of support. Why, then, did he oppose greater rearmament measures?

Acting on the COS (i.e., Hankey's) recommendation to educate the public on its defense policy, the Government issued its famous *White Paper on Defense* on 4 March 1935, as a prelude to the budget debates sure to come under heavy attack from the Labor Party for increasing defense spending and ignoring social needs. Widespread and violent demonstrations had erupted in January and February over Chamberlain's revised means test law, whereby the National Government took over the responsibility for administering the law from the more liberal local authorities, many of whom, including the London City Council, were controlled by the Labor Party. Increased defense spending would be exceedingly difficult to justify under the circumstances. Coming on the heels of steadily dwindling majorities in the by-elections since East Fulham, and several other losses,[63] the demonstrations against the means test increased the political sensitivity of the National Government to Labor's challenge.

The Conservative Party, whose stake in the National Government was enormous, was enlisted in the campaign to prepare the public for a moderate increase in defense spending from £114 million to £137million. In December 1934, under Chamberlain's direction, it published a pamphlet, *The National Government and Peace*, that defended the Government's role in the Geneva Disarmament Conference, and in March 1935, *The True Facts* appeared as a supplement to the *White Paper on Defense*. Intended to reassure the nation of its abiding commitment to peace through a prudent rearmament program, the *White Paper* failed to capitalize on the opportunity to educate public opinion. Calling attention to German rearmament, which "might produce a situation where peace would be in peril," the *White Paper* weakly apologized for the proposed increase in defense spending, citing the failure of the Disarmament Conference, notwithstanding the efforts of the National Government to keep it alive, as the reason for increasing defense spending.[64]

Developments abroad could not be ignored any longer. As the fifth ranking air power in the world, the current proposals for replacing, renovating, or re-equipping the existing forces were clearly inadequate to the military requirements of imperial defense, and new programs were needed. Both Hankey and Fisher were disappointed at the casual manner in which the paper was presented in Parliament. They felt that a great opportunity had been lost to educate public opinion.[65]

Understandably the Labor Party could not pass up the opportunity to score off the Government in the forthcoming debates. With a million and a half people out of work, Labor hoped to recapture the working-class vote stolen by MacDonald and the National Laborites in the betrayed election of 1931. The National Government was hard pressed to justify its request for additional defense spending while turning down the Labor Party's call for social programs and repeal of the means test. Eden regretted the narrow partisan line taken by Labor, but he paid little attention to their attacks. He understood that Labor took its position simply to oppose the Conservatives.[66] Chamberlain, however, was not as forgiving as Eden, and he chose to take Labor at its word for partisan reasons of his own. In fact, he welcomed their opposition.

Events abroad intervened to rescue the National Government from its uncomfortable dilemma. On 9 March, Hitler announced the existence of the German air force in defiance of the Treaty of Versailles and the League powers entrusted to enforce the treaty. To its credit, the French Government responded by increasing the conscription period from one to two years. Hitler retaliated by announcing German conscription, again in violation of the Treaty of Versailles. This was the atmosphere in which the House of Commons met to consider the air estimates, and though the Liberal and Labor parties dutifully opposed the Government's plans for increasing defense spending, public opinion began to shift more to favor air rearmament while still clinging to the illusion of collective security. Even the Liberal Party caught the drift and changed its position in May.[67] Henceforth, the Liberals ceased to oppose defense spending, at least to a level consistent with maintaining a force for collective security.

These events caused a slight rift in the ranks of Labor. The pacifist diehards, led by Arthur Ponsonby and George Lansbury, could not be convinced that the way to avoid war was to rearm. However, several leaders of the powerful Trades Union Congress (TUC) — Hugh Dalton, Walter Citrine, and Ernest Bevin —were willing to support a rearmament program in keeping with Britain's obligations to the League and the principle of collective security.[68] Their support was important because it took six months to train a skilled worker, and creating double shifts would boost production by 60 percent.[69] But Labor was not about to blindly jettison its most successful electoral issue since East Fulham without a compelling reason to do so. The gravity of the situation had not been sufficiently impressed on the country by the National Government to justify bipartisan foreign and defense policies. Baldwin's reassuring statements made to the House in November had lulled the nation into a false sense of security. As far as national security was concerned, therefore, the defense issue did not appear to be anything more than another political game, and the country slumbered through what Churchill called "the locust years."

Bevin, head of the Transport Workers Union, was not unalterably opposed to rearmament, but complained that the Government had not troubled itself to take the Opposition leaders into its confidence. He noted that "in the old days of the Liberals and Tories there was some consultation on policy, but since 1931 Labor has been treated like a caste apart. It was not for us to be supplicants; it was for them to come to us and for the first time recognize Labor as equals."[70] Just why the National Government failed to take this step underscores the sinister influence of Chamberlain, who by all accounts exhibited an undisguised contempt for the Labor Opposition. If the National Government itself did not sense the urgency of rearming, how could the public, or the Opposition, be expected to respond to its weak, half-hearted, and indecisive lead?

When Baldwin rose to defend the *White Paper* in the House, he sounded somewhat indifferent and ambivalent in stating the case for the Government:

The world has never been a more unsafe place for democracy than it is today. . . . I am quite convinced of this, that if our people as a whole feel that even the modest demands of this Paper, merely making your forces that you have got efficient — no increase in the Army, no increase in the Navy, an increase to at least the nearest striking force in Air — if they are not willing to do that, then I believe that the risks of our democracy perishing are great.[71]

It was not exactly a call to arms, but under the circumstances of an impending election, understandable. At no time during this early rearmament period, 1933–1935, did the National Government display its willingness to address the issue of national security purely on its merits. The defense program, coming increasingly under Chamberlain's control, continued to be shaped in the light of "finance and politics." In his diary he boasted that "he had to carry the Government on his back," and to his sister he wrote, that "he had become a sort of acting Prime Minister."[72] As long as Chamberlain remained in such a strong position, the defense program would never deviate from that track, effectively compromising the Government's efforts to respond to the serious threats confronting the country from abroad.

Following the release of the *White Paper* on 4 March 1935, Hitler vented his anger by catching a diplomatic cold, forcing postponement of a scheduled visit to Berlin by Sir John Simon of the Foreign Office and Anthony Eden. The meeting subsequently took place on 25 March, at which time Hitler dropped a bombshell by informing his British visitors that Germany had already achieved air parity with Great Britain, and would soon match the French air force. Although the Air Staff was skeptical of this information,[73] the Government had to treat the news with studied caution, especially after having been misled on its estimates of German air strength in 1934.

Confronted with this new situation, the Secretary of State for Air Lord Londonderry pressed for an expansion of the existing air scheme to keep pace with Germany. Premised on Germany achieving a front-line strength of 1,512 planes by 1937, the Air Ministry now proposed Scheme C, which would add 35 and a half squadrons by 1939 and build up its reserves thereafter.[74] That would still leave Germany with a numerical superiority by 1937 but the Air Staff felt that superior British organization, training, and equipment would offset the greater German numbers. At any rate, even though Germany might be a powerful menace by 1939, the German air force was not expected to be ready for a full-scale war until 1942.[75]

The Parliamentary debate on the new estimates for Scheme C, expected to cost £30 million annually, was put off by the Cabinet until after Hitler's speech on 21 May, for fear of giving offense to the unpredictable German dictator.[76] Chamberlain was relieved at the mild tone of Hitler's speech, which he thought had set out to "catch British public opinion and if possible, to drive a wedge between us and France."[77] He also felt his job had been made "much easier" by the speech.[78] That is, he did not think that Britain would have to rearm so quickly nor to such a great extent.

At this point it should be noted that the Cabinet had to be reshuffled because MacDonald's ill health forced him to step down as Prime Minister. Baldwin replaced him, but the rest of the Cabinet remained virtually the same. Chamberlain's steadying influence could best be exerted from the Treasury, where he decided to stay although he could have taken the more prestigious Foreign Office if he had wanted it. Simon, never popular among Conservatives, was eased out of the Foreign Office and moved to the Home Office, replaced by Sir Samuel Hoare who had instructions from Baldwin to "keep us out of war, we are not ready for it."[79] The only significant addition to the Cabinet was Phillip Cunliffe-Lister (later Lord Swinton), who replaced Londonderry at the Air Ministry. He proved to be a key player in the rearmament program until his removal in 1938.

Despite the German announcement of air parity and conscription, British leaders continued to exude optimism in public for an arms limitation agreement despite its implausibility. Baldwin informed the House of a Government proposal for an "Air Locarno"and a bombing pact,[80] again keeping public opinion from over-reacting to German militancy. An Air Locarno continued to be raised from time to time, even until 1939, in the rather naive hope of avoiding a devastating arms race. But the plain fact of the matter was that there could be no air pact as long as the Soviet Union was excluded from the talks. And neither Hitler nor the British Government was willing even to sit down with the hated Bolsheviks.

In June 1935 the British Government acquiesced to German demands for a naval agreement. Independently of her allies Great Britain recognized Germany's right to build a navy up to 35 percent the size of the Royal Navy. By signing the Anglo-German Naval Treaty, the British Government implicitly acknowledged Germany's right to rearm, notwithstanding the strictures imposed by the Treaty of Versailles. The effect on the Stresa Front and Britain's potential allies was debilitating. France was visibly upset at Great Britain's unilateral decision to flout the Treaty of Versailles, and Italy, the savior of Austrian independence in 1934 and a Locarno partner, was perplexed at the meaning of the British action. If Great Britain could not, or would not, stand up to unilateral German revisionism in naval matters, then where would Britain take a stand? Encouraged by this pusillanimous display of British diplomacy, Mussolini, already decided upon settling the long-standing dispute with Abyssinia, became emboldened to ignore British warnings not to use force in furtherance of his claims on Abyssinia, and commenced hostilities against Abyssinia later in the year.

The British decision to accept Hitler's formula for naval rearmament was sharply criticized by Churchill, a former First Lord of the Admiralty, on the grounds that it would tie down a large part of the Royal Navy in the North Sea that was desperately needed in the Far East. The point was not lost on the Admiralty. But for personal and political reasons, the Admiralty decided to go along with the Naval Treaty anyway. Sir Bolton Eyres-Monsell, First Lord of the Admiralty, was paraded out to downplay the German naval threat. Anxious to preserve his bargaining power in the Cabinet, he stated that he did not think the submarine threat constituted as great a threat as it did in the last war and that capital ships would not pose a threat for several years, by which time he hoped, Britain's air defenses would have been completed. Besides, what choice lay open to His Majesty's Government? Once Germany's right to build an air force and an army had been conceded, what could the British do to prevent German naval construction? The military option was never contemplated. Nor was the economic or diplomatic option seriously explored, either through the League of Nations or in concert with the Stresa powers, for fear of embittering Anglo-German relations. The Government simply assumed that nothing could be done to prevent Germany from rearming. So the next best thing was to try to contain it. Moreover, the treaty fit in neatly with the Government's attempts to court favor with public opinion by demonstrating its willingness to pursue arms limitation agreements and rebutting the Opposition's charges of "warmongering" sure to surface during the fall election.

Following on the news of German rearmament and the Anglo-German

Naval Treaty came the results of the long-awaited Peace Ballot on 28 June. The subject of much controversy, the Peace Ballot was an unqualified success in arousing public interest in the question of the League of Nations and collective security. More than 11 million votes were cast, or 37 percent of the electorate. Five leading questions were put to the voters.

QUESTION[81]	YES	NO
1. Should Great Britain continue to be a member of the League of Nations?	11,090,387	355,883
2. Do you favor a reduction in arms?	10,470,489	862,775
3. Do you favor a disarmament?	9,533,558	1,689,783
4. Do you favor the manufacture and sale of arms?	10,417,329	775,415
5. Do you favor sanctions?		
a. Economic and non-military	10,027,068	635,074
b. Military, if necessary	6,784,368	2,351,981

While 11,090,387 voted in favor of belonging to the League of Nations, 10,027,068 favored the imposition of non-military sanctions but only 6,784,368 favored using military sanctions if necessary. Undeniably the loss of over 3 million votes on the question of applying military sanctions entailed a significant but not unacceptable political risk. More than 60 percent of the voters approved question 5b by nearly a 3 to 1 margin, favoring the use of military sanctions, if necessary. Clearly, public opinion was on the side of the League of Nations, collective security, and sanctions. The respondents to the poll also favored disarmament and a reduction in arms, but by almost the same margin they wished to continue the manufacture and sale of arms (question 4). Either the public was confused by the ambiguous nature of the questions or uninformed about the implications of its responses. Such inconsistencies are not uncharacteristic of the fickle nature of public opinion. At any rate, the National Government did little to educate the public about the survey. It viewed the poll as a nuisance and distanced itself from the debate. Chamberlain called it "mischievous." Baldwin, though quiet for most of the time during the debate, put on his best public face and said he "welcomed" the results when they were presented to him by Lord Cecil.

It was now two years since the Government had decided to rearm, but the country was still relatively uninformed about the critical state of its defenses and, more important, about the need for a greater defense program. The voting pattern of the Peace Ballot suggests that, given the proper lead, public opinion might have been persuaded to support a greater defense initiative. Chamberlain apparently sensed the opportunity when he suggested to Baldwin that the Conservative Party should give the country a bold lead and make an issue of rearmament in the upcoming election.[82] While Baldwin generally deferred to Chamberlain's economic and financial expertise, his keen political sense took second place to none, and he wisely ignored Chamberlain's advice. Baldwin was content to downplay the rearmament issue, and allow the Conservative Party to address it at the annual party conference at Margate in October, in the confident expectation that it would endorse a strong defense program, as it had consistently done in the past.

The Abyssinian crisis helped to focus public attention more narrowly on the meaning of the Peace Ballot, and a small but perceptible change in public opinion began to take shape. Whereas the debate had been discussed earlier in somewhat abstract academic terms, the international situation provided an excellent opportunity for the public to consider the consequences of its policy choices in more concrete terms. The inherent contradictions and ambiguities between questions 2 and 5 gradually gave way to a more realistic appreciation for the need to rearm, at least for purposes of enforcing League sanctions should that become necessary. The political parties reacted accordingly. The Liberals, having refrained from opposing defense estimates in May, stopped short of supporting a major defense effort. As longtime supporters of the League in maintaining peace in the world, the Liberals reluctantly conceded that they could not logically oppose rearmament and support the League. And that Great Britain, as the most important League member, ought to be given the means with which to assume its obligations in fulfillment of that role.

Significantly, the most remarkable attitudinal changes occurred within the trade union affiliates and, to a lesser extent, in the Parliamentary Labor Party. Earlier in the year after learning of Germany's claim to air parity with Great Britain, the National Executive and General Council of the Trades Unions Congress (GCTUC) agreed with Dalton, Citrine, and Bevin to cease opposition to air rearmament necessary to ensure national security. Although no vote was taken Dalton claims to have been supported by the majority of those present, including Clement Attlee.[83] The Parliamentary Labor Party, seduced in part by Hitler's 21 May speech, and still under the leadership of George Lansbury, continued to oppose the air estimates in July, preferring to seek security not through rearmament but through disarmament. Nevertheless, on 24 July, the National Council on Labor gave assurances to the House that the PLP would back the Government on any stand it made at Geneva in support of the League policy dealing with the Abyssinian crisis.[84] This position was reaffirmed at the annual meeting of the Trades Union Congress (TUC) in September, despite warnings by Citrine and Bevin that it might mean war. The TUC pledged its support for "any action consistent with the treaties and statutes of the League to restrain the Italian Government and to uphold the authority of the League."[85]

While not actually endorsing rearmament, Labor for the moment held open the door of cooperation to the Government, which Baldwin was quick to recognize. Sensing an opportunity to win Labor's support for a stepped-up rearmament program then under consideration by the Cabinet, he met with Citrine a week later to explore the possibility of trade union cooperation for the defense program. He informed Citrine of the deplorable state of British arms, which were far below the minimum requirements of national defense, and of the politically unpopular cost of repairing those defenses.[86] Actually, Baldwin was hoping that Citrine might be able to do something on the TUC side.[87] Citrine then suggested a private meeting with TUC representatives so that Baldwin "could safely disclose what was in his mind."[88] Unfortunately, nothing emerged from these proposals, and the contacts were inexplicably broken off. Citrine left to visit the Soviet Union later in the month, and the two men did not meet again officially until late in 1936, and then, only to discuss the King's marriage problem.[89] In later years, Baldwin said he could not recall what had happened to his early efforts to win TUC support for the rearmament program.[90] Most likely, Labor's Soviet connection had a disquieting effect on Baldwin, but he was not exactly dealing from the top of the deck either. Unknown to Labor, election plans had already been laid for the fall. The move could hardly have been calculated to inspire Labor's trust in the National Government. The failure of the British Government to establish a good faith working relationship with Labor proved to be a costly mistake.

Italy's decision to resolve its dispute with Abyssinia by force placed the National Government in an uncomfortable position when it was forced to choose between a valuable friend and ally, and a weak League of Nations. Upholding League sanctions presented the unpleasant prospect of driving Mussolini into Hitler's arms and destroying the Stresa Front. To refuse to apply sanctions ran the risk of alienating a great body of public opinion that supported the League and collective security.[91]

Churchill, Vansittart, and most Conservatives agreed that Italy must not be alienated. But, when faced with an election in the fall, Baldwin gave in to political pressure and endorsed the League principles in his public utterances. The new Foreign Secretary, Sir Samuel Hoare, was in a tight spot. No matter which way he turned, he was stymied. He solicited advice from such diverse political shades of opinion as Churchill and Austen Chamberlain on the Right, to David Lloyd George, Herbert Samuel, and Lansbury on the Left.[92] And, of course, he sought advice from his colleagues in the Cabinet as he prepared a major foreign policy address for Geneva on 11 September. His search for a clear policy was not made any easier by France's uncooperative attitude. France was not about to destroy the Stresa Front, if for no other reason than to keep Germany isolated. Therefore, in desperation, Hoare tried to bluff his way through the crisis by coming down strongly on the side of the League of Nations against "all acts of unprovoked aggression," hoping to shore up French support for the League and, at the same time, to deter Mussolini from carrying out his threats against Abyssinia. Ultimately, Hoare came down on the side of public opinion. Mussolini was not impressed.

Hoare's speech was well received by Labor. At its annual conference in Brighton, 24 September to 4 October, the Labor Party went on record, by a vote of 2,168,000 to 102,000, "to support the League and to use all necessary measures, provided by the Covenant to prevent Italy's unjust and rapacious attack on the territory of a fellow member of the League."[93] The vote should not be interpreted for anything but for what it said — a vote for collective security and the League of Nations. But as Dalton, Citrine and Bevin had reminded the TUC earlier, support for the League might eventually lead to war, and Britain must be prepared to carry out its responsibilities under the League Covenant. The significance of this change in Labor's rearmament policy, though slight, has generally been overlooked by historians.

That point was not lost on George Lansbury, the sincerely pacifist leader of the party, who could not support the resolution; he resigned his position as a matter of conscience. Clement Attlee, his successor, was willing to support armaments for the League but not a "huge national rearmament program." Labor was positioning itself for a rearmament program necessary to resist aggression. Though apparently intended for use against Italy, it might also be adapted for defensive measures against Germany as well. When Italy finally invaded Abyssinia on 3 October 1935, the tide of public opinion had swung decidedly in line with the Government's policy laid down by Hoare at Geneva, though a handful of newspapers resisted the call for sanctions.[94]

Baldwin's timing of the national election was exquisite. It was announced barely three weeks after the invasion of Abyssinia. Hoping to capitalize on the patriotic fervor unleashed in the country by the King's Twenty-fifth Jubilee in June still sweeping the country, the Conservative Party effectively pre-empted Labor's best election issue — collective security and the League of Nations — by its opposition to Italian aggression. The National Government was brimming with confidence as it approached the general election, scheduled for November, and with good cause. The economy had shown marked improvement by the spring of 1935, at which time Chamberlain proudly proclaimed that Great Britain had recovered 80 percent of its pre-Depression prosperity. Aiding the recovery was a boom in the home building industry. Also, the furor unleashed by Chamberlain's new guidelines for welfare recipients which had triggered angry demonstrations against the Government in January, had subsided with the passage of a new Poor Law in the spring. All signs pointed to a relatively comfortable victory for the Government. Only the Abyssinian crisis presented a potential problem. By positioning the Government in line with the League and collective security, Baldwin effectively neutralized Labor's (and the Liberals') strongest appeal to the electorate. Labor was forced to campaign on domestic issues at a time of a steadily improving economy. Baldwin again demonstrated his political sagacity.

Attlee tried to revive the rearmament issue later during the campaign when he realized that he had been out-maneuvered by Baldwin, but to no avail. In frustration, Labor's attacks became more vicious and more personal. Chamberlain, in particular, was singled out, ironically, as a "war-monger" for the lead he had taken in the rearmament program. Inflammatory posters depicted babies wearing gas masks to enhance Labor's image as the party of peace, whereas the Conservative Party confidently went on record at its annual conference in support of a defense program of air parity and a British fleet capable of protecting its imperial interests.[95] Apparently, the peace issue and disarmament were dead issues. German rearmament and the invasion of Abyssinia had moved public opinion significantly closer to the Government's position on rearmament, and away from Labor. In the seven by-elections since March, rearmament had not played well for Labor candidates, who lost six of the seven contests. And, in the general election, Conservative members of Parliament made very few personal appearances and expended very little effort to explain to the voters why rearmament was necessary.[96]

Chamberlain's thoughts on the matter, more than two months before the election was announced, are worthy of note. In his diary he wrote:

Now, the Labor Party obviously intends to fasten on our backs the accusation of being war-mongers, and they are suggesting that we have "hush-hush" plans for rearmament which we are concealing from the people. As a matter of fact, we are working on plans for rearmament at an early date, for the situation in Europe is most alarming. Germany is rapidly rearming and the temptation to demand new territory may be too great in the next few years. Therefore, we must hurry on our own rearmament, and in the course of the next 4 or 5 years we shall probably have to spend an extra £120,000,000 or more in doing so. We are not yet sufficiently advanced to reveal our ideas to the public, but of course we cannot deny the general charge of rearmament, and no doubt, if we try to keep our ideas secret till after the elections, we should either find, or, if we succeed, lay ourselves open to the far more damaging accusation that we had deliberately deceived the people. In view of these considerations, I have suggested that we should take the bold view of actually appealing to the country on a defence programme.[97]

This extraordinary document seemingly depicts Chamberlain as a forceful advocate for a greater rearmament program. But a careful reading of the text also suggests something else. It reveals Chamberlain to be either naive or unwilling to meet the actual needs of the defense program when he contemplates spending only an extra £120 million over the next four or five years, while at the same time acknowledging that the situation in Europe is alarming and that "Germany is said to be borrowing over £1 billion a year to get herself rearmed."[98]

Yet if finance was thought to be the major stumbling block to rearmament, Chamberlain's decision to reduce the income tax raises serious questions about his commitment to rearm the country. His diary makes clear that he intended to continue to rely as much as possible on financing the defense program through the revenue, knowing that it fell far short of the DRC proposals to date. Later in his diary he revealed that he "had carefully abstained from any debate or specific commitments about defense."[99] In any case, it would be a mistake to characterize Chamberlain as a leading Government proponent of rearmament simply on the basis of his recommendation to make an issue of it in the 1935 election, as his subsequent actions make clear. His difference with Baldwin was over style and politics, not substance. Baldwin, the consummate politician, was out to capture the floating vote, while Chamberlain, the party man, wished to draw sharp lines between the Conservatives and Labor. By posing as a strong advocate of greater armaments, Chamberlain hoped to consolidate his position among the imperialist wing of the Conservative Party (Austen Chamberlain, Leo Amery, and Churchill) while still satisfying the appeasement wing of the party that saw socialism as a greater danger to the country than fascism.[100]

But Baldwin understood the importance of building public support for the National Government as it attempted to balance the security interests of the country against increasing taxation, scarcity of imported goods, and inflation — just some of the hardships to be endured in the next few years — and he saw no reason to excite a prejudice against Labor. Both men, however, agreed that Labor's fitness to govern should be one of the central issues of the campaign.[101] Strictly from a political point of view, Baldwin was wise to reject Chamberlain's suggestion to make defense a major issue in the 1935 election, since the country was riding the crest of a steadily improving economy. And, facing a divided Labor Party, the Conservatives had little fear of a Labor victory at the polls.

Prudence, it would seem, demanded caution where defense issues were concerned. Baldwin quietly acknowledged, in his Parliamentary role and in other speeches, that the Government was indeed rearming, but only to the extent necessary to fulfill its international obligation, especially in the context of the Abyssinian crisis. He gave his solemn pledge that there would be "no great armaments," to rebut Attlee's charge that the Government was planning huge armaments. Baldwin's campaign strategy paid off handsomely. The National Government won a convincing victory at the polls. Although Labor increased its representation from 46 to 154 seats, the Baldwin government still retained a comfortable majority of more than 250 seats with a five-year term in office to carry out its defense program.

But Chamberlain's concern for a mandate was well taken. Public support for the rearmament program was absolutely essential to its success. By making rearmament an issue in the election, the Government would be able to enact those controversial measures necessary to deal with the problems facing the defense program. Nevertheless, Baldwin could argue with some justification, as he did, that a mandate for rearmament had indeed been given. The Conservative Party conference had endorsed it, and Labor had made it an issue. The Labor Party had warned that a vote for the National Government was a vote for armaments and war.[102] The public had ample opportunity to weigh the differences between Labor and the Conservative Party on the issue of rearmament. The Conservatives, on the other hand, never tried to hide the fact that they intended to pursue a rearmament program adequate to the needs of the country. Many Conservative Party candidates adhered to the party position outlined at the Margate party conference and campaigned for a stronger defense program on their own. Conservatives like Churchill and Amery spoke in much stronger terms. If not directly, then at least by implication, Baldwin and the Conservatives could claim to have been given a mandate to push forward with the rearmament program, consistent with Baldwin's often repeated pledge of air parity with Germany, and sufficient arms to fulfill its obligations to the international community.

With the general election out of the way in November, one might have expected the poisonous influence of politics to have relaxed its grip on the rearmament program. Whereas "politics and finance" had shaped the defense program up to the general election, no British government could safely ignore the extremely vulnerable position of the British Empire in dealing with the increasingly aggressive actions of Germany, Japan, and Italy. Finance presented a formidable obstacle to the rearmament program, to be sure. But what was needed at the time was a clear statement of strategic and military objectives that would drive the rearmament program forward, at an affordable cost. Without it, the COS and the services would be stymied in their efforts to develop a coherent and appropriate preparedness plan to meet their responsibilities in time. The Abyssinian war amply demonstrated the need for such a clearly defined defense strategy.

Chamberlain's plan to increase the size of the air force to defend the home islands was ill-suited to a Mediterranean policy, where naval power was more important. By operating under carefully controlled financial, political, and economic imperatives, the rearmament program could hardly have been expected to provide the degree of security required by the threat confronting it. Having pledged the country to parity with Germany's ever-expanding air force, the Conservative-dominated National Government found itself at a competitive disadvantage with the German totalitarian methods of rearming.

Whereas the British government sought to provide for the exigencies of war through a market economy, the Nazi regime could compel the German economy to support its defense program with all of its resources, without fear of political opposition. It was the classic dilemma faced by leaders of free societies in dealing with totalitarian systems. The British Government was at a crossroad. By failing to take the necessary powers to fulfill its pledge of air parity, it could only expect to fall farther behind in the arms race it desperately sought to avoid. On the other hand, to join the race meant facing a long term of economic dislocation and the possible resurgence of the Labor Party.[103] Relying on Chamberlain's assurances, it chose the much easier path of *laissez-faire* rather than one of austerity and self-discipline. It was not so much a policy as it was of marking time.

NOTES

1. British investments in Shanghai alone totaled about £64 million in 1932.

2. Feiling, 236.

3. Maurice Cowling, *The Impact of Hitler* (Cambridge: Cambridge University Press, 1975), 24.

4. Roskill, *Hankey*, 540; Patrick Kyba, *Covenants Without the Sword* (Waterloo, Ontario: Wilfrid Laurier University Press, 1983), chs. 2 and 3.

5. CAB 23/76/38, 31 May 1933.

6. Kyba, *Covenants,* chs. 2 and 3.

7. DBFP, 2nd series, vol. 5, #5, 21, 30, 127, 223, 371, 448; CAB 24/239/52; CAB 24/241/129; CAB 24/242/198; CAB 23/76/35, 17 May 1933; CAB 24/242/184; CAB 23/76/48, 26 July 1933.

8. Roskill, 537.

9. NC 18/1/848, 28 October 1933.

10. Kyba, 57–58.

11. Ibid., 102.

12. NC 18/1/848, 28 October 1933.

13. CAB 23/77/62, 15 November 1933.

14. Ibid.

15. Kyba, 99.

16. CP 64(34). Only London and the southern part of England were covered under this plan. The northern part of the United Kingdom was to be without adequate air defense for five years.

17. *Debates*, 286: 2078, 8 March 1934. Hereafter cited as *Debates*.

18. Winston Churchill, *The Gathering Storm* (Boston: Houghton Mifflin, 1948), 117.

19. NC 7/11/27/29, 6 March 1934. Simon to Chamberlain.

20. Viscount Simon, *Retrospect* (London: Hutchinson, 1952), 179–181; Norman Rose, *Vansittart: Study of a Diplomat* (New York: Holmes and Meier, 1978), 188–189. Roskill, 75–76.

21. Roskill, 175–176.

22. Churchill, 114.

23. Ibid.

24. NC 2/23, 10 March 1934. Chamberlain was "firmly against it" (i.e., new elections at this time).

25. CAB 23/78/10, CP 64(34), 19 March 1934.

26. CAB 23/79/18, 25 April 1934.

27. CAB 24/249/113.

28. NC 2/23, 25 March 1934. After Munich, he reaffirmed this view, telling the Cabinet that ever since he became Chancellor of the Exchequer, he had been oppressed with the sense that armaments "might break our backs," and that he was still resolved to "remove the causes which were responsible for the arms race." CAB 23/95/48, 13 October 1938.

29. NC 2/23, 25 March 1934.

30. Ibid.

31. Ibid., 20 April 1934. The *Annual Report of the COS* in 1933 stressed the importance of the Low Countries to Britain's security. It warned that "limited participation in a European war would not be feasible, and to commit a portion of our slender military resources to the continent would . . . be fraught with the gravest danger." COS 310(33).

32. NC 2/23, 27 March 1934.

33. CAB 23/79/19, 2 May 1934. The members of this committee included Chamberlain, Hankey, Eden, Lord Londonderry, Quentin Hailsham, Sir Bolton Eyres-Monsell, Phillip Cunliffe-Lister, Lord Halifax, William Ormsby-Gore and Walter Runciman .

34. NC 2/23, 3 May 1934 and 6 June 1934.

35. Ibid., 12 May 1934; Gibbs, 110, 535. Gibbs also agrees that "Chamberlain was the strong man of the Party, and eventually got most of his own way."

36. DC(M) (32) 120, 20 June 1934.

37. NC 2/23, 6 June 1934; CAB 23/79/31, 31 July 1934.

38. NC 2/23, 3 May 1934; NC 2/23, 12 May 1934; NC 2/23, 6 June 1934. (See Feiling, 258).

39. NC 2/23, 16 March 1934; NC 2/23, 20 April 1934; NC 2/23, 6 June 1934. Apparently Chamberlain was prepared to recognize Japanese suzerainty over Manchuria and to acquiesce in a Japanese sphere of influence in China, despite its effect on Anglo-American relations. Bell, *Chamberlain, Germany and Japan,* 101–102.

40. CAB 23/78/13, 14 March 1934. Japan had just proclaimed the Amau Declaration, in which she announced that she would be the "sole judge" of foreign activity in China. This was one of Chamberlain's few setbacks in the Cabinet. Had Chamberlain been Prime Minister at the time, the outcome would have been very different indeed. [Ed.]

41. CP 70(34).

42. CAB 23/79/26, 27 June 1934; CAB 23/79/27, 4 July 1934.

43. DC(M) (32) 120, 20 June 1934.

44. CAB 23/79/26, 27 June 1934; CAB 23/79/28, 11 July 1934.

45. NC 2/23, 6 June 1934; CAB 23/79/31, 31 July 1934.

46. Gibbs, 106.

47. CAB 23/79/28, 4 July 1934.

48. Roskill, 111; Gibbs, 115, 120; CAB 23/79/29, 17 July 1934.

49. Debates, 238: 1075, 18 April 1934.

50. Shay, 42.

51. CAB 23/79/29, 17 July 1934; CP 205(34).

52. Gibbs, 115.

53. Ibid., 123–124; Kyba, 124.

54. CAB 23/80/41, 21 November 1934; CP 265(34)

55. CAB 23/80/42, 26 November 1934.

56. CAB 23/80/41, 21 November 1934.

57. CAB 23/80/42, 26 November 1934.

58. Debates, 295: 857, 28 November 1934.

59. The accelerated air program called for an increased expenditure of a mere £250,000 in the first year and of £500,000 in the second, but Chamberlain nevertheless warned his colleagues about assuming new obligations, as it was becoming extremely difficult to find additional revenue to meet the increased expenditure. CAB 23/80/42, 26 November 1934. The Admiralty asked for only £3,500,000 above the 1934–1935 estimates, since it had been forced to take a cut by the Exchequer in order to balance the budget. CAB 23/80/46, 12 December 1934; CP 291(34).

60. NC 2/23, 9 December 1934.

61. NC 2/23, 20 April 1934.

62. Sir Arnold Wilson, *Walks and Talks Abroad* (London: Oxford University Press, 1936), xxiv.

63. The National Government lost three of four contests between August 1934 and March 1935. Kyba, 119.

64. *Statement Relating to Defence,* CMD 4827 (London: HMSO, 4 March 1935).

65. E. C. Peden, "Sir Warren Fisher and British Rearmament Against Germany," 40.

66. Lord Avon (Anthony Eden), *Facing the Dictators* (Boston: Houghton Mifflin, 1962), 141.

67. Tom Stannage, *Baldwin Thwarts the Opposition* (London: Croom Helm, 1980), 244.

68. Hugh Dalton, *The Fateful Years,* vol. 2 (London: Muller, 1957), 134; Alan Bullock, *The Life and Times of Ernest Bevin,* vol. 1 (London: Heinemann, 1960), 562.

69. William Reader, *Lord Weir: Architect of Air Power* (London: Collier, 1968), 211.

70. Bullock, *Bevin,* 592.

71. *Debates,* 299: 35ff., 4 March 1935.

72. NC 2/23, 8 March 1935; NC 18/1/908, 23 March 1935.

73. CP 69(35).

74. CP 85 (35).

75. Ibid.

76. CAB 23/81/26, 8 May 1935.

77. NC 2/23, 26 May 1935. Hitler's speech hinted at a return to the League, support for Locarno, a willingness to accept air parity, and a Navy at 35 percent of the Royal Navy.

78. Ibid.

79. *Jones Diary,* 7 January 1936, 159. Jones was a private secretary and friend of Baldwin.

80. *Debates,* 302: 350ff. 27 May 1935.

81. Kyba, 149.

82. NC 2/23, 2 August 1935.

83. Dalton, 64.

84. Bullock, 562.

85. *The Times,* 5 September 1935.

86. Walter Citrine, *Men and Work* (London: Hutchinson,1964), 353.

87. Ibid.

88. G. M. Young, *Baldwin* (London: Rupert Hart-Davis, 1955), 204.

89. Ibid., 356.

90. Ibid.

91. NC 17/11/28/24, Hoare to Chamberlain, 18 August 1935.

92. J. A. Cross, *Sir Samuel Hoare* (London: Jonathan Cape, 1977), 209.

93. Dalton, 64.

94. They included *The Daily Express, The Daily Mirror, The Observer, The Saturday Review, The Scotsman, The Morning Post,* and *The Western Morning News.* Kyba, 154.

95. Ibid., 143.

96. Ibid., 127.
97. NC 2/23, 2 August 1935.
98. Ibid.
99. Ibid., 20 November 1935.
100. Ibid.
101. Stannage, 171.
102. Kyba, 176–180.
103. One of the reasons for the alliance with the Liberal Party in 1931 was so that "socialism would be forced to take a back seat for the best part of a generation." (Joseph Ball to Neville Chamberlain, 16 September 1931, CRD File F/1/A/1, quoted in Ramsden, 58).

Chapter 4

Labor Issues and Defense Policy

By late 1934 it had become apparent that Mussolini's designs on Abyssinia might well result in armed hostilities. This seriously deteriorating situation in the Mediterranean created a strategic problem for the National Government as it tried to fashion its defense policy. The immediate threat to British interests posed by Italy's belligerence required a strong naval presence in the area. Standing astride Britain's lifeline to India and the Far East, Italy could wreak havoc with British communications, threaten the Suez Canal from Libya, and disrupt British trade routes. Yet, the earlier terms of reference for the Defense Requirements Committee had not included Italy as a potential enemy. An anomalous situation had therefore arisen with regard to Britain's defense policy, which had been predicated thus far on strengthening its deficiencies in the air to meet the long-term, more dangerous threat from Germany's rapidly expanding air force, and not from Italy's naval threat in the Mediterranean.

The Chiefs of Staff had concluded in May that 1,400 more planes were needed to keep pace with Germany by 1937.[1] The Air Ministry backed the report by assuring the Cabinet that it would be possible to meet that figure without any appreciable reorganization of industry, although it admitted that some problems were to be expected with respect to recruitment and, to a lesser extent, ensuring supply.[2] Obviously, a decision to beef up the naval forces in the Mediterranean would exacerbate the problem. How could the needs of both services be met? How would priorities be assigned? Without a clear statement of objectives from the Cabinet, military and strategic policy had to be kept in abeyance. Consequently, the DRC asked for and received authority to work out a comprehensive defense program, providing the best security it could devise, by January 1939, the date by which the COS had targeted as the date beyond which it would not be safe to delay implementation of its rearmament programs. Financial considerations were referenced to be of "secondary importance."[3] For that reason, the program became known as the "Ideal Scheme."

Speaking for the Foreign Office, Sir Samuel Hoare tried, albeit unsuccessfully, to advance the date for completion of the rearmament program. He warned the Cabinet that all the information that he had at the Foreign Office pointed to a "critical" date earlier than was anticipated by the COS, "possibly as early as 1938."[4] Such information from the Foreign Office tended to be conveniently disregarded by the Cabinet, being interpreted as unduly pessimistic and inspired by the vehemently Germanophobic Permanent Undersecretary of State, Sir Robert Vansittart. Led by Chamberlain, the Cabinet chose to rely on an Air Ministry intelligence estimate that Germany would not be sufficiently prepared to launch a full-scale European war until 1942.[5] Limited wars, international incidents, and diplomatic threats were also ignored as the Cabinet implicitly affirmed its unwillingness to involve itself in matters not related to its immediate security interests.

After an interim report had been submitted, a third report of the DRC eventually found its way to the Cabinet on 21 November. Of the three services, the Royal Navy was in relatively good shape to defend the home base from attack, but it could offer little support in defense of its territories in the Far East. And even though the Admiralty entertained no doubts about its ability to prevail in offensive operations against Italy in the Mediterranean, should the Abyssinian situation warrant such action, it felt that its scarce resources could be more profitably employed elsewhere. The COS estimated that as many as four capital ships might be lost in any Mediterranean campaign in which Great Britain was the major player.[6] For that reason the COS stressed the importance of not imposing sanctions on Italy without the whole-hearted support of the French Government. What made the loss of four ships so critical was the time factor involved. Ships could take as long as four years to build, during which time the Royal Navy, already spread thin and with work on the Singapore naval base still lagging behind schedule, would not be able to respond to any hostilities in the Far East where Japanese militancy and arrogant behavior were still causing the British Government considerable embarrassment.

Efforts to reach a *modus vivendi* with Japan continued to interest British policy makers at Chamberlain's urging, but in the end floundered, largely because of the requirement to recognize (1) the Japanese puppet state of Manchukuo and (2) the difficulty of dealing with a military government.[7] Nevertheless, the COS concluded that in view of "our extremely weak position in the Far East . . . every possible effort should be made to overcome these political difficulties."[8] The memorandum may also have included the negative impact that a political arrangement with Japan would have on Anglo-American relations. Viewed in these terms, the DRC naturally subscribed to an ideal naval program known as the Two Ocean Standard, intended to project British naval power in Europe and in the Far East simultaneously. It called for the replacement of seven capital ships by 1939, the construction of four new aircraft carriers by 1942, and more destroyers, convoy ships, and smaller craft.[9] Scheme F was proposed as an "ideal" program for the Royal Air Force that would enable it to keep pace with Germany's expanding air force. It envisioned an increase in front-line planes from the approved number of 1,512 in Scheme C to 1,736, with a reserve component of 225 per cent of its front-line strength, whereas reserves for Scheme C had been postponed until 1939.[10] Finally, the third report of the DRC attempted to deal with the vexing problem of the Army. Of all the services, the Army was in the most deplorable condition. The Regular Army was under-strength by 10,000 men, and each year the manpower shortage threatened to grow worse by 3,000 recruits, while the Territorial Army (TA) component was short of its authorized strength by 42,000 men, not including the manpower to provide for the Air Defense of Great Britain (ADGB),[11] viz.,manning the anti-aircraft guns, searchlights, etc. In all, about 250,000 men were needed to support the Army's mission to defend the outposts of the Empire, the Low Countries, and the air defense of Great Britain. Yet, each year, the manpower shortage. threatened to grow worse as greater demands were expected to be made on the rearmament program.[12]

Hampering the Army's efforts to recruit soldiers were two factors. One was an image problem. During World War I, the TA had served as "wastage"— it was simply thought to be cannon fodder for a Continental army. The other recruiting problem had to do with the especially deplorable conditions of Army life in relation to the other services. Enlistments were for seven year terms, and discipline was harsh. Living conditions and poor pay also contributed to the shortfall in enlistments each year. The Committee for Imperial Defense rejected raising Army pay as a means of obtaining the necessary manpower because "it would compete with conditions in the labor market." Instead, it would rely on reforms and propaganda to meet its goal. Army enlistments were to be reduced to five years; more decent living quarters were to be built; and movies, pamphlets, and traditional propaganda methods were to be employed for the desired effect of raising Army morale and improving its negative image.[13] Conscription in peacetime was out of the question.

Ignoring these internal problems, the DRC recommended that the approved Continental force of four divisions plus one armored division should be supported by a reserve force of twelve divisions within twelve months. After all, what good was a Continental army without the reinforcements to back it up? Additionally, the DRC Report recommended that the TA take over the coastal defense and the anti-aircraft defenses of the country. The recommendations of the DRC were discussed again by the Cabinet on 4 December and raised a number of questions involving finance, manpower, and industrial capacity. The total cost of the Ideal Scheme was calculated at £417,500,000, a far cry from the £120,000,000 envisioned by Chamberlain in August. It was not enough simply to decide whether or how these programs could be financed. Where would the pilots come from to fly the additional planes? Would voluntary recruitment satisfy the manpower requirements for all the services, or would it be necessary to fulfill the requirements for the Ideal Scheme through conscription? Could existing facilities produce the required number of planes, ships, tanks, and tools, or would new ones have to be created? If so, would the Government be prepared to offer long-term contracts and credits to provide incentives for private investment? And, assuming that the industrial capacity could be found, where would the skilled labor be found to man the factories? Would military recruitment take precedence over civilian needs? These were but some of the vexing questions inherent in any scheme of defense predicated along the lines advocated by the DRC Failure in any one area, whether in finance, manpower, or industrial capacity, threatened to wreck the whole rearmament program. Careful consideration therefore had to be given to each of aspect of the DRC report for its impact on all aspects of British society.

With these concerns in mind, the proposal for the Ideal Scheme was sent to the Defense Policy and Requirements Committee (DPR), a newly created ministerial committee chaired by Baldwin. It proceeded largely under the direction of its chief adviser and consultant, Lord Weir, and of course Chamberlain, who boasted that "its policy has been guided by me."[14] Lord Weir came to the committee with excellent credentials on industrial problems related to defense. As Director General of Aircraft Production in World War I, and then as Air Minister, he possessed all the right qualifications for the job as far as Chamberlain was concerned. Currently he was serving in an advisory capacity to Lord Swinton at the Air Ministry on such matters. Not content to act simply as an expert on supply, he asked for and received the right to be associated with "the highest direction of rearmament in all its aspects, strategic, as well as industrial."[15]

Lord Weir's experience in World War I placed him in the forefront in dealing with the trade unions and their Parliamentary counterpart, the Labor Party, and only served to embitter his opinion of them. He was considered to be a "stern employer" and "uncompromising in trade union matters."[16] Weir was convinced that the decline of industrial Great Britain was due largely to the labor movement because "they were inefficient and unproductive, and for the social system they sponsored."[17] It was a point of view shared by many Conservatives, who persisted in their belief that the poor were undeserving and lazy, and that relief adequate to their needs would lure them from honest work.[18]

World War I had served as a persistent reminder to Weir of the disruption of the rhythm of everyday life caused by population drifts to urban centers. He understood that a transient workforce, wage and price inflation, profiteering and its accompanying popular discontent meant increasing labor unrest. Labor would have to be accommodated in the interest of preserving the existing order and maintaining industrial peace if the rearmament program was to be successful. The Government could not fulfill the requirements of the Ideal Scheme without giving labor its due, but it did not have the inclination to do so. Trade unions and labor leaders would have to be represented on boards and consulted by government officials in advance of any policy decision affecting the social order. It was a frightening prospect to Chamberlain. The coin to be used by the Government to preserve that relationship was to be more government programs for housing, education, and welfare. Nor did the Government wish to be saddled with these expensive social programs after the crisis had passed. For reasons such as these, Chamberlain felt that labor had to be restrained from the rearmament program as much as possible so as not to incur an additional political debt.

Lord Weir's credentials were all the more impressive when viewed from a conservative perspective. He certainly possessed the mental and political outlook necessary to ensure the proper direction of the rearmament program in such a way as not to unleash the turbulent political and economic forces that threatened to destroy the social fabric of the nation in the process. Of that Chamberlain could be sure, which is why he recommended Weir for the job.[19] In Weir, Chamberlain found a kindred spirit and valuable ally in his attempt to keep the rearmament program from wreaking havoc with the economy and destroying the social order.[20] The one kept his hand on the industrial machine, while the other managed the great engine of government. Together they made a formidable pair. Lord Weir supplied the technical argument for a scheme of limited rearmament while Chamberlain managed the political and bureaucratic aspects of the question. In their opinion, because of its socialist agenda, a heavily pledged Labor Party threatened a permanent dislocation of the economy, a weak defense system, and the inevitable disruption of the existing social order.[21]

Politics could not be divorced from the rearmament program as long as a national election hung in the balance. But that consideration could no longer be used to validate the rearmament debate after the 1935 general election. The powerful and decisive Treasury voice in defense matters must soon give way to a more compelling, national argument, or face the prospect of permanent inferiority in arms and the consequent loss of prestige in international affairs. When the report of the Defense Policy and Requirements Committee was submitted to the Cabinet on 12 February 1936, it reflected the pessimistic assessments laid down by Lord Weir and Chamberlain, noting Great Britain's inability to meet the needs of the defense program in five years "without a system of priority."[22] The Cabinet thereupon approved, with some modifications, a watered-down version of the Ideal Scheme that was careful not to interfere with the normal course of trade, even though Eden warned that they might not have five years to prepare.[23] Finance was not cited as the governing factor as strongly as it had been presented in the past. Manpower, industrial capacity, and skilled labor provided the rationale for the 1936 defense budget, which was not designed to provide security by 1939, only deterrence.[24]

Requiring huge amounts of manpower, the Army posed the greatest problem for the Government. The Cabinet, led by Chamberlain, showed little sympathy for the War Office's plight. Virtually ignoring the DRC's proposal to render the Army's Continental commitment credible, he used the Army's perennial recruitment problems to justify his argument for a force of limited liability. By pointing to the manpower shortage, he hoped to make an unanswerable case for limiting the Army's dreaded Continental role that threatened to destabilize the economy and, coincidentally, enhance labor's importance to the rearmament program. The labor question, more than any other reason, explains Chamberlain's determined and persistent effort to resist the attempts by the War Office to fulfill its Continental commitment under the Locarno Agreement and to defend its vital interests in the Low Countries.[25]

As part of its obligation to guarantee the Locarno Treaty, the British Government had established a Continental army of four infantry divisions and one mobile division largely as a symbolic peace-keeping force. But the volatile nature of European politics had thrust a new conception of its role on the War Office. As the prospects for a general European war became more realistic, and in keeping with the earlier Cabinet decision to ready the country for war by 1939, the Army concluded that it must make provision for resupply and reinforcement of the Continental force deemed necessary for that purpose by the DRC in its November 1935 report. The COS, drawing on the experience of World War I, defended its proposal for an expeditionary force by reiterating the strategic necessity of denying the Low Countries to Germany as forward bases from which to attack the British Isles by air and sea. They also recommended the proposal for its deterrent value of enabling British bombers to inflict heavy damage on military and industrial targets deep inside Germany that were difficult to reach under the present state of British air technology.

The noted military historian Basil Liddell-Hart took a somewhat different point of view. In a series of newspaper articles between November 1935 and January 1936, he advocated a theory of air power as a more effective deterrent to German aggression than an expeditionary force. He reasoned that in case of war, nothing could prevent Germany from overrunning the Low Countries, in which case an expeditionary force became useless. Scarce British manpower, materiel, and money, therefore, could be more profitably employed in furtherance of its air program. Chamberlain embraced Liddell-Hart's views whole-heartedly, but not completely, against those of Hankey and the COS because it lent support to his own views on limiting Britain's Continental commitment. But he had no intention of supporting an air program of the size and scope demanded by Liddell-Hart's strategy, which called for more offensive capability in the air.

The arguments from the Foreign Office supporting the War Office in terms of the debilitating effect that the DPR proposals would have on Britain's allies did little to dissuade the Cabinet from the Chamberlain–Liddell-Hart line of reasoning. Many Cabinet members retained vivid memories of Britain's disastrous experience with its Continental army in the last war, and were easily persuaded that the public would not support another involvement on the Continent. Trying to strike up the semblance of a compromise, a fatigued Baldwin gave way to Chamberlain's persistent and determined opposition, and decreed that since an increase in the size of the Army was largely a question of manpower and industrial output, and since it was impossible to complete the program in five years under peace-time conditions, the Government must simply "do the best it could for the Army in that period."[26] That settled the issue for the time being. The four regular divisions plus one mobile division were funded at a cost of £1,500,000 annually; the more costly program for modernization and equipment of the twelve TA divisions was postponed for future consideration since war was not expected to occur before 1939 at least.[27] And, by limiting the size of the

Continental army, the size of air and naval support facilities would automatically be limited as well.

The Admiralty did not pose as troubling a problem for the Cabinet. Of all the services, the Royal Navy was in the best fighting condition, and although its ability to project its power in the Far East had been compromised somewhat by the Abyssinian crisis, its ability to defend the home islands was unquestioned. Since it needed only 35,600 men by 1942 for an enlarged Navy, the manpower requirements for the approved program were not considered to be egregiously large. Although restricted by treaty from constructing new capital ships until December 1936, the British Government could have begun new construction earlier by declaring an emergency. But when he was asked by the First Lord of the Admiralty to do so, Baldwin told Sir Bolton Eyres-Monsell to check with Chamberlain before circulating his memo to the Cabinet. Afraid that the program would raise complications with the carefully controlled and managed rearmament program and play into the hands of those, who, like Winston Churchill, were calling for the appointment of a Cabinet-level Minister of Defense, Chamberlain rejected it.[28] Neither Chamberlain nor Baldwin wished to alarm the financial markets by raising the specter of war. Instead, the new naval program called for the replacement of five capital ships, more destroyers, two new capital ships scheduled for construction in 1937, and four new aircraft carriers by 1942.[29]

By reducing the Army's Continental role, more industrial capacity, skilled labor, manpower, and finance could now be diverted to the Royal Air Force. The new Air Force program, known as Scheme F, began to look like a truly deterrent force, matching up favorably with current intelligence estimates of German air strength. Churchill's blistering attacks in the House of Commons the previous November had done much to move the air program forward. Fortunately, Scheme F coincided with Chamberlain's own strategy of limited liability, which gave priority to air rearmament, called for an increase in the home squadrons from thirty to forty-eight (still insufficient) and a shift in emphasis to the bomber (1,022 out of 1,736 planes). The light bomber was to be replaced by the medium bomber. And, more important from the point of view of deterrence, it aimed at creating a reserve capacity of 225 percent.[30] Chamberlain took smug satisfaction in shaping the defense program, which he declared had been "materially modified as a result" of his efforts. He wrote in his diary: " I am pretty well satisfied now that, if we can keep out of war for a few years, we should have an air force of such striking power that no one will care to take risks with it. . . . I believe our resources will be more profitably employed in the air, and on the sea, than in building up great armies."[31]

The complexity of carrying through with the approved DPR program posed enormous problems for the Baldwin Government because of the limitations imposed on its implementation. Manpower, skilled labor, and industrial capacity were to be obtained without impeding the normal course of trade. And, in Chamberlain's judgment, financing for the program had to be provided out of the existing revenue as far as possible, that is, without deficit spending or borrowing. Without these self-imposed restraints, manpower suddenly appears, skilled labor is recruited, productive capacity enlarges, and money becomes available. But the social, political, and economic consequences of such a decision were deemed by Chamberlain to be so serious as to justify the imposition of these limitations. Consequently, the rearmament program was held in check by conveniently adhering to the decision not to interfere with trade.

Not all Cabinet members felt as confident as Chamberlain that these obstacles could be overcome. Lord Runciman of the Board of Trade expressed his misgivings in a memo to Baldwin, warning him that "the whole of our defense organization may collapse if due attention is not paid to these two important problems [manpower and finance], manpower in particular." And he wondered whether the present emergency ought not to be met by an emergency organization.[32] Labor Secretary Ernest Brown also anticipated problems. In a memorandum to the Cabinet in March 1936, he explained the labor issues involved in completing the program. Most troublesome, from his point of view, was not meeting current demand but the expansion of productive capacity. New factory construction would place a severe burden upon the building industry. For example, should new factories be built, or should construction of Army barracks have priority? If new factories were built, more skilled labor would be required. Perhaps bringing idle plants into use might lessen the demand for construction materials and skilled labor. But "even so, it was not possible to say whether there is sufficient manpower for completion of the entire programme, without harming the civil or export trade." And finally, Brown reminded the Cabinet that he placed the "highest importance" on the goodwill of the unions for the success of the defense program.[33] Anthony Eden, speaking for the Foreign Office, tried to move the Government to take the necessary steps to address these problems, but he was unsuccessful. Once again Chamberlain led the opposition.

In full awareness, therefore, of the difficulties confronting them, the Cabinet gave the Chamberlain-Weir program of shadow factories (without sufficient contracts), volunteerism, and imaginative diplomacy a chance to prove itself. Although the situation was bad, it was not yet thought to be desperate. As far as Chamberlain was concerned, it was a chance worth taking, so great were the domestic risks involved. A bewildered Cabinet went along, reassured by Chamberlain's confident lead that the Government would take the necessary steps to accelerate rearmament programs if the international situation grew worse.

At a cost of £394 million over five years, the defense budget was not out of reach. Funding for the program, as with the manpower problem, was not one of raising revenue but of determining the best method of doing it. Basically, three options were available: increased taxation, borrowing, or a combination of both. As Chancellor of the Exchequer, the decision was Chamberlain's to make. Fearing a taxpayer revolt if taxes were increased to pay for the defense program, Sir Warren Fisher urged Chamberlain to resort to the distasteful practice of borrowing, to prevent "destruction by external force."[34] To Fisher's credit, he continued to be the Treasury's "foremost advocate" of an accelerated rearmament program, despite its adverse impact on the Treasury, because he placed defense ahead of all other priorities.[35]   Fisher's advice struck a hollow note with Chamberlain, however, who in the past had rejected similar suggestions from Baldwin for a ten-year defense loan.[36] Since Chamberlain regarded loans as the road to destruction, Fisher's influence with Chamberlain began to wane and Chamberlain looked more to Frederick Phillips, Edward Bridges, and Richard Hopkins at the Treasury for financial advice with which to support his rearmament plans.

Chamberlain's faith in orthodox fiscal policy was unshakable. He continued to trust in conventional financial wisdom and gimmicks to finance the defense budget out of existing revenue for as long as possible, since these methods had been successful in bringing the country out of the Depression. By his own account the country had recovered about 80 percent of its 1929 prosperity by 1935 while increasing defense spending from £104 million in 1931 to £186 million in 1935. In fact, the 1934 and 1935 budgets managed to produce a surplus.

Unproven economic policies, such as those proposed by Lord Keynes that espoused public works spending, or using the defense program to alleviate unemployment, contradicted the prevailing orthodoxy and were shunned by Chamberlain. Nor did the Government show much interest in training the unemployed for defense work or for the export trades.[37] Chamberlain looked with disdain upon the recent French and American experiments in pseudo-Keynesian economics, and he took smug satisfaction in their continued distress and apparent failure at social engineering.[38] Chamberlain's opposition to borrowing related directly to his efforts to protect the export trade, which he hoped would supply him with the additional revenue needed to finance the rearmament program. The problem with borrowing, he argued, is that it forces interest rates to rise, causing inflation and making British exports more expensive and less competitive in world markets. Phillips lent his expert opinion to support Chamberlain's preferred course of action. He wrote: "[Borrowing]. . . reduces the national wealth. Goods and services are used up and the loss is permanent since expenditures on armaments will do nothing to increase the supply of goods and services in later years."[39]

Faced with an estimated annual expenditure of £158 million for maintenance costs at the completion of the defense program,[40] Chamberlain became alarmed at the prospect of meeting that bill with a crippled revenue base. Borrowing had to be resisted at all costs at this time, for psychological reasons as well as for those of sound finance. Instead, he chose to increase the income tax by a modest 3d, to 4s 9d, so as not to interfere too much with economic recovery then under way. An additional tax of 2d on tea and another raid on the Road Fund were expected to produce the additional £20 million needed to balance the budget for the coming fiscal year. Labor's main objection to the budget was the tax on tea, which fell most heavily on the backs of the poor.[41]

In announcing the 1936 *White Paper on Defense* in the House of Commons on 3 March, the Government did its best to assuage public fears of a developing international crisis that it knew was looming on the horizon. The

Abyssinian affair had driven home to the Government the imminent danger of war spreading at any time in the Mediterranean, and Japan continued to treat the British with disdain in the Far East. Moreover, another crisis was developing between France and Germany in the Rhineland, in which Great Britain could hardly be expected to stand aside. Rather than take the public into its confidence to build support for the ever expanding defense program, Chamberlain and Baldwin chose to downplay the critical state of British arms preparedness relative to the danger confronting the Empire. While this may have been a tactically sound political decision in 1935, it was hard to justify in 1936.

Prepared by Chamberlain, the 1936 *White Paper* began on a discouraging note. Conceding Great Britain's inferiority on land and lamenting its inability to intervene effectively in Continental affairs, it regretted that it was not possible simultaneously to recondition the Territorial Army and provide for the needs of the Regular Army, "owing to demands placed upon the capacity of industrial output." Then it made a faint-hearted appeal to British youths to enlist for reserve duty and to become apprentices in the skilled labor market. Toward industry and labor the *White Paper* was patronizing but non-committal: "What we have to do is to carry through . . . measures which will make exceptionally heavy demands upon certain branches of industry and upon certain classes of skilled labor, without impeding the normal course of trade. This will require the cooperation of Industry and the Trade Unions."[42] Without a compelling reason and a sense of urgency, the Government's plea for public support of its defense program could never hope to achieve its goals. In fact, Chamberlain refrained from mentioning the cost of the program in Parliament so as not to disturb public opinion. He simply said that it was more than any program yet announced, and that any attempt to estimate its cost was "premature." This explanation skirted the truth, to say the least. Chamberlain was well aware of exactly how much was going to be allocated for defense spending. What he feared was causing a panic in the country that would lead to a call for more arms, which would interfere with his hopes for an Anglo-German understanding.

Ramsay MacDonald did not share Chamberlain's extreme sensitivity to public opinion. He thought that the country would accept an increased military preparedness program "so long as it was convinced we mean peace."[43] And, speaking in the House, Hoare implored Baldwin to use his "great influence" to impress upon the country the urgency of the problems that faced them. If he did so, Hoare thought Baldwin would find a great body of support in the country. The speech struck a sour note with Chamberlain, who viewed it as a clumsy attempt by Hoare to get back in office after his recent dismissal.[44] Warren Fisher was another who deplored the fact that the public was "so little conscious of the dangers" that were looming everywhere. But, despite these discordant voices, Chamberlain's views prevailed.

The Government lost yet another golden opportunity to enlist sorely needed public support for its defense program when the *White Paper* announced the creation of a new position, that of Deputy Minister for the Coordination of

Defense. Public pressure for a Defense Ministry had been building ever since the Ideal Scheme came under Cabinet consideration in November 1935. Liddell-Hart's articles in *The Times* called into question Hankey's proposal for a well-balanced defense program, obliquely expressing a preference for the Chamberlain-Weir program of limited liability and more air power. Soon the public debate was joined in the editorial pages of *The Times*, *The Telegraph* and *The Morning Post*. Finally in February 1936, public pressure had mounted sufficiently in Parliament to warrant the attention of the Cabinet.[45] Calling the lagging defense program an "unexplained mystery," Austen Chamberlain led the call for a Minister of Defense to coordinate defense policy, strategy, and procurement in order to reassure the nation that everything was being done to prevent a recurrence of government blunders in the past (a reference to the Hoare-Laval Pact). Clearly something had to be done to reassure the country about defensive preparations.

Opposition to a Cabinet-level Ministry of Defense issued primarily from Hankey[46] and the COS, who stood to lose most by the proposal, and more subtly from Neville Chamberlain.[47] Each service jealously guarded its privileges and was reluctant to submit its traditional functions of supply, production, design, and mission to a "czar."[48] And even though Hankey and Chamberlain clashed over the Ideal Scheme, they shared a common interest in opposing a Minister of Defense. Chamberlain feared losing control over the defense program that threatened to interfere with his economic recovery programs. Hankey did not want to lose his influence in the COS to another minister. So the two men separately worked out compromise proposals calling not for a Minister of Defense but for a Deputy Minister for the Coordination of Defense. Only Swinton forthrightly favored a Ministry of Supply (i.e., Defense) to take charge of the supply function.[49]

The title of this new position was significant. The Deputy Minister would serve as Deputy Chairman of the DPR in place of the Prime Minister, who presumably was too busy to attend to the day-to-day concerns of the defense program. It was as if the defense question were nothing more than a nuisance to be suffered rather than a problem to be addressed. The Deputy Minister would also chair meetings of the COS and the Principal Supply Officers' Committee (PSOC). Ostensibly, his chief responsibility was to coordinate the competing claims of the services and industry for manpower and materiel. Actually, the position was designed to ensure that the defense program proceeded along without causing undue harm to the export trade or the Exchequer. The Deputy Minister was expected to be an agent for carrying out pre-approved Cabinet programs, over which Chamberlain's influence was by now decisive.[50] The Deputy Minister was not expected to be an independent voice in the Cabinet with a constituency and an agenda of his own, as a Cabinet-level Minister of Defense would have been. For that reason, such prominent names as Winston Churchill, Austen Chamberlain, and Samuel Hoare were by passed in favor of a relatively unknown lawyer possessing no expertise in defense matters, Sir Thomas Inskip.

When Inskip's appointment was announced on 9 March 1936, it was ridiculed as the greatest travesty since the Roman Emperor Caligula appointed his horse a consul. Eden regretted the choice because it would inspire no confidence in the House of Commons. Churchill was deeply hurt. No one had done more to arouse the House to the need for a Minister of Defense, nor did anyone possess more qualifications for the position than he did. But Chamberlain shrugged off the criticisms. While agreeing that Inskip's appointment would not excite enthusiasm, he knew that Inskip would be the safest choice because he would not create any problems.[51] And adding to the denigration of the office, Inskip was only provided with a small office staff consisting of a single deputy secretary and two typists. Great Britain's enemies were not impressed by this new creation. The decision to appoint Inskip was Baldwin's to make of course, but Chamberlain also concurred in the choice. Despite his lack of experience in defense matters, Inskip enjoyed a solid reputation for integrity and credibility. Somewhat naive in the ways of political intrigue, he was above all dutiful, loyal, and anxious to be a good team player, just the qualities that Chamberlain and Baldwin were looking for.

Labor's reaction to the 1936 *White Paper* was one of caution. On the one hand, it did not trust the Conservative Government, and on the other hand, it did not want to appear to be unpatriotic and obstructionist. To be sure, the Parliamentary Labor Party continued to oppose defense estimates in 1936, but not unequivocally. Taking its lead from the 1935 party conference, Labor members of Parliament could support arms for collective security but not for a massive rearmament program. Inasmuch as the National Government was not prepared to embark on a huge rearmament program along the lines proposed in the Ideal Scheme, there appears to have been some common ground for a bipartisan approach to the program.

Mr. Joyson Hicks, speaking for Labor, tried to pin down the Government's reference to the importance of seeking the cooperation of the trade unions. He asked the Government bench:

Is it [labor] to be sought, and how is it to be sought? Do the Government intend to consult the individual unions, or do they intend to consult, say, the TUC? Do they propose to meet with representatives of the trade unions, or is it that the Government do not propose to take part in any such consultations? . . . Do they propose to bring in employees or workpeople from the government training centers?[52]

Without any attempt to assuage the feelings of the Opposition, Chamberlain answered for the Government in his usual abrupt and arrogant manner. "If we have not yet approached the leaders of the trades unions, it is only because the time has not yet arrived."[53] In the light of subsequent developments, one has to wonder if there ever would be a proper time for such a meeting to Chamberlain's way of thinking.

The reaction from the unions was somewhat different from that of the PLP. The TUC were the pragmatists in the labor movement, while the latter were ideologues. The TUC were more concerned with jobs and job security than with politics. The trade union leaders Hugh Dalton, Walter Citrine, Ernest Bevin, and Herbert Morrison were instrumental in moving rank-and-file opinion away from the idealism and pacifism that characterized Labor's earlier foreign policy positions, to one based on a more realistic fear of the dangers inherent in fascism. They had seen how the Nazis had destroyed the trade union movement in Germany and were fearful of fascism's spread to Great Britain. They approved of the League of Nations taking strong measures toward Italy and were willing, if not anxious, to assist in the rearmament program. The PLP, on the other hand, cared more about improving the quality of life for the country.

While nothing had come of Baldwin's earlier meeting with Citrine, talk of a revitalized rearmament program encouraged speculation within the ranks of labor that they would be offered a role in the defense program.[54] Labor's hopes were encouraged by the many statements in Parliament and in public by Government officials stressing the importance of good relations with the trade unions.[55] In turn, the General Council of the Trades Unions Congress let it be known that it was interested in assisting the rearmament program in February 1936.[56]

The conflicting signals given by labor underscored the many-sidedness of the movement. The ideologically oriented PLP continued to view capitalism as its main enemy and tried to score points with the voters by standing for collective security and denouncing the scandalous actions of the capitalist profiteers. But the more pragmatic TUC turned a blind eye toward profiteering, apparently in order to sustain wages and employment.[57] The Parliamentary Labor Party and the Trades Unions Congress were also divided on the question of whether to support the *White Paper*. Dalton claims to have lost a close vote of 57–39 for its support while sixty other members of Parliament either were either missing or absent.[58]

Had the Government been sincere in its desire to rearm the nation and acted on its own words, recognizing the importance of the trade unions to the success of the rearmament program, the story of Munich and World War II might have been a very different one indeed. Ernest Brown, the Minister of Labor, laid out a course of action in 1936 that, if adopted, would have contributed materially to a defense program worthy of the name, and therefore bears quoting at length.[59]

It must be emphasized that labour is as essential for carrying out the defence programme as men are for the fighting forces. It has been indicated that there may be serious difficulties to be overcome in the supply and the necessary distribution of skilled labour during the forthcoming years. These difficulties, though grave, will not be insurmountable if careful regard is had in planning of the programme to the labour that can reasonably be expected to be available. This means that an attempt to produce all the requirements at a greater speed than the labour supply will make possible will defeat its own ends. What is needed, from this point of view, is so to plan the whole programme that there may be a steady and in the later stages a swift acceleration of production. If industry is given enough time it should be able to adapt itself to the new demands without seriously interfering with its normal output on civilian work. Within a year's time much can be done by industry itself in the reorganization of labour supply, which would greatly reduce labour difficulties and appreciably increase the [effectiveness of the] programme. If on the other hand, speed at all costs is attempted, very serious labour questions will be thrown up at once, with all the embarrassing consequences not only for the armament programme but for civilian industry. In short, therefore, there is nothing in the picture from the labour point of view, which would make it impossible to carry out the programme over a reasonable period and at a progressive rate of acceleration with complete success. If, however, the period is too severely limited, or the rate of acceleration at the start too rapid, the dangers of failure are very real.

Instead, the Government continued to treat labor with indifference and as poor relations to be shunned. At a DPR meeting in January, Weir advised against opening contacts with labor because it might create a crisis-type atmosphere.[60] Likewise, Humbert Wolfe, in his notes prepared for a Baldwin speech in the House of Commons, recommended that consultations with labor be avoided because "they would ask a high price both as to conditions and wages for their cooperation."[61] Another official at the Ministry of Labor warned against dealing with the TUC because they were concerned with politics and international affairs.[62] These recommendations not to include labor in its discussions were embraced by the Cabinet on many occasions.[63] Even the German march into the Rhineland and the admitted inability of the COS to intervene effectively[64] failed to impress the Cabinet with the urgency of their predicament and the need to do everything possible to ensure the success of the rearmament program with the least possible delay. In the final analysis, it was Chamberlain's insistence that nothing should be done to harm the export trade that really mattered.

The German entry into the Rhineland in March 1936 caused the COS to undertake an agonizing re-appraisal of its readiness to respond to such crises.[65] It found that the Army could send only two inadequately equipped divisions to the Continent, and the RAF could not spare even a token force for the Continent. The naval situation was the most serious. With Italy still at war in Ethiopia and under League sanctions, some parts of the Mediterranean were laid open to Italian air attacks, and the Admiralty had been forced to allocate some of its scarce resources to that region. Under these conditions the Admiralty did not feel very comfortable about taking a strong stand on the Rhineland. There was also some concern expressed about Japan taking advantage of a Mediterranean crisis to improve its position in the Far East. More naval construction was needed to meet the needs of collective security as well as of national security.

Yet the Cabinet approved a new construction program for only two battleships, five cruisers, and one aircraft carrier, at a cost of £36,345,450, but only £3,139,000 could be spent in 1936.[66] As Secretary of War, Duff Cooper argued forcefully, but in vain, for a readiness program for the Army. Only Anthony Eden offered a sympathetic ear to the "Cinderella Service." He warned that Germany's growing military might would subject Great Britain to humiliations in the years to come. Nevertheless, Chamberlain continued to adhere to the Liddell-Hart strategy that Britain's limited resources would be "more profitably employed in the air and on the sea, than in building up great armies,"[67] without defining the mission for such an air force. He argued successfully in favor of developing an air force "of such striking power" that "no one would care to run risks with it." It followed, therefore, that it really was not necessary to support a fully equipped Continental army. A token force would suffice when backed up by such an air force. The confident manner in which Chamberlain spoke on behalf of the air program easily dispelled any reservations that wavering Cabinet members might have entertained. In the light of his subsequent positions on the air program which tended to undermine the "striking power"of the air force, one must question whether Chamberlain's commitment to a strong program was sincere, or merely designed to elicit support for his efforts to reduce Britain's Continental commitment.

The problems that Weir had warned about in January began to surface almost immediately as Scheme F began to take shape. Calling for £50 million worth of new bomber squadrons with a reserve capacity of 225 percent, its demands on skilled labor and productive capacity stretched the limits of the rearmament program to the extreme. Brown cited problems in obtaining skilled labor for the rearmament industry, and he asked the Cabinet if "an orderly priority [could] be established for the best use of labor available."[68] The Minister of Health, Sir Kingsley Wood, expressed his concern that "the competition between building for defense and housing might force up the cost of housing,"[69] thereby jeopardizing Britain's economic recovery. Such remedies as wage and price controls, compulsory arbitration in industrial disputes, and the creation of new cooperative regulatory government boards might have established the kind of orderly process that Brown had in mind or eased Wood's concerns about inflation. But they were out of the question as far as Chamberlain was concerned, not only because of his natural reluctance to interfere with business practices but also because they invited cooperation with labor.

Baldwin was of little or no help. He was growing fatigued in the spring of 1936 and became more dependent than ever on Chamberlain, who readily moved in to supply the leadership for the rearmament program. Chamberlain effectively rebutted any suggestion of government controls by reminding his colleagues of the importance of the export trade to the needs of the defense program. He thought that it was premature for the government to take the powers of direction until all voluntary measures had been tried. Kingsley Wood and Brown retreated gracefully. Meanwhile the DPR and the Defense Policy and Plans Committee (DPP) became redundant when the Deputy Minister for the Coordination of Defense was appointed. The CID was then entrusted with the responsibility for developing a more efficient rearmament program. Inskip's job, originally conceived to coordinate supply, became bogged down with attempts to find the labor, industrial capacity, and military recruits for the rearmament program without causing an inflationary spiral that would harm both the general and the export trade.

As these problems mushroomed, the House of Commons witnessed stormy exchanges between Baldwin/ Chamberlain on the one hand and Churchill on the other. Churchill wanted to know what was holding up the rearmament plans in light of Germany's bold move into the Rhineland. Baldwin answered that the supply of "particular kinds of skilled labor" was causing some difficulty, but he expressed confidence that the industries themselves could settle the problem "without any menace to organized labor or to trade union standards."[70] The particular kinds of skilled labor that Baldwin referred to were mainly in the engineering industry. Meetings between the Engineering Employers' Federation (EEF) and the Amalgamated Engineering Union (AEU), beginning in August 1936, failed to produce a cooperative agreement like the one enjoyed by the building trades. The EEF complained of the erosion of engineering skills due to long-term unemployment, especially in the distressed areas, and that older workers had difficulty in reading blueprints or working to "fine limits," and had no experience in the new methods of work introduced since they had last been employed.[71] The AEU demand for higher wages and special allowances to compensate workers for relocating their homes or disrupting their family lives met stiff resistance from the EEF while the Government stood aside.

Dalton rejected the Government's claim that there was a shortage of skilled labor,[72] and a Ministry of Labor study seemed to bear him out. It listed 24,500 unemployed skilled engineers at the time.[73] It also noted that the transference of labor was not very great: only 20,000 in 1935 and 28,000 in 1936.[74] Apparently the labor was there but was not being utilized. Only the strong hand of the Government could break the impasse and provide the necessary labor for the rearmament program. Churchill wondered why the Government did not take the necessary steps to ensure supply. Chamberlain replied, that in such a situation, "you must. . .control. . .labor. . .[to get labor] where it is needed. There is no doubt that if powers of that kind were taken you could speed up the programme very materially . . . orders which would have to be canceled would go elsewhere, and in the future you might not easily regain the markets which we had set aside.[75] Not only was Chamberlain worried about the immediate effects of a command economy, but he feared its long-term effects as well. For him the defense problem was not to be viewed in a vacuum; the needs of posterity must be taken into account as well."[76] Therefore, to his way of thinking, any interference with the export trade that might result in a permanent loss of markets must be regarded as seriously as war itself.

Churchill was not impressed with Chamberlain's alarmist arguments. Defense and security needs came first. A strong defense backed by firm diplomacy was the best way to prevent war, he argued. And if labor problems were causing a disruption in the rearmament program, the Government should meet with the representatives of the TUC and gain their support. Austen Chamberlain supported Churchill's call for a meeting with labor. He recommended a secret session of the House on the defense question, in the hopes of uniting the country.[77] Neville Chamberlain demurred. He doubted that labor would attend, since it would bind them to the Government's position. Austen countered that since the Liberal Party would attend such a session, it would put the Labor Party in an "awkward position" to refuse. Neville argued against the proposal in the Cabinet and ended the discussion by saying that "it would be deplorable to let the country think that the government were not prepared to face their responsibilities."[78] He felt confident that skilled labor could be secured without seeking the cooperation of organized labor, and that it was premature at this point to think of resorting to the compulsory methods envisioned by Churchill. Once again his voice was decisive.

Ironically, Labor was more inclined to agree with Chamberlain at this time on the need to avoid compulsion. They saw expanded Government powers as a prelude to industrial conscription and feared this power would be used to break strikes, so they confined their attacks on the Government's rearmament program to profiteering while Churchill pressed on for a Ministry of Supply. Critics of the Government's policy were thus divided and the force of their arguments was blunted, making it easier for the Chamberlain to direct the course of the defense program.

Poor Inskip — he was caught between the undeniable demands of the service chiefs to meet the requirements of the mandated rearmament program and the chaotic manipulation of the workplace by both industry and labor. Nor did the Cabinet provide much help to the bewildered Defense Minister. By laying down the rule of non-interference with trade and by imposing budgetary restraints without a strategic plan to guide him, the Cabinet placed Inskip in an hopeless situation. Inevitably he came to rely more and more on Weir, Chamberlain, and Hankey for advice and guidance.

Compared with the other two services, the Royal Navy in 1936 was in the best condition and capable of defending Great Britain's home waters, now that the Abyssinian and the Rhineland affairs had passed. The Army's inability to take on a Continental role was not considered to be a critical need just yet, since the French and their allies held a military preponderance of power over Germany on land in 1936 and Germany was not expected to be able to launch a war until 1939 at the earliest. Only the Air Force needed immediate attention. Although the Royal Air Force was expected to provide the major defense against Germany's feared "knockout blow" from the sky, it lacked the numbers and the productive capacity to match Germany's dreaded Luftwaffe. Lord Swinton, the minister responsible for air preparations, resolved that all obstacles related to production be removed as quickly as possible, so that the Royal Air Force could discharge its responsibilities as defined by Scheme F. He found a great deal of sympathy but received little help. There were two alleged problems affecting the industry at the time: a shortage of skilled labor and profiteering.

Skilled labor was more of a problem for the Air Force than any of the other services. Air technology was undergoing a revolution from wood to metal and from double-wing to mono-wing prototypes. Gun mounts, bomb delivery systems, and panel instruments were also being revolutionized, so it was very difficult to find the necessary skills to keep pace with these modern developments. [The vaunted Spitfire, generally credited with winning the Battle of Britain in 1940, was in the pipeline at this time. It had been designed in 1935, but it did not come into large-scale production until the autumn of 1938.] Profiteering was also a problem for the acceleration of the air defense program. The aircraft industry had been dormant for over a decade, and now that it saw an opportunity to make enormous profits, it drove a hard bargain with the hard-pressed Air Ministry. Squabbling between the Air Ministry and the Society of British Aircraft Constructors (SBAC) over a pricing mechanism continued until 1938, causing further delays in the program. Also connected to profiteering were labor-related issues. By holding down wages, the employers could maximize their profits and keep inflation under control in accordance with the Government's policy.

The practical means by which industry sought to reduce wages and, not coincidentally, to weaken the power of the trade unions was through such practices as dilution, up-grading and de-skilling. This also explains the discrepancy between the claims of those who saw a shortage of skilled labor and those who denied the shortage. Industry tended to define skilled labor in such a way as to be able to hire on semi-skilled workers at a lower rate. Industry argued that many so-called skilled workers failed to meet current standards by which skilled labor was judged. Many of their skills had deteriorated because of prolonged unemployment, age, or obsolescence. There was some truth to this argument, but of course the trade unions saw it simply as an excuse for dilution. The failure of the employers to work these problems out with the trade union representatives became the source of more bitterness and strikes, further impeding the progress of the rearmament program, much to Swinton's distress. Even Lord Weir's influence with the SBAC was ineffective in convincing the employers to cooperate more whole-heartedly with the program, and problems in this area continued to plague the air rearmament program.[79]

Swinton came to the conclusion that a firm Government hand was needed to guide this program if it was going to meet the 1939 deadline.[80] He complained of his difficulties with the SBAC and pressed the Cabinet for more governmental powers to deal with them. The question was then referred to Inskip, who rather naively took an objective look at the problem without assessing its financial and social implications. He too was convinced, as was Swinton, that the urgency of the situation might require the Government to take new powers.[81] He had even explored the idea with Winston Churchill, who supplied him with a memorandum on 6 June 1936 on how a Ministry of Supply might work without using compulsory powers.[82] But the idea was quickly quashed by Chamberlain, who reassured Inskip that when the proper time came, he would take the new powers and create a Ministry of Supply. Until then, there must be no interference with trade. Gradually the dutiful Inskip fell into line and eventually became the Government's point man on defense matters.

Besieged on all sides for immediate solutions to the numerous problems holding back the rearmament program, Inskip hesitated. The COS were insistent that the mandated program should provide the services with the necessary recruits and weapons to carry out their responsibilities for defense. They were not easily placated with excuses about the difficulties encountered with respect to manpower problems, skilled labor, and industrial capacity. Inskip's promise to reconsider the policy of non-interference with trade if Germany rearmed with dangerous speed apparently reassured the COS;[83] they dropped their immediate objections to the policy and tried their best to work within the constraints imposed on them from above. Manufacturers wanted to know if they should give priority to war industry, but Inskip could only answer that he would "reserve his judgment"[84] on that question pending approval from the Cabinet. It never came until 1939. Until then, industry could not plan for expansion of its facilities, and the rearmament program fell farther behind.

Meanwhile, Inskip was feeling political heat in the House of Commons, where he was being criticized for failing to meet with the representatives of the trade unions on the questions of dilution and the transference of labor. He again sought guidance from his colleagues. Lord Weir and Ernest Brown thought that he should not meet with them until everything else had been tried.[85] Chamberlain also felt that it was "inadvisable" for him to meet with trade union representatives at this time. And despite assurances from Chamberlain that the Government would take the necessary powers "when the time comes," Inskip still expressed his concern that the country's defenses might not be ready in the next three years because of the inadequate supply of skilled labor[86] and the shortage of Army recruits.[87]

The termination of the Abyssinian affair on 9 June seemed to lift Inskip's spirits and his June progress report to the Cabinet was more optimistic. He was able to report that the outlook for defense was more "encouraging," although he noted some difficulty in finding skilled labor and military recruits. He hoped that the problem could be corrected somewhat by stepping up propaganda in films, schools, and the media.[88] But no matter how Inskip tried to gloss over the situation his weekly meetings with the COS and the PSOC continued to point to the need for direction, and he turned more and more to Chamberlain for advice. Chamberlain was only too happy to supply it.

Of the many incidents affecting the international situation during the inter-war period none could match the intensity and sustained level of public interest of the Spanish Civil War. The passions expressed from the Labor benches were reminiscent of Gladstone's speeches on the Bulgarian atrocities. The split in British public opinion re-opened old wounds in the conduct of British foreign policy that were just beginning to heal. Gone was the bitterness over the failure of the Geneve Disarmament Conference, thanks largely to a threatening and rearmed Nazi Germany. Gone was the myopic vision of a collective security arrangement under the auspices of the League of Nations. The failure of the League to redress the Manchurian grievance or to enforce the restrictions of the Treaty of Versailles on Germany, and finally its mishandling of the Abyssinian crisis, had done much to educate public opinion on the necessity of rearming. But despite the potential danger of a general European war arising out of the Spanish Civil War, the rearmament program failed to keep pace with these rapidly changing developments in Europe and the Far East.

The Spanish Civil War was more important, though, for its impact on Labor's defense policy, which became more militant. Those in the Labor Party who continued to oppose the defense estimates thereafter did so simply to oppose and embarrass the Government. At the annual Trades Union Congress meeting at Edinburgh in September 1936, Hugh Dalton was able to carry a vote for rearmament for collective security by 1,738,000 to 657,000 while continuing to pay lip service to the elusive goal of disarmament.[89] The decision to support the rearmament program was rooted in ideological as well as pragmatic reasons. Ideologically, it opened the possibility of assisting the Spanish Republican Government by allowing it to purchase arms in Great Britain, which was currently impossible with Britain's limited industrial production facilities. Practically, it offered the hope of providing jobs for 300,000 unemployed workers. No longer was there any question of whether to rearm, but to what extent. The Spanish Civil War provided the Government with the opportunity to carry public opinion forward in support of a more credible rearmament program. All that was needed was leadership, and it was that leadership which was found wanting, that ultimately encouraged German revisionism.

It was well known in European circles that Great Britain's defense program was experiencing difficulty and inadequate to her needs for years to come. Sir Robert Vansittart and Eden complained that their diplomatic efforts were being compromised as a result of Britain's military weakness. The current program was viewed as little more than window dressing by friends and foes alike. A typical example of derogatory foreign press accounts of the British rearmament program appeared in the *Muenchener Zeitung* on 16 May 1936. In effect the German newspaper treated British rearmament as "a joke." It reported that the Regular Army was short about one division and that the Territorial Army were "Sunday school amateurs." The Air Force was understaffed by 7,000 men. The *Muenchener Zeitung* even went so far as to question whether the Government would have the will to rely on force if necessary.[90]

The Government's failure to enlist Labor's support for the rearmament program at this time raises serious questions about its commitment to the rearmament program. After many pious declarations in the Cabinet and in its many committees on the need to secure the goodwill of the trade unions, it failed to take the necessary steps or make the timely overtures to a willing labor movement to ensure the success of its program. Holding the Government back from making the overture, apart from party considerations, was the price to be paid for the cooperation of Labor. At this particular time, Labor's asking price might very well have included British support for the Republican Government of Spain, which the Parliamentary Labor Party had gone on record as supporting in November 1936.[91] Labor's abhorrence of fascism was not their only sticking point with the Government. The Labor Party also felt that it had been unfairly manipulated by the Government during the Abyssinian crisis, when the Government took advantage of the situation to spring an election upon the country. Furthermore, how could Labor ask the boys to join up and support the rearmament program in light of the means test and the high rate of unemployment in the distressed areas?[92] On the other hand, it might well have dropped some of these objections in favor of the TUC's well-known interest in long-term employment security. Nevertheless, the question was a moot one, since the Baldwin-Chamberlain Government was determined not to become involved in the Spanish Civil War because of the danger of that conflict's escalating into a general European war. The whole strategy of British rearmament policy was geared to the avoidance of confrontation, at least until an orderly voluntary rearmament program could be implemented, by 1941 or 1942.

A tilt in British foreign policy toward Republican Spain also had the uninviting prospect of aligning the British Government on the side of international socialism and communism. Nothing could be more repugnant to a Conservative Government intent upon destroying socialism at home. To Clement Attlee it was clear that what the Government feared was "not aggression, but the success of the social experiment."[93] If the Leftist government of Republican Spain was to succeed in building a better Spain, might not other countries, including Great Britain, be tempted to initiate socialist programs also? Chamberlain argued that the time was not yet ripe to invite the cooperation of the trade unions, just as he had earlier rejected stronger Government controls over the economy as being premature. In the light of his subsequent actions one must seriously ask if the time would ever be ripe for the unions' cooperation. But without the voluntary cooperation of the trade unions the rearmament program could never become a credible deterrent force.

The Government was forced once again to deal with Churchill's call for a Ministry of Supply, which would resurface in the fall as a follow-up to the July meeting with a deputation of House members. While the tired Baldwin attended to the marriage problems of King Edward VIII, Chamberlain prepared for the November meeting of the Parliamentary delegation. But first Inskip had to be brought to accept the sacrosanct principle of non-interference with trade on which he had been wavering. Chamberlain spoke of it's being necessary to handle Inskip firmly.[94] Meeting with him on an almost daily basis, Chamberlain at last managed to bring Inskip to support his defense views. He even invited Inskip to meet with him on 19 October, while sick in bed, to "discuss a previous conversation concerning the RA and the TA."[95]Chamberlain laid out his rationale for maintaining the principle of non-interference in great detail:

apart from other considerations, we had not the manpower to produce the necessary munitions for ourselves and perhaps, if the U.S.A. stood out, for our Allies, to man the enlarged Navy, the new Air Force, and a million man Army. . . . We should aim at an army of 4 divisions plus 1 mobile division, and the necessary drafts to maintain its strength, no overseas work. . . .Territorials should be kept for AA work.[96]

Otherwise, "If we were to follow Winston's advice and sacrifice our commerce to the manufacture of arms, we should inflict a certain injury to our trade from which it would take generations to recover. We should destroy the confidence which now happily exists, and we should cripple the revenue."[97]

Chamberlain's lobbying paid off handsomely. When the Cabinet held a special meeting on 4 November to consider the merits of creating a Ministry of

Supply, Inskip had at last been converted to Chamberlain's policy. He told the Cabinet that he would ask for powers over industry only if he were told "to be ready for war in June 1937." Since that was not the case, he could not support a recommendation for a Ministry of Supply at this time.[98] Neither Hankey nor the COS pressed for it either.[99] They preferred to look out for their own interests and handle their own supply and recruitment problems rather than risk having regulations imposed on them by an independent government agency. Only Swinton continued to argue for some form of Government powers to accelerate aircraft production. When asked what kind of Government powers might be needed, he answered, "If we could, say, pick the eyes out of Singer's Sewing Machine Works, and certain other engineering forms, we should in a very short time get improved production." But then when Chamberlain asked what the effect of such a decision would entail, Swinton said that the immediate result would be unemployment in *those* factories, and the factories that depended on those products would also be affected.[100] Chamberlain rested his case; There must be no interference with trade just yet. The Cabinet agreed.

Also under consideration by the Cabinet at this meeting was a *Report of the Royal Commission on the Private Manufacture and Lending of Arms*. The Government had set up this commission to investigate Labor's charges of profiteering in the arms business. Though the *Report* rejected Labor's call for nationalizing the arms industry, it did ultimately recommend that the Government should set up a body "for the purpose of controlling supply and deciding the question of priority," in order to ensure rapid expansion in the rearmament program, because the problem "may well be insoluble by voluntary means."[101] It also concluded that this body should be presided over by a Cabinet-level minister. The main duties of this minister would be:

    a. To consider and decide on questions of supply and manufacture in time of peace
    b. To prepare regulations for an emergency
    c. To encourage private research
    d. To monitor a costing procedure to control pricing (inflation)   and prevent profiteering.[102]

It was not until 26 May 1937 that the *Report* was debated by the House. As was to be expected, it produced little result. There would be no Ministry of Supply, nor would there be any significant attempt to put curbs on profiteering until 1939, as long as Chamberlain had anything to say about it.

Unquestionably the economic consequences of a credible defense program were so serious as to warrant a policy of caution. But as evidenced by these internal discussions within the Cabinet on a semi-war organization, little attempt was made to ascertain just how far it was possible to ease the economic pain of conversion to a semi-war economy. It was simply assumed, on the word of the Chancellor of the Exchequer, that such schemes were "not feasible," or "impractical," or "premature." Churchill's suggestion for a 25 percent interference with trade initially elicited some interest from Inskip, but without Chamberlain's imprimatur the idea languished.[103] Even suggestions from such "friendly" sources as Bridges at the Treasury, who seemed to think there might be some tolerance in the engineering industry for some interference, were ignored.

The appalling lack of candor displayed by Chamberlain in dealing with the country's serious rearmament problems required that he should take the same line with Parliament and the press. Using his considerable influence at the Central Office of the Conservative Party and with the press lords, he disseminated his soporific views of a steadily improving defense system, assuring everyone that the Government was doing all that could be done to address the defense problems, and that whatever problems existed were purely local and temporary, and would soon be repaired. It worked. The huge Conservative majority in the House dutifully followed the Whip. Non-party Parliamentary criticism took on a partisan air and could easily be dismissed as political posturing. Churchill's witty, well-informed, and articulate outbursts failed to impress his colleagues, who were unaware of the risks being taken with national defense. With the exception of about thirty dissidents, the Conservatives supported the Government's policy whole-heartedly.

Non-intervention in Spain, appeasement of Germany, enough arms to repel an invasion of the British Isles, and business as usual satisfied their doubts about the cassandraesque pronouncements of Winston Churchill, whose record on recent issues called his judgment into question.[104] He had been on the "wrong"side of the India Bill and he was now on the "wrong"side of the King's marriage to Mrs. Simpson. What was next? Henry Channon, a loyal Chamberlainite, described Churchill's impact best: "Winston Churchill made a terrific speech, convincing, unanswerable, and his stock has soared, and today people are buying "Churchills," and saying once more that he ought to be in government, and it's too bad to keep so brilliant a man out of office, but were he given office, what would it mean? An explosion of foolishness after a short time? War with Germany? A seat for Randolph [Churchill]?"[105]

Nevertheless, Churchill would have to be treated with a certain amount of deference. As a Privy Councillor and member of the Air Research Committee, he had access to much privileged information. He could not be ignored publicly. Nor could Chamberlain's brother and former Foreign Minister, Austen, be dismissed lightly. So on 23 November, as promised in July, Baldwin invited the Parliamentary delegation to 10 Downing Street to respond to their questions about the state of the country's defenses. This time he was attended by Neville Chamberlain, Inskip, and Halifax. Conspicuously absent from this group were the Defense Ministers. Apparently, Swinton's willingness to interfere with business and Cooper's insistence on upgrading the Continental commitment raised questions about their value to the Government's prepared position, so Inskip was entrusted to handle the military and technical aspects of the defense program.

Of immediate concern to the Parliamentary delegation was the exposed position of London to air attack, which was exacerbated by a noticeable lack of TA personnel for antiaircraft defense. Churchill produced figures showing Germany with an advantage of 800 bombers to 372 for Britain, and Germany enjoying an even greater advantage in reserves and industrial capacity. Inskip conceded that German war potential was greater at present, although he thought Churchill's figures of the comparative air strength were probably too high. Nevertheless, the Government was now working at closing the gap. He explained that the present gap was largely attributable to filling orders for reserves and wastage, and that it was a difficult and expensive task. He also denied Churchill's allegations that quality was being sacrificed to quantity simply to justify the claims of air parity with Germany. Sir Edward Grigg noted that only 25 percent of the aircraft promised by 1937 would be available, but Inskip disagreed. He said the figure was closer to 80 percent. But under further questioning, Inskip admitted that most of the planes would be of the obsolete Hinds types.[106] Once again Inskip apologized, this time citing lack of equipment and not manpower as the problem. He acknowledged that if war came a large surplus of manpower was available,[107] notwithstanding Chamberlain's disclaimer.

Chamberlain was undoubtedly aware of the existence of a substantial pool of manpower through government surveys on the subject and his experience in the last war. The manpower question had come under review by the Sub-committee on Manpower of the CID, chaired by Sir Graham Greene, in 1934. On the basis of its findings, the Manpower Committee concluded that 500,000 men could be obtained for National Service without any serious dislocation of the economy, and that 1 million could probably be raised by voluntary means if necessary. However, the report went on to say that if more men were needed, "compulsory National Service would be necessary."[108] The report of the Manpower Committee also stated that present arrangements were inadequate to handle a sizable absorption of manpower and recommended that something must be done about it, not only in terms of securing the supply of labor but also to see that it was equipped. And if it appeared that war was likely to develop, "The earlier the system were introduced the better."[109]

Later manpower studies in 1936 recommended national registration of all men as a preliminary first step to National Service. The employment exchanges could carry it out. In all, the Manpower Committee estimated that 10,311,000 males between the ages of 18–49 were available for National Service though not all of them could be used.[110] And with unemployment at 1,300,000, the manpower was there if needed. Clearly manpower was not the problem it was made out to be. The real problem, as Lord Salisbury was quick to point out, was the need to equip and train those forces.[111] This is why the antiaircraft defenses were so neglected, and even if they were set up by voluntary means, they would have to be manned and trained, forcing the defense bill higher yet. Chamberlain recoiled at the prospect of any defense scheme that required such a huge influx of manpower.

Time and time again we see one excuse after another for not rearming the country to a level of defense required for its security. Cleverly manipulated by

Chamberlain, first with regard to finance, then politics, and then with manpower and industrial capacity, the rearmament program was held back by the Prime Minister-designate at great risk to the Empire. Manpower was available, but not on Chamberlain's terms. It had long been assumed that the defense program could not be funded out of normal budgetary processes. Thanks to Chamberlain's persistent efforts to control defense spending, the Government managed to avoid extraordinary financing schemes until 1937. But once the decision had been taken in February 1936 to move from simply repairing the worst deficiencies in defense to a more comprehensive defense force embodying the latest (and more expensive) technology, the defense bill could be expected to climb dramatically. And so it did, as the annual estimates from the services began to unfold in October.

Nothing gave Chamberlain so much cause for alarm as the TA problem and the proper role of the Army. Cooper's £90 million request for the War Office threatened to undermine the stability that Chamberlain had managed to impress upon the Government ever since the inception of the rearmament program. Its huge demands for manpower entailed a corresponding need for more equipment, industrial capacity, and skilled labor. For those reasons he wanted to maintain the Army in its present state under the umbrella of limited liability as he prepared his final budget. The Army's proposal had to be defeated. As Chancellor of the Exchequer, Chamberlain properly challenged the War Office's memorandum on financial grounds. He argued that the country's resources were limited, and that if the War Office proposal were accepted, the other services might be deprived of valuable resources. It was all well and good to train and equip the TA forces, but would not those resources be more profitably employed somewhere else? Preferably by concentrating on air defense. Never one to leave an issue in doubt, Chamberlain pressed the political question on the Cabinet as well. What about public opinion, he asked? Answering his own question, he did not think the country would support "continental adventures in the light of its unhappy experience during World War I. Would it not it be wise to study this proposal in the wider context of a comprehensive review of military policy?"[112]

Cooper thought the issue to be so quintessentially important to British security interests that he persisted in his argument for equipping the Territorials over Chamberlain's strong objections. Mindful of Great Britain's waning prestige abroad, highlighted by Belgium's recent declaration of neutrality in the aftermath of Germany's reoccupation of the Rhineland, and of the fig leaf policy of non-intervention in Spain, Cooper wondered how the Government intended to make good its commitment to defend the Low Countries and France under the Locarno Agreement. How were the five approved Army divisions to be reinforced on the Continent in case of war? Or were they to be left unsupported and "wasted"? Why for that matter have a TA at all if it was not able to perform its duties?[113] If the Government was really serious about preparing the nation's defenses by 1939, it must take the steps now to provide the industrial capacity because of the length of time involved in producing the equipment.[114]

Cooper's case for the TA was compelling, and even though the COS supported his position, it wilted in the face of Chamberlain's determined opposition. Chamberlain raised the question of maintenance costs again. "We should have to maintain in. . .peacetime, a permanent commitment, largely increased reserve stores of all kinds, and an increased capacity for munitions production in order that the seventeen divisions might be continuously supplied . . . and it is only too clear that overseas trade once lost will not be easy to recover."[115] Cooper's arguments failed to enlist any significant support from his Cabinet colleagues, who were anxious to remain on the good side of the Prime Minister-designate. Only Eden showed lukewarm support for the War Office. Baldwin referred the matter to a sub-committee of the COS for further study under some rather strict terms of reference.

Based on a January 1937 COS report which concluded that the Allies must be capable of putting considerable land forces in the field, supported by an adequate increase in the TA reserves, the COS recommended that the manufacturing capacity be increased to provide the equipment for the enlarged TA forces.[116] Another COS report gave a depressing account of the present state of Britain's armed strength. It revealed that most of its tanks were obsolete; only 61 of 76 approved antiaircraft batteries were operational; only 180 of 603 three-inch antiaircraft guns were available; 511 out of 2,036 searchlights were working; and Britain had 204 bombers, against 800 for Germany and 530 for Russia.[117]

Outflanked by the strategic arguments presented by the military experts, Chamberlain conceded that "admittedly security comes before finance, but the bill for armaments was running up very heavily . . . and the dangers of overloading the programme beyond the material capacity of the nation had to be considered. Was it really necessary to stick to 1939 for the date of the completion of our programmes?"[118] He also pointed to the lessening of tensions in international affairs as a hopeful reason for not rushing headlong into unnecessary, expensive, and disruptive defense planning.

Caught between the recommendation of the military chiefs on whose expertise in technical and strategic questions he relied in the CID, and Chamberlain's political and economic agenda, Inskip produced a compromise calling for the provisioning of two Regular Army and two antiaircraft divisions; the TA was to be trained in the use of the same weapons as the Regular Army; while there was to be"sufficient"equipment for twelve TA divisions (with no specification of the number of divisions or the dates of completion for modernizing the TA). The Cabinet accepted the proposal and directed the CID to cost out the program along with a time frame for reinforcing the Continental army. Cooper was not happy, but Chamberlain was elated with the result, as he revealed to his sisters a few days later.

I have at least got a decision about the Army, and it practically gives me all I want. The Regular Army is to be armed "cap-a-pie" with the most modern equipment, and is ready to go anywhere, anywhere. The Territorials are to have similar equipment, but only in sufficient quantity to enable them to train. In practice, this means that by withdrawing that equipment from all but two divisions, and concentrating it on them, they could be ready, if wanted, to go and reinforce the Regulars in four months after the outbreak of war.[119]

Not only had Chamberlain managed to curtail the Army's request, but he had won a delay in the implementation of the program, which was not reconsidered by the Cabinet until 28 April,[120] and then put off again until December. Meanwhile, the role of the Army remained largely undefined. Without a firm decision there could be no planning for the long term. Delay, that insidious bureaucratic death machine, became Chamberlain's constant companion in his quest for control over the rearmament program as each day brought him closer to the final "yes or no" as Prime Minister. Chamberlain could indeed say with some justification that "the policy of the Committee of Defense has been guided by me" as a tired, failing, and indecisive Baldwin stood aside.

Not to be outdone by the Army's bold move to secure funding for its programs, the Admiralty submitted a proposal for the construction of new capital ships[121] when it learned that German naval rearmament not only might be completed by 1940 but also exceeded British estimates.[122] The following week the Secretary of State for Air sought an increase of £50 million for Scheme H over the next four years, to keep pace with developments in Germany's air program. Citing British industrial intelligence reports confirming General Erhard Milch's earlier boast of Germany's growing air power, the Air Staff now estimated Germany's first-line air strength to be 2,500 by April 1937, of which 1,700 were bombers. Britain's air force, by comparison, would total 1,750 planes with only 1,022 bombers by 1939, far short of Baldwin's pledge of air parity.[123] The new proposal was deemed necessary because Scheme F was already behind schedule and could not be accelerated. Inskip attributed this problem to the firms, because they had not kept their promises.[124] If they failed to keep their promise, it was only because they had little to fear from a government that did not take its own rearmament program seriously. Scheme H proposed to expand the air program primarily by increasing its first-line planes at the expense of the reserve component, which was pushed back to 1941. The largest increase in Scheme H went for the production of bombers, raising its goal from 1,022 to 1,631.[125] French proposals for closer cooperation in the air were put off because the Cabinet deemed that the time was not yet ripe.[126]

Financial costs obviously escalated with each expansion of defense planning. But other problems also began to surface in relation to these programs. More industrial capacity was needed to accommodate the expansion of the defense industries that by now, could hardly keep up with demand. Inskip noted, for example, that a newly acquired factory in Spotswood could not produce for another year, and that it was "impractical" to complete naval antiaircraft rearmament.[127] Swinton continued to complain of shortages of skilled labor. Toolmakers, machinists, sheet metal workers, coppersmiths, and precision fitters were desperately needed.[128]

Arthur Robinson, Chairman of the Supply Board, despaired of meeting his responsibility to ensure proper equipment for the services. He complained to the DPR that "unless statutory interference in industry is adopted, little more can be done to affect problems drastically."[129] Inskip, in constant touch with the Minister of Labor to resolve these problems, warned the Cabinet that labor problems would only grow worse as the demands of the services escalated. Yet, as a good team player, he did not think the situation was so serious as to require some form of compulsion at this time.[130] Mr. Leggatt at the Ministry of Labor expressed amazement that apparently nothing was a being done to deal with this regrettable situation: "Incidents continue to arise showing the need of the central coordination of supply labor problems, and it is regretted that it appears to be accepted [by the Government] that it is humanly impossible to make any attempt to gain experience in such coordination until an emergency arises. "[131] Chamberlain acknowledged that present plans were placing a heavy strain on our resources and he cautioned his colleagues that any additional strain might put the present programs in jeopardy.[132] With pressure building for some form of compulsion, would the Government abandon its policy of non-interference with trade? Not as long as Chamberlain had anything to say about it.

Baldwin by now had practically abdicated his leadership position, waiting only for the proper moment to step down. Chamberlain had become the *de facto* leader of the Cabinet, and he was more determined than ever to keep the defense program from wrecking havoc on the economy and unleashing those social and political forces that he feared so much. [By October, Chamberlain was able to boast of a "general acceptance of [his] position of heir apparent and acting P. M." and "he was sending for people and endeavoring to conduct business as if [he] were in fact P. M." NC 2/23A, 6 October 1936. Ed. note]. The instrument that he used to bring the defense program under his control was the Treasury. None of the service proposals were approved at this time except for the tenuous compromise reached earlier with the War Office. Without a plan, orders could not be placed, factories constructed, manpower recruited, non-skilled labor trained. Meanwhile, Chamberlain was working on a plan of his own to control defense spending, thereby limiting the size of the defense program as he had consistently done in the past.

Until now the defense program had been financed without borrowing and by a relatively small increase in taxation. Clearly that practice would no longer suffice in a constantly expanding rearmament program. Another method had to be devised for financing the program. Chamberlain now proposed to fix a sum that, in his opinion, the nation could afford, then distribute it among the services under the watchful eye of Inskip. Orthodox fiscal policy taught that the amount of money the Government could borrow without inflation should be commensurate with national savings. Thus, by taking the national savings (about £450 million) and adding it to the expected revenue base (£1,100,000,000) over the next five years, approximately £1,500,000,000 could be raised for defense without setting off a destructive inflationary spiral. To finance the plan, he cautiously factored a 3d income tax into the revenue base, raising it to 5s per pound although Phillips at the Treasury cautioned that "taxation is already exceedingly high." Phillips would have preferred more borrowing.[133] Chamberlain also introduced a novel tax on business, the National Defense Contribution (NDC), which he called "the bravest thing [he had] ever done in public life." Chamberlain was well aware that the tax would not go down well with the party, where 181 out of 415 Government supporters in the Commons were directors of corporations.[134] His trusted confidant, Joseph Ball of the Conservative Research Bureau, also warned him against it,[135] as did Lord Montagu Norman of the Bank of England, when Chamberlain first discussed the idea with them in February. On the other hand, Simon's enthusiastic support for the idea paid off for him. He was tapped by Chamberlain to succeed him at the Exchequer.[136]

Nothing illustrates Chamberlain's independence of action more than the NDC business. While Chamberlain was certainly sensitive to his Conservative business constituency, he was driven more by his own personal agenda, as he had demonstrated when he proposed his social programs as Minister of Health. As expected, the reaction from the City and the House was uniformly negative when the NDC was announced on 20 April. It was even worse than he had anticipated. The attitude of the industrialists and business community as a whole was extremely embarrassing and hurtful to the Chancellor, jeopardizing his standing in the Commons. He told his sister that he feared he had "lost the confidence of the House."[137]

In a courageous effort to quiet the City, Chamberlain met with a group of industrialists a few days later to explain his position and win their support. He told them that he was rather surprised by the reaction of the business community to the NDC. After all, it was only a modest tax on the rate of profits gained largely through their defense contracts. Surely that was not too much to ask in these most difficult of times. But Chamberlain's desperate appeal to their patriotic sentiments did little to change their minds. Sensing that he was making little headway in convincing the group to cooperate with the NDC, he played his trump card, their fear of socialism. He warned them that, "We might end up with such concessions to Labor as would very seriously handicap our competitive trades."[138] It still did not work. Chamberlain suffered a rare political setback in failing to gain their support, and he had to modify his proposal to meet their objections. A 5 percent tax on profits was substituted, instead.

The attitude of Labor was constantly on Chamberlain's mind as he wrestled with the nation's defense problems. He confided to his sister that one of the reasons for the NDC was that it helped him to resist the Labor Party, "who are always crying out for bigger and better pensions:"

Up to quite recently there was little change in the cost of living, and I have been rather surprised that there has been little talk of profiteering. This is partly because Labor has been doing so well. But, it would be a fatal mistake to suppose that this state of things is going to last. Prices are bounding up now. . . subcontractors and sub-sub-contractors, who cannot be subject to the same control, are undoubtedly reaping a rich harvest. All the elements of danger are here. . . . .and I can see that we might easily run in no time into a series of crippling strikes ruining our programme, a sharp steepening of costs due to wage increases, leading to the loss of the export trade, a feverish and artificial boom followed by a disastrous slump, and finally the defeat of the Government, and the *advent of an ignorant, unprepared, and heavily pledged Opposition, to handle a crisis as severe as that of 1931.*[139] [Italics added]

That "heavily pledged Opposition," still searching for an electoral identity, had just published *Labor's Immediate Programme* in March 1937. Such measures as the forty-hour workweek, a raise in the age for leaving school from 15 to 16, nationalization of the Bank of England, help for the distressed areas, and paid holidays, only reinforced Chamberlain's determination to prevent Labor's coming to power. His thinly disguised contempt for Labor stemmed in part from his perception of Labor as a party of narrow self-interest, more inclined toward the advancement of the working class than of the nation.[140]

One way to resist Labor, was to deny it a meaningful role in the rearmament program, where its participation and cooperation might signal an appearance of legitimacy and acceptability for its radical social programs. Surprisingly, Labor's defense policy did not differ materially from Chamberlain's own plan for limited liability. In point of fact, Labor might conceivably have supported more armaments than Chamberlain was willing to concede. The *Immediate Programme* took the position that the Labor Party would "unhesitatingly maintain such forces as are necessary to defend our country and fulfill our obligations as a member of the British Commonwealth and the League of Nations."[141] Labor's opposition could no longer be characterized as obstructionist.

Labor's reaction to the 1937 defense budget showed a lack of intensity and passion that had characterized the earlier defense debates and indicated a subtle shift in Labor's traditional defense policy. Whereas Labor had insisted on disarmament and collective security in the early 1930s, repeated transgressions of the League Covenant forced the Labor movement to reconsider its utopian policy. The failure of the Geneva Disarmament Conference, the rise of National Socialism and German rearmament, Manchuria, Ethiopia, the Rhineland, and finally, the outbreak of the Spanish Civil War had all combined to demonstrate the need for a strong defense policy. The decision by the National Council on Labor on 28 October 1936 to withdraw its support for the Government's non-intervention policy confirmed the more militant shift in defense policy then taking place. Labor was quite prepared to fight for its ideals. The diehard pacifists like Lansbury and the ideologues like Sir Stafford Cripps, who opposed government rearmament programs, were soundly rejected by overwhelming majorities at their party conferences. Lansbury was forced to resign and he was replaced by Clement Attlee in 1935, while Cripps's steadfast refusal to accept the verdict of the Labor Party in 1936 led to his resignation from the Labor Council and finally to his dismissal from the party in January 1939. The amazing speed with which Labor managed to accomplish this transformation owed largely to the efforts of Dalton, Citrine, Morrison, and Bevin. But in a larger sense it was the daily reporting of the horrors of the Spanish Civil War that had convinced the rank-and-file members of the party to become more sensitive to the dangers facing the international labor movement from the forces of aggression.[142]

In March a deputation of TUC leaders met with Eden to lobby the Government to take a more forceful stand against the dictator states for violating the Non-Intervention Agreement. Eden confided that it would be impossible, owing to Britain's lagging rearmament program. The TUC leaders their gave their assurances for the "support of the bulk of the Labor Movement in a vigorous policy,"[143] but their voices fell on deaf ears as the Government rejected their overtures once again. Rather than include Labor in the defense program, Chamberlain told the House that he preferred to treat the problem in an "orderly and regulated manner" instead of "making violent advances which are often followed by violent collapses."[144]

So, in the debates over the defense budget in March and April 1937, Labor's response was more in the nature of a taunt or reproach than a question of principle. Attlee chided the Government on its decision to borrow £400 million for defense when he was told that to borrow £100 million for unemployment relief would bankrupt the nation. Instead of voting against the service estimates, the PLP executive voted 45–29 to abstain.[145] Other critics attacked the budget because it was inflationary or would destroy the Ottawa Agreement. Little opposition mounted against the Government's announced intention to enlarge its defenses. Whatever objections Labor made to the rearmament program in 1937 stemmed more from lack of trust in the Government than from unrelenting opposition to rearmament.[146]

John Gretton, a diehard Conservative MP, went to see Chamberlain in January, hoping to exploit the divisions within the Labor Party in order to seek support for the rearmament program. He reported to Chamberlain "that a number of them were *strongly* in favor of the government programme but that they felt hampered in supporting it by their ignorance of what really was being done."[147] According to Gretton, Labor mistrusted Stanley Baldwin, "whom they regarded as a Pacifist too much influenced by a desire to please Socialist nations about peace in our time." Therefore, they wanted to know how Chamberlain stood. Chamberlain asked for names. Gretton mentioned Bevin and Citrine;[148] Chamberlain acknowledged them as important, and told Gretton that he would take up the matter with Baldwin. Both leaders subsequently rationalized that Gretton was putting his own words in the mouths of the TUC, and the matter was conveniently dropped.

In July, Labor's Joint National Council issued a paper titled *International Policy and Defence*. Acknowledging the ineffectiveness of the League of Nations it reaffirmed its commitment to collective security. But Labor also recognized that Great Britain would have to rearm in order to organize the peace-loving states against the aggressor nations, either through a revitalization of the League or in alliance with other countries. Both the TUC and the PLP approved the report by overwhelming majorities in their respective conferences that fall, but Chamberlain showed no interest in their changed position as he prepared to succeed Baldwin at the head of the Government.

NOTES

1. CP 100(35), 21 May 1935.

2. Ibid., CP 103(35).

3. CAB 23/82/40, 24 July 1935.

4. Ibid.

5. CAB 23/81/24, CP 85(35), 17 April 1935. This assessment turned out to be quite accurate, but was misleading because it did not take into account Germany's ability to use this power for diplomatic purposes.

6. COS 421; Roskill, 176.

7. CP 12(36).

8. Ibid.

9. Ibid.

10. Ibid.; CP 144(35)

11. *Weir Papers* 17/1, 27 January 1936.

12. CP 92(36)

13. CP 26(36).

14. NC 2/23, 19 January 1936.

15. Reader, *Lord Weir*, 180.

16. *Daily Express,* 24 May 1935.

17. Reader, 180.

18. Pat Thane, ed., *The Origins of British Social Policy* (Totowa, N. J.: Rowan and Littlefield, 1978); *Jones Diary,* 28 October 1931, 20; Hankey also attributed Britain's decline in the 1920s to the dole and the increase in social programs. John Naylor, *Hankey: A Man and an Institution* (Cambridge: Cambridge University Press, 1984), 198-199.

19. NC 2/23, 16 December 1935.

20. NC 18/1/1003, 25 April 1937.

21. NC 2/23, 19 August 1935; ibid. 20 November 1935; *Harvey Diaries,* November 18, 1938, 222; P. K. Watkins, *Britain Divided* (New York: Thomas Nelson, 1963), 162. Keith Middlemas, *Politics in Industrial Society* (London: Deutsche, 1979), 221.

22. *Weir Papers* 17/1, Chamberlain in DPRC, 13 January 1936; Baldwin to DPRC, 16 January 1936.

23. CAB 23/82/10, 25 February 1936.

24. CP96(36).

25. NC 18/1/1003, 25 April 1937; *Hore-Belisha Papers* (hereafter cited as HB) 5/18, 19 April 1939.

26. *Weir Papers* 17/1, 16 January 1936.

27. CAB 23/82/10, 25 February 1936; CAB 24/259, CP 26(36).

28. Roskill, 194.

29. CP 26(36).

30. Ibid.

31. NC 2/23, 9 February 1936.

32. PREM, 1/196, Runciman to Baldwin, 17 February 1936.

33. CP 96(36).

34. Shay, 77.

35. Post, 236.

36. Shay, 42.

37. Peden, *British Rearmament*, 180.

38. Feiling, 284; Shay, 163. Yet, Keynes's views were not entirely unwelcome at the Treasury. Cf. R.A.C. Parker "British Rearmament, 1936–1939: Treasury, Trade Unions, and Skilled Labour," *English Historical Review*, 96 (1981): 316–317.

39. Quoted from Shay, 75.

40. Feiling, 284. Shay reported that £215 million was needed for maintenance costs, plus debt service and obsolescence. See Shay, 76.

41. *Debates,* 311: 422, 4 April 1936.

42. CP 62(36).

43. PREM 1/192, MacDonald to Baldwin, 17 February 1936.

44. Cross, *Hoare,* 268.

45. CAB 24/259/30.

46. CAB 24/260/36.

47. CAB 24/260/38.

48. Naylor, *Hankey,* 243.

49. CAB 24/260/37.

50. Post, 231.

51. NC 2/23, 11 March 1936.

52. *Debates,* 309: 2020ff., 10 March 1936.

53. Ibid.

54. Dalton, 87.

55. CAB 24/261/96; CAB 23/82/11, CP 62(36), 26 February 1936, *White Paper on Defense.*

56. J. F. Naylor, *Labour's International Policy: The Labour Party in the 1930s* (London: Weidenfeld and Nicolson, 1969), 152; Allan Bullock, *Bevin,* 543; Keith Middlemas, *Politics in Industrial Society* (London: Deutsche, 1979), 225–226.

57. Middlemas, *Politics in Industrial Society,* 251.

58. Dalton, 90.

59. CP 96(36), 8 April 1936.

60. *Weir Papers* 17/1, 27 January 1936, 7 May 1936.

61. Parker, "British Rearmament," 322.

62. Ibid.

63. CAB 23/82/9, CP 57(36),21 Feb 1936; CAB 23/83/28, CP 96(36), 8 April 1936.

64. CAB 24/261/81.

65. COS 441 and 442.

66. CAB 23/83/29, CP 103(36), 9 April 1936.

67. NC 2/23, 9 February 1936.

68. CAB 23/83/28, CP 96(36), 8 April 1936.

69. CAB 23/84/34, CP 113(36), 6 May 1936.

70. *Debates,* 309:1839–1840, 9 March 1936.

71. Parker, "British Rearmament," 330.

72. Dalton, 168.

73. Paul Inman, *Labour in the Munitions Industries* (London: HMSO, 1952), 22.

74. Ibid., 23n.

75. *Debates,* 311: 434–435, 23 April 1936.

76. NC 2/23, 25 October 1935.

77. NC 2/23, 5 July 1936.

78. CAB, 23/85/50, 6 July 1936. Instead, Baldwin agreed to meet with a selected group of members of Parliament later in the month.

79. For example; General Aircraft Ltd. had a contract in October 1935, for 89 Hawker Fury airplanes, but as of 20 November 1936, only 23 had been delivered. Martin Gilbert, *Churchill: A Life* (New York: Holt, 1991), 567.

80. CAB 24/260/37.

81. CAB 23/85/55, 29 July 1936.

82. Churchill, *The Gathering Storm*, appendix C, 679–680.

83. T. Taylor, *Munich,* 589.

84. CAB 23/83/28, 8 April 1936.

85. *Weir Papers* 17/2, 7 May 1936.

86. CP 96(36).

87. CP 92(36). He reported that "the situation is bad, but not desperate."

88. CAB 23/84/43, 23 June 1936.

89. Dalton, 104. Incidentally, the TUC also rejected Communist affiliation at this meeting. Bullock interprets the vote as abandoning opposition to rearmament. Bullock, 593.

90. Churchill, 186–187.

91. Dalton, 105.

92. Bullock, 592.

93. Watkins, *Britain Divided,* 162.

94. Ian MacLeod, *Neville Chamberlain* (London: Muller, 1961), 194.

95. NC 2/23, 26 October 1936.

96. NC 2/23, 25 October 1936.

97. Ibid., 26 October 1936.

98. CAB 23/86/43, 4 November 1936; CAB 24/265/297.

99. Roskill, 247.

100. CAB 23/86/43, 4 November 1936.

101. *Hankey Papers*, 8/34; "Royal Commisson on the Private Manufacture of and Trading in Arms Report," (London: HMSO, October 1936), Cmd. 5292.

102. Ibid.

103. CAB 23/84/41, 11 June 1936.

104. *Jones Diary,* 22 May 1936.

105. James, Robert Rhodes, ed., *Chips: The Diaries of Sir Henry Channon* (London: Weidenfeld and Nicolson, 1967), 575–576.

106. PREM 1/196, Baldwin meeting with Parliamentary delegation, 23 November 1936.

107. Ibid.

108. CAB 57/5/4, N.S. (LAB), 20 November 1934.

109. Ibid.

110. CAB 51/6, N.S. (v.) 13 October 1936.

111. PREM 1/196.

112. CAB 23/86/73, CP 326 (36), 9 December 1936.

113. Ibid.

114. CP 2 (37).

115. CAB 23/86/74, 16 December 1936.

116. COS 550; CAB 24/269/41.

117. COS 551; CP 58 (37).

118. CAB 23/87/5, 3 February 1937.

119. NC 18/1/993, February 1937.

120. CAB 23/88/19, 28 April 1937.

121. CAB 23/87/8, CP 61(37), 17 February 1937. The new construction sought approval for 2 aircraft carriers instead of one and seven cruisers instead of 5.

122. Roskill, 252.

123. CP 18(37).

124. CP 40(37).

125. CP 18(37), CP 69(37); CAB 23/87/9, 24 February 1937.

126. Gibbs, 624.

127. CAB 23/87/5, CP 40(37). 5 February 1937.

128. M.M. Postan, *British War Production* (London: HMSO, 1952), 96.

129. *Weir Papers* 18/5, 5 April 1937.

130. CP 40(37).

131. CAB 57/22, N.S. (w) 3, 16 February 1937.

132. CAB 23/87/5, 3 February 1937.

133. Peden, 79. But in February 1938 (after the Inskip Memorandum), Phillips came around to accepting higher taxation "here and now." Peden, 92.

134. Simon Haxey, *England's Money Lords* (New York: Morrison-Hilton, 1939), 35.

135. Ramsden, 87–88.

136. NC 7/11/30/115, 5 April 1937. Simon to Chamberlain.

137. NC 18/1/1003, 25 April 1937.

138. Shay, 148.

139. NC 18/1/1003, 25 April 1937.

140. Neville Chamberlain, *In Search of Peace* (New York: Putnam, 1939), 134.

141. Bullock, 597–598.

142. Ibid.

143. *Harvey Diaries,* 22 March 1937, 31.

144. *Debates,* 322: 1622, 20 April 1937.

145. Trevor Burridge, *Clement Attlee* (London: Jonathan Cape, 1985), 126.

146. Bullock, 582–586, 592–593; Kenneth Harris, *Attlee* (London: Weidenfeld and Nicolson, 1982), 133–134; 167.

147. NC 2/24A, 20 January 1937.

148. Ibid.

Chapter 5

Chamberlain's Government

Stanley Baldwin's long-anticipated retirement was announced on 11 April, but it was not until 28 May that Neville Chamberlain became Prime Minister in his own right. Though he exerted enormous influence on defense policy, he lacked the final "yes" or "no." Now he had that power. Essentially self-willed and obstinate, even by his own account, Chamberlain quickly brought his Cabinet into line and set the tone for its future meetings. He made clear that he intended to be master of his Cabinet and his own Foreign Minister.[1] He was well prepared to take over the Government, and he knew exactly what he wanted to do and how it was to be accomplished. He revealed his plans to his sister shortly after becoming Prime Minister: "I believe the double policy of rearmament and better relations with Germany will carry us safely through the danger period, if only the Foreign Office will play up."[2]

The words most often used by his contemporaries to describe Chamberlain were "dictatorial," "autocratic," "self-willed," and "obstinate." So concerned about his public image and reputation was the Conservative Research Department that Chamberlain was advised "to say something about democracy" in his acceptance speech because of the widespread feeling among the people that Chamberlain was an "autocrat at heart."[3] And when Winston Churchill, as the Senior Privy Councillor in the House of Commons, seconded the motion nominating Chamberlain as the new leader of the Conservative Party, he tactfully paid tribute to Chamberlain's tremendous achievement, as Chancellor of the Exchequer, in restoring Britain's financial position. But then in a thinly disguised reference to Chamberlain's dogmatic and arrogant personality, he reminded the party that its leadership had never been interpreted "in a dictatorial or despotic sense," and he appealed for the recognition of the rights of those who disagreed with the Government's policy. He continued, "We feel sure that the leader we are about to choose will, as a distinguished Parliamentarian and a House of Commons man, not resent honest differences of opinion arising between those who mean the same thing, and that party opinion will not be denied subordinate but still rightful place in his mind."[4]

Churchill's advice, no less than that of the Conservative Research Department, apparently made little impression on the Prime Minister. If anything, Chamberlain became even more autocratic as Prime Minister and less tolerant of criticism. James Margach, a lobby correspondent for forty years, noticed a significant change in his demeanor. He wrote, "As the war clouds grew, so did Chamberlain's obsession with the media. His own personality and the character of his news management underwent a startling transformation. The old, cozy, relaxed atmosphere with Lobbymen was replaced by a cold arrogance and intolerance."[5] On one occasion after becoming Prime Minister, Chamberlain appeared before the lobby correspondents "trembling and white with fury" at uncomplimentary press reporting of his appeasement policy. He thumped the table many times as he snarled in protest: "I tell you, I'm not dictatorial, I'm not autocratic, I'm not intolerant, I'm not overpowering. You're all wrong, wrong, wrong, I tell you! I'm the most relaxed and understanding of people. None of you, I insist, must ever say I'm dictatorial again."[6]

Lord Swinton, too, detected a "significant change" in Chamberlain's personality shortly after he became Prime Minister.[7] By the many who knew him, and even his sympathetic biographer, Chamberlain's administration has been described as a "one-man Cabinet."[8] David Margesson, who worked under Baldwin and Chamberlain as the Chief Government Whip, observed: "In Mr. Baldwin's Cabinet Chamberlain has been as powerful, if not more powerful, than his chief. In his own Cabinet, after he got rid of one [Eden] or two [Cooper] tiresome members, his was the only will that prevailed."[9] Hoare attested that "No Conservative Prime Minister ever had so strong a hold on his Party in the House of Commons as Chamberlain."[10] Only too sure of his own ability and his own carefully prepared positions, nothing could deflect him from his determined or, in many cases, predetermined course of action. Chamberlain found it difficult to seek advice from others, preferring to solicit opinions that tended to reinforce his own position.[11]

Lord Birkenhead noted that "there appeared in him when crossed, a streak of ruthlessness . . . and an autocratic tendency which led him to exercise an iron control over his Cabinet."[12] Chamberlain showed no false tolerance for persons holding an opposing point of view and he made little effort to conceal the fact. R.A. Butler, Undersecretary of State for Foreign Affairs and a loyal Chamberlain supporter throughout, regretted that Chamberlain

goes straight at the Opposition and expresses exactly what he means. The traditional soothing of members, by such phrases "the honorable and gallant gentleman will be aware," is usually erased [in the prepared speeches]. . . . In the Commons itself, where I used to sit next to him, he could not conceal his impatience with Labor and Liberal leaders. He would fidget and fume expletives in a manner, which brought to mind the famous physical eccentricities of Dr. Johnson.[13]

As is often the case with men of such strong character, they tend to be quite prejudiced.[14] Joseph Chamberlain, Neville's father, was known to have been anti-Semitic,[15] but whether Neville's behavior can be characterized as anti-Semitic is difficult to determine for sure. If not, it certainly comes close. Since he was careful to maintain a politically correct posture in public, the historian will find little concrete evidence to make a solid case for Chamberlain's anti-Semitism. On occasion one might find references to a "Jewish-Communist" conspiracy; but the closest Chamberlain came to letting his guard down appeared in a letter to his sister in which he confided that the "Jews were not a lovable people" and that "[he] did not care for them [him]self."[16] Expressions of anti-Semitism in themselves, of course, are not conclusive of anti-Semitic behavior, but when they are measured by Chamberlain's actions, they can help to identify a pattern of conduct that is unmistakably racist and prejudicial. Sometimes a failure to act also can speak to the subject. It need not be demonstrated that Chamberlain personally committed an anti-Semitic act to open him to the charge of anti-Semitism. If he failed to act to prevent and oppose anti-Semitism, does not this failure, in fact condone it?

An essential part of Chamberlain's appeasement policy toward Nazi Germany required that Nazi atrocities against the Jews, as well as other dissident groups, be watered down by the British press. In response to Chamberlain's subtle lead through Lord Halifax, Geoffrey Dawson of *The Times* admitted that he had kept things out of the paper to avoid offending Hitler and, in fact, added some of his own.[17] A senior BBC official also spoke of a "conspiracy of silence" to damp down British public opinion.[18] The manipulation of the press was not simply focused on anti-Semitism, to be sure, but anti-Semitic feelings certainly made it easier to adopt a press policy designed to insulate public opinion from the moral consequences of Nazism.

Aside from awkward remarks to the press about its susceptibility to "Jewish-Communist" propaganda,[19] Chamberlain personally showed little interest in, and was even annoyed to have "to say something" about Kristallnacht. He said he found it "difficult."[20] Sir Eric Phipps, the British Ambassador in Paris, used anti-Semitism to ingratiate himself with Chamberlain.[21] And in 1940, when Leslie Hore-Belisha, the only Jew in his Cabinet, became the target of a scurrilous anti-Semitic campaign engineered by *Truth*, Chamberlain failed to back his Minister of War. Hore-Belisha wrote to Chamberlain, hoping to put an end to the attacks and keep his job: "Frankly, Neville, I am completely perplexed. On the one hand, I have had throughout every assurance of your confidence in me; and on the other hand, you are prepared to accede to prejudice against me. You are delivering me to my enemies."[22] Chamberlain would not give Hore-Belisha any particulars in asking for his resignation but conceded that it was for reasons of prejudice.[23] Richard Cockett believes that Chamberlain's *real* political sympathies can be found in the pages of *Truth*,[24] a notorious anti-Semitic publication run by Joseph Ball and known to have been secretly controlled by Ball. Chamberlain even recommended it to his sisters.[25] *Truth* could have been silenced or at least toned down at any time by Chamberlain, but it was allowed to continue as long as he was Prime Minister. How different his attitude was to *Truth* than to his critics in the press! When the newspapers were critical of the Government's policy, Chamberlain would dispatch Horace Wilson, or Hoare, or Halifax to lean on the press, but there is no record that any attempt was ever made to intimidate or influence the publisher of *Truth,* with whom Chamberlain was on more intimate terms than anyone in the Government, with the possible exception of Wilson.

Chamberlain's prejudice toward Labor appears to have been directed as much at the leaders of the Labor Party as at its ideology. Chamberlain's reference to the Labor Opposition as "ignorant," "stupid," and a "pack of wild beasts" was not mere hyperbole.[26] He continued to treat Labor with "undisguised contempt," according to Hoare,[27] who knew him better than most. To Thomas Jones, Baldwin's private secretary, it appeared that Chamberlain was "much more prejudiced against Labor than Baldwin."[28] Alexander Cadogan spoke of Chamberlain's instinctive "contempt for the Americans" and his "hatred for the Russians,"[29] which he made no attempt to hide from those around him. His private secretaries, R. A. Butler and Arthur Rucker, shared his prejudices too (or they would not have been employed for very long).

As for friends, Chamberlain had none, according to his wife, Annie.[30] But he had many loyal and devoted followers who admired the efficiency with which he managed the government and the direction he provided for the party. Self-assured, supremely confident, and energetic, Chamberlain involved himself in every aspect of government and party business. These same qualities enabled him to persuade the press lords, the editors, and the lobby correspondents to cooperate with him in his search for peace through appeasement.

Indispensable to Chamberlain's highly personalized style of government were the people who were willing to "devil" for him.[31] That is, those who would speak for him without exposing the Prime Minister to criticism for the views expressed. Wilson, noted for the precise manner and measured response he applied to difficult problems, and for his unflinching loyalty to the Prime Minister, functioned as *alter ego* for Chamberlain, representing him at meetings, soliciting views, cajoling ministers, and maintaining a liaison with unofficial back-channel sources of government. Chamberlain was thus freed from taking responsibility for any potentially embarrassing disclosures of his personal initiatives, particularly in foreign relations. Typical of the manner in which he operated, Chamberlain revealed in his diary, an incident in which he "did not ask H[orace] W[ilson] who was the intermediary and he did not actually tell me, but [he] assumed it was Joseph Ball, who has once or twice before given me information of what Grandi [the Italian Ambassador in London], whom he knows well, is doing or thinking."[32]

Joseph Ball, of the Conservative Research Department, was another important functionary totally loyal to Chamberlain.[33] A former intelligence officer who was alleged to have been involved with the Zinoviev letter, Ball was a diehard ultra-conservative intent upon combating socialism.[34] He had worked for

Chamberlain at the Conservative Central Office and now ran a covert intelligence and propaganda service for him. Tapping phones,[35] disrupting the political Opposition,[36] passing and receiving sensitive information from foreign embassies for the personal use of the Prime Minister,[37] Ball enabled Chamberlain to carry on his policy of appeasement without going through the Foreign Office, long after the reasons for its justification no longer applied and could not be sustained in public. David Margesson also worked closely with Chamberlain and the Central Office to keep the party in line. Conservative members of Parliament who did not follow the party line were threatened with a withdrawal of support by the Central Office in the next election. Without that support, chances of re-election were very slim. Apparently Margesson performed his job quite well. Chamberlain's grip on the party was so strong that he was able to muster a Parliamentary majority of 81 votes even as the disastrous consequences of his policy began to unfold in the wake of the German advance through the Low Countries in 1940.

Among his Cabinet colleagues, Chamberlain was closest to Samuel Hoare and Kingsley Wood who often accompanied him on his daily walk through St. James's Park. But he did not confide in them as freely as he did in Wilson and Ball.[38] These sessions in the park were primarily designed to elicit support for his policy without his actually having to ask for it. Chamberlain had only to state his private, confidential views, and they proved only too willing to accommodate him. Unspoken assumptions about shared cultural, social, and economic goals provided the backdrop for their talks, which invariably permeated Cabinet discussions on sensitive matters. It was only after Munich and the Holland war scare that Hoare and Wood found the courage to stake out a more independent position without directly opposing Chamberlain.

Chamberlain's colleagues in the Cabinet and in the Government were expected to furnish support for his policies[39] When they wandered far afield and could no longer be relied upon to carry his policy, they were by-passed, or ignored, or even promoted (Vansittart, Fisher, and Hankey); or, forced to resign (Eden and Cooper); or unceremoniously replaced (Swinton and Inskip). Those who openly disagreed with his policy, like Churchill, were kept out of the Government.[40] Cadogan understood Chamberlain's managerial style only too well. When criticized for trying to get along with Wilson, although he resented Wilson's presence at foreign policy meetings, Cadogan explained, "If I tried to fight against him, I should only have been removed."[41] It was, indeed, a one-man Cabinet unequaled in the annals of British history. In such a setting, Chamberlain easily dominated his colleagues.

By any standard Chamberlain's outstanding bureaucratic and administrative skills enabled him to involve himself in every aspect of government, especially careful to keep the lid on the burgeoning rearmament program. Only a man of rigid competency could possibly have orchestrated such a large agenda through all of the unpredictable twists and turns and disruptions of the international order.[42]

While retaining the Baldwin Cabinet intact for the most part, Chamberlain made some important changes. The most important was to move the troublesome Cooper from the War Office to the Admiralty, where fewer problems were to be expected in terms of costly rearmament programs. He told his sisters that he "was anxious to remove D. Cooper from the War Office where . . . he and I have repeated differences."[43] Hore-Belisha, whom Chamberlain surmised was more anxious to advance his own political career, replaced Cooper at the War Office. But Hore-Belisha lacked stature, even in this tired and undistinguished Cabinet. To whom could he look for support of controversial programs? Chamberlain thought Hore-Belisha, a Jew, not well-connected socially, and not a part of the "old-boy network," could be counted on to carry out his program. In his rapid rise to the War Office, Hore-Belisha had established a reputation while a junior Minister of Transport for being a "boy wonder" and a man of action who got results. Those qualities were just what Chamberlain was looking for in the War Office. When Hore-Belisha interviewed for the position, Chamberlain emphasized the importance of "teamwork."[44] Chamberlain hoped that Hore-Belisha, unencumbered by club or other loyalties, would shake the troublesome War Office out of its preoccupation with a Continental role for itself and subscribe to Basil Liddell-Hart's views for a limited force.[45] The Prime Minister was initially well pleased with his dynamic Secretary of State for War. He told Lord Weir that he "believed that [Hore-Belisha] would do the job I sent him to the War Office for."[46] In other words, Hore-Belisha was on board, and could be counted on to go against the Army professionals and accept a limited role for the Army on the Continent. Chamberlain's shrewd assessment proved correct for the first year, but surprisingly, Hore-Belisha became more and more independent after Munich and proved exceedingly difficult to control.

Another major departmental change involved the Exchequer, where John Simon succeeded Chamberlain. Chamberlain allegedly chose Simon because of the political support that he could provide from the Liberals, and because he and Chamberlain had worked "so happily and effectively together."[47] But more than likely, Chamberlain judged Simon to be a sycophant who could be counted on to "devil" for him. Once again Chamberlain's uncanny judgment paid off. Sharing Chamberlain's concern for fiscal orthodoxy, Simon became his staunchest supporter in the Cabinet. Samuel Hoare, another loyalist, was moved from the Admiralty to the Home Office to make way for Cooper. Eden remained at the Foreign Office. Next to the Prime Minister, Eden was clearly the most popular man in the Cabinet and next in line to become Prime Minister. Inasmuch as he owed his position to the Hoare–Laval affair, his views were closely associated with support for the League of Nations and collective security, and carried wide appeal. Like Chamberlain, Eden sought to avoid a confrontation with the dictators, but he was not willing to go to the extraordinary lengths that his Prime Minister wanted in pursuit of his policy of appeasement.

Whatever personal shortcomings Chamberlain may have exhibited in office, none can deny the comprehensive, well thought-out, and consistent application of his ideas to the policy objectives he had set out to achieve. An important concomitant of his policy was to ensure its implementation through a careful management of administrative and bureaucratic personnel. What he wanted were people who would provide, "more support for [his] policy, and not a strengthening of those who don't believe in it."[48] He often met beforehand with key committee members to obtain their support for his agenda.[49] Whereas Baldwin allowed members and policy matters to drift, Chamberlain insisted on clear and unambiguous guidelines to be adhered to by his ministers. Whereas Baldwin was given to compromise and conciliation, Chamberlain was dogmatic and confrontational. Whereas Baldwin eschewed foreign affairs, Chamberlain ingested it.

Chamberlain's accession to the Prime Ministership was greeted with elation in Berlin, Tokyo, Rome, and Franco's Spain,[50] but created little enthusiasm on the British Left. These sentiments were not unfounded, as soon became apparent. Even Hoare had to admit that it would be "impossible" to conduct a national policy under this "intensely shy man" who harbored an undisguised contempt for the Labor Opposition, and little more regard for the independent Liberals or his critics within the Conservative Party.[51]

When Cooper renewed his request for an upgraded Continental force on 28 April 1937, an impatient Chamberlain barely managed to control his anger. He lectured the service ministers on their responsibility to keep their budgets within the £1,500,000,000 five-year limit, and warned them that the time had come when these budgets should be reviewed in the "light of both the financial situation and the manpower question."[52] Taking his cue from Chamberlain, Simon, the new Chancellor of the Exchequer, announced updated guidelines for defense funding. The services were informed that they should "estimate anew the time required for completion of their programs. These general estimates should then be examined by the Treasury and submitted to the Defense Policy and Requirements Committee (DPR), before being presented to the Cabinet. Meanwhile, discussions on new projects of major importance should be postponed."[53] Chamberlain gave a strong endorsement to the new procedure, which enabled him to control the rearmament program more effectively without exposing himself to the personal criticism of skimping on defense. Despite objections from the service ministers that the process was cumbersome and subject to more delay, the new procedure was adopted forthwith. It placed another obstacle in the path of Swinton's efforts to accelerate production of more airplanes, as he was already bogged down in lengthy negotiations with the Society of British Aircraft Constructors (SBAC). Simon's proposal was essentially a form of rationed defense in which the services were expected to prioritize among themselves, through Inskip, the most effective defense measures to be employed under the circumstances. In effect, the Treasury effectively managed the extent and nature of the defense program. Not surprisingly, the Treasury came under strong criticism, not only from the service chiefs, but also, later, from historians who could point to Treasury obstruction, rather than to Chamberlain, as the cause of the problems encountered in the defense program.

Having brought rearmament under control through the Treasury,

Chamberlain turned his attention to diplomacy, at the other end of his double policy. Colonial appeasement offered the most obvious and least obtrusive method of satisfying legitimate German grievances. The problem with this approach was that it was not popular with the public and ran into considerable opposition from the staunch imperialists within the Conservative Party. Here is yet another example that dispels the thesis that Chamberlain was merely carrying out the policies of the constituency that elected him. Industrialists, business interests, and imperialists were generally opposed to unilateral colonial concessions to Germany, although there was some support for mutually agreed-upon concessions in Europe. Yet Chamberlain was willing to take on their opposition if it would lead to the pacification of European problems. And although he preferred a *quid pro quo* arrangement with Hitler, he was prepared to acquiesce, if necessary, to stave off war. On 2 April 1937 he urged the Foreign Policy Committee not to reject the overtures from Hjalmar Schacht, President of the Reichsbank, to meet and discuss colonial mandates and access to raw materials, because it might lead to a general discussion of outstanding issues between Germany and Great Britain that he was anxious to pursue. Thus far, he noted quite correctly, too much attention had been paid to the colonial question in Anglo-German relations, when in fact it should be the last question on the agenda. He was perfectly willing to concede the greater part of German colonial demands if it would lead to a general European settlement. But Hitler showed no immediate interest in colonial appeasement. Subsequent meetings between Schacht and Frederick Leith-Ross, Chief Economic Adviser to the Government, bore little fruit because the Spanish Civil War kept getting in the way.[54] On 28 June, the Foreign Policy Committee concluded that the time was not yet ripe to pursue colonial appeasement, and talks were curtailed for the time being. But that did not discourage Chamberlain from seeking a *modus vivendi* with Germany. In answer to a question on the Government's German policy at the Dominions Conference in June 1937, he laid out German grievances, which included Austria, Czechoslovakia, Poland, Danzig, and Memel.[55] He expressed the confident hope that they could be redressed without the use of force, although William Strang of the Central Department of the Foreign Office had warned that if Germany could not achieve her goals through peaceful measures, she would try to achieve them through war.

While Chamberlain was wrestling with the German problem, Italian moves in the Mediterranean gave cause for more anxiety. Mussolini had strengthened Italian forces in Libya, threatening the Suez Canal, and Italian submarines had stepped up their attacks on ships in the Mediterranean, mocking the Non-Intervention Agreement to which Italy was a signatory power. Chamberlain was forced to admit that the situation was "disquieting" and that Mussolini had been "more than usually insolent" of late. But instead of taking strong action against Italy, Chamberlain informed the Cabinet that the way to deal with Mussolini was to get on better terms with Germany![56] Mussolini certainly was insolent. He boasted, later, that he had become "impudent" with Great Britain ever since the Abyssinian affair had revealed the extraordinary lengths to which the British Government would go to avoid a conflict.[57] As Italian actions in the Mediterranean brought the danger of war closer in the summer of 1937, the Sub-committee of Imperial Defense wrestled with the practical measures to be taken in case hostilities broke out. A suggestion by the CID to send modern aircraft into the Mediterranean region "as a show of progress in rearmament" was rejected by the Cabinet because the planes "could not be spared."[58] Chamberlain would do nothing that could be construed as provocative by the Italian Government.

Nothing, of course, could be done to produce ships or planes overnight, but manpower could be mobilized on relatively short notice. Inskip reported that some form of national registration would be helpful from the point of view of food rationing and air raid precautions.[59] He sought guidance from the Cabinet on this issue. "Was a scheme of national registration desirable and practicable from a political point of view?" he asked. "Or, should the Chairman of the Manpower sub-Committee be authorized to print forms and enrollment instructions of regular offices, notwithstanding that these measures would involve some measure of publicity?" And, third, "whether the Opposition parties should be consulted about either of the above."[60] The problem with national registration, from Chamberlain's point of view, was that it was generally seen as a prelude to conscription and was likely to be opposed by Labor thus raising public awareness of defense matters. Even the filling out of forms carried unwanted publicity and, unhappily, invited the cooperation of the trade unions, which Chamberlain rejected because it would "raise political difficulties." Nor was the mobilization of industrial labor to be contemplated, because it was "not only useless, but open to [political] objection."[61] Accordingly, a £20 million request for a three-month supply of food for a national emergency was turned down by the Cabinet,[62] and Labor was kept out of the defense program.

As invariably had happened in the past with the defense program, normal precautionary measures, as determined by the experts, became subordinated to the vicissitudes of party politics in pursuit of Chamberlain's goal of destroying the Labor Party. At no point in the defense program was an important proposal ever examined by Chamberlain and accepted simply because it was proper from a military or strategic perspective. Outside factors always seemed to take precedence over defense in the order of priorities as determined by Chamberlain. The Spanish Civil War was another such example.

The Spanish Civil War continued to be a source of embarrassment for the British Government in the summer of 1937. While Chamberlain was willing to suffer the indignities of a transparently weak foreign policy, Eden was not. Nor was British opinion, on either the Left or the Right, about to countenance the loss of British prestige to a second-class power like Italy. So, in concert with France — or, rather, because of French threats to abandon non-intervention — Chamberlain reluctantly agreed to a conference of Mediterranean powers, to assemble at Nyon, Switzerland, on 10 September 1937, to deal with "piracy" in the region.[63] The resulting agreement to step up multinational naval patrols in the Mediterranean was sufficient to deter Mussolini from further attacks on Mediterranean shipping immediately, almost as if by a miracle. Mussolini's attacks were simply designed to test British and French resolve to resist aggression. How different the course of British history might have been had the lessons of Nyon been impressed on Chamberlain. Eden, on the other hand, was encouraged by the instantaneous success of the Nyon Conference and determined to push ahead with his policy of firmness toward the dictators.

Meanwhile, trouble flared up again in the Far East. Japan had invaded China in July 1937 and, flushed with its early successes, became more truculent than ever toward Great Britain. The Sino-Japanese War dramatized the need for closer ties between the United States and Great Britain. Although Eden welcomed the prospect, Chamberlain recoiled from it. As always, Chamberlain predicated his foreign and domestic policy on measures designed to obviate the necessity for huge outlays of manpower and finance in the defense program. So, aside from his personal dislike of Franklin Roosevelt and the New Deal, closer ties with the United States had to be avoided for the same reason that Labor had to be resisted: to prevent larger rearmament programs from developing. Closer ties with foreign countries would render Great Britain susceptible to foreign pressure to increase its military preparedness program, and thus take some of the initiative away from the Prime Minister. Chamberlain would brook no interference with his policy from foreign sources any more than he would from domestic sources, or even his own Foreign Secretary.

Efforts by President Roosevelt to foster a closer relationship with Great Britain were greeted with varying degrees of skepticism in London. Both Chamberlain and Eden received the American initiative with studied caution.[64] Eden understood the diplomatic process and was willing to cultivate stronger Anglo-American ties for the long term. In the event of war, American assistance would be of enormous value, even if the United States was not directly involved at the outset. So he was willing to entertain weak American proposals simply for their cosmetic, psychological, and potential long-term value. Chamberlain, on the other hand, downplayed the American card. He deliberately placed one obstacle after another in the path of improved Anglo-American relations, though he was careful not to close the door.

But as strong expressions of public opinion in Britain and from the Dominions forced the Cabinet to take measures to deal with the deteriorating situation in the Far East, Chamberlain approved a Foreign Office inquiry to the U. S. Government on 30 September asking for its thoughts on a possible joint action in the Far East. Dissatisfied with the Foreign Office draft, he amended it to read, "We are not convinced that any such action would be effective, but we would be ready to examine matters with the U.S. Government if the latter thought it worthwhile," — completely changing its tone and purpose[65] Eden was unhappy with the addendum because he had hoped to affect a closer relationship with the United States. Chamberlain's draft sent the wrong message, so a second telegram was dispatched by Eden, in hopes of repairing any damage that might have been caused by the initial transmission. Eden's follow-up message welcomed the opportunity to meet with the U.S. Government if it felt "able to do so," and pressed for an early reply.[66] The reply was not long in coming. On 5 October, President Roosevelt delivered his famous "quarantine speech." Chamberlain's sister Hilda was "pleased" with the speech,[67] but her brother quickly put a damper on her enthusiasm. "I read Roosevelt's speech with mixed feelings," he wrote back. "What did it really mean? . . . . It was vague in 'essentials.' What does he mean by 'putting them in quarantine'?"[68] The next day the Cabinet heard from the Prime Minister that it would be unrealistic to expect anything more than words from the United States Government, and that appeasement efforts toward Japan should continue. Reluctantly, the Cabinet approved the continued sale of arms to Japan, but cautioned against alienating the U.S. Government in the process.[69]

In preparation for the Brussels Conference, due to open in November to deal with Japan's violation of the Nine Power Treaty, Eden recommended tying British actions to the extent that the United States was willing to involve itself, even if it meant a blockade. Chamberlain rejected the idea, saying that it would only expose Great Britain to retaliation in the Far East. He preferred to let China and Japan settle their differences among themselves. Besides, he thought the question was a moot one anyway, since the United States would not give assurances that it would be accept the consequences of whatever actions were agreed upon by the Nine Power countries.[70] He spoke more confidently at the next Cabinet meeting, though, when he reported that the United States "has no intention of taking decisive action in the Far East."[71] Consequently, he refused to allow Great Britain to be drawn into a futile policy of Japan-bashing at Brussels. Once the conference had gotten under way in November, he sent Malcom MacDonald, the Dominions Secretary, to replace Eden there in a thinly disguised attempt to sabotage the talks, which were proving to be extremely embarrassing and meddlesome to Chamberlain's preferred policy of unilateral appeasement.[72]

MacDonald's report on the Brussells Conference apparently confirmed Chamberlain's pessimistic view of American policy. He concluded that the United States only wanted to use "strong language," and was not prepared to take any action that required legislation because it had failed to move public opinion at home.[73] Chamberlain may have been technically correct in placing little faith in American words, but he completely ignored Eden's point about the symbolic value of an Anglo-American entente. Eden lamented that the Prime Minister "only prompted a further American psychological withdrawal."[74] But, of course, that was the point: Chamberlain eschewed closer American ties for fear of becoming an American dependency.[75]

Chamberlain moved eagerly to assert his control over foreign policy. He involved himself personally and directly in the process.[76] Working through his Press Officer, George Steward, he set up a secret back-channel to the German Government through Hesse at the German Embassy in London in order to represent his personal views in Berlin, which differed from those of the Foreign Office.[77] He did not call any meetings of the Foreign Policy Committee between late July 1937 and January 1938, thereby depriving Eden of any potential support or opportunity to build a consensus in the Cabinet for his policy of firmness toward the dictators. In these circumstances, Eden was forced to bring his views directly to the Cabinet, where he faced a hostile reception from the likes of Hoare, Swinton, Simon, and Wood, and about half of the Cabinet,[78] who were anxious to retain the Prime Minister's favor.

Without allies in the Cabinet, Eden was at a clear disadvantage. He was forced to go outside the Government to expound his views, much to Chamberlain's chagrin. The Prime Minister became angry when he learned that Eden was scheduled to make a foreign policy address to a Conservative Party rally at Llandudno, Wales, on 15 October. Only the intervention of the party chairman saved Eden from a serious rupture with his Prime Minister.[79] Chamberlain told Eden that he objected to his Foreign Secretary being used as a "party hack," which was somewhat disingenuous on his part, because he had on a number of occasions chastised Eden for not hitting the Opposition hard in debate.[80] What he really objected to was the substance of the speech, which might upset his efforts to appease the dictators. Eden proposed to use the occasion to promote his policy of taking a strong stand against Italy in Spain, since the Nyon Conference had demonstrated the efficacy of taking that line.[81]

Actually, Chamberlain was growing rather uncomfortable with his Foreign Secretary, who was clearly emerging as heir apparent. He contemptuously referred to Eden's coterie as the "glamour boys." Extremely popular in the country, Eden was widely respected among the PLP and enjoyed a great relationship with the press. Chamberlain, therefore, determined that Eden had to be restrained as much as possible, for fear that his views might attain widespread circulation outside of the Cabinet, thus affecting his own policy within the Cabinet. To adopt Eden's policy of encouraging closer relations with the United States, France, and probably the Soviet Union, ran counter to his own policy. It also carried with it the inevitable acceptance of those policies that he considered anathema: the New Deal in the United States, the Popular Front in France, and communism in Soviet Russia. Even if it were successful, would not an alliance or entente undermine the very principles that he was attempting to discredit in his own country? For these reasons, as well as for his own personal predilections, Chamberlain rejected Eden's policy and took the risks for peace that he did. Moreover, the formation of an alliance system, though it might actually strengthen the forces of peace, presented the unhappy prospect of a long and economically debilitating period of armed truce from which he thought it might take Great Britain generations to recover.[82] In fairness to Chamberlain, it must be noted that despite Germany's impressive military buildup, economic intelligence reports indicated that the volume and speed of the German rearmament program could not be sustained much longer,[83] and Germany might, therefore, be inclined to listen to the voice of reason. On the other hand, the possibility that Germany might attempt to resolve its problems by the use of force could not be discounted .[84]

The announcement of the Tripartite Agreement on 6 November was certainly an ominous sign for Eden, but not for Chamberlain, who became more determined to appease the dictators. Hence, Lord Halifax's visit to Berchtesgaden in November was seen as an exciting prospect for the success of Chamberlain's double policy. Halifax had received an invitation from Hermann Goering to attend a hunting expedition, during which time he hoped to meet with Hitler. Eden recalled that he "was not eager [to accept the invitation], but saw no sufficient reason to oppose it." At any rate it seemed to be an instance where he could demonstrate his willingness to cooperate with Chamberlain, who had complained in the past that the Foreign Office had shown insufficient resolve in developing better relations with Germany.[85]

While Eden was attending the Brussels Conference, a story that only could have come from the Foreign Office, appeared in *The Evening Standard*. In an apparent attempt to sabotage Halifax's visit to Germany, it revealed the context of the forthcoming talks (which proved ,in retrospect, to be amazingly accurate). Hitler, purportedly, would make no demands for colonies for ten years, as long as he was assured of a free hand in Eastern Europe.[86] Chamberlain became "exceedingly angry about the article," according to the German press attaché in London, Fritz Hesse.[87] Hitler, too, was angered by this premature disclosure, and considered aborting the talks. Only Chamberlain's determination to seek an opening to Germany prevented the collapse of the talks. He provided *The Times* and *The Daily Telegraph* with roseate accounts of the pending trip that suggested more than the Foreign Office was willing to reveal. Chamberlain apparently was prepared to accept German hegemony in Central and Eastern Europe as long as it was not achieved by the use of force.[88] Munich was in the making.

Returning from Brussels on 14 November, Eden was shocked to read in the newspapers the next morning "exaggerated accounts of the scope of the visit," while the Foreign Office notes stressing the informal and unofficial character of the visit to the press were virtually ignored.[89] Fighting off the flu, Eden arranged a meeting with Chamberlain on 16 November to represent the concerns of the Foreign Office in this matter. He mentioned that Yvon Delbos, the French Foreign Minister, had expressed his government's reservations about Halifax's trip, fearing that it represented a change in British policy. Eden was forced to deny the charge, but the recent press accounts hardly inspired French confidence in the British Government. Eden insisted that the matter be cleared up immediately by publishing a clear and unambiguous statement of the informal and unofficial nature of the visit. Chamberlain only agreed to "damp down" the enthusiasm of the press.[90] The Halifax visit proceeded on 17 November as scheduled, and the worst fears of the Foreign Office were soon realized. Despite Halifax's efforts to state the British position clearly, Germany came away from the talks satisfied that Great Britain was not interested in Central Europe.[91] Hitler's willingness to discuss colonies and disarmament at a later date was conditioned, in the final analysis, on Britain's acquiescence to Germany's revisionist demands in Eastern and Central Europe. In his memoirs, Eden expressed his regret at having "tolerated" the visit.[92]

Eden's meeting with Chamberlain on 16 November exposed other deep-seated differences between the two men. It was not the announcement of Japan's adherence to the Anti-Comintern Pact of 6 November, nor the impending visit to Berlin by Lord Halifax that disturbed him so much as his reading of a most secret memorandum compiled by the COS, "A Comparison of the Strength of Great Britain with Certain Other Nations as at January 1938."[93] Eden's main concern at the time was with the sad state of Britain's arms and the slow pace of rearmament, which were undermining his diplomacy.[94] He understood the dynamics of international relations in a way that Chamberlain never would. Without the force of arms to back it up, diplomacy could not of itself sustain the national security. The Chiefs of Staff's report, prepared for consideration by the CID and submitted to the Cabinet on 27 October, seemingly thrust an intolerable burden on the shoulders of the Foreign Office. Its main conclusion was that Great Britain's defensive obligations were truly overwhelming, and the COS could not foresee the time when its defenses would be strong enough to safeguard Britain's vital interests. In consequence, every effort must be made by the Government to limit the number of its potential enemies and gain the support of potential allies. Prepared under Inskip's direction, the report's conclusions echoed the views of the Prime Minister, with one difference. Inskip told the Defense Plans Sub-committee of the CID that if Germany rearmed with dangerous speed, "it might be necessary for us to accelerate our program, modify or reverse the Cabinet decision, and pass from a peace system to some form of war system."[95]

Eden had too much pride to carry out an obsequious foreign policy toward countries that Great Britain could easily deal with on equal terms in normal times. He tried to impress upon Chamberlain the need for more arms and allies so that Great Britain need not have to suffer the humiliation of a pusillanimous foreign policy of appeasement, which, once begun, could only end up in abject surrender of its vital interests. Chamberlain stiffened up. He acknowledged that the task was not an easy one, but he regretted the failure of the Foreign Office to be more creative. He placed little faith in allies and belittled Eden's efforts to improve Anglo-American relations at Brussels, calling it a "waste of time." Their meeting ended on an acerbic note, with Chamberlain telling his Foreign Secretary to "go back to bed and take an aspirin!" At the heart of their differences lay the perceived time frame within which the defense program could provide adequate security.[96] Chamberlain's optimism fed on the notion that Germany would be deterred from aggression by the reasonable prospect of achieving his objectives without having to fight a long, drawn-out war could hardly be expected to win. He was also encouraged by a COS report calling attention to Germany's weak economy and noted that her stocks of raw materials could only support a short effort under war conditions, and that no country would be in a position to launch offensive operations in 1938. "A Comparison of Strength" survey showed the following disposition of military hardware.[97]

Naval Strength

	Great Britain	Japan
Battleships	15	10
Aircraft carriers	5	5
Cruisers	59	32
Destroyers	161	121
Submarines	53	60

Air Strength (not including miscellaneous aircraft)

	Germany	France	Great Britain (metropolitan)
Long-range bombers	1074	228	216
Short-range bombers	550	228	156
Fighters	771	270	392
Total	1820	1195	1053

As far as Chamberlain was concerned, since the danger of war was not imminent, war measures were not called for. He also chose to ignore the more pessimistic sections of the COS report that warned of several scenarios which might well precipitate a conflict, such as

a. Internal difficulties in Germany that might decide its leaders to attack.
b. Germany's becoming aware of British and French deficiencies which might be an inducement to attack.

Chamberlain was not eager to seize on the recommendation of the COS to increase the number of potential allies, as Eden had recommended,[98] nor did he place much stock in French warnings that Germany might use new techniques of subversion against her neighbors, which only strong Anglo-French, and possibly Anglo-American, diplomatic pressure could prevent. The Prime Minister's mind had been made up to pursue appeasement, and no other policy was to be contemplated.

In keeping with the new policy guidelines for capping defense spending and obtaining Treasury approval for new programs, the defense estimates for 1938 were formulated by the services in late summer of 1937 and brought up for Cabinet consideration on 27 October. Chamberlain was ill and could not attend the meeting, so Simon took over. Simon was not happy with the aggregate defense bill of £1,717,000,000, which exceeded the limit of £1,500,000,000 set in the spring. He asked the services, including air raid precautions, to "estimate anew the period of time for completion of these programmes."[99] The matter was referred to Inskip for further study to balance the strategic requirements of national defense against its financial implications. Meeting with Hankey, the COS, and Chamberlain's trusted domestic adviser, Sir Horace Wilson, Inskip dutifully tried to stay within budget without paring down the estimates in such a way as to overtly compromise the effectiveness of the defense program that everyone, including Hitler,[100] already knew to be inadequate. Inskip's role was crucial to the success of Chamberlain's double policy. He was expected to supply the strategic arguments for the defense program without giving the impression that the Government was not merely seeking the cheapest defense, but the best under the circumstances. His job was not made any easier by Churchill's persistent and vigilant watch over the rearmament program.

On 12 October, Churchill had complained to Hankey, as a former colleague and as a Privy Councillor, that the air defense program was so pitiful that the Air Staff could not scrape up enough modern aircraft or trained crews to stage an impressive show of air strength for General Milch, a visiting German dignitary. Only one of each type could be displayed.[101] Hankey's amour propre had been wounded, and he fired off an angry response to Churchill, condemning the leaks at the Air Ministry. Nevertheless, Hankey had to admit the truth of the allegations. He informed Inskip of the Churchill letter on 14 October and confided to him that perhaps the time had come for relaxing the rule on the interference with trade and that "the imposition of compulsory industrial priorities was not so politically impossible as had been assumed, and in any event would be preferable to late in the day panic measures."[102] At last, Hankey was wavering. The COS were bound to follow.

Inskip's report, "Defense Expenditures in Future Years," was taken up during two Cabinet meetings on 22 December. More popularly known as the Inskip Memorandum, this document clearly articulated the second part of Chamberlain's double policy of limiting the size of the rearmament program. Steps toward implementing the first part of the double policy had been agreed upon earlier by the Cabinet when it accepted the COS report, " A Comparison of Strength with Certain Other Countries." Well aware of the risks inherent in this report, Inskip reminded his colleagues of their earlier decision in order to assure their support for the entire policy. "In the long run the provision of adequate defenses within the means at our disposal, will only be achieved when the long term foreign policy has succeeded in changing the present assumptions as to our potential enemies."[103] No mention was made of trying to enlist the support of potential allies or of the Dominions. Once again Eden tried to impress upon his colleagues the impossibility of carrying out his mission. He repeated his warning that Germany, Italy, and Japan had ambitions, and Britain stood in the way of their fulfillment.[104] The point was well taken, but it did not change matters.

Chamberlain's mind had been made up, and there was no doubt about which view was to prevail. Italy must be detached from Germany, if possible, and Japan was not to be provoked into taking some rash action. All agreed that the Foreign Office was placed in a most difficult diplomatic position, but it must buy time for the rearmament program to take effect.

As far as the defense program was concerned, Inskip sought to preempt the anticipated criticism from the service ministers by taking refuge behind the Treasury argument limiting defense spending to £1.5 billion. Yet he was careful to avoid giving the impression that this five-year proposal was crafted only in terms of finance. In deciding

whether or not we can afford this or that programme, the first question to be asked is how much this programme will cost; and the cost of the programme is then related to the sums which can be made available from the Exchequer sources, from taxation, or exceptionally, from the proceeds of loans. But the fact that our real resources consist not of money . . . but of our manpower and productive capacity, to maintain our credit and the general balance of our trade. . . . while, therefore, it is true that the extent of our resources imposes limitations upon the size of the defense programmes which we are able to undertake, this is only one aspect of the matter. . . . The maintenance of our economic stability . . . can properly be regarded as a fourth arm of defense, alongside the three Defense Services, without which purely military effort would be of no avail.[105]

The words of the Memorandum may have belonged to Inskip, but the substance was pure Chamberlain. Predicated on the assumption that Germany would be in a position to strike in 1939, the terms of the memorandum were not calculated to provide the greatest security, but only enough defense to avoid a knockout blow. Its principal purpose was to act as a deterrent by confronting Hitler with the prospect of having to fight a long, drawn-out war. It went on to say, "Nothing operates more strongly to deter a potential aggressor from attacking this country than our [economic] stability. . . . But were other countries to detect in us signs of strain, this deterrent would at once be lost."[106] In consequence, the memorandum stipulated that the service departments should be guided by the following criteria in formulating their programs:

FIRST: To maintain the security of the United Kingdom.
SECOND: To preserve the trade routes on which Great Britain depends
             for her imports and raw materials.
THIRD: To provide for the defense of the British overseas territories.
FOURTH: To cooperate in the defense of the territories of her allies.[107]

Notwithstanding the omnipresent German threat, these guidelines were intended to meet Great Britain's defense needs for the next five years. Implicit in the memorandum was a decision to abandon the commitment to guarantee the Locarno Treaty, which was last in the order of priorities of the overall defense plan. Also hit hard by the memorandum were the Dominions, whose security interests would have to be subordinated to needs closer to home. It also meant that

Great Britain would lose a substantial amount of political leverage with friendly countries once they learned that Britain was weakening its Continental commitment.

The Inskip Memorandum was drafted with one goal in mind: limiting the size and scope of the defense program. By elevating finance, the fourth arm of defense, to the level of the three defense services, Inskip was able to dignify the memorandum's strategic and tactical concept with a credible alternative to a very serious military problem. The Treasury argument, skillfully employed by Chamberlain, Simon, and Inskip, did not admit the inability of the country to meet the defense bill. Rather, it was predicated on the curious notion that the Treasury's resources should not be squandered now, but should be held in reserve until the actual outbreak of hostilities, in order to make it easier to obtain foreign credits during the war! The prospect of Britain's ability to draw on foreign credits was expected to provide a powerful deterrent to aggression no less than Britain's air force. Yet, paradoxically, Chamberlain maintained a cold and indifferent attitude toward the United States, on which he expected to call for financial assistance when the going got tough.

Sources of revenue for the defense program were available from increased taxation and/or additional borrowing. At 5s per pound the income tax stood where it had been in 1932, and far from the 7s that it had reached during World War I. Borrowing had been introduced earlier in the year, and presented an awkward political problem. But it did not pose a financial hardship any greater than the one facing the defense program. Significantly, this Treasury view, which figured so prominently in the rearmament program, and was used with such great effectiveness to counteract the views of the military experts and the Foreign Office, never categorically stated its inability to meet the defense bill. The £400 million loan subscribed earlier in the year represented only the amount of money that the Treasury determined could be borrowed without an appreciable rise in the rate of inflation, not an absolute figure. Phillips reported that borrowing £80 million per year was well within the country's ability without the fear of producing inflation.[108] Chamberlain emphatically supported the conclusions of the Inskip Memorandum, especially the part that stressed the importance of maintaining economic stability as an essential element in defensive strength. The debate was settled on Chamberlain's strong endorsement of the report. There was nothing more to be said. The fate of the defense program was sealed.

One by one the service proposals submitted in October were subjected to reexamination according to the priorities established by Inskip's committee. The Navy, expected to provide the first line of defense, had submitted two proposals for consideration. One was based on strengthening existing forces (Hypothesis A), and a second (Hypothesis B) called for adoption of a Two Ocean Standard. Predicated on the assumption that it might have to wage war in Europe and in the Far East simultaneously, and with the situation in the Mediterranean threatening British lines of communication to the Far East, the Admiralty pressed for a Two Ocean Standard, which would require an additional three battleships, two aircraft carriers, and seven cruisers, at cost of £90 million above the pre-approved standard for the quinquennium.[109]

Naval Forces of Great Britain and Japan[110]

	Great Britain		Japan
	Hypothesis A	Hypothesis B	
Battleships	15	+ 3	10
Aircraft carriers	5	+ 2	5
Cruisers	59	+ 7	32
Destroyers	161	—	121
Submarines	53	—	60

Cooper made a strong case for the Admiralty, but Simon noted that Hypothesis A would raise the cost of the five-year plan to £1,605,000,000, and Hypothesis B, the Two Ocean Standard, would cost £1,884,000,000. Neither plan was acceptable from the Treasury's point of view. In lawyer-like fashion, Inskip produced a compromise for the time being. Since new naval construction could not be laid down until the next fiscal year, he recommended that a decision on the Two Ocean Standard be postponed until a modified proposal could be reviewed. In the meantime the Admiralty should consider retaining and modernizing some of its ships due to be scrapped, and cost out its additional needs.[111] Cooper, of course, was not happy with the decision, but neither were the COS. They had learned that Japan was building a 42,000-ton battleship with 16-inch guns,[112] larger and more powerful than any British battleship.

Chamberlain's decision to move Cooper from the War Office to the Admiralty paid an early dividend. Hore-Belisha, the new Secretary of State for War, offered relatively little resistance to the low priority assigned to the army's defense needs. Only too anxious to prove himself as a reliable team player, he raised few objections to Inskip's proposals for the reallocation of funds for the Territorial Army. Since the defense of the United Kingdom was listed as the number one priority in defense planning, the Inskip Committee had actually redefined the role of the Army by assigning the TA to the air defense of Great Britain (ADGB) instead of equipping and training it as a reserve for the Continental army or for reinforcement of its imperial garrisons. Hore-Belisha's easy compliance with Inskip's proposal was influenced by a visit he had recently made to France to observe army maneuvers there; he had been impressed with France's ability to defend itself behind the Maginot Line. Moreover, he reasoned that this fortress would allow the French Army to allocate its reserves for the

Army of its obligation to ensure the defense of the Low Countries and the Channel ports. Hankey, incidentally, had come to accept this view as well, having realized that Chamberlain would never budge from his opposition to a Continental commitment, and that he would have to accept the constraints imposed by the Inskip Memorandum.[113] He now threw his support to a revitalized air program as the lesser of two evils.

To accept Hore-Belisha's proposal meant a virtual abandonment of the Army's Continental commitment. As Eden was quick to point out, this was a rather new concept of Britain's Continental role, and therefore the French Government ought to be notified of the Cabinet's decision.[114] Eden feared the diplomatic consequences of such a decision on Britain's allies. Belgium had already loosened its ties to the Western democracies by declaring neutrality following Germany's march into the Rhineland. What other defections might follow Great Britain's decision to weaken its Continental commitment? How might Eastern European countries interpret this move? Might not France be driven to seek an accommodation with Nazi Germany? Strong Anglo-French ties should not be taken for granted. There were very strong feelings on the French Right against the Popular Front Government of Leon Blum that might just prepare the way for a *rapprochement* with Germany. Their slogan was "Better Hitler than Blum." Nor could the prospects of a Nazi-Soviet *rapprochement* be ruled out.[115]

The most difficult problem for the Cabinet to address was the Air Ministry's proposal of Scheme J. According to Swinton, Scheme F had been rendered obsolete by the October revelations of General Milch, that Germany had achieved superiority over Great Britain in the air, and a new air program was needed to keep pace. British intelligence sources confirmed that Germany would have an advantage in front-line aircraft of 3,240 to 1,736 by 1939. But even more ominous than the facts presented was Milch's boast that Germany was capable of doubling its production at a moment's notice.[116] The Air Staff was confronted at once with the de facto inferiority in the number of aircraft, and also an ever increasing disparity in numbers thereafter. To deal with this problem, the Air Staff urged Swinton to reconsider the system of industrial priority that was frustrating their efforts to meet the threat from the Luftwaffe. It was basically the same recommendation that Hankey had made to Inskip in October.

Although Swinton sympathized with their problem, he knew that Chamberlain would never sanction any proposal to interfere with trade at this time, at least not until the new diplomacy had been given a chance to work its magic. He therefore instructed the Air Staff to prepare a proposal that would not cause a severe disruption in the civil trade. Their proposal, called Scheme J, was, as Swinton was careful to point out, designed "to avoid the control of industry and interference with normal production to meet civilian requirements."[117] By reducing the number of reserves and postponing deliveries of overseas orders, the Air Ministry hoped to achieve a front-line metropolitan strength of 1,442 bombers and 532 fighters by 1941. Still far short of Germany's expected front-line strength, Scheme J represented the best that Swinton felt could be achieved under strength, Scheme J represented the best that Swinton felt could be achieved under the circumstances. What he wanted was for the Government to apply strong pressure on certain civil industries to give priority to the air program, without taking statutory powers.

In line with his earlier attempts to persuade Chamberlain to relax the rule on interference with trade, Eden gave strong support to Swinton's proposal. Petulantly, Chamberlain directed the Cabinet Secretary to record that the Foreign Secretary's argument had been presented orally. Halifax and Hoare also offered qualified support for Scheme J, while Cooper appeared to be too preoccupied with the Admiralty's plight to lend outright support. More money for the RAF translated into less money for the Admiralty. Hore-Belisha, still very much in awe of the Prime Minister and anxious to remain on his good side, also stayed out of the debate for the most part. The inability of the service ministers to work together for stronger defense played to Chamberlain's advantage in keeping a lid on the rearmament program. Individually there was little that could be done to overcome the well-prepared position of the Prime Minister.

Notwithstanding the technical advice of the experts, Simon reacted vigorously to Swinton's proposal. At a cost of £650 million as compared with £467 million for Scheme F, Scheme J threatened to break the fetters of the Treasury. Simon insisted on maintaining the integrity of the defense budget as the "fourth arm of defense," and was strongly supported by Chamberlain. Nevertheless, security admittedly took precedence over finance, and a more credible case needed to be made for limiting the size of the air program in terms of strategy and defense while not appearing to be made solely on the narrow grounds of finance. It was left to Inskip, therefore, to supply the strategic and technical arguments for rejecting Scheme J.

Inskip dutifully questioned the feasibility of Scheme J on technical grounds. According to his estimates, 13,100 officers and pilots would be needed to staff the proposal, but he reckoned that only 12,000 could be obtained by voluntary means; and of 114,000 airmen, only about 96,000 could be supplied. He also doubted that the skilled labor for an accelerated program could be obtained even "if we were prepared to compel by other means a large scale diversion of civil factories to armament work."[118] It was clear that the voluntary system of recruiting could not keep pace with the accelerated program envisioned by the services. Even so, if the funding for a larger defense budget were suddenly to become available, it would not materially affect the rearmament program, since the additional spending could not be absorbed into the current system of voluntary administration and production.[119] Inskip summed up the problem for the Cabinet. If heavy expenditures exceeding the currently approved levels were contemplated, "it must appear that we. . .envisage measures of compulsion on industry and labor, measures not only most difficult politically, but threatening the maintenance of that stability which is an essential defense interest to preserve."[120] However, Inskip injected a note of optimism into an otherwise depressing report by noting that the rather large increases in the 1937 defense program had been met with reasonable success (i.e., without dislocating trade). He felt that a continuation of those measures would carry the defense program through 1938, *as long as there was no further deterioration of the international situation.* The "reasonably successful"measures included a closer liaison between the defense departments and industry, and more de-skilling and dilution. In light of the misgivings of the COS, it is difficult to accept Inskip's optimistic expectation of "reasonable success" in meeting the defense requirements by voluntary means as anything more than wishful thinking. Inskip knew better. He was in daily contact with military and industrial leaders to deal with specific problems related to the defense program, but not with Labor. He knew that Hankey and Admiral Chatfield and the COS were becoming increasingly restive at the diminishing margin of safety offered by the defense program, which they believed would not give security in time.[121] And he was also aware of the acute difficulties the industrial firms faced in obtaining skilled labor.[122] Yet, as Deputy Minister for the Coordination of Defense, his job was to articulate the views of the Prime Minister, and as long as there was the slightest hope for success of the Prime Minister's policy, he would support it.

The practical effects of the Cabinet decision on 22 December to adhere to the £1.5 billion Treasury figure therefore were (a) to limit the size of the Army's reinforcement capability for its Continental divisions; (b) to assign the Territorial Army to the ADGB; (c) to delay new naval construction; and (d) to reduce its bomber and reserve squadrons. Simon asked that the new estimates be submitted to the Treasury by 20 January, so that the 1938 defense budget could be examined by the Cabinet in the first two weeks of February and be ready for presentation to the Commons in March.

The stratagem of the Inskip Memorandum was brilliantly employed by Chamberlain to win Cabinet support for his double policy of limited rearmament and appeasement by raising finance to a level on par with the service departments as the "fourth arm of defense." Such a proposition, made by Inskip or Simon, would have been indefensible under the circumstances without the support of the service chiefs or the Foreign Office. But, when articulated and engineered by Neville Chamberlain, it encountered relatively little opposition in the Cabinet. The opinion of the COS had been successfully muted by a rigid bureaucratic process imposed and cleverly manipulated by the Prime Minister. Clearly upset with the process, Admiral Chatfield could only present his views to Hankey, the Chairman of the COS, who was expected to make his case to Inskip at the CID. Chatfield wrote to Hankey on 6 January that "the time has come to consider our position once more" (i.e., with respect to the rule on the non-interference with trade).[123] Afraid that the existing programs would not provide security in time, the COS recommended that the Government order double shifts, which would increase arms production by 33 percent within three months. When Chatfield wrote his memoirs after the war, he reflected on the "mistakes"of the past. He complained bitterly that in the future some way should be found to "enable the technical opinion of each Chief of Staff to be confidently expressed to Parliament . . . when he considers the country is being misled, and that Imperial defense will no longer be placed at the mercy of party politics."[124]

Hankey agreed to press Inskip, on behalf of the COS, to seek a relaxation of the rule on non-interference with trade. He wrote to Inskip on 14 January, reminding him of his repeated pledge to the COS to seek Cabinet approval to relax the rule on non-interference with trade when the international situation became precarious:

We are at the parting of the ways. Either we must change our foreign policy or increase the tempo of our rearmament by dropping the principle that trade and industry are not to be interfered with. . . . unless the number of our potential enemies can be reduced at once, I submit that our rearmament policy must be changed. . . . A decision to press forward without regard for trade considerations might prove a decisive factor in deterring war, or if it came, in averting disaster.[125]

Inskip discussed the matter with the Prime Minister and Chamberlain persuaded Inskip to stay the course by assuring him that the number of Britain's potential enemies was about to be reduced. Once again Inskip was caught between the COS and Chamberlain as he attempted to pare down the estimates along the lines laid out in the Inskip Memorandum. Inskip explained his dilemma to the Cabinet at the 9 February meeting (CAB 24/274/24):

We are faced with an inexorable choice between two courses. The first involves heavily increased taxation, and the straining of our economic system, leading perhaps to another crisis [as in 1931], or a long and painful period of bad trade. The second course, in so far as it might be interpreted as a decision to restrict the defense programme might react upon the prospect of successful negotiation, and might therefore, be fraught with the danger of war. If heavy expenditure over such a figure [£1.5 billion] were contemplated, it would appear that we must envisage war measures of compulsion on industry and labor, measures not only most difficult *politically* but threatening the maintenance of that stability which it is an essential interest to preserve.

Tactfully, Inskip produced another of his many compromises. He reduced the estimate from £1,800,000,000 to £1,570,000,000 and awarded an additional £80,000,000 for ARP. But, instead of spreading the total over five years, he approved of more spending in the first two years, provided that the industrial capacity, manpower, and skilled labor could be found without interfering with the normal course of trade. Treasury officials were disappointed that their efforts to convince Inskip to hold the line were not as satisfactory as they had hoped.

Under the new terms of reference Hore-Belish meekly accepted a further reduction in the Army's Continental role from four Regular Army divisions, one mobile division and three antiaircraft divisions, to two RA divisions, one mobile division, and two antiaircraft divisions, plus slowing down the rate of reinforcement.[126] He also repeated Chamberlain's familiar but gratuitous argument that public opinion would not accept a large Continental commitment. Swinton proposed to alter Scheme J by postponing increases in overseas air squadrons, reducing the number of bombers, and cutting back on reserve forces, and he made it clear that this new Scheme K was not structured by the needs of the Air Ministry, but by what was financially expedient.[127] Scheme K, in short, was much like Scheme J. The major difference, aside from its cost-cutting feature, was moving up the date of its completion from 1941 to 1940, at the expense of the reserve component.

The Admiralty proved to be more difficult to accommodate. Cooper, removed from the War Office for being a maverick, lived up to his reputation and would not be intimidated by the Treasury. A self-assured politician by reason of his social position, Cooper played his hand for all it was worth. As the head of the senior and most prestigious service, and aware of its crucial importance to the impending Imperial Conference, Cooper resisted cuts beyond those proposed in December. He reminded his colleagues that the Admiralty was already operating under last year's minimal standard for national security, and that the international situation had deteriorated since then.[128] He insisted on a decision by the Cabinet to define the Admiralty's responsibility for a Single Ocean or a Two Ocean Standard, but none was proffered. Instead, Cooper was given another chance to come up with a financially acceptable naval program.

He returned the following week and obtained approval for the construction of two capital ships instead of the three he had asked for, and fewer destroyers.[129] But Cooper was still unhappy. He had failed to obtain a long-term commitment from the Cabinet for a definitive role for the Admiralty. Was the Navy to provide only for the defense of the home waters, or was the Empire to be protected as well? Cooper had suffered through this kind of indecision at the War Office, and he was not about to repeat that indignity as the head of the senior service. Without a proper role, long-term planning became impossible, and for the Navy, long-term planning was more critical because of the lengthy time factor involved in the construction of capital ships. His plea for a definitive answer to that question drew a sharp rebuke from the Prime Minister. Chamberlain argued that "it would be wrong to build up the Navy at a great expense over the rearmament period to such a size that it would be clearly beyond our means to maintain the fleet once it had been built up to a new level."[130] The rising maintenance cost of the rearmament program also was a cause of great concern to Chamberlain. It was variously estimated at between £200 and 250 million per year, and Chamberlain feared that "the annual cost of maintenance, after we had finished seemed likely to be more than we could find without heavily increased taxation for an indefinite period."[131] It was one of the most powerful influences acting on him to limit the size of the rearmament program.

Chamberlain's apparent lack of urgency in dealing with the nation's defense problems stemmed from the facile optimism with which he viewed the future prospects for an Anglo-Italian *rapprochement*. If Italy could be removed from the list of Britain's potential enemies, the growing restlessness within the COS might be silenced and the nation's scarce resources could be more profitably employed elsewhere. An Anglo-Italian *rapprochement* might also apply the brakes to German adventurism and open Germany to more reasonable diplomatic initiatives. To Chamberlain, a "new level" of rearmament would have imposed an unacceptable economic risk on the country for years to come, perhaps generations, and therefore had to be resisted as much as war itself. Appeasement appeared to be a much more attractive policy under the circumstances.

Finance, though a problem, was not so great a problem as skilled labor. Money could be found; skilled labor could not — at least, not without the cooperation of Labor. In fact, the Army had been able to spend only £35 million of the £81 million available because it could not place the orders for its equipment without causing a disruption in the civil trade.[132] The Air Ministry also had been unable to spend all the money allotted to it for air defense between 1935–1937.[133] Clearly the most important problems for Inskip (and Chamberlain) were the consequences of an expanded rearmament program if it was enlarged to the extent envisaged by Swinton and Cooper. By now, most of the shadow factories had been secured. Tools and machines could be obtained, but only after a fifty or sixty-week delay. The only resource lacking was skilled labor. Some form of government action, such as wage and price controls, direction, dilution and de-skilling regulations, or a relaxation of union rules in the workplace, was required to produce these workers. But without the cooperation of Labor, such schemes were not feasible.

Nevertheless, Chamberlain was still vehemently opposed to any scheme that would bring Labor into the defense program as an equal partner or major player. Not only was he content to restrain the growth of the rearmament program because of its injurious effect on trade for generations to come, but he was also bent on destroying the Labor Party as the agent of reckless social change. Chamberlain had hoped to be able to avoid taking that route by continuing to rely on market forces to supply the skilled labor for the defense program. A recession in 1937 was expected to release a significant number of workers, but it did not. Unemployment had risen to 1,665,407 in January 1938, an increase of 200,000 since December 1936.[134] Clearly, an anomalous situation had arisen with respect to the rearmament program, but apparently social policy continued to take precedence over rearmament policy. Belatedly, Chamberlain brought Sir Reginald Bruce-Gardiner into the government to help persuade the employers to be more resourceful in their efforts to procure skilled labor. Bruce-Gardiner came at the recommendation of Sir Montagu Norman, head of the Bank of England, and was well connected to the industrialists.[135]

Also, Inskip approached Sir Charles Craven, President of the Electrical Employers' Federation (EEF) and Chairman of Vickers-Armstrong, one of the leading and more favored defense contractors, to suggest ways and means of obtaining skilled labor. Craven explained some of his difficulties to Inskip, with whom he worked very closely. He reported that at present, 3,333 skilled and semi-skilled workers were required at Vickers-Armstrong, and when new machines were delivered for double shifts, 4,325 skilled and semi-skilled, and 4,458 unskilled, would be needed. Moreover, prospects for recruiting skilled labor in the near future were not very promising. There were only 5,025 indentured apprentices to the skilled trades, and another 2,317 being trained as machinists.[136] The COS reported much the same problem in obtaining skilled labor. A new factory in Scotland revealed that it could find only 70 skilled workers but needed 522 to work at full capacity.[137]

The suggestion to use double shifts was rejected because it would only exacerbate the demand for skilled labor. Instead, Craven hoped to ease the shortage by de-skilling, dilution, and withdrawing skilled labor from work not connected with the rearmament program. He had taken note of the fact that the unions had not offered much resistance to dilution lately. The Electrical Engineering Union (EEU), expected to provide the bulk of the skilled labor for the defense program, experienced relatively minor difficulty in finding employment for its members. The only questions for them were relocation and job classification. Craven, however, needed help from the industrialists to relax their standards for skilled labor. He therefore told Inskip that he would appreciate a strongly worded letter from the Government to that effect. A few days later, after discussing the problem with Inskip, Craven reported to the EEF that the Government was not satisfied with the rate of progress in armaments, but had not indicated "any intention of interfering with the Employers' control over the industry."[138] This was not the strong response that Craven was hoping for. Chamberlain's refusal to involve the Government more directly in the industrial aspects of rearmament, despite the urging of Swinton, Weir, Eden, and the COS, underscores his deep-seated hostility toward Labor.

Before the British Government could set the modest proposals of the Inskip Memorandum in motion, events abroad conspired to render its terms practically useless. In January, Chamberlain's Italian initiative hit a snag, and the Japanese Army committed a fresh outrage in Shanghai. And, unexpectedly, President Roosevelt tried to lend the prestige of the United States to ease international tensions. He sent an inquiry to London on 11 January hoping to obtain British backing for his plan to hold a conference of world powers for the purpose.[139] Distrustful of the United States and confident of his own plan, Chamberlain was not favorably disposed toward the American initiative even though the British Ambassador to the United States, Sir Ronald Lindsay, urged "a very quick and cordial acceptance." Without waiting for Eden's return from the South of France, Chamberlain and Wilson discussed the note with the new Permanent Undersecretary of State for Foreign Affairs, Sir Alexander Cadogan, who had just replaced Vansittart in that position.[140] Cadogan's soft draft was replaced by a polite rejection. Eden was informed of the initiative, but only after it was too late to change its impact. Upon returning to London, Eden voiced his strong objections to the Prime Minister's handling of the note, and forced a meeting of the Foreign Policy Committee on 19 January to review the decision. He later recorded that his relations with Chamberlain "were seriously at odds" for the first time.[141] At the heart of their differences lay Eden's desire to cultivate U.S. goodwill for future needs, while Chamberlain determinedly sought to avoid an arms race by reducing the number of Britain's potential enemies.[142]

Chamberlain felt confident of being able to detach, or at least to neutralize, Italy by recognizing its claims in Ethiopia, which he considered a small price to pay with such large stakes at issue. Secretly, Chamberlain had received word from Count Galeazzo Ciano, Italy's Foreign Minister, through his sister-in-law in Rome,[143] and from Count Grandi, the Italian Ambassador in London, that the moment was propitious for such an initiative. Shortly thereafter, Austrian Chancellor Kurt von Schussnigg's visit to Berlin on 12 February dramatized the need for quick action. Schussnigg had been subjected to a tirade of abuse and intimidation by Hitler, which Chamberlain believed might have been prevented by an Anglo-Italian agreement.[144] And inasmuch as Hitler was scheduled to visit Italy in May, Chamberlain felt that the opportunity for an understanding would pass if not seized now. He therefore resolved to conclude an Anglo-Italian agreement at once. Eden would have to drop his objections and give whole-hearted support to Chamberlain's policy, or resign. The issue was joined, and the matter was placed before the Cabinet on 19 February. Eden was quite willing to pursue an Italian agreement, but he insisted on some reciprocal gesture from Italy, such as the removal of some of its troops from Spain, before he would agree to it. Chamberlain wanted an agreement at any price. He was willing to take Mussolini at his word, but Eden was not. The Cabinet were caught unaware of the deep-seated differences between the Prime Minister and his Foreign Secretary, and were forced to vote a vote of (no) confidence for the Prime Minister's policy. Chamberlain asked each member for his views and "marked them as they spoke." According to Chamberlain's count, "none supported Anthony," while fourteen supported the Prime Minister unequivocally, and four others, MacDonald, Zetland, Morrison and Eliot, did so "with reserve."[145]

In the final analysis, Eden did not share Chamberlain's optimistic assessment of the international situation or his confidence in reaching an accommodation with the dictators, except at a humiliating loss of prestige around the world. Eden was primarily concerned with the disastrous effect that Italian appeasement would have on the state of public opinion in the United States, as well as on the U.S. Government, which was afraid that it might encourage more bold Japanese initiatives in China.[146] Chamberlain, on the other hand, was obsessed with the urgency of closing a deal with Italy that was apparently within his grasp, and thought Roosevelt's international conference was too provocative.[147] Chamberlain's anti-American feelings undoubtedly colored his action. He had long been suspicious of American motives, which, he felt, were calculated to move America into Britain's economic position in the global economy.

That Eden's resignation did not arouse a firestorm of protest owed largely to Ball's clandestine efforts in persuading the media to report the resignation as a difference over means and personalities rather than of policy. Ball could congratulate himself on a job well done.[148] Eden's silence and noble sufferance also helped to deflate the issue. Unaccompanied by any other resignations, except for several undersecretaries at the Foreign Office, the incident died almost as quickly as it arose. Conservative members of Parliament, with the exception of Churchill and a few others, had little choice but to support their Prime Minister, who explained their differences as being of means and not of substance.[149] Once again, Berlin and Rome had cause to rejoice in their man in London.

When the German armies marched across the Austrian border on the night of 11/12 March, the dynamics of European politics changed dramatically. Germany flanked Czechoslovakia on three sides and had projected its power into Central Europe. Moreover, the Anschluss was made possible by Mussolini's acquiescence, a fact pointing out the futility of Chamberlain's efforts to detaching the southernmost member of the Axis from the list of Britain's potential enemies. Yet, Chamberlain could only think of what might have been. He told his sister, "If Halifax had been at the Foreign Office the Anschluss might have been averted."[150] He believed that Eden's failure to appease Mussolini had pushed Italy more dangerously into the German orbit. As far as Chamberlain was concerned, the Anschluss only served to confirm the correctness of his policy, not its weakness. He was taken by surprise at the timing and the manner in which the Anschluss was carried through, and his initial reaction was one of relief that the vexing Austrian question was now out of the way.[151] To some extent, Halifax shared these sentiments. He told the Cabinet that the Anschluss had not really changed the international situation too much, since it had long been assumed at the Foreign Office that the union of Germany and Austria was inevitable. But he did express his regret at the manner in which the Anschluss had been carried out.[152]

British opinion was nearly unanimous in its condemnation of the forceful manner in which the Anschluss, was effected. On the eve of the Anschluss, even Chamberlain's devoted sister Hilda understood that " if Germany gets away with her scheme to swallow Austria, far from being responsible, she will be impossible to do anything with."[153] *The Daily Mail* and *The Daily Mirror* both went so far as to endorse conscription if the Government would abandon its policy of appeasement.[154] The Leftist press seized the opportunity to enlist public support for its anti-Fascist Spanish policy and called for stronger defense measures by the Government. But when the Right and moderate press, including *The Times*, joined in the public denunciation of Nazi tactics and supported the need to rearm, Chamberlain was placed in the uncomfortable dilemma of having to show tooth and yet keep the door open to Germany, something that Eden had said all along was impossible to achieve.

Personally, Chamberlain was willing to accept the ignominious consequences of the Anschluss, ignoring centuries of traditional foreign policy, conceding the shift in the balance of power toward Germany in Central Europe, and risking the loss of British prestige abroad.[155] He was determined not to allow anything to stand in the way of getting on better terms with Germany, but he could not ignore the groundswell of opinion building against the Government. Reports were circulating that even the City was losing confidence in the Prime Minister.[156] At an emergency Cabinet meeting called on Saturday, 12 March, all had agreed that nothing could be done for Austria. Chamberlain then posed two questions for consideration:

    a. What steps should be taken to guide public opinion?

    b. How were we to prevent similar action being taken in Czechoslovakia?[157]

But he cautioned his colleagues against giving the impression that the country was faced with the immediate prospect of war. In other words, public opinion had to be restrained and not educated to the nature of the crisis facing the nation. While the clouds of war were thickening over Europe, the Royal Air Force was lagging two years behind the Luftwaffe and anti-aircraft defenses practically nonexistent, Chamberlain deliberately chose to hide these facts from an unsuspecting public, for fear of stampeding the country into taking war measures that, even if successful in deterring Hitler's ambitions, would have inflicted such changes on British society that Great Britain would have turned into a drastically different country. Britain would still be obligated to maintain its huge military establishment for an indefinite period, at a great financial and social cost.

    Chamberlain had been careful to rein in the press in accordance with his policy of appeasement. Using his personal and private contacts with the lobby correspondents, the editors, and especially the press lords, Chamberlain had effectively cultivated a smooth and insidious working relationship with the press. When he could not meet with them, he sent Joseph Ball or Horace Wilson in his place, but he resented other Ministers who tried to do the same.[158] Whenever foreign correspondents reported information damaging to the process of appeasement, the press lords would either sit on the story or water it down. J. L. Garvin of *The Observer* admitted writing under the "strictest reserve."[159] Halifax maintained a close liaison with Geoffrey Dawson of *The Times,* and Hoare helped to restrain the Beaverbrook press. It was not until after Munich that their comfortable relationship began to deteriorate because they no longer shared Chamberlain's continuing faith in appeasement. Thereafter, Chamberlain's letters began to fill with annoyance, exasperation, and anger at those in the press who opposed his policy of appeasement. In the meantime, the British people were allowed to continue without any idea of the risks their Government was taking on their behalf, notwithstanding the attempts by Churchill, Eden, and other discordant voices to alert them. Not surprisingly, the Home Secretary's call for a million volunteers on 14 March produced only 400,000 men in the next three months.[160] Appeals to patriotism and nationalism proved to be insufficient inducements to National Service, lacking the compelling theme of a national emergency.

    When the Cabinet reconvened on Monday (14 March) to consider measures from the service ministers for accelerating the defense program, any hopes that Chamberlain might reverse his policy of non-interference with trade were quickly dashed. Taking advantage of Cooper's absence, Chamberlain summarily dismissed the Admiralty's request for increased naval construction on the grounds that he "himself" did not think the Admiralty's arguments outweighed those of the air and anti-aircraft defenses and unless any of his colleagues "took a contrary view," the meeting would move on.[161] Of course, no one challenged the Prime Minister.

In regard to the situation in Czechoslovakia, the Cabinet learned that Churchill intended to support an Opposition inquiry into the (in)adequacy of the Air Force program. Chamberlain thereupon indicated that he would favor an increase in the Air Force and an acceleration of AA defenses in the hope that "Mr. Churchill can be approached with a better prospect of . . .getting him to temper his criticism in the House of Commons."[162] Chamberlain then instructed the service ministers to prepare appropriate memoranda for consideration at the next meeting, "on the assumption that. . .it may possible to find the means for withdrawing skilled labor from ordinary industry to armament work."[163] Chamberlain showed more interest in damage control than in dealing with the very serious problems raised by the Anschluss.

Hore-Belisha, responding to Chamberlain's patient handling and anxious to retain the Prime Minister's confidence,[164] did not recommend any specific plan for accelerating AA defenses at the 14 March meeting. Instead, he laid out a discouraging account of the present state of AA defenses and left it to the Cabinet to decide which of three courses to adopt and their possible position in three months.[165] They included plans

    a. Without taking special measures
    b. Giving special priority to AA equipment
    c. For acceleration on an emergency basis.

Chamberlain suggested that these options needed further study since they would have to be integrated into the five-year plan, to which Hore-Belisha readily agreed. But outside of the Cabinet, in notes that he had prepared for the meeting, Hore-Belisha was more forthcoming. He commented on the Prime Minister's objections and wrote, "It is all well and good to have a five year programme, but shall we have five years for it?"[166]

The most important problem for the Cabinet to consider was Swinton's accelerated version of Scheme K, rejected in February for financial reasons. At a cost of £567 million, slightly less than the £576.5 million proposed for Scheme K, the new proposal would increase front-line strength at the expense of the reserves by March 1940 instead of 1941.[167] There was one drawback to this proposal. Swinton told his colleagues that it could be implemented only "if sufficient personnel was provided for double shifts and priority given in certain raw materials, particularly special steels and alloys." To accept "double shifting" meant interference with the normal course of trade. Swinton estimated that about 70,000 skilled workers would be needed for his accelerated plan.

After discussing the problem with Sir Alexander Ramsay of the Electrical Employers Federation, Inskip concluded that such a large influx of workers could not be obtained without the dilution of labor, "perhaps with compulsion in the background." And in such cases the trade unions were likely to resist and "make conditions; e.g., they might demand that the Government should undertake to use the arms in support of Czechoslovakia or insist on the question being dealt with by the League of Nations."[168] On balance, Inskip did not feel that he could support Swinton's request for double shifts at this time, although he sympathized with Swinton's problem. If he had given his approval, he would more than likely have been replaced.[169]

Nevertheless, Swinton persisted in his efforts to release skilled labor to the defense industry, much to the annoyance of Chamberlain. He urged his colleagues to take powers to divert the civil trade where feasible, and even then, he warned, they would only be deciding on a program that was "below what was regarded by the Air Ministry as minimum insurance."[170] Speaking for the Treasury, Simon argued forcefully for maintaining the £1,650 million limit on defense spending as the fourth arm of defense. He explained that in case of war, "we could [then] adopt unorthodox measures, such as excessive borrowing, inflation of currency and so forth."[171] Inskip expressed concern that an accelerated air program would create problems for the other two services. He claimed that "it would mean the allocation of so much of the available money to the Air Force as to reduce the quota available to the Army and Navy very seriously," and "would wreck the rearmament programme recently adopted by the Cabinet."[172]

Somewhat disingenuously, Chamberlain permitted Swinton to proceed with Scheme K on the specious assumption that it might be possible to find the skilled labor for rearmament, knowing full well that it was impossible to achieve as long as the rule of non-interference with trade was allowed to stand. Apparently counting on rising unemployment to supply some of the demand and noting a softening TUC opposition to dilution, Chamberlain hoped to satisfy Swinton just enough to keep him in line. To be sure, for all of his foot-dragging tactics in the defense program, Chamberlain was desirous of providing an adequate air program, but only for defensive purposes. It was a calculated risk, especially as long as the rule against interfering with trade remained in place. In a letter to his sister, he revealed his thinking: "We don't need offensive forces sufficient to win a smashing victory. What you want are defensive forces sufficiently strong to make it impossible for the other side to win except at such a cost as to make it not worth while."[173]

Ever since the rearmament program had begun to take shape in 1935, skilled labor had been expected to be a major stumbling block. It was one of the reasons for bringing Lord Weir into the Government. When Lord Weir consented to take on the position of Industrial Adviser to the Air Ministry, he had done so with the understanding that rearmament was to be carried out under peacetime conditions. He played a key role in limiting the size of the rearmament programs, but with the caveat that rearmament would be accelerated if the foreign situation deteriorated any further — unlike Chamberlain, who was determined to limit the size of the rearmament program regardless of the foreign situation. And, like Hankey, following the Anschluss, Lord Weir was forced to question the Government's policy of not interfering with trade. Weir told Swinton, and Chamberlain as well, that "up until now we did not consider ourselves justified in creating a war regime. . . .The present organization of the Air Ministry is quite capable of handling the existing programme under peace conditions, which has been the basis of our national policy. Such policy since [Anschluss] becomes a proper subject of review."[174]

After deliberately excluding Labor from the rearmament program, and under pressure to demonstrate the Government's credibility in supplying the needs of the defense program without having to interfere with trade, Chamberlain was at last forced to acknowledge labor's indispensable and legitimate role in the rearmament program. Reluctantly, he informed the Cabinet that "no particular programme should be decided on, but that investigation should be set on foot at once and conversations should be entered into with the trade unions and the aircraft industry to ascertain whether extra skilled labor could be obtained by voluntary agreement and to what extent."[175]

During the next two months, Wilson, Inskip, Swinton, and Weir met with various representatives of the Society of British Aircraft Constructors, the Engineering Employers' Federation, and the Trades Unions Congress to seek ways to provide the 70,000 skilled workers needed for the air defense program. And, after careful preparations for talks with the TUC representatives had been made, including secret coaching sessions by Citrine,[176] Chamberlain finally met with the TUC leaders (not with the PLP, however!) on 23 and 28 March. Although Bevin characterized Chamberlain's reception at these meetings as "cool,"[177] Wilson pronounced them "satisfactory," inasmuch as the TUC leaders appeared willing to accept modest downgrading and some dilution.[178] Citrine's suggestion to set up a "sort of Council of State," which would include representatives of the trade union movement, to enable the various interest groups "to appreciate the international situation and its implications," was rejected by Chamberlain as a "dangerous innovation."[179]

Since the Amalgamated Engineering Union (AEU) had not attended the earlier meetings with the TUC, its critical support had not been obtained. At Citrine's suggestion, therefore, Inskip met with Jack Little, President of the AEU, on 4 April to seek the AEU's voluntary support for the rearmament program. Inskip's fear of opening discussions with the AEU, because "they would impose conditions" on the conduct of foreign policy, proved to be unwarranted. Little informed Inskip that the real reason for the AEU's reluctance to accommodate the Government was not its Spanish policy, but the Government's betrayal of its promises to the unions in the last war. He told him:

You are asking this union to relax the rules, possibly agreements and some privileges which it has taken many, many years to secure. We have the experience of the War behind us; it is not too pleasant a thing to think of now because promises were made by the Government . . . to help the Union to restore the privileges and rules and regulations that had been relaxed, were never given effect to, and we are suffering from that even today. We had at that time, too, certain guarantees from the Government, some of which were embodied in an Act of Parliament. Up to now, we see very little reason for recommending any kind of relaxation to our members, because frankly, we are not satisfied with your policy, if you call it a policy.[180]

Little also questioned the Government's contention of a shortage of skilled labor. He pointed to the large numbers of unemployed engineers and blamed the employers for not utilizing their services properly. Little's attitude, though skeptical, was not obstructionist.

On 27 April, Citrine asked, on behalf of the General Council of the Trades Unions Congress (GCTUC), if the Prime Minister would receive another TUC delegation and explain his foreign policy dilemma to them. Chamberlain agreed to receive them, but the meeting did not take place until 26 May, almost a month later. By then, the international situation had improved, at least as far as Chamberlain was concerned, and the newly developing dialogue with the labor leaders was downplayed, and eventually terminated. On 25 May, a meeting between representatives of the Engineering Employers' Federation and the Shipbuilders and Engineering Unions, was held to discuss Ramsay's request for dilution, transference of labor, sub-contracting, employment of women, and more overtime. Both parties agreed on more sub-contracting, or taking work to labor, which would help alleviate unemployment in the distressed areas, but not on much else.[181]

The next day, Chamberlain met with the representatives of the General Council of the TUC to explain his foreign policy. The GCTUC wanted some assurances that their cooperation would be used to oppose the dictators rather than lending them support. The publication of the Anglo-Italian Agreement on 26 April, while thousands of Italian troops were still engaged in Spain, did little to inspire their confidence. The question of profiteering surfaced again, and Chamberlain agreed to look into it. And, finally, the TUC leaders could not let pass their long-standing grievance about the failure of the Government to consult with them earlier.[182]

But not all the representatives of the TUC were suspicious of the Government's motives. Bevin, of the Transport Workers Union, was much more interested in the jobs that a first-rate rearmament program would create than in the politics of rearmament. That aspect of rearmament could be dealt with by Attlee and the PLP. Although the Government and the unions were dealing at arm's length with one another, they shared a common ground in trying to find skilled labor without having to resort to Government controls. The TUC, for all its willingness to cooperate with the program, did not trust Chamberlain with compulsory powers, which would include wage controls and dilution, among other unacceptable practices. They continued to look in vain for a signal that the Government's policy had changed. Chamberlain came away from the meeting sure that "we shall get their help all right because the TUC reps left in high good humor, laughing and joking." He felt that the meeting had been a "complete success."[183] He was mistaken.

A week later, Chamberlain finally agreed to receive a delegation of leaders from the Parliamentary Labor Party for, the first time to discuss the defense program. This meeting was not only embarrassingly late, but maladroit as well. Chamberlain's greeting produced a chilling effect on the group: "I assume you have come to see me from patriotic, and not from political motives."[184] Dalton remarked that "it was obvious that he disliked us, and we him, profoundly."[185] Nothing came of the meeting. Later, Chamberlain characterized the Labor back-benchers as a "pack of wild beasts."[186] And, as the Czech crisis subsided in May, so did Chamberlain's interest in a rapprochement with Labor.[187] Chamberlain's failure to involve himself more decisively in the negotiations between the employers and the Trade Unions was a fatal blow to the defense program. Never one to shy away from a fight, or to make difficult decisions, Chamberlain showed a reluctance to involve the Government in the negotiations between the employers and the unions that was just plain inexcusable. It certainly was not oversight, or careless neglect, that prevented him from doing so. It had been understood at the outset of the rearmament program that Labor would have to be consulted at some point, and he himself had acknowledged this after the Anschluss.

Obviously, something more important was on his mind as Chamberlain consistently and deliberately refused to take that path of appeasement toward Labor even at that late hour. Why he did not take strong steps to force both parties to reach industrial accord under the threat of Government intervention is not difficult to understand. If successful, such steps might dislocate the economy. But if the threat to legislate industrial matters failed, he would be compelled to act on that threat, and bring into existence the very situation he had successfully managed to avoid throughout the rearmament period — government controls over the economy. And, if he was personally repulsed by the prospect of dealing with that "ignorant pack of wild beasts," some other members of the Government could have been entrusted with that responsibility. The truth of the matter is that Chamberlain feared Labor more than he did Hitler, especially since détente with Labor would wreck his policy of appeasement. It was a subject on which Chamberlain, the most rational of men, became immensely irrational. He gloated over the Opposition's fumbling in debate,[188] and took their criticisms personally as an attempt "to denigrate the Prime Minister."[189] Any decision likely to elevate the status of Labor, therefore, was rejected. Only when the GCTUC complained of the Government's setting up of the Ministry of Supply on the very eve of war did Chamberlain order the Government departments to seek TUC cooperation and allow its members to serve on committees.[190]

When a modest proposal for a voluntary National Register was considered by the Cabinet in April, it was again rejected as being impractical from a political point of view.[191] For the same reason, the demands of the PLP and dissident Conservative back-benchers for a Ministry of Supply also were rejected. Chamberlain maintained that such proposals would be ineffective without controls, and he told the Cabinet that they had no "special value in time of peace." He even questioned whether the Government could obtain those powers,[192] alleging that there would be labor unrest and disruption of the rearmament program. If Chamberlain had seriously entertained the notion of winning Labor's support for the lagging rearmament program, he certainly went about it in a very strange way. Speaking at the Annual Conference of Women's Conservative Associations on 12 May, he launched into a vitriolic attack on the Labor Opposition. He told his audience, "They pay lip service to the cause of peace, but with them, party interests come before the country, and they don't scruple to misrepresent the motives of the Government, if by doing so, they think they can discredit it with the electors."[193]

Chamberlain's supporters were disappointed with his behavior. Miss Maxse, Chief Organization Officer of the Conservative Central Office, lamented that the "PM was hitting up Labor just when their support was necessary for his rearmament policy. [The] Government was purely a one-man show."[194] Even Baldwin complained of Chamberlain's failure to pursue a national, rather than a party, policy.[195] Halifax regretted the Prime Minister's intense partisanship and did his best to keep open the lines of communication between the Government and Labor. He described Attlee as being "very sensible and intelligent,"[196] and in his private conversations as well as in his public appearances, he acknowledged Labor's contributions to the rearmament program.[197] Conservatives such as Hoare, Weir, and Baldwin had been able to set aside their personal feelings about socialism. Only Chamberlain remained adamantly opposed to a *détente* with Labor.

Chamberlain's obstinacy certainly exacerbated the problem of securing skilled labor for the rearmament program through voluntary means, and even endangered the prospects for compulsory methods. The only explanation for his irrational behavior lies in his genuine abhorrence of the Labor Party, its leaders, and all that it stood for.[198] Pinning his hopes on the success of his appeasement policy, Chamberlain felt that Labor could safely be ignored, even to the point of Britain's accepting an inferior position *vis-a-vis* Germany.[199] Attlee was not far from the truth when he charged Chamberlain, in a speech at Barnesby on 16 June, with being "blinded by class prejudice to the duty to organize the democratic powers to resist the dictators."[200] How different the course of history might have been if the self-righteous Prime Minister had exhibited the same determination to resist the demands of Hitler that he had shown in resisting the demands of labor. If rearmament was such a high priority with Chamberlain, as it was with Eden and the service chiefs, or even Halifax and Weir, prudence demanded, at the very least, some conciliatory gesture from Chamberlain toward labor, such as the repeal of the Trade Disputes Act of 1927, a more aggressive war on profiteering, or a lowering of political rhetoric. Without such a signal labor could hardly be expected to cooperate with Chamberlain in the rearmament program. And what if labor's cooperation had succeeded in hastening completion of the rearmament program, and the danger from the dictator had passed? Would labor then be left at the mercy of the employers, bereft of government protection? Chamberlain would give no assurances.

Whether Chamberlain's *détente* with labor would have succeeded in accelerating the defense program is not open to question. Chamberlain's failure to play this card must cast serious doubts on his commitment to the cause of rearmament and the national security, notwithstanding the economic hardship sure to follow. But as Cooper, Hankey, and Weir had pointed out, it would have been preferable to late-in-the-day panic measures or war. For these same reasons, Chamberlain never even sought to ascertain the economic benefits to be derived from adopting a larger defense program. Admittedly, such benefits would have been short term, but when weighed against the national interest, they certainly deserved to have been explored more carefully.

The Anschluss focused attention immediately on Czechoslovakia, but it did not discourage Chamberlain from seeking an accommodation with the dictators. It just made things more difficult for him. Despite the pressure from the COS and service ministers (with the exception of Hore-Belisha and Inskip) to relax the rule against interfering with trade, Chamberlain remained steadfast in his adherence to the double policy of gradual rearmament and appeasement. On the day following the emergency Cabinet meeting of 12 March, he mused in private that "we must show some determination not to be bullied, by announcing some acceleration (not expansion!) in rearmament,"[201] but it was not followed up by any specific measures. Yet in the same breath he resolved "to pursue our relations with Italy," which he did follow up on. He also expressed the confident hope that he might be able "to avoid another coup in Czechoslovakia."[202]

Pressure from Churchill and the PLP in the House of Commons mounted on the Government to abandon its policy of appeasement in favor of some form of collective security. Churchill's proposal for a "grand alliance" of the major and Eastern European countries was rejected largely on grounds that nothing could be done to prevent Czechoslovakia from being overrun, and therefore the only result of such an alliance would be to ignite a general European war. Even if war was temporarily averted by the alliance, the effect would be to divide Europe into two warring camps, requiring huge armaments over a prolonged period of time (a cold war, so to speak), with formidable maintenance costs thereafter. Chamberlain was not about to embark on that tortuous road, especially since he was trying so desperately to stay off it now. He offered appeasement as the only solution to Britain's predicament, and he would not abandon it even though he recognized that "force is the only argument that Germany understands."[203] Additional pressure mounted from France and the Soviet Union, both of which wanted to enter into conversations with the British Government concerning the German threat to Czechoslovakia. And from across the Atlantic, Ambassador Lindsay reported that the Anschluss had increased American isolationism.[204]

The Foreign Policy Committee met daily between 18 and 20 March to discuss its options. No conclusions were reached, pending a military assessment from the COS. But the arguments against making any commitments to Czechoslovakia were already very strong, whatever the views of the military experts.

Only Oliver Stanley spoke strongly, but ineffectively, in favor of a new commit-ment. On 21 March the COS issued its report,"The Military Implications of German Aggression Against Czechoslovakia." Its terms of reference had been carefully scripted by Chamberlain to produce the expected result. Italy was presumed to be either hostile or neutral, and Japan unfriendly, while, incredibly, Poland and Russia, both tied to France by alliances, were to be completely ignored by the COS in its planning, and the United States was effectively discounted at the outset of war, ostensibly because of its Neutrality Act. This episode provides a good example of Chamberlain's ability to manipulate and control government policy. The only conclusion that could possibly be reached by the COS, was, of course, that there was nothing Great Britain could do to prevent Germany from overrunning Czechoslovakia. The report served to reinforce Chamberlain's appeasement policy. Not surprisingly, this was the same line taken the day before by Chamberlain in a letter written to his sister: "You only have to look at the map to see that nothing that France or we could do would possibly save Czechoslovakia from being overrun by the Germans, if they wanted to do it."[205]

Cadogan, at the Foreign Office, was able to predict at an even earlier date, on 16 March, that the Cabinet would take this line of least resistance with regard to Czechoslovakia, and do nothing.[206] One of the more compelling reasons for the COS's pessimistic report was the woeful state of British armaments, except for the Navy. It acknowledged that

our A/A rearmament measures are far from complete. The Army still has a long way to go in the process of reorganization and re-equipment. In the air, the expansion of re-equipment of the Air Force still falls far short of the stage at which it will be adequate for the protection of this country; while the incomplete state of our passive defense arrange-ments and of our A/A defenses, both at home and throughout the Empire are well known.[207]

General Ironside called the paper on the rearmament program "the most appalling reading." He wondered "how we have come to this state." It was "beyond believing . . . . no foreign nation would believe it." [208] As long as industrial and financial constraints continued to operate, the COS, much to its chagrin, could only support the pusillanimous policy of appeasement. But Hankey was not happy. In April, he complained to his son Robin that rearmament was improving, "but not satisfactory." The Government "had started too late, were much too easy-going in the early stages."[209] Hankey's views had changed considerably since a year earlier when he had written to Robin that the rearmament program was "not too bad."[210] Consequently, the Cabinet agreed to discourage the French from going to the aid of Czechoslovakia, "a disagreeable business which had to be done as pleasantly as possible."[211]

The French were informed the next day that if they went to war in defense of Czechoslovakia, British participation should not be presumed, although it was more than likely that Britain would be drawn in because its vital interests were tied to France. And on 24 March, in one of his strongest statements to the House of Commons, Chamberlain reiterated the Government's position, as much to warn Hitler as to impress public opinion with his firm resolve:

When peace or war are concerned, legal obligations are not alone involved, and if war broke out, it would be unlikely to be confined to those who have assumed such obligations . . . .The inexorable pressure of facts might well prove more powerful than formal pronouncements, and in that event it would be well within the bounds of probability that other countries, besides those which were parties to the original dispute, would almost immediately become involved.[212]

Churchill was not impressed with the speech. He challenged the Government to give effect to its words. If Britain and France were indeed locked into a special relationship of mutual security, "Why not say so? . . . Are we to have all the disadvantages of an alliance without its advantages, and to have commitments without full security?"[213]

Chamberlain went on to reassure the House that rearmament "would have first priority in the Nation's effort," echoing the Cabinet decision of the previous day that seemingly permitted some interference with normal trade. The speech was a great success with the House and with the public in general. But the speech was also disingenuous because it did not commit the Government to any specific course of action. Nor did it reach out to the Labor Opposition, as Chamberlain had apparently agreed to do on 14 March. Neatly packaged for domestic consumption, it soft-pedaled the Spanish question and seemingly promised more than it was prepared to deliver, much to the annoyance of the PLP. Despite these objections, even such a staunch Chamberlain critic as Oliver Harvey had to admit that the speech had gone over well.[214] The Liberal *Manchester Guardian* and *The Times* both agreed that Chamberlain had overcome the enemies in his own camp on the strength of that speech.[215] But when Arthur Mann, editor of *The Yorkshire Post* and a Conservative, interviewed Chamberlain on 27 March and implored him to "rally the democratic world and avoid war," Chamberlain stared at him "with no friendly eye," leaving the impression that the Prime Minister was "obstinately and feverishly determined to do nothing that will be bold and foreseeing."[216] For the time being, at least, Chamberlain managed to gain more time to pursue his elusive double policy. But he had to be careful not to alienate public opinion in France and the United States in the process.[217] In those countries, any overt signs of appeasement were likely to be greeted with strong disapproval.

Chamberlain's double policy was pulling in both directions at once, causing confusion, apprehension, and doubt to all except the dictators and his ever shrinking band of loyalists. Chamberlain's 24 March announcement to the House that defense would receive the highest priority, "especially in that of the Royal Air Force and the AA defenses," was certainly misleading. The impression it conveyed was that the Government was at last abandoning its policy not to interfere with trade and was taking all the steps necessary to accelerate its defensive preparations. In point of fact, as the service chiefs soon learned, finance, manpower, and industrial capacity still set the parameters of British rearmament policy for 1938, notwithstanding news of Germany's rapidly expanding war potential.[218]

When Hore-Belisha attempted to accelerate the recruitment and equipment for the ADGB, he faced strong opposition to his request from Chamberlain and Simon, even though the new responsibilities for providing anti-aircraft batteries for the defense of new airfields, squadrons, and port facilities had thrust a greater burden on the War Office. In addition, the increased demand for anti-aircraft batteries, supply of which was already far behind schedule,[219] competed with the demands of the Admiralty and the Field Force for newer guns with greater range and efficiency. This demand for more guns required a greater industrial capacity than currently existed, with a corresponding need for more skilled labor. The same, of course, was true for the other service requirements. Anxious to ingratiate himself with the Prime Minister, Hore-Belisha wrote to Chamberlain on 9 April: "As you discussed this matter with me and as the attached statement is of such grave importance, I feel certain you would like to see a copy [i.e., of the cuts in approved Army programs]. I have dispatched the original to the Treasury with a heavy heart, but you will see the *extent of our desire to cooperate*."[220] [Italics added. Ed.]

Overriding the objections of the military experts, Hore-Belisha proposed to achieve these reductions largely at the expense of the Army's Continental commitment of two TA divisions plus one mobile division. The TA divisions earmarked for reinforcement of the other two TA divisions were to be converted to duties assigned to the ADGB, such as maintaining order and security from German air attacks, and for evacuation purposes. The French, of course, would have to be informed of the decision, which in effect rendered the two remaining TA divisions for Continental defense useless because of the inability of the British to replace their combat losses due to the conversion of the two TA divisions. Hore-Belisha was forced in the end to accept the cuts when Chamberlain promised that if the situation continued to deteriorate, the War Office could re-apply for funding.[221]

Unlike Hore-Belisha, Cooper did not stand in awe of the autocratic Prime Minister. He was a forceful advocate for the Royal Navy and not easily placated by Chamberlain's smooth evasions. Displaying the same courage and tenacity that had characterized his tenure at the War Office, he continued to resist the Treasury decision to cut his naval programs. The Cabinet's decision to accept the rationing concept inherent in the Inskip Memorandum forced the Admiralty to make the necessary cuts. But the Anschluss provided Cooper with another opportunity to press forward with his proposal for a Two Ocean Standard.[222] Without it, he argued, he did not see how the Navy could carry out its mission to defend the home waters and the trade routes so vital to the economic security of the Empire. But what he really wanted, above all, was a clearly defined role for the Navy instead of the piecemeal, *ad hoc* arrangements constantly plaguing the long-range planning departments of the Admiralty. Capital ships could not be produced overnight or bought abroad; they had to be planned for well in advance. His request for a £31 million increase over budget for the fiscal year was countered by a Treasury recommendation in April to cut his total proposal by £80 million.

Unable to control his frustration with the concept of rationing any longer, Cooper fired off an angry memorandum that he intended to circulate to the Cabinet, challenging the shaky premise upon which the Treasury memorandum was based. The Treasury tried to suppress the document but was unsuccessful.[223] He argued that "the notion that the Treasury could spend only so much money, and that the Services would have to tailor their programs to that amount was a pernicious and dangerous idea." While admitting that it was a difficult choice between defense and stability (i.e., non-interference with trade), he insisted that defense must take precedence over all else, because it leads to "complete destruction," while economic instability "can only lead to severe embarrassment, heavy taxation, and the lowering of the standard of living and reduction of social services."[224] Under Chamberlain, the Government was prepared to do neither. He dismissed Cooper's memo as highly exaggerated and unduly pessimistic, and continued to place unbounded faith in the role of diplomacy to reduce the risks attendant on the defense program.

But Cooper's persistence paid off. Chamberlain could not risk losing another important member of the Government at this time, so he backed off slightly and agreed to work out a compromise. The Cabinet decided that Cooper, Chamberlain, Simon, and Inskip should meet and decide on a proper role for the Navy, given the limitations imposed by the Treasury. Later in July, the Cabinet approved a new standard costing less than the £452 million requested by Cooper but more than the £355 million allotted by the Treasury. Cooper was well satisfied with £410 million.[225] His requests were easier to satisfy than those of the other Services, since they were long-term in nature, and did not involve an immediate excessive and outlay of funds; nor did they place an undue burden on the productive capacity of the rearmament program as a whole because the demand for skilled labor in the shipbuilding program was not as acute as it was for the junior services. The additional industrial, labor and manpower requirements would not kick in until 1939, giving Chamberlain more time for his policy of appeasement to work.

The air program fared a little better after Anschluss, but mostly on paper.[226] It was more "window dressing" designed by Chamberlain for the purpose of quieting domestic concerns rather than impressing the Germans. Under the terms of reference laid down in the Inskip Memorandum, the British Government had abandoned all pretense of maintaining its pledge of air parity with Germany. Overriding the advice of the Air Staff for an offensive capability to inflict comparable damage on German targets, Chamberlain, through Inskip and Simon, forced the Air Ministry to accept a limited, defensive role for the Royal Air Force. The Air Staff argued that its deterrent value would be lost if an adequate number of heavy bombers was not provided with sufficient reserves. Aside from the fact that four fighter planes could be built for every heavy bomber, the drawback to having more bombers rested on its drain on manpower and skilled labor. Bomber crews were larger and more difficult to train and to maintain; their losses, not as easily replaced. The dependence on skilled labor, already in short supply, would become more acute, leading to inflation and all of its accompanying dangers. Social policy continued to drive the rearmament program no less than military exigency. Of course, these dangers could have been managed to some extent by strong and vigorous government action to control industry and labor, but such measures were rejected out of hand by Chamberlain. To him, the danger of a dislocated economy was no less debilitating than the military threat from Nazi Germany, and had to be resisted at all costs. Only by gradual rearmament did he hope to avoid that pitfall. Appeasement would have to buy time to complete the rearmament program. He told his cousin, "Until our armaments are completed, we must adjust our foreign policy to our circumstances, and even bear with patience and good humor actions which we should like to treat in a very different fashion."[227]

Of all the services, none attracted as much public attention and Parliamentary criticism as the Air Ministry. Fear of the dreaded knockout blow from Germany was reinforced by recurring scenes of savage destruction of the civilian populations in Spain and China by aerial bombardment. Chamberlain complained to Lord Weir that he was concerned "over the growing body of criticism, ignorant, and well-intentioned, which the Air Ministry was attracting."[228] Some public announcement, therefore, of air defense preparations had to be made to reassure the public regarding security concerns. Swinton's new proposal, Scheme L, became the beneficiary of this concern. Essentially the same proposal that he had submitted as Scheme K, Scheme L called for an increase in front-line strength at the expense of reserve capacity. Treasury objections to the £60 million increase in the Air Ministry allotment were overridden by a special committee composed of Chamberlain, Swinton, Inskip, and Simon, and the Cabinet routinely approved the decision on 27 April.[229] Apparently, financial concerns were not as critical as they had been made out to be in the Inskip Memorandum. The new plan called for the production of 4,000 aircraft in the first year, and 12,000 by April 1940. The numbers appear to be quite impressive at first glance, but upon further scrutiny, were qualitatively inadequate. Kingsley Wood later admitted that many of the planes were obsolete and continued in production only to keep the factories going.[230] If Scheme L was meant to send a message to Hitler, it was a weak one indeed. Hitler was hardly impressed by the new plan as he continued his saber-rattling against Czechoslovakia.

Another weakness of the plan was the false optimism upon which Scheme L was built. On the basis of their discussions with industry and labor leaders, Inskip and Wilson fed Chamberlain's optimism. Wilson noted that "with few exceptions, there appears to be no labor shortage of the kind that calls for any action by the Government."[231] Swinton, however, did not share the optimistic pronouncements of Inskip, Wilson, Simon, and Chamberlain. Unable to secure enough skilled labor even for Scheme F, he was not at all confident that the additional 100,000 men now needed for Scheme L could be found without taking measures to compel the diversion of labor. His attempts to coerce the employers to accept more skilled labor did little to endear him to the SBAC. Industrial capacity also caused problems for Swinton. Although the machinery and floor space were adequate for the air programs of 1936–1937, they were clearly inadequate for Scheme L.[232] Relations with the aircraft industry went from bad to worse for Swinton. Production quotas had not been filled, and delays in transporting the planes continued to plague the air rearmament program. And, after two years of negotiations, a satisfactory pricing arrangement for Government contracts had not yet been reached. While Swinton's heavy-handed style and rather abrasive personality certainly contributed to his problems with the SBAC, the ad hoc, indecisive nature of the air program, coupled with Treasury and military/technical interference, also caused problems.

Incensed by the Cabinet decision of 13 April to purchase aircraft from the United States and Canada, and worried by Swinton's determination to seek controls over the industry, Bruce-Gardiner fired off a list of SBAC grievances to Swinton the following week, turning up the heat on the embattled Air Minister.[233] The timing was unfortunate for Swinton. The Anschluss had exposed the deficiencies in the air program to strong public and Parliamentary criticism. An ineffectual Lord Winterton had to rise in the House of Commons to defend the Air Ministry for the second time in three months because Swinton sat in the House of Lords and was unable to speak in the House of Commons. Additionally, Swinton's position had been weakened by publication of the Cadman Report on 9 March. Although critical of civilian air policy and practices not directly affecting the defense program, the report nevertheless focused public attention on the Air Ministry as well as any Parliamentary inquiry into the deficiencies in the air program could have done, and contributed to the undermining of public confidence in Swinton. The SBAC now went public with its attacks on Swinton. Warren Fisher also joined in with a cowardly attack. He wrote a letter to Chamberlain blaming Swinton for all the problems in the air defense program, and even tried to enlist Hankey in the campaign to oust him, but Hankey declined.[234]

The debate on the air defense program opened on 12 May. Chamberlain sought Swinton's resignation on 14 May, claiming that he needed an Air Minister in the House of Commons to defend the air program. Swinton's resignation was followed immediately by Lord Weir's resignation in sympathy. Quite frankly, Chamberlain was relieved to have rid himself of such a strong threat to his policy of non-interference with trade. Swinton later attributed his dismissal to Chamberlain's desire to maintain unchallenged supremacy in the Cabinet.[235] Weir's biographer concurred. "It may be fair," he wrote, "to see Weir as one of the casualties, and not the least important, of Neville Chamberlain's drive to dominate public affairs."[236] As with Eden, the price for not supporting the Prime Minister's policies, proved to be extremely costly for Swinton. He was replaced at the Air Ministry by one of Chamberlain's closest friends in the Cabinet, Kingsley Wood. The most disturbing aspect of the Swinton affair for Chamberlain, however, was the growing body of dissent within the country, drawing attention to the beleaguered air defense program. Hankey was sorry to see Swinton go. He thought the Air Minister had done a "first class job."[237]

NOTES

1. Lord Birkenhead, *The Life of Lord Halifax* (London: Hamish Hamilton, 1965), 362; *Harvey Diaries*, 11 October 1938, 212; Eden, 510; *Amery Diary*, 292; *Jones Diary,* quoting Chamberlain to Lady Astor shortly before becoming Prime Minister, 30 May 1937, 350.

2. NC 18/1/1014, 30 July 1937.

3. Ramsden, 66; Margach, 59.

4. Gilbert, *Churchill: A Life*, 577.

5. Margach, 52.

6. Ibid., 59.

7. Cross, *Swinton*, 114. Also, cf., NC 18/1/1015, 8 August 1937. Chamberlain boasted of his power to his sister, "Now I have only to raise my finger and the whole face of Europe is changed."

8. Feiling, 305; Roskill, 75; *Harvey Diaries*, 12 October 1938, 213; Macmillan, *The Winds of Change, 1914–1918* (London: Macmillan, 1961), 468.

9. *Margesson Papers* 1/5.

10. Templewood, 386.

11. Chamberlain's biographer also noted this character flaw, but he chose to place quite a different construction on it. He wrote, "Chamberlain was too masterful a man to look much for policy to others, but true that he valued the measuring of any nice question by an intellect the tranquility and firmness of which he admired, and whose precision of expression he found congenial." Feiling, 327.

12. Birkenhead, 362.

13. Ibid.

14. Cf. Adorno, *The Authoritarian Personality*.

15. Fuscher, 12–13.

16. NC 18/1/1110, 30 July 1939. Also, cf. 18/1/1078, 4 December 1938.

17. Margach, 53 and 31–32.

18. West, 41.

19. Margach, 53.

20. NC 18/1/1076, 13 November 1938.

21. John Herman, *The Paris Embassy of Sir Eric Phipps: Anglo-French Relations and the Foreign Office, 1937–1939,* (Brighton: Sussex Academic Press, 1998), 134.

22. R .J. Minney, *The Private Papers of Hore-Belisha* (London: Collins, 1960), 276.

23. Ibid., 269–270.

24. *Truth* was a journal operated by Joseph Ball, who, next to Horace Wilson, was Chamberlain's most trusted confidant. For more about Ball and *Truth,* cf. Richard Cockett, "Communication: Ball, Chamberlain and Truth," *Historical Journal* 33, no.1 (1990): 131–142.

25. NC 18/1/1108, 23 July 1939.

26. Cowling, *The Impact of Hitler*, 304.

27. Cross, *Hoare*, 1294; also, cf. *Amery Diary*, 353.

28. *Jones Diary*, 30 October 1938, 418.

29. *Cadogan Diaries*, 53.

30. *Harvey Diaries*, 29 December 1938, 233.

31. Percy, *Some Memories*, 149 (quoted in Ramsden, *Conservative Party Policy,* 43). Also, cf. Ramsden, ch. 4, "Chamberlain's Private Army."

32. NC 2/24A, 18 February 1938.

33. Since Ball destroyed most of his records, knowledge of his role in the Chamberlain Government is somewhat sketchy. Nevertheless, there is still enough evidence to lay out the scope of his activities. Cf. Cockett, "Communication. "

34. CRD File F/1/A/1, Ball to Chamberlain, 16 September 1931, quoted from Ramsden, 58.

35. Cockett, "Communication;" Robert Shepherd, *A Class Divided* (London: Macmillan, 1988), 135.

36. NC 2/24A, 18 February 1938.

37. Ibid.

38. Templewood, 329.

39. NC 18/1/1006, 30 May 1937; NC 17/11/30/144, Chamberlain to Weir, 15 August 1937; NC 7/11/30/143, Weir to Hore-Belisha, 4 November 1937; NC 11/31/124A, Halifax to Chamberlain, 11 October 1938; NC 18/1/1073 and 1074, 8 and 15 October 1938; NC 18/1/1089, 12 March 1939.

40. NC 18/1/1106, 8 July 1939; NC 18/1/1111, 5 August 1939.

41 Cadogan Diaries; 53, Margach, 103.

42. Douglas Home, *The Way the Wind Blows* (New York: Quadrangle, 1976), 59; Roskill, 75; *Margesson Papers* 1/5; Templewood, 329; Post, 237, 313.

43. NC 18/1/1006, 30 May 1937. "I was anxious to remove D. Cooper from the W.O. where he has been a failure. . . .On the Role of the Army, he and I have repeated differences."

44. HB 1/4, 25 March 1937.

45. Chamberlain had sent Hore-Belisha a copy of Liddell-Hart's book outlining the theory of limited liability for Great Britain. Hore-Belisha wrote back that he was "impressed by his general theories." NC 17/11/30/76, 1 November 1937.

46. NC 7/11/30/144, 15 August 1937, Chamberlain to Lord Weir.

47. NC 2/24A, 19 March 1937.

48. NC 18/1/1072, 15 October 1938.

49. Trying to console his sister about encountering a particular difficulty in one of her social committees, he wrote, "I suppose it is very difficult for you to do any lobbying before meetings . . . as I have done. . . . people seen alone and reasoned with can often be convinced and committed beforehand." NC 18/1/1089, 12 March 1939. Also, HB 1/5, 14 March 1938.

50. Watkins, 101. Mussolini even sent a personal, hand-written note of congratulations, NC 7/11/30/108. He told his sisters that Berlin and Rome would be happy to learn that Vansittart had been removed from his post; NC 18/1/1031, 20 December 1937. The Japanese Ambassador, Shigeru Yoshida, confided that he preferred to deal with Chamberlain rather than the Foreign Office because "he knew Chamberlain was anxious for an agreement." NC 2/23, 25 October 1936. Harvey recorded that the Germans were expecting a change in policy when Chamberlain became Prime Minister. *Harvey Diaries*, 23 February 1937, 15.

51. Cross, *Hoare*, 1294; NC 7/11/32/13, Mr. Blackwood, a National Labor MP, to Chamberlain, 8 March 1939; NC 18/1/1003, 25 April 1937; NC 18/1/1050, 8 May 1938; NC 18/1/1088, 5 March 1939; NC 18/1/1094, 15 April 1939; NC 18/1/1057, 25 June 1938; Dalton, 170; *Harvey Diaries*, 14 January 1939, 244; *Jones Diary*, 30 October 1938, 418.

52. CAB 23/88/19, 28 April 1937.

53. CAB 23/89/28, 30 June 1937.

54. Ian Colvin, *The Chamberlain Cabinet* (New York: Taplinger, 1972), 39–40.

55. Parker, *Chamberlain and Appeasement*, 74–75.

56. CAB 23/89/29, 7 July 1937.

57. DGFP, series D, vol. 1, #2, 2 October 1937.

58. CAB 23/89/30, 14 July 1937.

59. CP 177(37).

60. CAB 23/89/30, CP177(37), 14 July 1937.

61. Ibid.

62. CAB 23/89/31, CP192, 21 July 1937.

63. It also helped that British intelligence had learned of Mussolini's order to cease attacks on British ships.

64. CAB 23/89/35, 29 September 1937; CAB 23/89/36, 6 October 1937; CAB 23/89/37, 13 October 1937; CAB 23/89/38, 20 October 1937.

65. *Harvey Diaries*, 2 October 1937, 48–49.

66. Ibid.

67. NC 18/2/1039, 7 October 1937.

68. NC 18/1/1023, 9 October 1937.

69. CAB 23/89/36, 6 October 1937.

70. CAB 23/89/37, 13 October 1937.

71. CAB 23/89/38, 20 October 1937.

72. CAB 23/90/42, 17 November 1937.

73. CAB 23/90/43, 24 November 1937.

74. Avon, 606.

75. Kennedy, "British Net Assessment," in Murray and Millett, *Calculations*, 41, 42; Newton, *Profits of Peace*, 121. For a good discussion of Anglo-American relations during this period, see Ian Cowman, *Dominion or Decline, Anglo-American Relations in the Pacific, 1937–1941* (Berg: Oxford University Press, 1996); and William Rock, *Chamberlain and Roosevelt, 1937–1940* (Columbus: Ohio State University Press, 1988). The most recent study by J.C. McKercher, *Transition of Power* (Cambridge: Cambridge University Press, 1999), is much better on economic questions than for political analysis.

76. The American note was not the only example of Chamberlain's desire to be his own Foreign Secretary. In July, Chamberlain had taken the liberty of sending a personal note to Mussolini without first discussing it with his Foreign Secretary.

77. Raymond Sontag and James Beddie, eds., *Documents on German Foreign Policy* (Washington, D. C.: U.S. Government Printing Office, 1949), hereafter cited as DGFP, series D, vol.4, #251, 12 October 1938. Steward is described as a "confidential agent of NC."

78. *Harvey Diaries*, 15 October 1937, 50. Later, Simon and Hoare visited *The Sunday Times* to spread rumors of ill health as the "beginning of the end for A[nthony] E[den]," 17 November 1937, 61. Chamberlain was aware of the intrigue, and may well have encouraged them.

79. Ibid.; 22 September 1937, 47; Avon, 523.

80. Avon, 549.

81. Ibid., 533–535.

82. NC 2/23, 26 October 1936.

83. CAB 24/273/296.

84. Ibid.; CID 1366-B.

85. Avon, 577.

86. Cockett, 34–38.

87. DGFP, series D, vol. 1, #29, 18 November 1937.

88. NC 18/1/1030, 26 November 1937.

89. Avon, 580.

90. Ibid.

91. DGFP, series D, vol. 1, #31, 20 November 1937, 58; #38, 24 November 1937, 75. Hitler was told that Britain was not unalterably opposed to a change in the status quo in Eastern Europe, as long as it was accomplished peaceably. For Halifax's report to the Cabinet, cf. CAB 23/90/43, 24 November 1937.

92. Avon, 585.

93. CID 1366-B; CP 296(37). Eden had seen a draft copy on 28 October. Colvin, 60.

94. Avon, 552–560.

95. DP(P) 12, 12 October 1937.

96. Avon, 562. The Foreign Office expected that Germany would be a menace by 1939, while Chamberlain continued to rely on assessments by the COS that Germany would not be ready to launch a full scale war until 1942. But there was a great difference between a menace, and going to war.

97. CP 296(37).

98. Ibid.

99. CAB 23/89/39, 27 October 1937.

100. "Hossbach Memorandum," DGFP, series D, vol. 1, #19, 10 November 1937, 33.

101. Gilbert, Churchill, 581–583.

102. T. Taylor, Munich, 606.

103. CAB 23/90/48, CP 316(37), 22 December 1937.

104. Avon, 565.

105. CP 316(37), para.16.

106. Ibid.

107. Ibid.

108. Peden, British Rearmament and the Treasury, 79.

109. CAB 23/90/39, 27 October 1937.

110. A Comparison of the Strength of Great Britain with that of certain other Nations as at January, 1938, CID memorandum 1366-B, CAB 24/273/296.

111. CAB 23/90/48, CP 316, 22 December 1937. Chamberlain's growing impatience with Cooper prompted him to write a stinging rebuke to Cooper for a speech he made urging British intervention in Spain, hoping to force his resignation. NC 18/1/1030, 17 December 1937.

112. Roskill, 307.

113. Ibid., 291.

114. CAB 23/90/48, 22 December 1937.

115. Harvey Diaries, 26–28 January 1938, 80. Anthony Eden was told by Burckhardt, the High Commissioner for Danzig, that Josef Goebbels was inclined towards a rapprochement with Soviet Russia and even Goering was amenable to the idea under certain conditions.

116. CAB 24/273/316. When World War II broke, Germany had 3,600 front-line aircraft.

117. CAB 23/90/39, 27 October 1937.

118. CP 316(37).

119. In fact, the 1937–1938 budget returned a £20 million surplus for approved military spending that was unable to be absorbed by the defense industry. Shay, 194.

120. CAB 24/274/24.

121. Gibbs, 306–308; Shay, 183.

122. PREM 1/238, 11 January 1938; CAB 21/644; Gibbs, 310–312; Parker, "British Rearmament," 330.

123. Gibbs, 306–307. Chatfield had earlier lamented the state of Britain's defenses to his colleagues in an off-the-record comment, for which he was reprimanded by Inskip.

124. Lord Chatfield, *It Might Happen Again* (London: Heinemann, 1947), xii, 206.

125. Quoted from Shay, 191.

126. CP 26(38).

127. CP65(38).

128. CP 29(38).

129. CAB 23/92/6, 23 February 1938.

130. Ibid.

131. NC 2/24, 19 February 1938.

132. Gibbs, 308; Peden, *British Rearmament,* 172.

133. Peden, 154; also cf. appendix IIIb.

134. These figures were supplied by the Board of Trade Advisory Council. CAB 24/274/13.

135. NC 11/12/1, Bruce-Gardiner for Mrs. Anne Chamberlain @ 1954.

136. Gibbs, 308–311.

137. Ibid.

138. Parker, "British Rearmament, 1936–1939," 334.

139. The precise nature of Roosevelt's plan was not very clear, however. *Cadogan Diaries,* 11 January 1938, 35–36.

140. Vansittart was removed from that post in December because he was a stumbling block to Chamberlain's policy of appeasement. He was then appointed to an honorific post as Chief Diplomatic Adviser to the Prime Minister. Chamberlain told his sisters that Van's removal would be greeted favorably in Rome and Berlin, where the rejoicings would be "loud and deep!" NC 18/1/1031, 12 December 1937.

141. Avon, 554.

142. Ibid., 555.

143. Ivy Chamberlain, Austen's widow.

144. PREM 1/276, Wilson to Chamberlain; CAB 23/92/5, 16 February 1938; NC 18/1/1041, 13 March 1938.

145. NC 2/24A, 19 February 1938.

146. CAB 23/92/3, 24 January 1938.

147. NC 2/24A, 19 February 1938. Chamberlain wrote, "Germany and Italy might use it [Roosevelt's proposal] to postpone conversations with us and if we associated with it, they would see in it another attempt on the part of the democratic bloc to put the dictators in the wrong."

148. NC 7/11/30/10, 21 February 1938; Ramsden, 87; *Harvey Diaries,* 27 February 1938, 102–103.

149. Later, Cooper said that he did not appreciate the larger issues at stake in this matter, and if he had, he would have resigned along with Eden. But Eden stoically maintained his silence for fear of causing dissension in the Party and isolating himself from

the Conservative Central Office, should he wish to return to the Government. Margach, 101.

150. NC 18/1/1041, 13 March 1938. But, he also acknowledged that "force is the only argument that Germany understands."

151. CAB 23/92/12, 12 March 1938.

152. Ibid. The Cabinet had been informed that the future of Austria and Czechoslovakia had been discussed during the Anglo-French talks, and that the French expected that Germany would intervene in some way in Austria and Czechoslovakia. CAB 23/90/45, 1 December 1937.

153. NC 18/2/1062, 11 March 1938.

154. Peter Dennis, *Decision by Default* (Durham, N.C.: Duke University Press, 1972), 180–191.

155. NC 18/1/1030, 26 November 1937. He told his sister "of course they [Germany] want to dominate Eastern Europe."

156. *Harvey Diaries*, 15 March 1938, 117; 16 March 1938, 118; *Jones Diary,* 20 March 1938, 395.

157. CAB 23/92/12, 12 March 1938.

158. Cockett, *Twilight of Truth,* 6, 9. Margach, 51.

159. Cockett, 54–55; 82–83.

160. Templewood, 238. He repeated the call in June, with minimal results.

161. CAB 23/92/13, 14 March 1938.

162. CAB 23/92/12, 12 March 1938. Coincidentally, Churchill's name began to surface more in the press and in the drawing rooms for a ministerial position, which Chamberlain was determined to resist. *Harvey Diaries*, 16 and 17 March 1938, 117–118, 119. Churchill was dropped by *The Evening Standard* but Lord Camrose picked him up for *The Daily Telegraph*.

163. Ibid.

164. HB 1/5, 10 February 1938, 14 March 1938; 9 April 1938; Minney, 105, 193.

165. CAB 23/92/13, 14 March 1938.

166. HB 1/5, 14 March 1938.

167. The revised Scheme K called for 1,320 bombers and 544 fighters for the Metropolitan Force by March 1939 and adequate reserves by April 1941. CP30(38).

168. CAB 23/92/13, 14 March 1938.

169. In January 1939, when Inskip finally caved in to the enormous pressure building on the defense program, he was removed by Chamberlain before he could give his formal approval for a Ministry of Supply.

170. CAB 23/92/13, 14 March 1938.

171. Ibid.

172. Ibid. The Air Ministry showed a £28 million surplus for the year. CAB 23/93/18, 6 April 1938.

173. NC 18/1/1108, 23 July 1939.

174. NC 7/11/32/294, 11 April 1939, Lord Weir to Chamberlain.

175. CAB 23/92/13, 14 March 1938.

176. Citrine, 367.

177. Bullock, 624.

178. PREM 1/251, Wilson notes on Chamberlain's meetings with the TUC on 24 and 28 March 1938.

179. Burridge, 130.

180. Ibid.

181. PREM 1/251, Special Conference Between the Employers and Shipbuilders Union, 25 May 1938.

182. PREM 1/251, Chamberlain with TUC, 26 May 38; Bullock, *Bevin*, 625–626.

183. NC 18/1/1054, 28 May 1938.

184. Dalton, 170.

185. Ibid.

186. Middlemas, *Diplomacy of Illusion*, 290.

187. NC 18/1/1056, 18 June 1938.

188. NC 18/1/1046, 9 April 1938. "The debate in the House was disastrous for the Socialists . . . .Greenwood made one of the worst speeches . . . [whereas Chamberlain] got an enthusiastic applause."

189. NC 18/1/1050, 8 May 1938. Chamberlain wrote to his sister, "I had not expected such a violent personal attack by Attlee, but evidently it was part of a concerted plan to denigrate the PM."

190. Bullock, 642–643.

191. CAB 23/93/19, 13 April 1938.

192. CAB 23/93/24, 18 May 1938.

193. Chamberlain, *In Search of Peace*, 134.

194. *Harvey Diaries*, 3 May 1938, 135.

195. Ibid., 15 March 1938, 117–118.

196. Ibid., 12 March 1938, 115.

197. Ibid., 12 May 1938, 139; 19 May 1938, 141.

198. NC 2/23, 20 November 1935; NC 18/1/970, 18 July 1936; NC 18/1/1050, 8 May 1938.

199. NC 18/1/1053, 22 May 1938.

200. *Manchester Guardian*, 16 June 1938, quoted in Cowling, 211.

201. NC 18/1/1041, 13 March 1938.

202. CAB 23/92/13, 12 March 1938.

203. NC 18/1/1041, 13 March 1938.

204. Rock, *Chamberlain and Roosevelt*, 91.

205. NC 18/1/1042, 20 March 1938.

206. *Cadogan Diaries*, 16 March 1938, 63.

207. CAB 23/93/16, COS 698, 22 March 1938.

208. *The Ironside Diaries*, 29 March 1938, 53–54.

209. Roskill, 310–319.

210. Ibid., 252. Apparently, Hankey's less than enthusiastic support induced his resignation from the Cabinet, and he was pensioned off with a seat on the Suez Canal board of directors.

211. CAB 23/93/16, 22 March 1938.

212. *Debates*, 345: 1399 ff., 24 March 1938.

213. Ibid.

214. *Harvey Diaries*, 25 March 1938, 123–124.

215. Middlemas, *Diplomacy of Illusion*, 206.

216. Quoted in Cockett, *Twilight*, 63–64.

217. NC 17/11/31/158, Chamberlain to Lord Kemsley, 22 March 1938. Chamberlain thanked Kemsley for sending him his notes of Lloyd George's speech in France favoring intervention in the Spanish Civil War. He told him to "Let me know if you

hear of its effect on French public opinion."

218. CAB 24/277/177, 24 May 1938; Cross, *Swinton*, 209. On 31 March 1938, Hoare pointed out in a CID. meeting, that Germany was producing 500 airframes and 1,000 engines per month, while Great Britain was producing only 118 and 250 respectively. Martin Gilbert, *Winston S. Churchill*, vol. 5 (New York: Houghton Mifflin, 1976), 930–931; Gibbs, 482.

219. E.g., of 352 3.7-inch guns, only 7 had been delivered. The bulk of the anti-aircraft guns and howitzers for the Field Force were of the 1905 variety. Gibbs, 478.

220. HB 1/5, 9 April 1938.

221. CAB 23/92/21, 27 April 1938.

222. CP 92(38).

223. PREM 1/346.

224. Ibid.

225. CAB 23/94/34, CP 170, 27 July 1938.

226. CAB 23/96/53, 7 November 1938. One year later, the Air program was still far behind schedule, largely because labor supply was 130,000 less than needed to meet its goals. Gibbs, 582 . Also, NC 7/11/32/294, 11 April 1939, Lord Weir to Chamberlain: "I know the Air figures . . . . [there has been] no genuine acceleration."

227. Chamberlain's letter to an American cousin, 16 January 1938, quoted in Feiling, 322–323.

228. Cross, *Swinton*, 205.

229. CAB 23/93/21, 27 April 1938.

230. CAB 23/96/53, 7 November 1938.

231. PREM 1/251, undated note from Wilson to Chamberlain, Spring 1938.

232. Postan, 21.

233. Cross, *Swinton*, 207–208.

234. Ibid.,209. In fact, Hankey went further. He wrote Chamberlain a letter in support of Swinton.

235. Middlemas, *Diplomacy of Illusion*, 249. Swinton told Stephan Roskill that he was let go so Chamberlain could appoint "an easy person." Cf. Roskill, 355–356f.

236. Reader, 294.

237. Roskill, 319.

Hugh Dalton. From Kenneth Morgan, *Labour People* (1987). Reproduced courtesy of Labour Party Archives.

Clement Attlee. From Kenneth Morgan, *Labour People* (1987). Reproduced courtesy of Labour Party Archives.

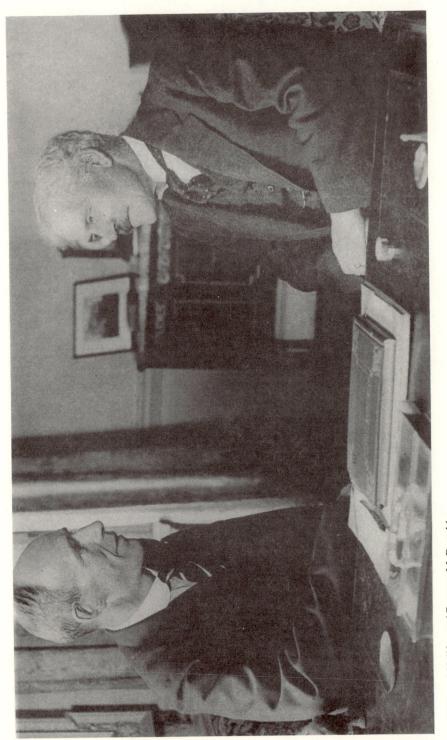

Lord Edward Halifax and Ramsay McDonald

Duff and Lady Cooper

Sir Nevile Henderson

Chamberlain and Hitler at Bad Godesburg.

Chamberlain returns from Munich.

Sir Horace Wilson and Sir Nevile Henderson.
AP/WIDE WORLD PHOTOS.

Sir Samuel Hoare

Chapter 6

Appeasement over Rearmament

The Czech problem continued to drive British foreign policy during the spring and summer of 1938. President Eduard Benes ordered the partial mobilization of Czech troops on 21 May in response to provocative German troop movements along the Czech border that were a blatant attempt to disrupt the elections scheduled for the next day. Lord Halifax sent a message to Joachim von Ribbentrop through Ambassador Nevile Henderson, reminding him of Chamberlain's 24 March statement not to count upon Britain from standing aside from a European conflagration.[1] Suddenly, the May crisis fizzled almost as quickly as it had risen. When Germany did not intervene in the Sudetenland, Great Britain was generally credited by the German and the foreign press with forcing Hitler to back down. Halifax and Chamberlain went to great lengths to persuade the British press not to play up the incident as a British victory so as not to offend Hitler. But the impression had already been created, and Hitler was furious. In a fit of anger, he ordered his military leaders to prepare a plan to smash Czechoslovakia by the fall.

The May crisis was also a close call for Chamberlain. He was angry with the Czech Government for taking matters into its own hands. He then determined to insinuate a restraining arm against further unilateral decisions by the Czech Government that might involve Great Britain in hostilities with Germany. The French Government was asked to press the Czechs to come to terms with the Sudeten Germans. In addition, William Strang, an official of the Foreign Office, was sent to Berlin and Prague to assess the situation. Strang reported that military action by Germany in the near future was unlikely because she was not ready, but he believed that the Sudetenland must inevitably become a German province. The only question that remained was the method of incorporation.[2] Neither Chamberlain nor Halifax thought a plebiscite was "feasible." They were leaning toward neutralization, which would relieve France of her obligation to aid Czechoslovakia and, in turn would ease pressure on Britain becoming involved in Central

Europe.

The Czech question had been under discussion by the Foreign Policy Committee (FPC) ever since the Anschluss. But any decision was taken out of its hands on 16 June when Chamberlain adjourned the committee, which was not to be reconvened until November. Before adjourning, however, the FPC agreed to appoint a "distinguished mediator" between the Czechs and the Germans. That man was Lord Runciman, an unofficial observer possessing no governmental authority to act on behalf of His Majesty's Government. The idea was ingenuous. Lord Runciman could use his quasi-authority to restrain the Czech Government and to encourage the Czechs to satisfy the Sudeten German demands, while the British Government retained the flexibility to deny any words or actions that might cause it severe embarrassment. The Runciman mission departed on 2 August amid warnings of German military preparations against Czechoslovakia. Meanwhile, Parliament had adjourned for its annual August recess (not to be reconvened until the Czech crisis forced its recall on 27 September). The Cabinet also adjourned for the month of August, leaving Chamberlain in control of the Government through a hand-picked Inner Cabinet, including Halifax, Simon, and Hoare. The Inner Cabinet was another example of Chamberlain's skillful manipulation of those around him. It met, but it did not decide anything. It merely conveyed the impression of collegiality and allowed Chamberlain to rebut charges of dictatorship.

Despite the darkening clouds of war gathering over Europe, Chamberlain chose to look to the silver lining of diplomacy. "Hitler had missed the bus," he wrote to his sister after the May crisis. Either Germany wasn't ready for war, or didn't want it.[3] He credited the Anglo-Italian Agreement signed in April, recognizing Italian suzerainty over Ethiopia, as having had a steadying effect on the Czech situation. Chamberlain told his sister that he had "no reason to expect an immediate explosion. . . .evidently Musso can't want a war."[4] When Hitler's personal adjutant, Captain Fritz Wiedemann, visited London in July, he held out the prospect of a state visit by Hermann Goering as further proof of improving Anglo-German relations, and Chamberlain was quick to clutch at it. As for the Spanish Civil War, it looked as if that conflict was about to end in a Franco victory, thus removing a major obstacle to improving Anglo-Italian relations and opening the way for the quick implementation of the recently signed Anglo-Italian Agreement. The situation in the Far East, though far from happy, presented no immediate danger of war. The British Government needed only to refrain from giving Japan cause to initiate hostilities. Consequently, China was refused a £10 million loan.[5]

Nevertheless, the May crisis caused political problems for Chamberlain. The Parliamentary Labor Party called for an inquiry into the air defense systems, and in the ensuing debate on 25 May, the Government was hard pressed to defend itself. The record was clear for all to see. After more than two years of serious rearmament, Great Britain was more at risk of the dreaded knockout blow than before. Hugh Dalton led the attack. The Air Ministry was in shambles, he said.

It had no engineer, nor anyone with practical flying experience, to lead it, with the possible exception of the new Undersecretary of State for Air — who, by the way, had been sent to India for the transparent reason of deflecting criticism of the air program. Dalton also ridiculed the highly-touted shadow scheme as a "farce" inasmuch as the Government continued to fall far behind Germany in providing adequate training and equipment for the RAF. He quoted figures given by Sir Frederick Sykes, formerly Chief of Air Staff, in the 5 April issue of *The Daily Telegraph*, that put Germany's front-line air strength at anywhere from 2,500 to 3,000 as against 1,750 for Britain— and the difference was growing larger each month.[6] He even went so far as to support the 1937 *Royal Commission Report on Armaments* for Government controls over industry in order to expedite the rearmament program.

When the Government tried to place the blame for these problems on the shortage of skilled labor, a spokesman for the Amalgamated Engineering Union (AEU) answered that unemployment among its members had increased by 669 in the last month alone.[7] Afraid that the Government might then use the crisis as an excuse to adopt compulsory measures to obtain skilled labor, Mr. Kirkwood, a Labor member of Parliament (MP), spoke boldly to the point: "The engineers will not tolerate any idea of any negotiations which will give any body the power to do away with the power to strike, withhold their labor, with collective bargaining, nor will they agree to the dilution of labor."[8] When Lt. Col. Moore-Brabazon, a dissident Conservative MP, stated that the Ministry of Supply was not intended to take away from labor "any of the rights which they at present enjoy," Kirkwood responded, "If that is all that is wanted, you can depend on the engineers."[9] Unknown to Kirkwood, Chamberlain had no intention of using Government powers to obtain skilled labor. He was determined to rearm without labor's help in order to avoid having to make concessions to them. Col. Wedgewood, a Labor MP, also tried to counter Government charges that Labor obstructionism was responsible for the deplorable state of British armaments at the time. He reminded the House that when Baldwin said he could not get the Labor people to agree to a rearmament program in 1935, "It was a lie! Labor is only too anxious to defend itself . . . democracy and . . . England. . . . What are the Government playing at the present time? Is it a party game, or does the Prime Minister not believe that the proposition is sufficiently serious for an enquiry, for a new system of supply, and above all, an air force?"[10]

Government spokesmen pointed to the huge outlay on defense spending and the heavy influx of men and equipment into the program to rebut the Opposition charges, but they could not deny that the margin of safety had narrowed perceptibly at the same time. Oliver Harvey commented on the debate: "Labor is perfectly ready to cooperate, but will not do so with the present PM."[11] The motion for an inquiry was defeated by a solid vote of 329–144. Chamberlain's grip on the House had not been shaken despite Labor's well-aimed blows.

The Anschluss was followed by a war of nerves against the beleaguered Czechoslovakian state. The summer of 1938 passed with Chamberlain in good spirits and more hopeful for the prospects for peace. He told the House of Commons, "I believe that we all feel the atmosphere is lighter, and throughout the Continent there is a relaxation of that state of tension which six months ago was present."[12] As usual, Chamberlain was expressing a fervent hope rather than a well-founded belief. The Czech situation was moving towards a *dénouement*, and he knew it. He could hardly take much comfort from Britain's embattled defense preparations.

It was not long before alarming new evidence of Germany's military preparations against Czechoslovakia prompted Chamberlain to call an abrupt end to the Cabinet's summer recess. On 30 August, Ambassador Henderson was recalled from Berlin to present his personal assessment of the situation, especially since his views were likely to reinforce the Prime Minister's. The French had already taken military precautions by calling up some reservists. What would the British do? Informed sources recommended that the Government should take the same strong action towards Germany as it had done during the May crisis, lining up solidly behind the French and the Czechs, and remind the Germans of its 24 March statement. Great Britain's stand at that time, though reluctant, was generally credited as the decisive factor influencing Hitler's decision to back down from his demands against Czechoslovakia. The fact was confirmed by information received from dissident German sources. Major Ewald von Kleist,[13] one of the dissidents, in mid-August told Vansittart, who in turn reported to Halifax, that a strong show of British resolve in the ensuing crisis would be all that was needed to help the dissidents overthrow Hitler. The dissidents did not think Hitler would be able to withstand another diplomatic setback like the one he had experienced in May. Theo von Kordt,[14] a more credible German dissident, repeated the plea a week later to Horace Wilson, who was sufficiently impressed by the quality of the information to pass it on to Chamberlain. Vansittart's intelligence sources also advised the Government to take a strong stand, along with Czechoslovakia and France, to warn Hitler against using force to achieve his objectives. These recommendations were ignored, in part, because the state of intelligence gathering was not sufficiently advanced,[15] but it is more likely that ultimately Chamberlain had the final say about which information to act on and which to discard.[16] For Chamberlain to have acted on Vansittart's advice or the warnings of the dissidents would have undermined his appeasement policy, which he felt was beginning to show signs of promise after the dark days of May. He exuded confidence in his policy because "recent accounts of the change in public opinion [are] in our favor," and also because of the "desire of the American President to do something to help."[17] Therefore, he chose to place quite a different interpretation on any information he received advocating a more forceful policy toward Nazi Germany. He likened the German dissidents to the Jacobites at the French Court.[18]

Chamberlain told the Cabinet that if Britain were to adopt a strong line toward Germany, it should be prepared to plunge the country into war. It was too risky to take that road, he added, both militarily and politically. Inskip backed him up. He reported that the armed forces would not be ready for war for another year.[19] Chamberlain also expressed his concern over the divisive effect that a "get-tough" policy might have on the country and on the Dominions.[20] Of course, his careful management of the news had done little to prepare his countrymen for the dangers confronting them, thereby preventing a consensus of opinion contrary to his own views from developing. In summing up the matter, he offered his personal opinion that Germany would not launch an attack against Czechoslovakia because it was disadvantageous for her to do so, since it would turn world opinion against her, particularly in the United States.[21] It was clear then, that Great Britain would not repeat its warning of May as long as Chamberlain was in control. And as long as the rearmament program languished under a policy of limited military preparations, Chamberlain could always justify his policy of appeasement on grounds of Britain's military weaknesses.

Little consideration was given to the strategic implications entailed in the loss of the Sudetenland to Germany. Was Hitler seeking to satisfy a legitimate grievance, or was he attempting to dismantle the French alliance system? Evidently, it made little difference to Chamberlain. He made no attempt to ascertain the answer to this question. It would not have made any difference anyway, since Chamberlain had already decided that Czechoslovakia "was not worth the bones of a British grenadier." He had told his sisters that the Germans intended to dominate Eastern Europe. And, as far as Chamberlain was concerned, he was prepared to acquiesce on that point.[22] The Runciman mission offered proof of his willingness to dance to the German tune. Runciman's main objective was to weaken the Czech position and force Benes to make concessions to the Sudeten Germans. Now that the Czech problem had assumed manageable proportions, Chamberlain determined that it should not be allowed to get out of hand again, as it had in May. He would see to it personally. He resolved to take control of the situation. Chamberlain had a plan, revealed only to a few trusted colleagues, to have a private meeting with Hitler. It was known as Plan Z.[23]

When the Cabinet met to deal with the rapidly escalating Czech crisis, Cooper's request to mobilize the fleet and take the warships out of reserve was turned down as too provocative. Instead, it was agreed to move up the dates for previously scheduled naval maneuvers by several days. The Cabinet, in Halifax's words, intended to "keep Hitler guessing" as to the Government's position in the developing crisis, and to wait on Hitler's 12 September speech before considering its next step. But of course Hitler did not have to guess very hard. The Halifax visit had already convinced him of Britain's disinterest in Eastern Europe, and the Anglo-Italian Agreement, the Wiedemann visit, and limited rearmament confirmed his prognosis of Britain's abdication of a Continental role. Actually, Hitler had correctly diagnosed British strategy earlier, as one of conflict avoidance. Following the Halifax visit in November 1937, Hitler had issued a memorandum for the Foreign Ministry outlining its position to be taken in future meetings. He predicted, quite accurately in retrospect, that when faced with war on three fronts, Great Britain will "place a restraining hand on France and seek a settlement with Germany."[24] And, in a letter to Mussolini on 7 September, Hitler warned that

"Britain was determined to get rid of one or the other of the two totalitarian nations as soon as she has completed her rearmament."[25] No, Hitler did not have to guess British intentions very hard.

If the British Government was at a loss for policy initiatives, labor was not. At its annual congress held at Blackpool, 5–9 September, the TUC adopted resolutions to support an accelerated rearmament program, and to join with France and the Soviet Union in resisting German aggression, "whatever risks are involved."[26] Labor's approach to foreign affairs had certainly come full circle from its position in the early 1930s, when it had relied on the twin panaceas of disarmament and collective security to form the basis of its strategy for world peace. But with the brutalizing events in Abyssinia, Spain, and Nazi Germany, idealism gave way to pragmatism. Disarmament was de-emphasized and collective security recycled, but in a different way. Reliance on the League of Nations was replaced by a system of collective security based on an alliance of all peace-loving nations determined to resist aggression. Labor urged the Government to form a closer relationship with France and the Soviet Union.

Whether this conversion was more apparent than real may be debated. What is important, however, is that foreign policy now offered Labor a highly visible political platform upon which to challenge the Conservative Party. Labor's new policy easily adapted itself to the high moral ground in international relations of law and morality, justice and freedom. This newly developed policy of collective security and rearmament stood in stark contrast to the weak-kneed policy of appeasement offered by the Chamberlain Government. By wrapping itself in the flag of self-righteousness and moral rectitude, Labor was able to camouflage any feelings of personal animosity it may have harbored toward Chamberlain, and to assume a more statesmanlike posture in its attacks on the Government. This attitude was not helpful to an embattled Prime Minister struggling desperately to keep his finger on a steadily deteriorating international situation. Not only must he prevent a military confrontation from developing, but he must also do so in a way that carried the support of the nation.

After Hitler's Sportspalatz speech on 12 September, Chamberlain decided to go ahead with Plan Z. The idea of summit diplomacy was not exactly a new idea. It was very rarely employed, though, and dangerous, given Britain's military weakness and Chamberlain's well-advertised intention of avoiding a confrontation of any kind with the dictators. What did Chamberlain hope to achieve by this dramatic gesture? He certainly did not have Czechoslovakia's welfare in mind. Czechoslovakia had been written off as least as early as the Halifax visit to Germany in November 1937. Only Britain's immediate interests mattered to Chamberlain. More to the point, it was only Britain's interests, as defined and interpreted by Chamberlain, that really mattered. War had to be avoided at any cost.

Chamberlain prepared his political ground carefully, so as to advance his goal of appeasement and limited rearmament without having it subjected to the scrutiny of many differing points of view and terms of reference. He sprang the news of his whirlwind decision to meet personally with Hitler at the 14 September Cabinet meeting, although he had been considering it for several weeks. He announced that he would fly to Berchtesgaden on the morrow. What could anyone say? The die had been cast. Simon called Plan Z "brilliant." Only Walter Eliot offered mild criticism. He complained of the way in which Cabinet meetings like this were called with nothing on the agenda but the innocuous term "International Affairs." Without being given time for adequate consultation and reflection, "we were being led by pressure to do something which we would not have done of our own free will."[27]

To impress further on the Cabinet its wisdom in going along with the decision, Chamberlain produced a memorandum from the COS outlining Britain's military position.[28] Not surprisingly, the outlook was very bleak from a military point of view. The COS reported that only two Army divisions could be spared for action on the Continent at present; but they lacked proper reserves and equipment. Air defense for the Empire was incomplete, and the ADGB was entirely inadequate. Lack of searchlights, barrage balloons, water pumps, modern aircraft, and antiaircraft guns placed London at great risk. The Navy, while able to defend the home waters, was unable to send more ships to the Mediterranean or the Far East. Of fifteen capital ships, only ten were operational. The COS reaffirmed its position of last March, that there was nothing Britain could do to affect the military outcome in Eastern Europe. Germany's weaknesses were ignored. It was the same argument that had been used during the Rhineland crisis. The COS report did not address the question that Oliver Stanley wanted answered: What would the international situation be a year from now? In other words, what impact would the loss of Czechoslovakia have on the peace and security of Europe? Would it be more favorable to confront Germany now than later?[29]

Nor did Chamberlain mention the attitude of the U.S. Government, which was willing to be of assistance. Ambassador Ronald Lindsay had cautioned that a weak stand would cause a serious diminution of American friendliness (i.e., public opinion). Also, . . . President Roosevelt told us "we could have everything except troops and loans."[30] In the light of Chamberlain's subsequent reluctance to implement Britain's guarantee to Poland in September 1939, it is doubtful that his actions at Munich would have been very different even if Britain's defenses were stronger. Chamberlain was widely believed to be a "peace at any price man." Roosevelt believed it, and so did Eden.[31] Hitler obviously believed it, too, because he premised his risky policy on it. Was Chamberlain's feeble rearmament program in fact a justification for his appeasement policy rather than a reason for it? At every crucial moment, even after war had begun in 1939–1940, the Chamberlain Government was criticized for not resisting the dictator states while still entertaining peace proposals,[32] using the same argument of military weakness to justify its policy.

When Chamberlain departed for Berchtesgaden on the 15 September, therefore, his mind had already been made up. Fortified by the Runciman Report that legitimized Hitler's demands, he resolved that Czechoslovakia must acknowledge the harsh realities of the international situation and make concessions to Hitler. Chamberlain's job was to secure the best terms possible for Czechoslovakia, images of Canossa notwithstanding. It quickly became apparent at Berchtesgaden that autonomy and neutralization were out of the question for the Sudeten Germans. Nothing less than a partition would suffice. The talks centered on various proposals for an immediate plebiscitary settlement of the question; the British proposals were virtually ignored by Hitler.

Chamberlain returned to London the next day and met with his Cabinet on 17 September to brief them on his talks with Hitler. Many of the members were surprised to learn that Chamberlain had exceeded his instructions not to discuss the idea of a plebiscite, and that none of the proposals drawn up by the Cabinet on 14 September were considered at Berchtesgaden. They were afraid that such talk would lead to further demands for plebiscites from the Hungarian and Polish minorities in other parts of Czechoslovakia.[33] But Chamberlain defended his actions on the plausible grounds that it was impossible to go to war to prevent self-determination, which Hitler apparently was set on doing. Reflecting a growing pessimism about the Prime Minister's policy, Inskip noted in his diary that Chamberlain had, in fact, been "blackmailed."[34] Gloom settled over the meeting as the bitter truth of Eden's warning became clear — diplomacy, unsupported by arms, could only lead to deep humiliation and endanger the national security. Lord Edward Winterton lamented their failure to take rearmament more seriously during the last three years, but no one paid any attention to him, according to Inskip.[35]

Oliver Stanley, Earl De la Warr, and Cooper spoke against the idea of a plebiscite and in favor of preserving the Czechoslovakian state, not from moral principles, but as a matter essential to Britain's national interest, which, as Cooper reminded Lord Hailsham, had always been to prevent any European power from achieving hegemony on the Continent. Sir Warren Fisher, now without influence, also abandoned support for Chamberlain's policy, forwarding his reservations in writing to Chamberlain.[36] Other aspects of the question resurfaced in the discussions. Simon worried about the effect a plebiscite might have on the Empire. Would India and the Arab states take advantage of the European situation and insist on self-determination for themselves? Inskip advanced yet another reason for avoiding war. If Britain went to war to stop Hitler, Hitler would be destroyed, but there would be no winners "except Moscow and the Bolsheviks."[37] Reluctantly, the Cabinet gave its approval for Chamberlain to continue his discussions with Hitler for some form of autonomy for the Sudetenland.

Following the Cabinet meeting, Chamberlain faced the disagreeable task of explaining his policy to the Opposition leaders and to his French allies. Accompanied by Halifax and Wilson, he briefed the more amenable labor leaders, Citrine, Dalton and Herbert Morrison on his Berchtesgaden meeting with Hitler. The National Labor Council had just concluded its meeting by reaffirming the Blackpool Declaration adopted by the TUC, urging Chamberlain to stand up to

Hitler. Dalton pressed that line on Chamberlain, but he was told that if Britain stood behind Czechoslovakia, "Germany would then come for us" and "we were not yet ready for war." Admitting that Britain's defenses were inadequate to meet the German threat, Chamberlain rationalized the Government's failure to rearm in time by calling attention to the even more pitiful state of France's air program. Nor did he place much faith in Soviet offers of assistance to support Czechoslovakia.[38]

Citrine described the meeting as "one of the frankest" that he had ever attended,[39] but it had not gone well. Unable to conceal his irritation with the labor leaders, Chamberlain failed to win their support. According to Citrine, "The three of us came away from the interview feeling a good deal of anxiety, both as to the readiness of the Government to face the issue and as to the state of our preparedness."[40] Attlee joined with Churchill in imploring Chamberlain to reconvene Parliament, but Chamberlain did not want any more complications to his policy. He refused to consider their plea. Next, he briefed the French on the Berchtesgaden visit. Prime Minister Daladier and Foreign Minister Bonnet had arrived on 18 September. They showed themselves to be quite willing to follow Chamberlain's lead in preserving the peace, but were anxious to save as much of the Czechoslovakian state as possible.[41] Their preferred solution was cessation rather than plebiscite, because self-determination would only encourage separatism among the other minorities. Chamberlain was relieved to hear this. He confidently wrote to his sister on 19 September that "things were going pretty much the way I want."[42]

The duty of asking President Benes to accept the dismemberment of his country without a fight was left to the French, pending approval by the French Cabinet the next day. Benes was prepared for the worst. Secretly he had made his bottom line known to the French. He had even prepared a map delineating those areas of Czechoslovakia that could be given up while the integrity of his country remained intact.[43] But when the contents of the Anglo-French plan were made known to him, Benes balked. To agree to a plebiscite or cession in principle was one thing, but the details were something else. Some areas about to pass under German domination were strategically important for the defense of his country and could not be handed over to Germany. Benes was given only one day in which to reply to the Anglo-French proposal, for fear that Hitler might not stay his hand any longer. If he agreed to the terms, Britain and France would guarantee the independence (not integrity!) of Czechoslovakia. If he refused, Britain and France would wash their hands of the affair and take no responsibility for what followed. Only the Soviet Union took a firm stand. Maxim Litvinov declared that Russia would stand behind its treaty obligations to Czechoslovakia, but only if France honored its treaty obligations as well. Whether the Soviets really intended to honor their word is still the subject of considerable historical controversy.

Bowing to a *force majeure*, Benes agreed to accept the principle of the transfer of territory. The British Cabinet met on 21 September to discuss the issues likely to be raised at Godesberg and to prepare instructions for Chamberlain on how to address these issues. Among the issues discussed was the question of other minority claims against Czechoslovakia. Poland and Hungary had made known their interest in securing the right of self-determination for their minorities living in Czechoslovakia. What if Hitler were to champion those groups as well as his own? In that case, the Cabinet agreed, Chamberlain must refuse to entertain those claims; or, if the discussions progressed well enough, Chamberlain could discuss a proposal to maintain an international force in the affected districts. Failing this, he should return home for further consultations with his Cabinet. The meeting closed on the ominous note that Italy was moving large numbers of troops into Libya, posing a threat to Egypt and the Suez Canal.[44]

Since Parliament was not in session during these critical weeks, the PLP demanded, and received, the right to be informed of the rapid developments now taking place in international affairs. Halifax met with a deputation of labor leaders including Citrine, Dalton, and Morrison, following the 21 September Cabinet meeting. He restated the Prime Minister's position of not backing Czechoslovakia more firmly in the continuing crisis. Great Britain simply could not risk a war now, due to deficiencies in its rearmament program.[45] The delegation was not moved, however, and continued to insist on collective defense measures involving France and the Soviet Union as the best way to deal with Hitler.[46] It was, in all, "a most disagreeable meeting," according to Dalton.[47] The same could be said of Chamberlain's meeting with the PLP leaders, Attlee and Greenwood, on the same day. Angrily, Attlee charged the Prime Minister with "simply giving way to Hitler," and said that Great Britain would have to bear the responsibility for Germany's overrunning Eastern Europe.[48]

Unfazed by Labor's objection to his policy, Chamberlain departed for Godesberg on 22 September for his second meeting with Hitler. Brimming with confidence in his ability to achieve a peaceful settlement of the Czech question, he received a rude shock in his next encounter with Hitler. Hitler was not interested in discussing the Anglo-French plan for cession of Czech territory. He presented his own demands for the immediate evacuation of the Sudetenland by Czechoslovakia on 28 September and, as feared, he pressed the claims of the Polish and Hungarian minorities. Instead of returning home for further consultations, as instructed by the Cabinet, Chamberlain stayed on until 24 September for further discussions with Hitler, so intent was he on preventing hostilities from breaking out. But Hitler refused to budge on his demands, except to extend the deadline for the invasion to October 1. A distraught Chamberlain was forced to carry the bad news back to London in pouring rain — an appropriate metaphor for the occasion. Hurriedly the Cabinet assembled to assess the situation; there was little time to lose.

Anticipating their objections, Chamberlain told his colleagues that he was not trying to "disguise the fact that if we now possessed a superior force to Germany, we should probably be considering these proposals in a very different spirit."[49] It was for this reason, he told them, that he stayed at Godesberg rather than break off the talks and risk the imminent danger of war. Chamberlain's proposal to pressure the Czech government into accepting those terms produced a chilling effect on the Cabinet, who had been made uncomfortable by the realization that the Prime Minister had been blackmailed. It was one thing to stand aside helplessly and watch a friendly country disappear, but it was another to assist in the destruction of that country. As long as Hitler's demands had assumed a semblance of legitimacy, based on a sense of a generally perceived injustice, as the Runciman mission had attempted to demonstrate, or on the democratically accepted principle of self-determination, responsible Government officials could pretend that their acquiescence to those demands was a positive and constructive contribution to world peace and, however distasteful those actions may have been, were morally and practically defensible. But when the methods employed by Hitler at Godesberg vitiated the very foundations of the democratic process, its pretensions could not be squared with Britain's national honor.

What had become clear to most of the Cabinet was that Hitler had aims beyond Czechoslovakia, and that he intended to dominate the Continent. Consequently, the Czechs must decide for themselves whether to accept the Godesberg terms or not, and if war resulted, so be it. It would no longer be a war to save Czechoslovakia, as Chamberlain had interpreted the policy, but a war to check Hitler's ambitions. For the first time Chamberlain encountered stiff resistance to his policy, and the Cabinet decided to refrain from pressuring the Czech Government not to mobilize or take other measures of self-defense. After discussing the Godesberg terms with Cadogan on the way home after the Cabinet meeting, Halifax had an epiphany. He, too, had come to the realization that Hitler aimed at nothing less than the destruction of the Czechoslovakian state and the domination of Central Europe. Meanwhile, the Czechs had wasted no time in rejecting Hitler's humiliating terms, "absolutely and unconditionally," relying on the "two great Western democracies, whose wishes we have followed much against our judgement, to stand by us in our hour of trial."[50]

The next day Chamberlain opened the Cabinet meeting unaware of Halifax's overnight conversion. He called upon Halifax for an assessment of the rapidly deteriorating international situation, hoping to lay the premises for abandoning Czechoslovakia. Instead, in a startling development, Halifax openly deviated from Chamberlain's line and recommended against acceptance of Hitler's terms. Chamberlain was taken completely by surprise. Unable to hide his chagrin, he passed a hastily scribbled note to his Foreign Secretary: "Your complete change of views since I last saw you last night is a horrible blow to me, but of course, you must form your opinions for yourself." Then, in a petulant and disturbing manner, he added, "It remains, however, to see what the French have to say."[51] If Halifax would not carry his policy, then the French must do it. They must press the Czechs to accept the Godesberg terms.

The defection of Halifax, one of Chamberlain's most trusted and loyal supporters in the Cabinet, accentuated the growing pessimism in the Cabinet and in the country about Chamberlain's policy. It was indeed a horrible blow for Chamberlain. No longer could he count on the unquestioned loyalty of the

Cabinet to support his policy *ipse dixit*. His policies would be subjected to a more rigorous and critical consideration warranted by the exigencies of international developments. No longer could his views be superimposed on events in order to conform them to his personal ideological construct of world events and domestic goals. They would have to be defended more on their merits than on narrow personal, partisan lines. Nevertheless, Chamberlain still possessed sufficient authority to lead the Cabinet, but not in his accustomed manner.

Joining with Halifax in his refusal to press the Czechs to accept Hitler's ultimatum were Cooper, Eliot, De la Warr, Stanley, and Winterton. But since they had expressed earlier objections to appeasing Hitler, their position did not come as a surprise, and Chamberlain could tolerate their minority dissent as an annoyance and not as a threat. More serious for Chamberlain were the positions taken by Hore-Belisha and Hailsham in support of Halifax, and the less than ardent support that received from such loyalists as Inskip, Hoare and Kingsley Wood. Only Simon and Zetland backed the Prime Minister wholeheartedly. The Cabinet was literally in revolt over the Godesberg terms, and as many as six ministers considered resigning.[52]

The split in the Cabinet mirrored the change in public opinion that had surfaced after the Godesberg meeting. Hitler had revealed himself as a bully and a threat to the peace of Europe, and had to be restrained. Indicative of the change that had occurred, *The Times* published the Godesberg Memorandum on 26 September, with an accompanying editorial opposed to its humiliating terms. In its opinion, the Anglo-French plan was bad enough, but Godesberg was "quite incapable of fulfillment."[53] *The Daily Telegraph* called the Godesberg Memorandum "an abject and humiliating capitulation."[54] Noisy demonstrations were being organized and angry crowds appeared in the streets of London for the first time. Labor, without a Parliamentary forum to express its opinion, held a huge rally at Earl's Court on 26 September urging the Government to stand by the Czechs. Not only had Chamberlain's hold over the Cabinet been badly shaken, but his ability to lead the country down the road to more appeasement had been compromised.

Nevertheless, Chamberlain would not be deflected from his policy of peace at any price. Shaken but undeterred, he urged upon the Cabinet the importance of maintaining a united front in light of the upcoming talks with the French later in the day. Meanwhile, the Czechs had to be kept under control. Halifax asked for, and received, Czech assurances that any further responses to the Godesberg terms should be channeled through 10 Downing Street. Wilson called Henderson in Berlin and told him to inform Hitler that he should ignore any reports concerning Czechoslovakia unless they came from the Prime Minister.[55] Daladier and Bonnet arrived in London on 25 September, stiffened by public outrage of the Godesberg terms in their country and the rejection of the Godesberg terms by the French Cabinet. Chamberlain and Simon took turns at playing devil's advocate, reminding the French of their military weakness and their lack of a credible plan to save their Czech allies from a German occupation. Halifax played only a small part in the conversations because of his recent defection from the Chamberlain policy, a point not missed by the French delegation. Skillfully, Chamberlain's cold logic chipped away at the French resolve to honor their commitment to Czechoslovakia. What do the French propose to do if Germany attacks Czechoslovakia, he asked. What will you fight with? What is your offensive plan? Will it be enough to save Czechoslovakia? How do you expect to cope with Germany's overwhelming superiority in the air? Unable or rather, unwilling, to answer these questions, the French ministers referred them to the French Chief of Staff, General Maurice Gamelin, who met with the British ministers on the next day. Gamelin made a brave effort to maintain France's national honor, but in the end, it boiled down to the fact that France could not conduct any offensive operations against Germany, even if it wanted to, without British support. France would have to follow Britain's lead. Chamberlain summed up the two days of discussions with the French for the Cabinet this way. He thought it significant that the French had never once put the question, "If we go to war with Germany, will you come in too?" — implying that the French were looking for a way out of their dilemma without going to the aid of Czechoslovakia. Cooper disagreed with the construction Chamberlain placed on the Anglo-French talks, which "all tended to one conclusion and excluded other facts which tended the other way."[56] It was Chamberlain at his best.

The next day, with the Cabinet's support, Chamberlain informed the French leaders of a last-ditch effort to avoid hostilities. Would they object, he asked, or like to add to his new proposal to Hitler to set up an International Control Commission to expedite the transfer of Czech territory, coupled with a warning that if Germany should attack Czechoslovakia, and France became engaged in hostilities with Germany as a consequence, Britain shall feel obliged to support them? Daladier agreed to the initiative, which Chamberlain had already presented to his Cabinet as a *fait accomplit* on 26 September. Although Chamberlain was not very optimistic about a favorable response to his proposal from Berlin, he dispatched Wilson to deliver the message to Hitler in person.

After much discussion about precautionary measures to be taken, the Cabinet decided to approve several emergency measures to protect London from a sudden air attack. Army reserves were called up for air and coastal defenses, and steps were initiated to mobilize the fleet. The Prime Minister was authorized to carry out whatever mobilization measures he deemed necessary without prior Cabinet approval.[57] It was also decided that Parliament should be reconvened at last, after a two-month recess, an indication that events had passed out of Chamberlain's control and war was a distinct possibility. Also, a state of emergency was declared by an Order-in-Council: 38 million gas masks were distributed, plans to evacuate the children were activated; 1 million feet of slit trenches were dug, and hospitals were readied to receive tens of thousands of casualties. Chamberlain listened anxiously to the radio for an indication of whether Hitler showed any interest in his latest plea. His worst fears were realized as Hitler proceeded to castigate the bastardized offspring of Versailles in the most vituperative terms. President Benes was singled out for the most severe abuse. Chamberlain derived small comfort from Hitler's patronizing remarks praising the British Prime Minister for his efforts to preserve peace.

Reluctantly and with heavy heart, Chamberlain took to the air on the next day. He told the nation, "How horrible, fantastic, incredible it is that we should be digging trenches and trying on gas masks here because of a quarrel in a far-away country between people of whom we know nothing."[58] Yet in the same breath, he clung to the desperate hope that war could be avoided by "the value of our promise" to guarantee the future of the Czechoslovakian state. And in another pathetic plea, intended more for the ears of the Nazi dictator than for the British people, he reiterated his determination to go to the last mile in the interest of peace, if he "thought it would do any good." He even offered to make a third visit to Germany. Was Hitler listening? He could have all he wanted without the risk of war. Britain and France would see to it that Czechoslovakia did not stand in the way of peace by offering a guarantee to Czechoslovakia if Czechoslovakia did not stand in the way of peace and accepted Hitler's humiliating terms. But just why Czechoslovakia should accept a shaky guarantee in place of a more binding negotiated settlement did not seem to matter to Chamberlain. Czechoslovakia had effectively become a British client state during the crisis and could safely be ignored.

When the House of Commons reconvened on "Black Wednesday," it was more reminiscent of a scene scripted in Hollywood than of a real life drama.[59] Before a packed House, the Prime Minister rose to review the events of the past two months. After reading from a carefully edited version of the Czech crisis for over an hour, he suddenly interrupted his speech when he was handed a note informing him of Hitler's willingness to attend a Four Power Conference at Munich the next morning. Czechoslovakia and the Soviet Union, France's allies, were not invited, nor were the good offices of the United States solicited. The announcement, of course, was greeted with a profound sense of relief in the House and in the country. Stunned, the Labor Party had no choice but to join in the chorus of well-wishers. Attlee offered a qualified blessing to the Munich Conference. But he cautioned that the preservation of peace should not include the sacrifice of important principles. One of the few who did not get caught up in the euphoria of the moment was Eden, who reportedly walked dejectedly out of the House, knowing that the fate of Czechoslovakia and Europe had been sealed, and wondering how many more humiliating Munichs would have to be endured.

The agreement signed at Munich on 30 September was a gigantic cover-up. All that was left to decide was the timetable and the conditions under which Czechoslovakia should cede its territory to Germany. Under the guise of self-determination, the German occupation of the Sudetenland was to be effected over a ten-day period instead of on the 1 October deadline set by Hitler at Godesberg. The disputed areas were to be resolved by an ill-defined International Control Commission, which Hitler completely ignored after Czechoslovakia's defenses had been abandoned.

Nevertheless, the charade was sufficient to quiet the nerves of a tense nation for the time being. Chamberlain was widely acclaimed for his efforts to preserve peace while Hitler's image suffered accordingly. But to the more enlightened observers, the Munich agreement was an ominous sign of more appalling concessions down the road unless accompanied by a drastic change in Government policy. Thirty dissident Conservatives joined with the Labor and Liberal Opposition in an effort to dislodge that policy during the Parliamentary debate that followed. The euphoria surrounding the Munich Agreement soon subsided under the sober realization that the country had narrowly averted the most serious threat to its national security since the Spanish Armada. The emergency call-up had revealed gaping holes in British defensive preparations. The AA batteries were seriously undermanned and poorly equipped. Gas masks were in short supply, and the balloon barrage was virtually non-existent. Preparations were made to evacuate 500,000 children in case war should break out, but then it was discovered that transportation and other auxiliary services had broken down or had been otherwise rendered ineffective by a lack of organization and volunteers.

For the first time the British people had come face-to-face with the magnitude of the danger confronting them. Conservative Thomas Jones admitted that the "country got such a fright during the crisis that in its present mood it could be got to accept vigorous defense measures."[60] Until Munich, public opinion had been assiduously misled by the Government with the help of the press lords and opinion makers, under the mistaken belief that they were assisting the Government in the pacification of Europe.[61] The Government had gone to extraordinary lengths to restrain public opinion throughout the rearmament period for fear of driving the rearmament program out of control and derailing the appeasement process. John Coatman, an official at the British Broadcasting Corporation (BBC), spoke of a "conspiracy of silence" in which he and his colleagues in the press had unwittingly participated, preventing the public from understanding the true state of the dangerous international situation.[62] Sir Jonathan Reith, the respected Chairman of the BBC, although he was anxious and willing to assist the Government as best he could, was forced to resign because he would not compromise the integrity of the BBC by turning it into a propaganda organ for the Government.[63] Reith's support for the Government was not good enough for Chamberlain, who expected unquestioned loyalty to his policy,[64] as Rex Leeper, head of the News Department at the Foreign Office, soon found out. Leeper had been held under restraint by Halifax after the Anschluss, but then removed from his post after Munich and reassigned to other duties because his efforts to educate public opinion ran counter to Chamberlain's attempt to control it.

Munich forced the toothpaste out of the tube, so to speak. People could see for themselves the dangers to which they had been exposed,[65] and any newspaper or broadcast that attempted to obscure that fact would have lost its credibility.[66] Henceforth, newspapers became more independent, but not necessarily anti-Government, and began to articulate the public's concerns for greater security measures. In October, a Gallup Poll reported that, by an overwhelming margin of 72–18 percent, that the public favored "increased expenditure on armaments," and 78 percent favored a National Register of everybody available for civilian or military service.[67] Unofficial, less sophisticated newspaper polls also confirmed a more militant public spirit than the Government was prepared to acknowledge. *The Observer* came out for conscription and a greater rearmament program.[68] A *Daily Mail* poll revealed that 50.2 percent supported a voluntary scheme of National Service, while 49.8 percent favored a compulsory program of National Service.[69] Even the more sympathetic dailies, such as *The Times* and *The Daily Telegraph,* were urging the Government to abandon its futile attempts to appease the dictators and step up its rearmament program.[70] Jones, like most Conservatives, expected a "thorough-going program of air defense" after the Munich scare.[71] He also felt "that the country could be got to accept some form of National Service if led in that direction."[72] But he, too, had been misled.

Little did the public understand how its interests were being systematically subverted and misled by the willful Prime Minister, who was doing all in his power to resist such commonsense and popular measures as National Service, registration of all those eligible for military service or outright conscription, and providing more protection for the civilian population against aerial bombardment. The same Gallup Poll that showed a strong preference for rearmament also gave Chamberlain a personal vote of confidence with an approval rating of 56 percent. The ambivalence of this situation posed somewhat of a problem for the Prime Minister, who was determined to carry out a policy at variance with the public mood. Should he capitalize on his personal popularity and call for a new election?

Afraid that Chamberlain might try it, Hoare and Halifax urged him to broaden his Government instead, and make it truly "national" in composition.[73] The opportunity to broaden the government presented itself when three Cabinet vacancies were created by Lord Stanley's death and Lord Hailsham's ill health, and Cooper's resignation in a noble but futile protest against the Munich Agreement. The force of Cooper's resignation had been blunted by the fact that inasmuch as Cooper would have preferred a showdown with Hitler at Munich, the country was relieved that Chamberlain had managed to avoid war. Cooper's resignation, therefore, did little to change things. Without other Cabinet defections, which Chamberlain managed to contain,[74] Cooper's action failed to impress on an unsuspecting public the need for a more broadly based Government and, consequently, a new policy.

Disregarding the advice from Halifax and Hoare to broaden his Government, and from Baldwin, to use his time wisely (i.e., broaden the government and rearm),[75] Chamberlain told his sister not to expect any "drastic" revision in the reconstruction of his Cabinet.[76] He conceded that it was becoming exceedingly difficult for him to find the "extra strength" for his Cabinet. "Anthony" and "Winston" were ruled out because he wanted more support for his policy, "not a strengthening of those who don't believe in it, or at any rate, are harassed by constant doubts." He was having "enough trouble with the present one."[77] Subsequently, he appointed Lord Stanhope to the Admiralty, Lord Runciman as Lord President, and Sir John Anderson as Lord Privy Seal. Jones recorded the disappointment of the Cliveden Set with the "tepid reconstruction of the Cabinet."[78]

Speculation continued to abound that Chamberlain was about to spring a general election in the hopes of capitalizing on his momentary rise in popularity after Munich. In anticipation of such a move, Churchill met with Liberal and Labor leaders to discuss a common plan of action if the Government decided to go ahead with the election. Chamberlain was kept informed of the "conspiracy" by the clandestine efforts of Ball. Working through the Conservative Central Office, Ball managed to keep potential dissidents in line by tapping their phone lines and threatening to run candidates against them at the next election, while the Chief Whip, David Margesson, threatened to use the whip against defectors.[79] The dissidents, including such high-profile figures as Eden, Cooper, and Leo Amery faced the harsh political reality with studied caution, and in the final analysis lacked the courage of their convictions to resist such pressure. Only Churchill dared to risk a break with the Central Office, which only made it more difficult for the Conservative dissidents to associate with him. And without a core of Conservative support, Labor was reluctant to throw in with him.

Fears of a surprise election proved unfounded, however. Chamberlain understood that an election now would only raise embarrassing questions about Britain's appalling lack of defensive preparations. Members of his own party, under the pressure of public opinion, would be forced to acknowledge the urgency of repairing the country's defenses, creation of a Ministry of Supply (or Defense), and conscription. Taking a hard look at the political ramifications of an election, Chamberlain concluded that it was "tactically" unwise to hold one at this time, though he "eagerly" sought an opportunity to hold one.[80] What he needed was a conciliatory gesture from the dictators, so that he could go to the country for a vote of confidence in his policy. Unable to manipulate the press and his own Conservative constituency in his accustomed manner, Chamberlain turned to the dictators for help in promoting his policy of appeasement and limited rearmament. It was not unusual for Chamberlain to look to Berlin or Rome for help. On more than one occasion he submitted a draft of a speech to be given for their comments. This time, Wilson asked the German Government if Hitler would "give the Prime Minister some support in forming public opinion in Britain in his forthcoming speech at the Sportspalast?"[81] Hitler, of course, was only too happy to oblige. He responded by denouncing the warmongers — Churchill, Eden, and Cooper— by name for advocating alliances and more rearmament, and then used the opportunity to urge the German people to step up their own rearmament measures. It was not what Chamberlain had in mind. He did not need any help from Hitler in keeping Churchill or Eden out of the Government. He needed some overt act, not words, by Hitler to persuade his colleagues and the press that appeasement was bearing fruit. The German Embassy passed word to Hitler that he should not attack Churchill, Cooper, or Eden in the future, since it was counter-productive. Chamberlain could safely ignore them.[82] And, perhaps, if Chamberlain had success on the disarmament question, he would find an opportunity for a general election, with his position so strong that even fanatical anti-Germans or political intriguers would not be able successfully to oppose any attempt by Chamberlain to arrive at a lasting agreement with Germany on the basis of the Munich protocol.[83] Hitler knew that, but he was driven by the dynamics of his own agenda, and could not possibly have given Chamberlain the help that he so desperately needed to continue with appeasement. He held the advantage and he had to press it before Britain could complete its rearmament program.

The German Ambassador in London, Herbert von Dirksen, was well pleased by the way Chamberlain had conducted himself during the Czech crisis, "circumventing the Foreign Office and ignoring provisions in the British Constitution and customary Cabinet usage."[84] Chamberlain could be relied upon, not only to prevent British interference in Eastern Europe but also to exercise a restraining influence on any French attempts to prevent German revisionism in Europe. Chamberlain, unwittingly, had become an adjunct, and a very important one of Hitler's drive for autarky. Without Chamberlain in such a dominant position in the British Government, it is highly unlikely that Hitler would have taken the military risks involved in overriding the objections of his generals. Confidently, Dirksen reported later that as long as Chamberlain remained Prime Minister, "a relatively moderate course is assured."[85]

But as Chamberlain's policies found little acceptance in the press and in the country after Munich, especially as Germany made a shambles of the protocol so quickly, his grip on the Cabinet weakened accordingly. Lacking the fervor and the single-minded purpose with which Chamberlain pursued his policy, Cabinet ministers wavered in their personal allegiance to him and began to question the wisdom of his double policy. Chamberlain characterized the Munich debate as "a trying ordeal" because he had to fight constantly to prevent the defection "of weaker brethren in the Party."[86] Election results in the two months following Munich confirmed the dramatic reversal of the Government's fortunes. The London municipal elections went to Labor. In the eight by-elections, the Government lost two seats. The Central Office of the Conservative Party advised against a general election at this time, warning that "only a small turnover of votes would defeat the Government."[87]

Since his policies could not be sustained alone in the long run, Chamberlain turned more and more to his trusted lieutenants, Ball and Wilson, for help. Ball's murky fingerprints are all over Chamberlain's persistent efforts to manage public opinion, Parliamentary criticism, and foreign policy in furtherance of his policy of appeasement.[88] Unfortunately, Ball did not write his memoirs. He burned all of his papers before his death, so it is difficult to pin down his role with the precision that the historian would like. However, enough peripheral data have been unearthed to provide at least a thumbnail sketch of his activities.[89] In addition to a covert intelligence-gathering operation for Chamberlain that kept him informed of any dissident moves to unseat him or otherwise obstruct his policies,[90] Ball also ran a news service called *Truth*, to rebut and counteract any derogatory press accounts of Chamberlain. Ball's activities also extended to foreign policy, where he maintained a close liaison with the Italian Embassy through George Steward. He even carried on private negotiations with Count Grandi for Chamberlain.[91] When M15 informed Cadogan of Steward's clandestine activities in November 1938, Cadogan told Halifax, who in turn reported this information to Chamberlain. Cadogan suspected that Steward was acting on behalf of Ball. Chamberlain feigned surprise at the news, but the business was abruptly terminated. Inexplicably, however, Steward was allowed to remain at his post until 1940, when Chamberlain resigned.[92] On another occasion, Oliver Harvey was "curious" about a press campaign about Italy that issued from Ball through the Conservative Central Office, and not from No.10 Downing.[93] Chamberlain was undoubtedly well aware of Ball's activities. Ball had often accompanied Chamberlain on his fishing vacations, and it would indeed be a stretch of the imagination to believe that their only concern was the catch of the day.

Wilson was Ball's reporting channel to Chamberlain, thus enabling Chamberlain to deny any connection with Ball should embarrassing disclosures surface. Steward told Prince Phillip of Hesse at the German Embassy to deal directly with him and not through the Foreign Office.[94] Chamberlain also mentioned in one of his letters that on receiving some news from Wilson, he presumed that it came from Ball.[95] Like Ball, Wilson did not publish his memoirs. If anyone could have provided more insight, or help, in rehabilitating the tattered image of Chamberlain, it would have been Wilson and Ball. They were completely devoted to the Prime Minister and anxious to preserve his legacy, so one can only conclude from this wall of silence that Chamberlain's actions, born out of desperation, obduracy, and prejudice, were so thoroughly discredited as to have no redeeming social, political, or diplomatic value. Had there been an identifiable, defensible, national interest, surely the ever loyal Wilson or Ball would not have passed up the opportunity to set the record straight. Ball, in fact, said as much to Chamberlain after the latter was forced to resign in 1940. His letter bears quoting at length.

I am very proud to have been so closely associated with you in your great work during the past 10 years or more. The work of the CRD [Conservative Research Department], the establishment of . . . the National Publicity Bureau, and, finally, the greatest privilege of having played a definite part of my own in helping you in your great search for peace. But, in the course of this long association we have both made many powerful and unscrupulous enemies, some of who are in high places today! But I have no intention of "giving them best," and I am fully determined, that come what may, the full great truth about your great and sustained effort to save the peace of the world . . . shall be told. . . .I am determined that whatever abilities I may possess in matters of political controversy and propaganda should be devoted to placing before the country . . . the true facts of *our* [italics added] single-handed search for peace.[96]

But, of course, the world still awaits the "full great truth" of Chamberlain's effort to save the peace of the world.[97]

      Hitler's actions after Munich caused more problems for the beseiged Prime Minister, who was desperately trying to sell his policy to a nation determined to resist Nazism. It could be done only by subterfuge and chicanery. The ink had hardly dried on the Munich Agreement when, on 1 October, Germany proceeded to ignore the ill-defined and hastily convened International Control Commission and began to dismember Czechoslovakia. Helpless and frustrated, President Benes resigned on 5 October, since the Allies could offer only weak protests in the face of superior German military force in the disputed areas. If the critics of appeasement were hopeful that Hitler's gangster tactics in the Sudetenland would at last lift the scales from the eyes of their misguided Prime Minister and spur the Government to adopt a more credible defense program, they were mistaken. Chamberlain remained as steadfast as ever. When asked for his support in the House of Lords, Swinton told Chamberlain that he would support the Munich Agreement as long as it provided a breathing space for the rearmament program. Chamberlain replied, "But don't you see, I have brought back peace."[98] Later in October, he wrote, "A lot of people seem to be losing their heads, and thinking as though Munich has made war more, instead of less, imminent."[99] As far as Chamberlain was concerned, peace was an end in itself, at any price.

      In the first Cabinet meeting after Munich, Eliot tried to energize his colleagues to step up rearmament plans to avoid another Munich, but Chamberlain immediately challenged Eliot's proposition and set the line to be taken in future discussions of the Government's policy. Although he recognized "the need to make good our deficiencies, it was not the same as saying that we should at once embark on a great increase in our armaments programme."[100] He was hopeful that the contacts made with the dictators at Munich would preclude the necessity for embarking on an expensive and destructive arms race. Ordinarily, that lecture would have been sufficient to stifle any further discussions of the matter, but the Cabinet had been shaken to its foundations as a result of Munich. The Prime Minister's iron grip on the Cabinet had been loosened during the crisis, and he had to tread more carefully in matters of national security. He could no longer control Cabinet decisions by the force of his own personality or position, especially as the service ministers became more sensitive to their own departmental liabilities. With the clouds of war thickening on the horizon, the military advisers were becoming more restless and confrontational. Only a man endowed with Chamberlain's extraordinary talent for managing the government and his iron-willed obstinacy could have survived the Munich crisis undeterred. His political courage was undeniable, but his judgment was obscured by an *idee fixeé* of peace at any price.

Nevertheless, Chamberlain had to seem to trim his sails in order to retain the public's confidence. He promised the House a "thorough inquiry . . . military and civil" into the defense program to see what further steps might be taken "to make good our deficiencies in the shortest amount of time . . . so that we may be able to defend ourselves and make our diplomacy effective."[101] But to the Cabinet he conveyed quite a different message, reminding his colleagues of the larger issues at stake and the reasons that they had initially signed on to the double policy: "Ever since I became Chancellor of the Exchequer, I have been oppressed with the sense that armaments might break our backs. This was one of the factors which had led me to the view that it was necessary to resolve the causes which were responsible to the arms race."[102] He was not about to abandon the course now. There would be no interference with trade, and appeasement of the dictators would continue. He directed Inskip to undertake a review of the existing defense programs and report on their deficiencies that needed to be made ready by August 1939. However, he cautioned that any increase or acceleration of existing rearmament programs had to be measured against the availability of skilled labor and manpower resources.

Since these problems had plagued the rearmament program ever since the Ideal Scheme was introduced, it came as no surprise when the Minister of Labor submitted a Progress Report (DPR 289) on 19 October, which repeated the warnings issued in his 1936 report[103] that the existing labor supply was "inadequate to meet the demands of the War Office and the Air Ministry unless the labor now engaged in civil work was turned to munitions." The report went on to say, that "the crux of the problem lay in making proper use of our existing capacity" and "the responsibility for solving the problem should not be put on the shoulders of the Trade Unions."[104] The report indirectly lent strong support to the on-going debate over the creation of a Ministry of Supply, to which Chamberlain was vehemently opposed.[105] Worried about rumors that a Ministry of Supply was about to be created, a group of industrialists met with Horace Wilson to offer their cooperation in the rearmament program.[106] In November, Chamberlain set up a Panel Group of Industrial Advisers to help resolve the question of labor supply and distribution. No such consideration was extended to the labor community, however, an omission that in normal times might have been excused on political grounds but, given the recent scare during the Czech crisis, was hard to justify at this time.

Labor's support was invaluable. Its most important asset was its control over human resources. So much of the Government's defense planning depended on voluntarism. About one million volunteers were needed for home defense, evacuation, and reserve duty, not to mention their importance for any scheme of dilution or transfer of labor. How any national leader could have ignored such an important resource in time of national emergency is difficult to explain. It bordered on criminal negligence.[107] The only plausible explanation is to be found in Chamberlain's stubborn determination to resist labor's challenge to the existing political and social order. By denying labor its legitimate role in the rearmament process, Chamberlain could claim full credit for his party's role in defending the country and, if appeasement worked, in preserving the peace. Labor's social agenda would then have to be placed on hold indefinitely.

Pressure for a Ministry of Supply and for National Service also came, indirectly, from a most unlikely source — Sir Samuel Hoare, one of Chamberlain's most reliable supporters. As Home Secretary, Hoare was responsible for air raid precautions, and his office came under heavy criticism for the deplorable state of home defense preparations exposed during the emergency call-up. His complaints to the Cabinet about the heavy burden imposed on his office by ARP contributed to the growing realization that the issue of a Ministry of Supply could not be postponed much longer. But Chamberlain did not think the time had arrived for such a drastic step. He argued that both the employers and the unions would object, and that all avenues had not yet been tried. Pressed on all sides for action, Chamberlain asked Inskip to prepare a memorandum on the feasibility of creating a Ministry of Supply at this time.[108] It was a stalling tactic. As usual, Chamberlain set the terms of reference. He wanted to know (as if he did not already know),

    a. What deficiencies existed;
    b. What steps should be taken for accelerating those programs;
    c. Whether the existing programs could be extended, and how.

When the Cabinet met on 26 October to consider the feasibility of setting up a Ministry of Supply and how to remedy the deficiencies in the approved service programs by August 1939, the ministers had fallen into line. Earl Stanhope, newly appointed to the Admiralty, did not see the need for "material change." Fortunately for Chamberlain, Cooper was no longer at the Admiralty to push for the Two Ocean Standard. In the air, Kingsley Wood proposed to advance the dates of completion of front-line fighter planes from April 1940 to August 1939, again at the expense of reserve strength.[109] However, many of the planes would be of inferior quality. Nevertheless, Inskip dutifully reported that air defense preparations would be "adequate" by August 1939. He concluded, therefore, that a Ministry of Supply was not needed at this time. In fact, he argued that a Ministry of Supply would have the opposite effect of slowing down the rearmament program for a number of months while the machinery for coordinating supply problems was being prepared, thus losing valuable months in the defense build-up. He also threw out a prognosis that might well have come from Chamberlain: What if war didn't come?[110] The country would then be burdened with a weighty bureaucracy, the export trade ruined for generations, and the economy gutted in the process. The memory of 1931 was paraded out once again to remind his colleagues of the reasons that originally led them down the path of limited liability and appeasement.

Hore-Belisha, on the other hand, was beginning to show signs of independence since being rattled by the Czech crisis. Spurred on by the Army

Council and stiffened by the COS, he could no longer remain silent in the face of a failed policy. The emergency call-up on 26 September had exposed glaring defects in Britain's home defenses, and as the service responsible for the ADGB his department came under a great deal of public scrutiny and criticism. Years of neglect had finally caught up with the "Cinderella Service." Earlier in the year, Hore-Belisha, against the advice of the COS, had meekly accepted £70 million in cuts from the Army's five-year budget proposals in accordance with the strategy laid down in the Inskip Memorandum. This economy had been achieved largely in two areas: the ADGB and reinforcements for the Continental army. In practical terms it meant producing 300 anti-aircraft guns less than the total recommended by the Army Council, and of the smaller total, 320 AA guns would be of the obsolescent 3-inch type.[111] It was also learned that out of the 352 modern 3.7-inch AA guns approved in 1937, only 44 were in service during the Munich crisis. Even the obsolete 3-inch guns were under strength. Of 990 approved two-pounder barrels, only 50 were in service, as were 140 of 450 barrage balloons and only 1,430 of 4,128 searchlights.[112] And the list went on in every conceivable sector of civil defense, including gas masks, rations, hospital beds, and manpower. The Army was still 20,000 men short of its established strength.[113]

These embarrassing disclosures were followed by another unpleasant fact for the Army to consider. The Munich Agreement had resulted in the elimination of Czechoslovakia's "Little Maginot Line" and the effective loss of thirty Czech divisions considered to be of high fighting quality, as well as of the Skoda munitions works, among the finest in Europe. To offset these losses, Hore-Belisha proposed to restore the cuts made in the TA earlier in the year. Without thirty Czech divisions to occupy German troops on the eastern frontier, the German Army could concentrate its forces on the western borders. Hore-Belisha found it difficult, if not irresponsible, to accept the military consequences of limited liability any longer. He pointed out to the CID that one of the reasons for the shortage of AA batteries was the inability of industry to produce sufficient numbers of field artillery guns and AA guns simultaneously. One type would have to be produced at the expense of the other.

Despite Chamberlain's pledge to accelerate rearmament plans after the Anschluss, its effect on rearmament had been negligible thus far. The Government's attempt to secure voluntary cooperation between the employers and the unions had not been successful either. Nor had the industrialists been persuaded to abandon their profitable enterprises, either civil or military, for new or additional ones. Consequently, in many cases it was more profitable for them to continue to produce obsolescent aircraft, or the 3-inch AA guns, than to retool their factories and produce more modern equipment without long-term guarantees from the Government that would maintain their profit margins. Nor were the industrialists persuaded to accommodate the rearmament program by the threat of compulsion.[114] Swinton had used that weapon and failed. Only after Munich did they begin to take the threat somewhat more seriously, when they agreed to serve on Chamberlain's panel of industrial advisers. Meanwhile, the unions continued to be treated as outsiders and interlopers. The failed talks with labor in the spring were not about to be resumed just yet.

Hore-Belisha had finally come to the same realization that had prompted Hankey and the COS to question, earlier in the year, whether the time had not at last arrived to consider interfering with the civil trade and setting up a Ministry of Supply to coordinate the supply and distribution of raw materials, skilled labor and manpower. He had therefore raised this very sensitive issue on 6 October in the CID, where Inskip was forced to deal with it. But even though Chamberlain pronounced against a Ministry of Supply in the Cabinet meeting of 19 October, Hore-Belisha, in a remarkable display of courage, took his case public in a speech to the County of Glamorgan Territorial Army and Auxiliary Air Force Association on 21 October, and was backed by the Beaverbrook press. Chamberlain was furious. The next day he summoned Hore-Belisha to 10 Downing Street for a meeting of the minds. With Wilson on hand, Chamberlain tried, unsuccessfully, to get Hore-Belisha to abandon his advocacy for a Ministry of Supply.[115] Hore-Belisha was too committed by now to back off. His responsibilities were too great to set aside for purely personal considerations or out of loyalty to the Prime Minister. As much as he admired Chamberlain, he could not accept the military risks inherent in his policy. Instead, he urged that if Chamberlain could not see his way to setting up a Ministry of Supply at this time, he should go to the House and inform it that the Government was doing everything in its power to increase arms production.[116] Chamberlain assured him he would do so.

Meanwhile, Hore-Belisha continued to argue in the Cabinet for a Ministry of Supply with compulsory powers.[117] However, he was something of a loner in the Cabinet, and as long as Inskip continued to support Chamberlain's policy, there was not much he could do to effect a change. Hore-Belisha's opposition had to be honored, so an *ad hoc* Committee on Defense Programmes and Acceleration was set up to study the problem at length, especially its financial implications. The composition of the committee, however, left little doubt about its ultimate conclusions. Chaired by Inskip, it also included Simon, Brown, Hoare and the three service ministers: Hore-Belisha, Kingsley Wood, and Stanhope. It was highly unlikely that a recommendation for a Ministry of Supply, with or without compulsory powers, would follow.

The Opposition was not convinced that the Government was sincere in its efforts to rearm the country. On 2 November, Morrison moved a vote of censure against the Government for its lack of preparations to protect the civilian population, but the motion failed along predictable party lines. Chamberlain once again demonstrated his firm control of the House, although the same could not be said for his standing in the country. Henry "Chips" Channon, one of Chamberlain's most devoted followers in the House, noted a "cleavage" in London society regarding Chamberlain. And a week later he thought that the "wave of anti-Chamberlain feeling, though largely confined to London society, seems to be growing."[118] Chamberlain was forced to make a small concession to his critics. At last he was willing to consider a voluntary system of National Service. Though long opposed to National Service, he now felt that it would be helpful in preparing the country against air raid attacks. Police, fire, Red Cross, and ambulance services required extensive planning and coordination.[119] These measures, he hoped, would have the cosmetic effect of showing the country that the Government was actually doing something for national defense. Subsequently, the Home Secretary, Sir John Anderson, was named to the post of Lord Privy Seal in charge of National Service and also put in charge of ARP.[120]

The Cabinet considered Inskip's deficiencies report at its 7 November meeting.[121] The Army's request for TA training and equipment was deferred pending a CID study on whether to re-define the Army's role after the loss of Czechoslovakia. The Admiralty offered no new significant measures to improve its readiness to respond to a crisis. Since the shipbuilding capacity was fully occupied, it could not take on new construction even if it wanted to. Only the Air Force proposal, Scheme M, for more bombers came under much discussion. Chamberlain was reluctant to increase the bomber squadrons because "it was difficult to stress this part of our force as in any way defensive."[122] He was afraid it might antagonize Hitler (as would a Ministry of Supply).[123] Such a move would only encourage Germany to build "more and heavier bombers" and involve the two countries in an arms race similar to dreadnoughts prior to World War I, and "it wasn't certain that we could beat Germany in an armaments race, which was not only a question of money but also of industrial capacity and the labor force."[124] And, of course, it would destroy his appeasement policy. Another, more practical reason for rejecting Scheme M was that bombers required more skilled labor and manpower to produce, equip, and train than fighters, a situation that might then lend support to the idea of a Ministry of Supply. However, in the final analysis, the Cabinet was apparently more persuaded by the Treasury argument to produce more fighter planes, which cost 300 percent less than bombers, so Scheme M had to go back to the drawing board.

At any rate, finding more labor for the accelerated air program was still a formidable problem as long as the rule of non-interference with trade prevailed. Chamberlain acknowledged that sufficient labor could be obtained by compulsory methods, but he was afraid that it "would give rise to a lot of trouble" with the trade unions.[125] Kingsley Wood told Chamberlain that he had not experienced much difficulty with the unions, and that maybe they could be bluffed into cooperating with the Government. Hoare also thought that perhaps the time to take the Opposition into its confidence had arrived, but Chamberlain brushed the suggestion aside and told the committee that he would consider voluntary measures "at a later date."[126] Although pessimistic about obtaining labor's cooperation, Halifax thought "it would be worth pursuing, whether it failed or not," because "our hand" would then be "stronger."[127]

Chamberlain's lack of urgency in fulfilling his post-Munich promise to accelerate the defense program was reinforced by several considerations. First, he continued to regard Munich as a vindication for his policy of appeasement,[128] that could be repeated indefinitely, if necessary, until Britain's leisurely rearmament program could be completed. Second, he was encouraged by earlier intelligence reports indicating that Germany would not be prepared to fight an all-out war until 1942, although 1939 would still be a dangerous year.[129] And finally, should diplomacy succeed, it would "allow us to stop arming and get back to the work of making the world a better place."[130] Britain's feeble rearmament program did not escape the attention of the German press, which ridiculed Chamberlain's rearmament efforts were ridiculed as "puny."[131]

In November, Halifax informed the Foreign Policy Committee of a number of disturbing intelligence reports indicating that Hitler was becoming more hostile to Great Britain for its interference during the Czech crisis because it had deprived him of a great personal military triumph. But Chamberlain, as usual, tried to place the most conciliatory construction on these reports. He cautioned the FPC that this information was by no means as precise as that received during the summer, and "there was no suggestion that Herr Hitler contemplated any immediate aggressive action."[132] At any rate, he concluded that it became all the more important to get on better terms with Italy, since Kristallnacht had derailed further Anglo-German initiatives for the time being.

On 9 November, a Nazi official in Paris was assassinated by a Jew named Grynszpan. Joseph Gobbels used the incident to whip up anti-Jewish hysteria in Germany, unleashing a violent outburst of destruction and mayhem on the Jewish population of Germany. World opinion was outraged by the incident. Kristallnacht "horrified" Chamberlain, but he was more concerned about framing an appropriate public response than in addressing the moral outrage that it sparked in Great Britain. He did not want to close the door to appeasement by condemning the Nazi regime, yet he had to speak for the nation under the watchful eye of foreign opinion, especially in America.[133] He was not pleased at the prospect, however. He told his sister that it was "difficult," but "he supposed" that he would have to say "something" on the subject the next day.[134] The Cabinet only agreed to study the problem.

Throughout November and December reports continued to be received revealing Hitler's bellicose designs. From Berlin, Sir George Oglvie-Forbes reported that Hitler had abandoned any hope of improving relations with Great Britain as a result of the storm of indignation over Kristallnacht and Munich. As the British press became more critical of his double policy, the strain on Chamberlain became more noticeable. His sister Hilda commented that "the foreign news and the press have made large demands on your equanimity."[135] He replied, "You are quite right in supposing that I have found the newspapers especially depressing this week," especially in their reporting of Cooper's speeches abroad.[136] Chamberlain's appeasement policy was wearing thin with the press, Parliament, and the British people, although his personal popularity remained quite high. Little did they know of Chamberlain's clandestine efforts to appease the dictators and resist rearmament.

When Ivone Kirkpatrick returned from the Berlin Embassy in December with an alarming report that Hitler intended to bomb London in March,[137] his warning could not be ignored. For the first time Chamberlain took a discouraging intelligence report seriously enough to act upon its merits without trying to fudge it. He passed it on to the CID, where it was considered in a most secret session on 17 December. Later the Cabinet approved a long-delayed acceleration of air raid precautions to the tune of £20 million. Defense at last took precedence over finance or politics. It was made easier by the fact that ARP could in no way be construed by Hitler as a provocative act, and it still kept open the door to future appeasement initiatives. Nor would it involve excessive demands on skilled labor or industrial capacity, except possibly in the case of providing more AA guns.

Another problem for Chamberlain surfaced on 10 December, when Dirksen informed Halifax that Germany was exercising its option to lift the restrictions imposed by the Anglo-German Naval Agreement on its submarine fleet. It was a severe personal blow to Chamberlain. He complained to his sisters of the "venomous attacks by the German press, and the failure of Herr Hitler to make the slightest gesture of friendliness."[138] Nevertheless, he quietly pursued his latest initiatives aimed at appeasing Germany's economic appetite. Germany was known to have been suffering from severe economic problems. But whereas most intelligence sources predicted that Germany would attempt to solve the problem through aggressive action, Chamberlain saw this as an opportunity to hold out the proverbial carrot (without an accompanying stick) by offering Germany generous trade concessions and colonial adjustments. Similar attempts had been made in the past, without success. But Chamberlain persisted in his efforts to court Hitler's favor. Circumventing the Foreign Office once again, he used Horace Wilson to brief Lord Norman of the Bank of England along those very lines for his forthcoming visit to Germany[139] which was meant to follow up on the Government's attempt in October to ease Germany's exchange and credit problems. Later, Frederick Leith Ross, Chief Economic Adviser, continued with this initiative, which eventually culminated in the abortive Hudson-Wilson-Wohlthat talks in July. Hitler simply was not interested. His goal was autarky and power, not economic servitude.[140]

Faced with annoying votes of confidence in the House in November and December, Chamberlain derived small comfort from Churchill's failure to enlist any significant backbench support against the Government's policy. But the indefatigable Churchill continued to press his attacks on the Government in especially harsh terms. In a speech on 11 December, following Germany's denunciation of the Anglo-German Naval Treaty, he charged that the Government's policy was dividing the nation at a time when it should be pulling it together, and that it was "hampering the whole progress of national defense *for fear of having to invite the cooperation of the Opposition parties*" [italics added].[141]

Stung by the speech and another vote of no confidence on the following day, Chamberlain tried to stem the steady erosion of his support in the country. The Government had not fared well in the recent by-elections, and even the City and the House were becoming more apprehensive about Chamberlain's policy.[142]

Adding to the Prime Minister's problems in courting public opinion was the fact that Eden had just departed on a visit to the United States, where he was received with great fanfare. His meeting with President Roosevelt was described by the British Ambassador there as a "major sensation."[143] American disenchantment with Chamberlain's appeasement policy could not have been expressed more clearly. Yet Chamberlain refused to be moved. He downplayed the significance of Eden's trip and took the offensive on 13 December. Ignoring comments from the Foreign Office on a speech to be delivered at a Foreign Press Association dinner, he presented a defense of his appeasement policy. He acknowledged that he was perceived as an advocate for an understanding with the dictator states, but he denied that he favored such systems. He told the group that he was faced with two choices: either accept war as inevitable, or try to remove the possible causes of war, which he was trying to do. And finally, he expressed the hope that more rearmament would not be required.[144]

The audience applauded in all the "wrong" places as far as Chamberlain was concerned.[145] His references to France and the United States were cheered, while his mention of appeasement was greeted with silence. He realized that the speech had been a "flop" and regretted having made it,[146] although Simon, as usual, wrote him a letter expressing his support, for which Chamberlain was grateful.[147] To his sister Ida he admitted that it had been "a pretty awful week between external and internal affairs, and he will be glad when the House closes down for a month."[148] These developments were mirrored in public in a disappointing manner, pointing up the importance of conducting foreign policy in a more broadly based manner. The call for volunteers for National Service had not gone well. By December, only a 81,000 of 300,000 men needed had responded to the clarion call of National Service.[149]

Chamberlain was able to withstand the growing body of criticism only because his critics were hopelessly divided. Any thought of removing Chamberlain floundered on the question of his replacement.[150] The plain fact, which could not be obscured, was the overwhelming majority enjoyed by the Conservatives in the House of Commons and the tight control exercised over its members by the Government whips and the Conservative Party Central Office. Who among the Conservatives could assume the reins of leadership? Certainly not Churchill. His inflammatory speeches against the Government had alienated many party loyalists, and his judgment was questioned because he had been on the "wrong" side of many high-profile issues, such as the India Bill and the King's marriage. Halifax might have been an acceptable choice, but his peerage handicapped his chances. Realistically, only Eden possessed the experience, stature, and talent to lead a reconstructed Conservative Party government. (And he was liked by the Labor Party as well!) However, the very qualities that enabled Eden to enjoy such widespread support were at once detrimental to the cause of the Cabinet reconstructionists. He would not associate himself publicly with Chamberlain's enemies in order to position himself for a return to the Government. Yet he continued to urge the Government to abandon its "business as usual" policy and take those steps deemed essential for national defense by the experts. Chamberlain took smug satisfaction in noting that while Eden was loudly cheered by the Opposition, "he did himself no good with our party."[151] Halifax expressed interest in Eden's return to the Government, but Chamberlain would not consider it unless Eden was willing to support his double policy unconditionally — and he did not think that Eden would accept such conditions. He was right. Eden told friends that "it would be impossible for me to return to play the part of an ostrich, or to cheer on party warfare which I regard as stupid, if not criminal, at this time."[152]

Meanwhile, a political storm of major proportions was brewing. On 11 December Chamberlain revealed that a junior minister had threatened to resign, along with others, unless he got rid of two, and preferably four, of his colleagues.[153] Harvey reported that five Parliamentary under-secretaries, Robert Hudson, Lord Strathcona, Captain Harry Crookshank, Kenneth Lindsay, and the Marquess of Dufferin were threatening to resign because of their dissatisfaction with the slow pace of rearmament, the failure of the Munich policy, and agricultural policy.[154] The story broke two days later when *The Evening Standard* carried the front page headline, "Junior Ministers in Revolt." Chamberlain met with the dissidents on 17 December and he managed to talk them out of their decision to resign.

The chief objects of the revolt were Inskip and, ironically, Hore-Belisha, who among the major Cabinet officers had recently become the most forceful advocates for a greater rearmament program in the Cabinet. Apparently the junior ministers mistakenly attributed the slowness and ineffectiveness of the rearmament program to these two service ministers. However, it is difficult to imagine that they were unaware of Chamberlain's role in the rearmament program, and therefore one has to wonder whether the attack on Hore-Belisha and Inskip was not really meant to be an attack on those individuals, but rather on the Prime Minister himself. Chamberlain was finding it more difficult to contain the criticism of his rearmament program.

The junior ministers incident was not discussed formally by the Cabinet. By 21 December the revolt had quietly died down when none of the letters of resignation were sent, nor were the dissidents fired (as they perhaps had hoped!).[155] Chamberlain was shaken by the revolt. He wrote to his sister Ida, "I have succeeded in staving off all resignations of junior ministers but I shall have to spend some of the holiday in considering whether it is possible or desirable to make some changes and if so what."[156] In any event, Chamberlain seemed to have gotten the message that changes in the defense program had to be made and confidence in his Government restored. He adopted a firmer tone in Parliament. Even such a harsh critic of his policy as Harvey noticed the change: The "PM's speech in the House last week . . . was much stiffer than his wont and he was even more outspoken at the luncheon with the lobby correspondents," and that "He is certainly pressing on with rearmament, but not as fundamentally as the situation demands."[157] Chamberlain's ability to control the rearmament agenda was rapidly unraveling as the year came to a close.[158] He looked eagerly toward his Italian visit for a boost to his sagging policy.

Chamberlain and Halifax arrived in Italy on 11 January to a staged reception. Chamberlain's desperate attempt to drive a wedge between Mussolini and Hitler only increased the Italian dictator's contempt for the decadent Empire. Ciano described the British visit as a "big lemonade."[159] The visit accomplished little. Chamberlain reported it as "highly successful" to Parliament. He was satisfied that the journey had definitely strengthened the chances of peace.[160] But Halifax did not share the Prime Minister's optimism. Laconically, he told the Cabinet that he had nothing to add to the Prime Minister's report.

NOTES

1. Sir Nevile Henderson, *Failure of a Mission* (New York: Putnam, 1940), 137–138.

2. CAB 23/93/26, 25 May 1938.

3. NC 18/1/1054, 28 May 1938.

4. NC 18/1/1051, 13 May 1938.

5. Yet Turkey was given £6 million to "keep them out of German hands." NC 18/1/1054, 28 May 1938; CAB 23/93/23, 11 May 1938.

6. *Debates*, 356: 1234 ff., 25 May 1938. Note: That figure closely paralleled the Government's own estimate.

7. Ibid.

8. Ibid., 1297–1298.

9. Ibid., 1306.

10. Ibid., 1304.

11. *Harvey Diaries*, 26 May 1938, 145.

12. *Debates*, 339: 2693, 26 July 1938.

13. Kleist, a retired German officer, was a Prussian Monarchist and "violently anti-Hitler," according to Chamberlain.

14. Theo von Kordt, a counselor in the German Embassy in London, put patriotism ahead of his loyalty to Hitler. He tried to overthrow Hitler because he considered Hitler's policies to be dangerous for the German people.

15. See Christopher Andrew, *Her Majesty's Secret Service: The Making of the British Intelligence Community* (New York: Viking Press, 1985); and Wark, *The Ultimate Enemy*, 207.

16. Kennedy, "Net Assessment," 49.

17. NC 18/1/1059, 9 July 1938; CAB 23/94/35, 27 July 1938.

18. CAB 23/95/36, 30 August 1938.

19. Ibid.

20. Ibid.

21. Ibid.; NC 18/1/1059, 9 July 1938.

22. NC 18/1/1030, 26 November 1937; Feiling, 322–323.

23. NC 18/1/1067, 3 September 1938.

24. DGFP, series D, vol. 1, #93, 2 January 1938.

25. DGFP, series D, vol. 2, #415, 7 September 193 D8.

26. Harris, 153; Cowling, 212.

27. CAB 23/95/38, 14 September 1938.

28. Ibid.; COS 765.

29. The best analysis of the military, strategic, and economic dimensions of the problem can be found in Murray. He has made a strong case demonstrating the wisdom of confronting Germany in 1938, rather than later. See Murray, *The Change in the European Balance of Power*, ch.7.

30. *Inskip Diary 1*, 13 September 1938.

31. Rock, *Roosevelt and Appeasement*, 111; *Harvey Diaries*, 10 September 1938, 175; T. Taylor, *Munich*, 771.

32. NC 18/1/16, 10 September 1939; NC 18/1/24, 8 October 1939.

33. CAB 23/95/38, 14 September 1938.

34. *Inskip Diary 1*, 17 September 1938.

35. Ibid.

36. Peden, *British Rearmament and the Treasury*, 191.

37. CAB 23/95/39, 17 September 1938.

38. PREM 1/264, Chamberlain meeting with labor leaders, 17 September 1938.

39. Citrine, *Men and Work* (London: Hutchinson, 1964), 360.

40. Ibid.

41. CAB 23/95/40, 19 September 1938.

42. NC 18/1/1069, 19 September 1938.

43. Igor Lukes, *Czechoslovakia Between Stalin and Hitler* (New York: Oxford University Press, 1996), 221; T. Taylor, *Munich*, 777.

44. CAB 23/95/41, 21 September 1938.

45. PREM 1/264, Halifax meeting with labor leaders, 21 September 1938.

46. Dalton, 188.

47. PREM 1/264. Chamberlain with labor leaders.

48. Harris, *Attlee,* 154.

49. CAB 23/95/42, 24 September 1938.

50. DBFP, series D, vol. II, #1092, 25 September 1938; *Harvey Diaries*, 25 September 1938, 197.

51. *Cadogan Diaries*, 25 September 1938, 105.

52. Cowling, 198: *Inskip Diary 1*, 17 September 1938. Jones mentioned only 5 resigning. *Jones Diary*, 23 September 1938, 409; Winterton told Amery that four or five of his friends contemplated resigning. *Amery Diary,* 268–269.

53. *The Times*, 26 September 1938.

54. *The Daily Telegraph*, 26 September 1938.

55. DGFP, series D, vol. 2, #610, 25 September 1938.

56. CAB 23/95/44, 25 September 1938.

57. Ibid.

58. Chamberlain, *In Search of Peace,* 174.

59. There has been some speculation that Chamberlain must have known of Hitler's reply before he addressed the House. Martin Gilbert and Richard Gott, *The Appeasers* (Boston: Houghton-Mifflin, 1963), 173–175. Chamberlain had received a letter from Hitler the previous evening encouraging him to continue his efforts to preserve peace if he thought it would do any good.

60. *Jones Diary*, 30 October 1938, 418.

61. Cockett, *Twilight of Truth*, 12, 80.

62. West, *Truth Betrayed,* 41.

63. Cockett, *Twilight of Truth*, 82–83.

64. Reith, *Into the Wind*, 311–313, 320. In his place Chamberlain appointed Sir Allan Powell, a man thought to be wholly unqualified for the job.

65. Ibid., 341.

66. For the human dimension, cf. Ben Wicks, *No Time to Wave Goodbye* (New York: St. Martin's Press, 1988), and *The Day They Took the Children* (Toronto: Stoddart, 1989).

67. G.H. Gallup, ed. *Gallup International Public Opinion Polls, Great Britain, 1937–1975,* vol. 1 (New York: Random House, 1976), 10. Public opinion also opposed returning German colonies by 85–15 percent.

68. Stephen Koss, *The Rise and Fall of the Political Press in Britain*, vol. 2 (Chapel Hill: University of North Carolina Press, 1984), 583.

69. Dennis, 149.

70. *The Times*, 18 October 1938.

71. *Jones Diary*, 5 October 1938, 413.

72. Ibid., 30 October 1938, 418.

73. NC 11/31/124A, Halifax to Chamberlain, 11 October 1938; *Harvey Diaries*, 11 October 1938, 212; Macmillan, 518.

74. NC 18/1/1072, 15 October 1938.

75. NC 11/31/124A, Halifax to Chamberlain, 11 October 1938; Feiling, *Chamberlain*, 161.

76. NC 18/1/1072, 15 October 1938.

77. Ibid.

78. *Jones Diary*, 5 November 1938, 420.

79. NC 18/1/1071, 9 October 1938; John Charmley, *Churchill: The End of Glory* (New York: Harcourt, Brace, 1993), 355.

80. NC 18/1/1072, 15 October 1938.

81. David Irving, ed., *Breach of Security* (London: William Kimber, 1968), 50.

82. DGFP, series D, vol.4, #250, 11 October 1938, 304. Dirksen to Weizacker.

83. Ibid., #252, 15 October 1938, 311, Dirksen to Weizacker.

84. Ibid., #251, 12 October 1938, 306, Hesse to Dirksen.

85. Ibid., series D, vol. 6, #35, 18 March 1939, 39, Dirksen to Weizacker.

86. NC 18/1/1071, 9 October 1938.

87. Parker, *Chamberlain and Appeasement*, 189.

88. The German Embassy reported that during the Czech crisis, Chamberlain had acted entirely alone with his two intimate advisers (Wilson and Ball). DGFP, #251, 12 October 1938, 306. Hesse and Stewart conversations.

89. See Cockett, "Communication: Ball, Chamberlain, and Truth," *The Historical Journal*, 33, #1 (1990): 131–142.

90. Sheppard, *A Class Divided*, 135. Ball admitted tapping phones of Chamberlain's perceived enemies, including Eden and many in the press. Also, see Margach, 103.

91. Ramsden, 86; NC 2/24A, 18 February 1938.

92. Cockett, *Twilight*, 15.

93. *Harvey Diaries*, 10 February 1938, 87–88.

94. DGFP, series D, vol.4, #251, 12 October 1938, Hesse and Steward conversation.

95. NC 2/24A, 18 February 1938.

96. NC 7/11/33/19, Ball to Chamberlain, undated, summer of 1940.

97. Feiling, Chamberlain's official biographer, attempted to do so with little success. Also Charmley, *Chamberlain and the Lost Peace* is way out of line.

98. T. Taylor, *Munich,* 926.

99. NC 18/1/1072, 15 October 1938.

100. CAB 23/95/48, 3 October 1938

101. *Debates*, 339: 474, 6 October 1938.

102. CAB 23/95/48, 13 October 1938.

103. CP 96(36), 26 March 1936.

104. CAB 23/96/49, 19 October 1938.

105. NC 18/1/1074, 29 October 1938; NC 1/20/1/186, 5 November 1938, Chamberlain to Mary Endicott Chamberlain.

106. PREM 1/336, 21 October 1938.

107. Messersmith (U.S. State Department official) to Geist, 3 February 1939, quoted from Hill, 131. Messersmith said that "the stupidities which are being committed are so great that they are more than criminal," and he accused Chamberlain of "criminal participation in Hitler's aggressive plans."

108. CAB 23/96/49, 19 October 1938.

109. CP 218(38).

110. CAB 23/96/50, CP 234(38), 26 October 1938; NC 18/1/1074, 29 October 1938.

111. Gibbs, 481.

112. Postan, *British War Production,* 55–56.

113. CP 234(38).

114. NC 11/21/1. Bruce Gardner to Mrs Neville Chamberlain, @1954.

115. NC 18/1/1074, 22 October 1938; Minney, 158–159.

116. HB 1/5, 24 October 1938.

117. CAB 23/96/51, 31 October 1938.

118. *Channon Diaries,* 3 and 8 November 1938, 176–177.

119. NC 18/1/1074, 29 October 1938.

120. CAB 23/96/50, 26 October 1938.

121. CP 240(38).

122. CAB 23/96/53, 7 November 1938.

123. Kingsley Wood to Austin Hopkinson, *Nicolson Diaries,* 24 November 1938, 374.

124. CAB 23/96/53, 7 November 1938.

125. Ibid.

126. Ibid.

127. NC 11/31/124A, Halifax to Chamberlain, 11 October 1938.

128. NC 18/1/1072, 15 October 1938. He wrote, "We are nearer to the time when we can put all thoughts of war out of our minds."

129. Wark, 116.

130. NC 1/20/1/186, 5 November 1938. Chamberlain to Mary Endicott Chamberlain (a cousin).

131. CAB 27/624, 14 November 1938; *Harvey Diaries,* 13 November 1938, 218; Sir Ivone Kirkpatrick, *The Inner Circle* (London: Macmillan, 1959), 135.

132. *Cadogan Diaries,* 14 November 1938, 125.

133. CAB 23/96/55, 16 November 1938; CAB 23/96/56, 23 November 1938.

134. NC 18/1/1076, 13 November 1938.

135. NC 18/2/1103, 9 December 1938.

136. NC 18/1/1079, 11 December 1938; *Harvey Diaries,* 24 November 1938, 223.

137. DBFP, series 3, vol. 3, #403, 8 December 1938; *Cadogan Diaries,* 15 December 1938, 130.

138. NC 18/1/1079, 11 December 1938.

139. *Harvey Diaries,* 4 January 1939, 235.

140. PREM 1/332, Hitler to Lord Kemsley, 27 July 1939.

141. Robert James, ed., *Churchill: His Complete Speeches*, vol. 6 (London: Chelsea House, 1974), 6049.

142. NC 18/1/1078, 4 December 1938. Chamberlain described the mood in the House as "very odd." Also, *Harvey Diaries*, 11 December 1938, 226.

143. Rock, *Chamberlain and Roosevelt*, 141–142.

144. Chamberlain, 240–244.

145. *Harvey Diaries*, 14 December 1938, 228; *Cadogan Diaries*, 13 December 1938, 129–130.

146. *Harvey Diaries*, 17 December 1938, 228; *Cadogan Diaries*, 14 December 1938, 129–130.

147. David Dutton, *Simon* (London: Aurum Press, 1992), 256.

148. NC 18/1/1080, 17 December 1938.

149. CAB 23/96/57, CP 262(38), 30 November 1938.

150. NC 18/1/1078, 4 December 1938.

151. NC 18/1/1075, 6 November 1938.

152. James, *Anthony Eden*, 206.

153. NC 18/1/1079, 11 December 1938.

154. *Harvey Diaries*, 13 December 1938, 227. Rob Hudson claims that there were eight involved instead of five. Minney, 162. In a separate unrelated development, Vansittart also informed Halifax of his desire to resign. Halifax urged him to stay on as Chamberlain shuddered at the thought of his going into Parliament. *Cadogan Diaries*, 21 December 1938, 131.

155. Strathcona was let go by the War Office on 31 January 1939, despite Hore-Belisha's intercession with Chamberlain to retain him. Minney, 164–165.

156. NC 18/1/1080, 17 December 1938.

157. *Harvey Diaries*, 25 December 1938, 229. Harvey apparently was referring to the recent £20 million appropriation for ARP.

158. The Japanese Ambassador in London also noticed that Chamberlain was losing his grip on the country. Roger Parkinson, *Peace for Our Time* (New York: David McKay, 1972), 86.

159. Hugh Gibson, ed., *The Ciano Diaries, II,* vol.2 (New York: Doubleday, 1946), 12 January 1939, 9–10.

160. NC 18/1/1082, 15 January 1939.

Chapter 7

Unraveling the Double Policy

Whatever benefits Chamberlain expected to reap from his Italian conversations were dispelled immediately upon his return to London. More disquieting evidence of Germany's aggressive intentions had surfaced since Kirkpatrick's bombshell in mid-December. Although most signs pointed to trouble in the East, the possibility of an attack on the West could not be discounted. Hitler was known in London to have been upset with Chamberlain's intervention in the Czech crisis[1] because Chamberlain had deprived him of an opportunity to demonstrate Germany's military power. Munich had also served notice on Hitler that in any subsequent forays eastward he would have to reckon with intervention by the Western powers. Therefore, he might be tempted to launch a preemptive strike against Great Britain well before her armaments were completed. This view explains why Hitler was not more helpful in accommodating Chamberlain's domestic efforts to gain wider support for his appeasement policy. Time was running against him, and he knew it. Additionally, British officials generally feared Hitler was highly unstable and certainly capable of a "mad dog" act. There was no telling what he might do next.

Among others, Mason MacFarlane reported from the Berlin Embassy that an attack in the East was imminent, but it would probably be launched in the West first, because Germany regarded England as enemy number one.[2] The British Ambassador in Paris, Sir Eric Phipps, could not exclude the possibility of an action in the West.[3] Ogilvie-Forbes reported that "Hitler was relying on our lack of preparedness for a major war this year." He anticipated an eastward putsch by Germany in order to obtain valuable raw materials for the nation's war machine but he also thought it possible that Hitler would attack in the West first, perhaps by March.[4] Inskip had information that fixed the date of operations on 21 February, and he found it "hard to believe that these reports are fabricated."[5] The signs were all too convincing to ignore. The German war machine was gearing up, and whether in the East or West, it boded ill for Britain. The German Army had canceled leaves, reservists were put on stand by, and transportation facilities were placed under military jurisdiction. These reports did not appear to disturb Chamberlain unduly. He had resigned himself to German hegemony in Eastern Europe a long time ago, though he wished it would be accomplished without the use of force. And even if Hitler managed to establish his position in Eastern Europe, it would not necessarily compromise Britain's interests there as long as Britain and Germany maintained a cordial relationship based on a common policy of anti-Bolshevism and elitism. German revisionism, therefore, was not an entirely unwelcome prospect as far as Chamberlain was concerned. Once Germany had established itself in Eastern Europe, it would then be forced to contend with the Soviet menace, allowing Britain to rearm at a leisurely pace without making concessions to labor or having to rely on foreign support (especially from the United States). The Empire could thus be preserved without having to make the difficult choice between destruction by external force or economic dislocation. Lord Halifax did not appear to be overly concerned with these reports either. He told U.S. Ambassador Joseph Kennedy that Great Britain was not about to do anything to prevent German revisionism in Eastern Europe[6] because it would give Britain more time to rearm. In addition, if Hitler established hegemony in Eastern Europe, it would also provide Europe with a bulwark against Bolshevism.

By the middle of January, signs of a German attack on Holland grew stronger. Intelligence reports specifically mentioned Holland as a zone to be occupied by Germany in early spring, as insurance against Western interference.[7] Colonel Josef Beck's cordial reception in Berlin on 5 January and the steady deterioration in Anglo-German relations lent credibility to this interpretation. The prospect of military action within six weeks time caused a major shift in Cabinet thinking at its 18 January meeting. The matter was referred to the Foreign Policy Committee the next day. What if Germany should attack Holland? How should Great Britain respond? On the one hand, the COS acknowledged that there was nothing that Britain (or France) could do to prevent a German attack from running over Holland. On the other hand, if Britain did not do anything, the consequences would be much worse. The COS warned that the

failure to intervene would have such moral and other repercussions as would seriously undermine our position in the eyes of the Dominions and the world in general. We might thus be deprived of support in a subsequent struggle. In our view it is hardly an exaggeration to say that failure to take up such a challenge would place Germany in a predominant position in Europe and correspondingly lower our prestige throughout the world. We have, as we see it, no choice but to regard it as a direct challenge to our security.[8]

The Government's duty was clear. An attack on Holland should be treated as a *causus belli*. If Holland could not be saved, every effort must be made to secure Belgium and northern France in order to deprive Germany of submarine and air bases from which to attack Great Britain. Also, a German occupation of Holland could jeopardize Britain's Far Eastern position "if Germany should make a present of the Dutch East Indies to Japan."[9] The impact on the Dominions would be devastating to the Empire. The dangerous course that Chamberlain had laid out in 1936 now came back to haunt the Cabinet. Apparently, Holland and Belgium had no faith in British promises to guarantee them against a German attack, and they politely declined British attempts to initiate discussions. They were fully aware of Britain's inability (or unwillingness) to fulfill its Continental commitment, and they preferred to trust in neutrality as the lesser of two evils.

The fact which could not be obscured, however, was that a German attack on the Low Countries was as much a matter for Britain's national security as it was for France's. France was doomed at the outset of a purely Franco-German struggle due to the preponderance of German military, industrial, and human resources. France could withstand a German onslaught only with British help. But in Chamberlain's strategy of limited liability, the only real assistance Britain could provide for France was at sea, in the form of a blockade that would take effect in two years, too late to be of any assistance. The Royal Air Force was concentrating on building fighter planes, which would be able to defend only the home islands and not be of much assistance on the Continent. And the Army was not prepared to accept a Continental commitment. France would have its hands full in fighting Germany, which most likely would be supported by Italy, and possibly by Franco's Spain. France could not possibly defend the Low Countries alone. These concerns had been raised by the French at the 24 November ministerial meeting, but were effectively rebutted by Chamberlain. Now they carried more weight.

Halifax raised yet another frightening prospect should the Government fail to strengthen its Continental commitment. Bearing in mind the signing of the Franco-German Declaration of Friendship Treaty on 6 December, he could not discount the possibility that France might decide to cut a deal with Germany if the situation seemed hopeless.[10] Clearly, Britain would now have to step up its Continental commitment or face the consequences outlined in the COS report. In January, the French renewed their requests for British Army support in the light of these recent developments, and the British Government was forced to reconsider its policy. The COS analyzed the French request on 12 January, and while acknowledging the problems just outlined, they offered no solution because they were not asked for a recommendation. However, the COS did urge that talks with France should be expanded.[11]

Hore-Belisha, still smarting from the revolt of the junior ministers, sensed the opportunity to make a case for the long neglected Continental army and decided to press on with it. He had recently returned from an inspection tour of French fortifications and came away from the trip more impressed by the depth and construction of the German defenses on the Siegfried Line than with the Maginot Line, because the former had demonstrated how much could be done in a short span of time. At present, Britain proposed to send two ill-equipped divisions to the Continent at the outbreak of hostilities and two or three later, without adequate provisions for long-term reinforcement. The Army Staff could not responsibly send these troops into battle under these conditions. They would merely be "wasted."[12] By alleging shortages of manpower and industrial capacity, Chamberlain had been able to resist the cry for a Continental commitment. However, a recent study by the Manpower Committee assured the COS that there was a considerable surplus of manpower and industrial capacity. At the time only 30 percent of the engineering capacity was employed in arms production.[13] Chamberlain's objection to the Continental army evidently was based more on political grounds than on its merits.

Hore-Belisha seized the opportunity to renew his plea for a Ministry of Supply as the only way to remedy these deficiencies in the shortest period of time. He had already begun to take inventory of the Army's deficiencies. On 9 January he had asked every member of the Army Council for a "frank" statement of any difficulties which may be hampering the progress of the Army's rearmament program, especially those of a financial or administrative nature.[14] On 19 January, he passed on to the Prime Minister the gist of their reports, which in general were critical of the meddlesome role played by the Treasury in the Army program. Chamberlain offered little sympathy, inasmuch as the Army required £60 million for reorganizing and supplying adequate forces for a Continental role.[15] Hore-Belisha came away from the meeting feeling "a bit depressed."[16] The Secretary of State for War must have been very naive indeed to have expected a sympathetic hearing from Chamberlain on a new role for the Army. However, when he met with Chamberlain again on 24 January, the Holland war scare had changed the situation in the Cabinet, and Chamberlain approved the acquisition of more AA guns on 28 January, a transparent effort to head off a larger request for the Continental army.[17]

It seemed to Hore-Belisha that Chamberlain's world was coming apart in January.[18] Chamberlain was besieged on all sides to abandon his policy of limited liability because appeasement had not succeeded in detaching any of the dictators from the others. Britain was therefore forced into a closer relationship with France against her wishes. The French meanwhile took advantage of this new leverage and stepped up their pressure for a greater land commitment from the British, to which they now added a call for conscription. Backed by the COS report, which implicitly endorsed the concept of a Ministry of Supply, Halifax was inclined to agree with their position. Unnerved by the junior ministers' revolt and under pressure from the COS, the War Office, and the Foreign Office, Inskip also reluctantly concluded that the time had finally arrived to recommend a Ministry of Supply. He reported for the CID that because the situation had grown worse since Munich, "further large scale measures of industrial mobilization might well have to be taken in an emergency [i.e., the Holland scare]; and that in his view, both this situation and the pressure of public opinion, might well force the Government to set up a Ministry of Supply."[19]

Inskip has not been treated very well by historians, and unfairly so. His duty was to relieve the Prime Minister of the weighty problems involved with the day-to-day details of the defense program, and to be his spokesman in

Parliament and in the many committees requiring his presence. He did so in a masterful fashion. A tireless worker and a gentleman, he was respected by all with whom he dealt for his integrity and evenhandedness. All received a fair hearing in his committee. He defended the Prime Minister's policies admirably against the most cynical critics of the defense program with his lawyer-like precision and expertise, and his devotion to the Prime Minister was second only to his love of country. But, as an honorable man, he now found it exceedingly difficult after Munich to balance the requirements of national security against his loyalty to the Prime Minister. Relying on Chamberlain's promise, he had always told the COS that he would recommend a Ministry of Supply when the proper time came. With reports of war being only a matter of weeks away, Inskip felt, as did Hore-Belisha, that the time had now arrived. Mistakenly, he assumed that Chamberlain shared the same sentiments. So when Inskip opened the door to a Ministry of Supply, even one without compulsory powers, Chamberlain abruptly decided to let him go, as he had done with Eden and Swinton for not giving full support for his policy. Chamberlain met with Inskip on 17 January and informed him of his decision to replace him as Minister for the Coordination of Defense because his "position in the House of Commons, in the country and in the press has gone bad lately," and not because he had any criticism of the job that he had done.[20] Disappointed and hurt, Inskip accepted the Prime Minister's decision with good grace but was shocked when Chamberlain told him that he was appointing Lord Chatfield to the vacant position. Chatfield was not a member of the House of Commons, which had been given as one of the reasons why Chamberlain had asked for Swinton's resignation. Chamberlain explained that Chatfield's appointment would give the country confidence because Chatfield was a military man.

Chamberlain's reason for removing Inskip from the CID should not be accepted without reservation. He had given considerable thought to making a Cabinet change since the revolt of the junior ministers had caused a great deal of unrest among the backbenchers. Like Swinton, Inskip became the scapegoat for the embattled rearmament program and deflected criticism away from Chamberlain. His dismissal also offered Chamberlain an excuse to buy more time for his program of limited liability by arguing, as he did, that the new minister needed more time to study the defense program.[21] In an ill-disguised attempt to soften the blow to Inskip, Chamberlain tried to make light of it. He told him that while it was true that his position had gone bad lately, so had Hore-Belisha's, and there would not be as great an "exaltation at your departure as there would be if Hore-Belisha was to be going."[22] Chamberlain then offered Inskip the post of Dominions Secretary in place of Malcom MacDonald, who was allowed to keep the Colonial Office. Inskip was crushed by the suddenness of the decision but accepted the position nevertheless. Mrs. Inskip was furious, because Chamberlain had reassured her husband of his job after the junior minister's revolt.

At the Cabinet meeting of 25 January, it was agreed that a German attack on Holland should be treated as a *causus belli*, but no decision was reached on what action ought to be taken in consequence of that information, except to inform the United States of the situation. Although he did not want to commit the country to Holland's defense, Chamberlain could not afford to challenge his colleagues directly. Sensing the growing militancy in the Cabinet, he conceded that Britain must resist German aggression against Holland, but then countered, "What if Holland chose not to resist?" referring to that country's refusal to enter into discussions with Britain. He also questioned the quality of the intelligence he was receiving, which had proved wrong at times in the past and which, in certain circumstances, might be "embarrassing."[23] Chamberlain was being driven against his will to support a policy that he felt to be wrong, and was doing everything in his power to resist the inexorable flow of events. But his arguments no longer carried the weight they had before Munich. The COS were now asked to study the military implications of a German attack on Holland the next day, and to forward their report to the Foreign Policy Committee and the CID.

The FPC concluded that the struggle with Germany on the Continent was an uneven one for France and the Low Countries. And in order to combat French defeatism and reinforce French morale, a strong commitment should be given and Anglo-French staff talks initiated. The French welcomed the military talks but pressed the British for a conscription bill as evidence of their new policy. The CID concerned itself with the practical aspects of providing military assistance on the Continent. Since there was neither adequate equipment nor reinforcement for these divisions, at present, Hore-Belisha argued that steps should be initiated immediately for the proper training and equipment of the Territorials, since it would take about a year to produce significant results. He therefore proposed the creation of a Ministry of Supply, this time supported by Halifax, Brown, Stanley and Wood.[24] Lord Stanhope was also wavering in his support for the Prime Minister's policy. Now, only Simon could be counted on to support Chamberlain's policy in the Cabinet with any degree of conviction.

Chamberlain recoiled at the thought of taking the last remaining steps on the road to rearmament, and the vast and irreversible social and economic changes that would follow. With keen insight, Harvey explained why he thought Chamberlain was so reluctant to set up a Ministry of Supply.

The position, as I see it is this. If there is a war of any length, those classes [i.e., Conservative and business] will almost certainly be ruined; if there is not a war, though they will not be ruined, their standard of life will nonetheless be greatly reduced by the cost of defensive re-armament and by the changeover to more totalitarian methods of production and industry. The second point. . .is that. . .we cannot carry through the drastic rearmament and the changes of method in industry as a whole. . .unless, we have a confident and keen Labor movement behind us.[25]

Just as the Munich crisis had emboldened several key members of the Cabinet to assert their independence from the Prime Minister, so the Holland crisis (in which Switzerland was included) confirmed the widening breach in their ranks. Persuaded more by the coolheaded logic of Halifax than by Chamberlain's crisis management style, the Cabinet acknowledged Britain's responsibility to validate its Continental commitment and recommended approval of Hore-Belisha's plan to reorganize the Army in a manner consistent with its newly defined role of defending the Low Countries.[26] The Continental army, at present, existed only as a token paper force, incapable of defending itself for more than several months in the field. During the November talks with Daladier and Bonnet, the French had been coldly informed by Chamberlain that the British could provide only two RA divisions at the outset (i.e., within three weeks of war), and two more later, plus one mobile division; he then pointed to Britain's enormous contribution of naval power and air power to the allied cause as compensation for lack of a greater force on land. Although the four RA divisions and one armored division were fairly well trained and equipped for war on the Continent, the TA was only partially equipped for that role, since its chief responsibility was to defend the colonies and provide for home defense. It would have to be retrained and reequipped in greater numbers and for a different kind of warfare. Based on the experience of World War I, twelve TA divisions were considered sufficient for a Continental war for a single year. But, as Britain's support for its allies constituted the least important priority of the four categories assigned in the Inskip Memorandum, the TA was furnished only with sufficient equipment for training purposes. In case of war, therefore, the TA could not be sent into battle because it lacked proper equipment, which would take upwards of a year to produce under the rule of non-interference with trade, which is why Hore-Belisha advocated a Ministry of Supply organization to speed up the re-equipment of the Army. While the FPC approved in principle the sending of a *bona fide* army to the Continent, it was left to the Secretary of State for War to flesh out its design.

As chief spokesman for the Government, Chamberlain had to articulate those views in his public utterances, whatever his personal feelings might be. But when he did so, as in his 28 January speech at the height of the Holland war scare, he often understated the Cabinet position so as not to offend Germany and close the door to appeasement. He spoke of the great strides being made in the defense program but regretted that "it should be necessary to devote so much time and so vast a proportion of the revenue of the country to warlike preparations instead of to those more domestic questions that brought [him] into politics."[27] In an oblique reference to the Holland war scare, which he characterized as "rumor," Chamberlain reiterated his desire to "pursue the path of peace and conciliation." Harvey thought that speech was "again very weak."[28] A less biased voice at the Foreign Office, Cadogan, initially thought the speech "quite good enough." But two days later he was having second thoughts about it.[29] Halifax could not find anything wrong with the speech, but thought that it failed to signal the new get-tough attitude developing in the Cabinet. Halifax insisted on a stronger statement meant to reassure the French of Britain's recent commitment to defend northern France and the Low Countries, and warn Italy that Britain would not stand aside if the Franco-Italian dispute should result in hostilities.

Chamberlain responded remarkably well to the urging of the Foreign Office. He could not do otherwise. He told the House of Commons the following week that any threat to the vital interests of France would invite the immediate intervention of Great Britain. The House was astounded, even Harold Nicolson, one of Chamberlain's severest critics, was taken aback. He wrote, the "speech was superb. . . .[He] never felt more happy than for months. . . . This is a complete negation of [Chamberlain's] 'appeasement' policy. . . . It can only mean that he realizes that appeasement has failed."[30] Harvey also was impressed.[31] He reported that the "gulf between the Government and the Eden group has been much reduced," as a result of the Prime Minister's speech.[32] Cadogan was also hopeful that it might be a turning point.[33]

But Nicolson and the optimists were wrong to think that appeasement was dead. Chamberlain's speech was a tactical move designed to bolster his sagging support in the country and in the Conservative Party as later became clear. Nevertheless, it succeeded in quieting criticism of his policy for the time being. Chamberlain never had any intention of abandoning appeasement. Sir Nevile Henderson was sent back to his post as Ambassador to Germany on 13 February after having been recalled during the Czech crisis. Henderson was *persona grata* in Berlin and could be counted on to revive Chamberlain's dying policy. He dutifully reported that Germany was not contemplating any wild adventure and that "their compass is pointing towards peace." If treated right, Hitler would gradually become more pacific.[34]

The report, coupled with earlier intelligence reports indicating a lessening of tension in Europe,[35] revived Chamberlain's spirits in February. He sensed a "brightness" that he had not felt for months. The Holland war scare was apparently over, and although Danzig, Memel, and Czechoslovakia continued to be hot spots, they were not considered to be fraught with the danger of a general European war. On 28 January, the Anglo-German Coal Agreement was signed promising closer economic cooperation between the two countries. More good news fueled Chamberlain's optimism. The Cabinet learned that Japan had turned down a proposal to sign a Tripartite Pact with Germany and Italy.[36] And, as the Civil War in Spain was winding down, the Cabinet decided to recognize the Franco regime on 2 March, thereby removing a major stumbling block to improving Anglo-Italian relations.

Exuding confidence once again and seeking vindication for his policy, Chamberlain wrote to his sister in glowing terms of the improving prospects for peace: "All the information I get seems to point in the direction of peace."[37] Chamberlain thought that perhaps it might now be possible to follow up on Lord Norman's recent visit to Berlin and offer some economic concessions in Eastern and Central Europe to encourage Germany to resolve her problems peacefully. Frank Ashton-Gwatkin, Chief Clerk and the Government's chief economist in the Foreign Office, was sent to Berlin 19–26 February to lend support to the efforts of British industrialists to establish better trade relations between the two countries. Ashton-Gwatkin reported that his meetings with Goering and

Ribbentrop were "friendly," and he did not detect any signs of imminent German aggression.[38] As a result, his trip was to be followed up at the ministerial level by Oliver Stanley of the Board of Trade, on 17 March. Chamberlain's spirits rose accordingly.

Unable to restrain himself, he assumed a more active role in promoting his policy of appeasement. On 9 March, he made a rather awkward attempt to create a favorable climate for Stanley's mission, and to influence public opinion at home in the direction of appeasement. At the very least he hoped that it would prevent public opinion from hardening any further against the dictators and in favor of more rearmament, as was likely to result when the Army estimates were announced in Parliament. He gave an interview to the lobby correspondents in which he rendered an optimistic assessment of the international situation for the coming year, and stated that he hoped there would be a disarmament conference in the not too distant future. At Chamberlain's urging, Hoare elaborated on the same theme the following day, in a speech to his constituents on the improving relations among the four major European powers that were leading to a "golden age"of peace.

These sentiments took the Foreign Office by surprise. Halifax was upset, not only with the false impressions conveyed in these speeches but also with the insidious manner in which they were conveyed. Cadogan had met with Horace Wilson just prior to Chamberlain's interview, and he reported that Wilson gave "no inkling of what the Prime Minister intended to say," although Wilson was privy to Chamberlain's most private thoughts. Chamberlain knew the Foreign Office would object to his characterization of the present state of international affairs, so he simply by-passed it, as he had done so often in the past. When Halifax learned of the interview, he tried to meet with Chamberlain for an explanation, but he was told by Wilson that Chamberlain had left for Chequers. Halifax then dispatched a "reproachful" letter reminding the Prime Minister of the importance of speaking with one voice on foreign affairs, and that in the future the Foreign Office should be consulted in advance.[39] Chamberlain agreed to do so, but he would not disavow his statements. Halifax's private secretary recorded that "H. [was] amused and (?)[sic.] half-convinced." [40] As long as Chamberlain remained in power, Hitler could be assured of having his own way in Europe. All eyes in Berlin were focused on Chamberlain. Goering wanted to know what assurances the British Ambassador could give that Chamberlain would remain in office, and that he would not be succeeded by a Churchill or an Eden government.[41]

When Hore-Belisha's "Role of the Army" was presented to the Cabinet on 2 February, supported by the FPC and the CID, he should ordinarily have had an easy time with it, but he did not.[42] Simon, Chamberlain's last remaining shill in the Cabinet, was brought out to challenge the proposal on the familiar grounds of financial responsibility. The cost of £81 million, Simon noted, was double the Army budget for 1937–1938. Next year's budget, therefore, would produce a huge deficit, and each year thereafter, would swell maintenance costs to such a level as could not be met out of the revenue, even in time of peace. The

Chancellor of the Exchequer reminded his colleagues that finance was still the"fourth arm of defense"and "one of the strongest weapons in any war not over in a short time."[43] Halifax rejoined, somewhat surprisingly, that he would rather be bankrupt in peace than beaten in war — the same sentiments expressed earlier by Eden and Cooper. Harvey noted with obvious delight that "Halifax is unrecognizable from the Halifax of a year ago."[44] And Halifax was the one man in the Cabinet whom Chamberlain could not afford to alienate.

Chamberlain took the position that Hore-Belisha's proposal for a Continental army was a rather "new conception of our role."[45] To be sure, he said, an unanswerable case could be made for all the services, but the line had to be drawn somewhere. Certainly the Cabinet had understood the dilemma when it accepted the Five Year Plan in 1937. Halifax countered that the Cabinet was faced with a whole new set of circumstances that negated the previously agreed-upon plan. Chamberlain gave ground grudgingly. Tacit approval was given for the full equipment of the twelve TA divisions (which still could not be equipped for six months to a year), but other aspects of the proposals, especially for the ADGB, were to be considered after the new Minister for the CID, Lord Chatfield, had had a chance to acquaint himself with his new duties.

A hand-picked committee consisting of Chamberlain, Simon, Chatfield, and Hore-Belisha was set up to work out a compromise with the Army. Hore-Belisha had been placated earlier by an initial appropriation of £16 million to be used for badly needed training equipment for the twelve TA divisions, and two weeks later he received approval for a supplemental appropriation of £64,600,000.[46] With the new monies, plans for a reorganized Continental army could go forward for four fully equipped RA divisions to embark within 21to 60 days; two smaller armored divisions; and full equipment for four TA divisions to embark in six months instead of four.[47]

At first glance it might appear that the Army had won a significant victory in preparing itself for a meaningful Continental role. But a closer examination reveals that the decision to appropriate the necessary funds does not, in fact, guarantee that those funds would actually be spent. The Treasury still retained strict control over Army appropriations,[48] and under Simon's watchful eye, they could be subjected to the most stringent bureaucratic procedures, which in turn might discourage the producers and cause them to look elsewhere for military contracts, effectively slowing the Army's program. Also, the sudden infusion of such large appropriations presented labor problems. Where would the skilled workers be obtained? The Royal Air Force had not been able to meet its production quotas owing largely to this problem. Nor could industrial capacity be expanded overnight simply by throwing money at it.[49] This is not to say that larger defense expenditures were unimportant. They were a significant first step. Later developments would determine whether they were meaningful or not. The only way to guarantee effective use of the funds was to establish a Ministry of Supply. Without it, spending could accomplish little. Chamberlain and Simon were well aware of this. Without a Ministry of Supply they could delay implementation of the Army programs, perhaps indefinitely, if Germany could be appeased.

Each man opposed a Ministry of Supply, but for different reasons. Simon's opposition to the new role of the Army at least went with the job. His departmental responsibilities required that he should be an advocate for the Treasury and fight hard to insure its integrity, just as each of the service ministers was expected to advocate programs that he considered essential to the success of his particular mission. Chamberlain's opposition to a Ministry of Supply, however, was much more insidious. (It has been discussed elsewhere and need not be repeated here). Those views had not changed even at this late hour. Together the two ministers, virtually alone, fought a rearguard action against the Army's new role. Chamberlain selected the targets and pulled the trigger while Simon supplied the ammunition.

On the revised role of the Army, Simon legitimately and properly pointed out the extremely serious financial consequences of increased defense spending. Nevertheless, he was unsuccessful in persuading the Cabinet to reject the Army's proposals at the 2 February meeting. He delivered a somber warning about future defense spending at its next meeting. He anticipated a whopping £280 million budget deficit for 1939, which additional taxes, direct and indirect, could not satisfy. Since only £200 million remained of the National Defense Contribution funds, he asked for, and received, authority to borrow an additional £400 million, which he estimated would last through the 1940–1941 budget year, assuming that the level of defense spending did not escalate any further.[50] Such huge outlays might have been avoided if prudent steps had been taken earlier to rebuild the country's defenses.

In contrast to Simon's forthright position, Chamberlain often had to resort to subterfuge, half-truths, and misrepresentations in order to advance his personal agenda. More Machiavellian than he is generally portrayed by historians, Chamberlain pursued a policy out of step with the Foreign Office, the Cabinet, and the country, but he could not overtly oppose or thwart the Cabinet's decision to rearm more heavily, nor isolate the French, nor ignore domestic and foreign opinion. Instead, rather than change direction, Chamberlain gave the impression of conforming to the conventional wisdom of preparing for the worst while hoping for the best because he passionately believed that his policy was the only way out of Great Britain's dilemma. He told his sister just two days before Prague, "I know I can save this country and I do not believe that anyone else can."[51] But no one was buying his policy now, and he was finding it increasingly more difficult to justify it. Since Munich the press had become more independent, but was not immune to political manipulation. In his present difficulties Chamberlain tended to blame the press more and more frequently for his troubles. Annoyed with *The Times* and *The Telegraph* over a series of articles that they were running on trying to understand point of view of the workingman in the defense industries, he characterized them as "humbug." The idea "sickens me, and of course is . . . pure invention from beginning to end."[52] Here again we see Chamberlain's terrible obsession with the Left, which was growing worse as his policy was being scuttled.

Although Hitler would have been only too glad to bolster Chamberlain's domestic position, he was driven by his own agenda to acquire lebensraum before the democracies had time to complete their rearmament.[53] The dismemberment of Czechoslovakia had been in the works before the ink on the Munich Agreement had dried. On the night of 14 March, German troops crossed the Czech border and Prague was occupied the following day. Czechoslovakia ceased to exist as a sovereign state. The news was received in London just prior to the weekly Wednesday meeting of the Cabinet. Chamberlain's cherished Munich Agreement lay in shambles. For the first time, Hitler had incorporated non-Germans into the Third Reich. Until now, his revisionist demands had been couched in the language of self-determination, carrying a semblance of legitimacy. In that context, excuses for his behavior could be made with some justification, and appeasement rationalized. But not any longer. The beast was out of the belly. British and world opinion had been pushed to its palpable limits. Mussolini had to admit that "it is now impossible to present to the Italian people the idea of an alliance with Germany," and that "even the stones would cry out against [it]."[54]

No longer persuaded by the logic of appeasement, and stunned by talk of a "golden age of peace," the British press began to question the Government's policy more aggressively and to reflect more accurately the mood of public opinion by calling for such commonsense measures of national defense such as alliances, increased rearmament programs, and conscription. *The Times, The Daily Telegraph, The Sunday Times, The Observer,* and *The Daily Mail,* which had been among Chamberlain's most reliable supporters in the past, now urged him to abandon appeasement.[55] The conservative *Daily Mirror* came out for conscription and a change in leadership,[56] and the Liberal *Manchester Guardian* and the Labor dailies urged Chamberlain to go a step further and organize foreign support against Hitler. Labor's *Daily Herald* was even prepared to accept conscription if the Soviets were brought into the coalition.[57] Thus, a sedated public opinion, one of the main props of Chamberlain's unilateral government, collapsed, and the very fear that haunted him throughout the rearmament period came to pass — a frightened country demanding war measures, and with them an end to "limited liability."[58]

Chamberlain faced an unusually hostile reception in the House when it convened on 15 March, following Germany's march into Prague. For the first time back-benchers were openly expressing their feelings, much to the alarm of the Government whips.[59] Even Hankey was forced to admit that Churchill's speeches had captured the House and that he "may end up pushing out Chamberlain . . . .not a very reassuring thought."[60] Trying valiantly to maintain his double policy, Chamberlain sought to keep the door to appeasement slightly ajar. He expressed his "regret" over the moral breach of the Munich Agreement, but quickly added that Britain should not "on that account be deflected from our course."[61] He tried to explain away the British guarantee to Czechoslovakia on the rather technical grounds that the Munich Agreement no longer applied because the Czechoslovak state had voluntarily disbanded. His speech did little to inspire the confidence of the House. One member of Parliament noted that "the feeling in the lobbies is that Chamberlain will have to go or completely reverse his policy."[62] Sensing that the time was at last ripe for a change in policy, Eden repeated his call for a Government of national unity.[63] Speaking for Labor, Dalton quickly rejected the idea unless there was a new Prime Minister and a new policy.[64] But Dalton had no need to worry. There would be no Government of national unity as long as Chamberlain was Prime Minister.

Chamberlain misjudged the public mood as well as the House's reaction to Prague, and he was forced to adopt a tougher line than he intended in a speech to his Birmingham constituents just two days later. Responding to his critics, who charged that Prague had demonstrated the failure of his Munich policy and who held him personally responsible for the fate of Czechoslovakia, he sent a belated but weak warning to Germany: "It would be a mistake to suppose that, because the [British Government] believes war to be a senseless and cruel thing, this nation has so lost its fibre that it will not take part to the utmost of its power in resisting such a challenge if it were ever made."[65] Without an accompanying announcement committing the British Government to a specific course of action, Hitler was not impressed by the strong words. It had been reported in the Cabinet that Hitler sneered at Britain's attempt to rule the world with fifteen battleships,[66] and that he predicted that if Great Britain did not introduce conscription by spring, the days of the British Empire were numbered.[67]

Following the Birmingham speech, Chamberlain hurried back to London, where he convened a special Cabinet meeting for Saturday afternoon. Reacting to the dramatic change in public opinion in the country and trying to maintain his hold over the Government, Chamberlain changed direction abruptly. Prague had seriously undermined public confidence in his leadership. Nevertheless, he had to keep the Cabinet in line, so he told it what it wanted to hear:

Until last week we had proceeded on the assumption that we should be able to continue with our policy of getting on better terms with the Dictator Powers, and although these powers had aims, those aims were limited. We had all along, in the back of our minds that this might not be the case, but we felt we had to [try it]. . . .[Chamberlain] had now come to the conclusion that Herr Hitler's attitude had made it impossible to continue to negotiate on the old basis with the Nazi regime.[68]

Yet his actions belied his well-chosen words. Chamberlain's apparent conversion to a tougher line was just another tactical maneuver to allow him to retain the confidence of his Cabinet and party in order to continue his furtive policy of appeasement. The next day he wrote to his sister that he had a plan to put to the Cabinet, the purpose of which was "as always, to gain time, for I never accept the view that war is inevitable."[69] Temperamentally, he was unable to abandon his policy. He had invested too much in it. Self-willed, obstinate, only too sure that he was right on every issue, and driven by a messianic zeal to achieve peace, Chamberlain eschewed any change in his policy. To go back on it now was tantamount to a repudiation of all that he had worked toward in shaping Britain's defense policy and a frank admission of his own personal failure. His hubris simply would not allow it.

The reason for this highly unusual meeting was to discuss an alarming report from Romania's Minister in London, Virgil Tilea, that Germany had presented Romania with an ultimatum for economic concessions. Tilea reported that Germany demanded a monopoly of her exports in exchange for a German guarantee of Romania's borders.[70] But when the Foreign Office inquired about it in Bucharest, the Romanian Foreign Minister flatly denied the allegation. Until now, British attention had been focused on Poland as Germany's next objective, since the destruction of Czechoslovakia had exposed Poland's southern flank to German military pressure. The Tilea incident forced Halifax to weigh carefully the effects of this indirect aggression against Romania for its impact on the balance of power in Central Europe, and ultimately for the entire Continent. Hungary was already becoming a German client state,[71] and from there, with Bulgarian support, Romania could be subjected to enormous German political and economic pressure.[72] Suddenly, all of the Balkan states lay exposed to German penetration, thus negating any pressure that a British blockade might bring to bear on Germany's aggressive designs.

The question Halifax put to the Cabinet was "whether Germany intended to obtain domination over the whole of Southeastern Europe," and if so, "what action should be taken in consequence of that behavior."[73] It is the same question that Stanley and Cooper had wanted answered during the Czech crisis. There could be no question of the Government not taking some concrete action. Since Prague, the country had been roused as never before, and foreign governments were asking what Britain was going to do.[74] The French, Soviet, and U.S. governments were particularly interested.

Having raised the issue in January in conjunction with the Holland war scare, the French Government was expected to renew its demands for a more substantial Continental commitment when President Albert Lebrun and Foreign Minister Bonnet visited London on March 21–22.[75] Bonnet did not disappoint his host. Apologetic but firm, Bonnet insisted on some evidence of Britain's resolve to increase its support for a Continental army, as it had promised in January. France had called up some reservists, set up a Committee of Production with compulsory powers, and raised additional troops in North Africa in response to the dismemberment of Czechoslovakia. What concrete steps had the British taken? Chamberlain pointed to the great success achieved in expanding the Royal Air Force. From a monthly total of 250 in September 1938, the British were now producing around 600 planes per month while the French were producing only one hundred per month at present, compared to Germany's estimated production of 850 to 950 per month.[76] Chamberlain also noted that the role of the British Army had been expanded in February as a result of the Holland war scare. The French were not impressed without the corresponding steps to provide the manpower and the industrial capacity needed to meet the expansion. Only a Ministry of Supply and conscription could ensure its effectiveness. These measures would be the litmus test by which the sincerity of Britain's commitment to the anti-German coalition would be judged. Lingering doubts about "Perfidious Albion" were fueled by German and French right-wing propaganda that "Britain was prepared to fight to the last Frenchman." The talks nearly broke off,[77] but fortunately, for the sake of Anglo-French solidarity, the two sides resolved to work harder to improve their defenses. Staff talks began on 29 March, continued until 3 May, recessed, and were revived again after the Nazi-Soviet Non-Aggression Pact had been signed on 23 August.

Cadogan viewed the international situation as a crisis worse than the one experienced in September. "It was more critical and more imminent, and more acute. . .but the public don't know it."[78] Chamberlain found it increasingly difficult to resist the swelling chorus of opinion for the inclusion of the Soviet Union in a system of collective security against German expansion in Eastern Europe. That view found its way into the Cabinet on 18 March in conjunction with the Tilea incident. Chatfield stressed the importance of obtaining support from Poland, Russia, and Turkey in opposing Germany in Romania.[79] But Halifax agreed to deal the Russians in only if Poland could be persuaded to go along. Hore-Belisha, Stanley, Eliot, and Hoare came out for a Russian alliance notwithstanding Poland's intransigent anti-Soviet attitude.

Chamberlain was quick to exploit the opening presented by Halifax to cut short any talk of a Soviet alliance. Unwilling to deal with the Soviet Union, he came up with a proposal that seemingly would satisfy the proponents of a Soviet alliance while not adumbrating his own goal of accommodating Hitler. He wondered whether "we could obtain sufficient assurances from other countries to justify us in a public pronouncement that we should resist any further act of aggression on the part of Germany. . . .It would have the advantage of giving us a breathing space."[80] Without the benefit of a military or strategic assessment, Chamberlain arbitrarily declared Poland to be the "key" to a security system in Eastern Europe, and he readily secured Cabinet approval to contact Russia, Poland, Yugoslavia, Romania, Turkey, and Greece with an eye toward resisting German aggression.[81] By-passing the Foreign Policy Committee and complaining that the Foreign Office was "as usual, pretty barren of suggestions," Chamberlain conceived of what he described as a "pretty bold and startling idea,"[82] which he easily pressed on a small, hand-picked ministerial committee consisting of Halifax, Simon, Stanley, and himself. He wished to limit Britain's obligations in Eastern Europe by dropping the Balkan states from the list of countries to be consulted during a crisis. This abrupt change in policy was apparently inspired by Chamberlain's obsession for an Anglo-Italian *rapprochement* that might be jeopardized by the Cabinet proposal of 18 March to align with the Balkan states. His "bold and startling idea" included using the good offices of Mussolini, once again, to restrain Hitler.[83] He therefore sought Cabinet approval for the Italian initiative, which, if successful, would buy more time for rearmament and lessen Britain's dependence on the Soviet Union.

Unhappy with the Foreign Office draft (he called it a "monument of clumsiness"), because it warned Italy that a conflict with France would precipitate a war with Britain, he (and Wilson) drafted a more conciliatory letter. Cadogan "struggled against the drafts" because it might look like Britain was "asking for another Munich."[84] But Chamberlain's views eventually prevailed, and the letter was sent.[85] The Italian initiative could also be adduced to neutralize the pro-Soviet voices now surfacing in the Cabinet, since Mussolini presumably would regard such a move as an unfriendly act. Chamberlain was able to convince the Cabinet that Mussolini did not want war,[86] nor did the Italian people, who were deeply shocked by the German march into Prague.[87] The Cabinet was persuaded to go along with this initiative because it offered some glimmer of hope, and because it was being pushed very aggressively by the Prime Minister. Consequently, there was some good reason to expect that Mussolini might indeed be receptive to such an initiative. And if Mussolini did in fact succeed in restraining Hitler, so much the better. And if not, Chamberlain hoped that he might at least drive a wedge between the two dictators. It was indeed a "bold and startling" idea born of desperation.

The Soviet proposal for a Six Power Conference in the wake of Prague was not seriously entertained by the Cabinet. Instead, Chamberlain offered a Four Power Declaration pledging the signatory powers "to consult together if it appears that any such action" affecting the peace and security of Europe was threatened.[88] The French Ambassador was horrified at the proposal to "consult." And Halifax candidly admitted that "a pledge to consult" was not a "very heroic decision." Nevertheless, after some alteration in the language, the proposal went out to Paris, Warsaw, and Moscow for their reactions. The Russian response was predictable. The Soviet Foreign Minister Maxim Litvinov was quite "perturbed" that the British Government had not been more enthusiastic over his proposals for a Six Power Conference. Halifax agreed that "we should get closer to their point of view," and promised to do more to retain Russian goodwill. Nevertheless, the USSR agreed to participate in the discussions if Poland would agree also.[89] But the Poles, not surprisingly, were adamant about not dealing with the Soviet Union, for historical and ideological reasons, as well as out of fear of German retaliation. Poland proposed, instead, a bilateral agreement between the two countries to consult in event of a German threat, which eventually led to the British decision to offer a unilateral guarantee of Poland's independence.

Meanwhile, Stalin was growing more impatient with the democracies and their foot-dragging tactics. On 23 March, *Pravda* issued a stern warning that unless Britain and France showed more devotion to collective security, Soviet suspicions of the democracies would be further aggravated.[90] Soviet suspicions of Britain had been increasing steadily since Munich. Speaking in Moscow on 6 November 1938, Vyacheslav Molotov had fired off an angry warning to the democracies. He accused them of using their military weakness as a pretext for not intervening seriously against the aggressor, because *"they are still more afraid of a workers' movement."*[91] [Italics added]

Hitler adroitly exploited the divisions between the USSR and the West.

At his New Year's Day reception, for example, he spent more time talking to the Soviet Ambassador than anyone else, and in his much-anticipated speech on 30 January, he omitted his customary anti-communist diatribe against the Soviet Union. Charles Corbin, the French Ambassador in London, told Cadogan that it was an "ominous" omission.[92] Stalin responded to Hitler's overture by delivering his strongest warning to the Allies yet. At the Eighteenth Congress of the Communist Party on 10 March, he reviewed the events in the Far East and Europe and interpreted them as an indication of the desire of the democracies to encourage the aggressors "surreptitiously "to make war on the Soviet Union. He pointed to the extraordinary interest being shown in the Western press over the nagging Carpatho-Ukraine question, on which the West pinned its hopes of igniting a Nazi-Soviet conflict, and then warned that "the big and dangerous political game started by the supporters of the policy of non-intervention [i.e.,the West] may end up in a serious blow for them."[93] Despite these and other signs, Chamberlain steadfastly refused to entertain any notion suggesting the possibility of a Nazi-Soviet *rapprochement.*

If Britain was not listening, Hitler was. When Czechoslovakia was dismembered, Hitler awarded Ruthenia to Hungary on 16 March, as a reward for its adherence to the Anti-Comintern Pact, thus ending the brief interest in a Carpatho-Ukraine Republic and quieting nerves in the Kremlin. Stalin's hand was growing stronger while Britain's was diminishing. No longer content to play the role of a supplicant, Stalin insisted on being treated as an equal among the Great Powers. Yet Chamberlain continued to treat the Soviets with the same contempt he had shown for his Labor Opposition. Ivan Maisky blamed Chamberlain personally for this state of affairs. He predicted that as long as Chamberlain was Prime Minister, Britain would never sign a treaty with the USSR.[94]

Poland's intransigent attitude toward any policy associating with the Soviet Union was not unwelcome to Chamberlain, for now he could with some justification allege that the exclusion of the Soviets from an Eastern European security system "comes not from ourselves but from other quarters."[95] On 24 March Chamberlain was forced to deny in the House of Commons the obvious conclusion that the Soviets were being ignored for ideological reasons. Two days later, he revealed his true feelings in a letter to his sister, to whom he confessed "the most profound distrust of the USSR."[96] Whether Chamberlain did, in fact, eschew a Soviet alliance for ideological reasons may be questioned. But the result was the same. Germany could expect little more than moral condemnation for its expansionist policy in Eastern Europe as long as Chamberlain was Prime Minister.

The FPC was reconvened on 27 March, after a seven week hiatus, to discuss a new plan to replace the defunct Four Power Pact. Their new proposal for an Eastern European security arrangement envisioned an Anglo-French guarantee to Poland and Romania if those countries would also agree to a mutual assistance pact that would take effect if the independence of either country was threatened by Germany. The plan had received the backing of the COS, who were asked to prepare a recommendation assuming the Soviet Union to be a

188 Neville Chamberlain and British Rearmament

"friendly neutral." This rather narrow frame of reference obviously was adopted to give the appearance of a militarily feasible and strategically sound policy, but it was quite misleading. The COS concluded that a second front consisting of Poland and Romania was militarily feasible for a short period of time, but only if the Western powers took the offensive.[97] Their report was flawed, however, because it rested on such an unlikely frame of reference. The Allies had no offensive plans. Russian friendship could hardly be presumed under the circumstances, and allowances for Soviet neutrality, or even alliance with Germany, should have been made. A more objective study might have called for an evaluation of the military value of Poland and Romania *vis-a-vis* Russia; or of Russia's observation of strict neutrality (as the Western powers had done in Spain). That only came later in May, after the policy had already been formulated to devalue the Soviet contribution to an anti-German front.

Hoare, a former Foreign Secretary, shed his political bias against the Soviets and spoke strongly in favor of a Soviet alliance at the FPC meeting on 27 March. From a military point of view, he welcomed its deterrent effect. Diplomatically, he feared the consequences of driving Russia into isolationism, which would be construed "in many quarters as . . . a considerable defeat for our policy." And finally, he argued for the alliance on the grounds that it would help with the left wing, both at home and abroad.[98] Chamberlain's vehement opposition to the Soviets, coupled with his Italian initiative, was sufficient to keep the FPC in line. Only Stanley supported Hoare, while Halifax, Simon, and Inskip reluctantly followed the Prime Minister's lead. Halifax's position was crucial to the policy. Having expressed himself initially in favor of making overtures to the USSR, he was nevertheless unprepared to enter into an alliance with a country he did not trust. Trying his best to retain Chamberlain's confidence, Halifax felt that it was important to tie down Poland and Romania first, and bring the Soviet Union into the alliance later. Nor did he wish to alienate Italy while Chamberlain awaited an answer to his letter of 20 March. So he, too, deferred to Chamberlain's lead, but he was not unalterably opposed to an understanding with the Soviets.

Without waiting for Cabinet approval, the new proposal was cabled to the British Ambassadors in Bucharest and Warsaw late that night. The Cabinet was informed of the new policy on 29 March, rendering it virtually impossible for dissenting opinions to be heard. The same arguments were repeated. A choice had to be made between Poland and Russia, and since Poland had been arbitrarily singled out as the "key," the FPC had chosen to guarantee Poland along with France, leaving Russia in the cold. It was argued that there was too much foreign opposition to a Russian alliance. At any rate, the Cabinet was assured by Chamberlain and Halifax that a way might be found to accommodate the Soviet Union at a later date.[99] There was little to be said by the dissidents in the Cabinet. Lacking the expertise, the information, or the time to digest the swift current of events, potential critics of the policy, such as Hoare, Hore-Belisha, and Stanley, were effectively silenced for lack of a well thought-out alternative policy.

Later that day, two important messages were received, that called for yet another round of British foreign policy initiatives. U.S. Ambassador Kennedy passed information to Halifax that Germany was planning to attack Poland.[100] The information was reinforced by information received from Ian Colvin, a correspondent for the *News Chronicle,* who reported that Germany was stocking supplies in East Pomerania, a situation pointing to an attack on Poland "in twelve hours, three days, a week or a fortnight."[101] Colvin went on to describe the consequences of Germany's inevitable annexation of Poland. It would be "followed by the absorption of Lithuania, and then other states would be easy prey. After that would come the possibility of a Russo-German alliance. . . . Finally, Britain would fall into the German orbit."[102]

Halifax and Chamberlain were sufficiently impressed by the information to call an emergency session of the Cabinet the next day. The meeting had been called, the ministers were told, because the Government had received information of a "possible *coup de main* against Poland."[103] Characteristically, Chamberlain was not telling the whole truth. He had been in possession of information concerning Germany's threat to Poland for several weeks but had not acted on it, relying an earlier COS assessment that such moves were aimed at Danzig rather than Poland.[104] Nor did the French place much credibility on the threat to Poland.[105] What really alarmed Chamberlain was the prospect of Poland acquiescing to a German ultimatum, [106]or worse, France becoming involved in a war with Germany over Poland, in which Great Britain must necessarily become involved. By singling out Poland as the "key" to his foreign policy, Chamberlain could pretend that he had a second front. Otherwise, he would have to accede to the demands of the Left and rely on the Soviet Union for a second front. So no matter which way the situation turned — whether in fact Germany did attack Poland, or Poland capitulated to German demands — the result would be disastrous for Chamberlain's policy. The guarantee to Poland also gave Britain diplomatic standing in a Polish–German dispute, allowing Chamberlain to place a restraining hand on Poland if necessary (a la Munich?). Consequently, Chamberlain felt compelled to make some clear declaration of intention to aid Poland as the only way to prevent such a situation from developing. The object of this declaration, he said, was twofold: (a) to forestall Hitler and (b) to educate public opinion.[107]

Halifax had the unpleasant duty of informing Ambassador Maisky of the Polish declaration while at the same time asking Soviet approval for it, so that when questioned about the Soviets in the House of Commons, Chamberlain could assure the Opposition that the Soviets had been "consulted." After having been kept waiting all morning, Maisky was finally greeted by Halifax on 31 March just before going to Parliament. As expected, Halifax's diplomatic effrontery was matched by Maisky's diplomatic evasion. Maisky would say only that he could not give a reply to the British guarantee on such short notice, and that he would have to contact his Government and await further instructions. Minutes later, Chamberlain arose in the House of Commons to announce the unilateral guarantee of Polish independence: "In the event of any action which threatens Polish independence and which the Polish Government accordingly considered it vital to resist . . . His Majesty's Government would feel themselves bound at once to lend the Polish Government all support in their power."[108] In answer to the question of the attitude of the Soviet government, Chamberlain replied that the Soviet Government "fully understood and appreciated " the statement. It was hardly reassuring to the Left. Privately, Litvinov told Ambassador Seeds in Moscow that the USSR had had enough, and would henceforth stand apart from any commitments.[109]

Those who looked to the Polish guarantee as a second front were soon disappointed by the failure to include the Soviet Union, since there was no way to effectively implement the guarantee. Obviously, the guarantee was given primarily for its deterrent effect and not for the specific military purpose of establishing a second front. A COS study concluded that Poland would be overrun in two or three months at most.[110] The guarantee, given publicly, was intended to prevent war by confronting Germany with the prospect of having to fight a European war against a coalition of British states led by Britain. Chamberlain had hoped to restrain Nazi warmongers from reckless adventurism without Britain having to rely on Soviet support. And, if he was successful, the country might yet be spared the dreaded effects of a social revolution sure to be the inevitable consequence of a vastly increased program of military preparedness. And, if the Polish declaration was not successful in deterring German aggression, the Soviet Union might yet be brought in at a later date to supply a more credible second front. David Lloyd George was not persuaded. When briefed by Chamberlain on the situation, he warned that "your statement of today [is] an irresponsible game of chance which can end up very badly."[111] Even the more compliant Cadogan labeled it "a frightful gamble."[112]

At first glance it appears that the declaration automatically committed Britain to the defense of Poland, but a closer reading suggests other interpretations. As Chamberlain was careful to point out, the guarantee was predicated on two conditions. First, Poland's independence had to be threatened; and second, Poland must feel it vital to resist Germany's threat.[113] In answer to objections that this declaration would place British foreign policy in the hands of a foreign power, Chamberlain answered that it was not so, because "it would, of course, be for us to determine what action threatened Polish independence, and this left us some freedom of manoeuvre!"[114] Thus, if Poland should become embroiled with Germany over Danzig, for example, Britain could argue that it was not a threat to Poland's independence, only to her territorial integrity, and the British guarantee would not, therefore, apply. Nor should it be presumed that Britain was committing itself to war. The guarantee only committed Britain to provide all the assistance *in its power*. And, of course, it was for Britain to decide what assistance it could provide. Without Russian support, it could mean that since Britain could not render any effective aid to Poland, the guarantee could not be implemented — a rather cynical policy, as Cadogan admitted.[115] As far as

Chamberlain was concerned, therefore, the declaration was merely meant to be a line drawn in the sand. But as inevitably happens, such lines are often blurred by the changing winds of time. Nevertheless, the reaction to the Polish guarantee in the House and in the country was electrifying. It was Chamberlain's greatest moment since Munich.

Chamberlain's second objective, educating public opinion was somewhat belated and disingenuous. Never once during the rearmament period had he evinced any desire to educate public opinion. In fact, the record shows just the opposite. Special care was taken not to disturb public opinion for fear of creating a backlash that would push the rearmament program beyond the carefully controlled limits imposed by the Treasury.[116] Ever since Munich had lifted the scales from the eyes of a docile press, Chamberlain's correspondence had resounded with bitter criticism of the "fourth estate." He complained to his sisters that a *Sunday Times* article critical of the Air Force program was "most unfortunate;"[117]*The Daily Telegraph* continues to pound "extremely mischievous and stupid" articles;[118] "I have found the newspapers exceptionally depressing this week and I wish that I could censor it;"[119] "I wish the press could be controlled a bit better."[120] When Neville Chamberlain talked of educating public opinion, he really meant cajoling it.

On the day following the Polish guarantee, *The Times* urged Poland to get on better terms with Germany. It was not the first time that *The Times* had been used by Chamberlain as a conduit for his personal diplomacy.[121] Memories of Munich must have haunted the Polish Prime Minister, Josef Beck, as he prepared for his meeting with Chamberlain on 4 April. The meeting proved to be as exasperating for Halifax as it was gratifying for Chamberlain. Beck once again categorically rejected a Russian alliance. Chamberlain could, therefore, continue to oppose closer ties with the Soviets while placing the onus on Poland and neighboring countries, thus enabling him to deny any ideological or political animus. But in his report to the Cabinet, Chamberlain still admitted to a "considerable distrust of Russia."[122] Chamberlain was also pleased with Beck's agreement to a mutual assistance treaty, which would afford Great Britain a second front in the unlikely event that Germany attacked Great Britain first. However, Halifax was disappointed in his failure to persuade Poland to guarantee Belgium, Holland, Yugoslavia, or Romania against German aggression.[123] Sensitive to the fragile state of Anglo-Soviet relations and the recent criticism by Litvinov, Halifax told the Cabinet that he would see the Soviet Ambassador "more frequently to avoid any suspicion that we are cold-shouldering her [the USSR]."[124]

More worrisome than foreign complications, from Chamberlain's point of view, was the widespread talk of conscription among "our people . . .without knowing exactly what is meant by it."[125] Obviously, they had not dwelt upon its impact on posterity and the Empire as thoroughly or as deeply as had the Prime Minister. Of all the difficult issues confronting Chamberlain during the rearmament period, none was more threatening to the unraveling of his policy than conscription. Not only did conscription stand astride his attempts to gain Hitler's confidence, but it was also inherently incompatible with his concept of limited liability, by which he had hoped to control the social, political, and economic outcomes of the rearmament program.

Thus far, the efforts of the employers, the Trades Union Congress, and the Panel of Industrial Advisers to secure skilled labor for the Air Force and more recruits for the Army had been unsuccessful in meeting the demand, and was daily growing worse as the new role of the Army placed an even greater burden on the rearmament program. But Chamberlain continued to rely on voluntarism to meet that demand; he set up the Committee on Defense Acceleration to assist the panel of industrial advisers in its task of finding supply.[126] Halifax urged him to go further and meet with leaders of the TUC which he agreed to do, although he did not think it would be very helpful.[127] The Minister of Labor, Ernest Brown, who had been in conversations with labor representatives since January, supported the recommendation. He readily conceded that labor would resist compulsory measures, but it could be counted on, nevertheless, to cooperate with the Government's call for volunteers to accelerate defense preparations if the Soviet Union was brought into the discussions.[128]

Three days later, Chamberlain's reliance on voluntarism received another setback. Afraid that Hitler might try a "mad dog" attack, Chamberlain quietly alerted the air raid precautions defenses on 21 March to guard against a surprise air raid.[129] The Cabinet was shocked to learn that the country was practically defenseless for the first twelve hours of an emergency. Clearly, an understaffed, voluntary TA was inadequate to the task of defending the home base, listed as the number one priority in the Inskip Memorandum. Stronger defenses were in order, making it exceedingly more difficult for Chamberlain to promote his laissez-faire policy in the Cabinet. Talk of conscription resurfaced at the next Cabinet meeting. This time Chamberlain told his colleagues that while he personally favored conscription, he was afraid that it might upset everything,[130] because he had noticed of late that labor had been "turning a blind eye" to a number of practices to which it would normally have objected.[131] Chamberlain, of course, had no intention of introducing conscription. Never once in his voluminous correspondence or in any committee meetings, or privately to his colleagues, did he ever indicate his support for such a proposal. He was merely attempting to maintain control over a rapidly deteriorating situation. When Chatfield offered the expertise of the CID to study the problem, Chamberlain said he "welcomed the idea."[132] In turn, Chatfield expressed surprise at learning that such an important issue had not been examined earlier. Chamberlain was in no position to object to such a sensible proposal.

Nor could he ignore the swelling chorus of opinion for a more broadly based government and an accelerated rearmament program, which now included his former ally, Lord Weir. Weir, who had returned to Chamberlain's good graces after supporting the Munich Agreement,[133] now felt that Hitler's occupation of Prague had unmasked his true intention to dominate Europe; therefore, he urged Chamberlain to abandon the "halfway house between war and peace" and take the unavoidable last step of "asking the country to adjust itself to work as it would do in war."[134] Knowing Chamberlain as well as he did, Weir deliberately avoided using strong language to lay out his ideas for compelling the diversion of labor. Tactfully, he preferred to let Chamberlain draw the conclusions for himself. But when Chamberlain announced the Polish guarantee two weeks later, Weir expressed his "surprise" that "it was not followed by new proposals outlining new domestic steps, such as the conscription of labor and possibly of wealth," and telling the country that the measures were imperative "to readjust. . .to new conditions."[135]

Such advice, coming from such a staunch Conservative, an industrialist and a friend of business, once again dispels the notion that Chamberlain's policies simply reflected the interests of the Conservative constituency that elected him, and therefore he should not be held personally responsible for the policy that he steadfastly pursued. There were many Conservatives who shared Weir's patriotic views, and were willing to set aside their personal prejudices and take the necessarily prudent steps to prepare the country for war. For most Conservatives, rearmament was not an issue of class, although Chamberlain treated it as such. Chamberlain had moved far ahead of his party on this issue. Conservatives, in general, consistently favored stronger rearmament measures throughout the period. Chamberlain was probably much closer ideologically to the far Right crypto-fascists — such as the Duke of Buccleuch, the Duke of Westminster, Lord Brocket, and Lord Arnold Wilson, who wanted closer ties with the dictators — than to the rank-and-file Conservatives, though they did not necessarily oppose stronger defense measures. (This connection, if there was one, still needs to be explored).[136] Chamberlain admitted that he had actually entertained the idea of an alliance with Germany, "provided it was based on confidence that the policy of force was given up."[137] Was he merely carrying out the policies of the Conservative Party that he represented, or did he have his own political and social agenda in mind? Clearly, it was the latter.

As he had promised Halifax, Chamberlain agreed to meet with the TUC leaders on 23 March, in a bold move to head off compulsion. Conceivably, all the recent talk about conscription had convinced the unions to become more receptive to schemes of voluntary National Service and dilution. Although he sought their contribution, Chamberlain had no intention of including them in the defense program in any meaningful way. To his sisters he conceded that, "Anything we do can only be done by agreement with at least the TUC. I have an idea of the way to approach them, but I am not going to be hustled into rash or foolish commitments which might do us infinite harm."[138] Hopefully, the unions might drop their long-standing objections to the use of women, apprentices, and other semi-skilled workers to satisfy the demands of the employers without having to resort to compulsory measures. The moment was propitious for a *détente* with labor, but only on Chamberlain's terms.

As Brown had predicted, the discussions with the TUC leaders invariably turned to the Soviet Union. They wanted to know why the unions should cooperate with a Government so obsessed with appeasing the dictators. If national security interests were so serious as to justify a relaxation of union rules and practices, should not the same urgency compel the Government to enlist the aid of the Soviet Union and seek other allies? Chamberlain's facile attempt to gloss over the Soviet question failed to convince Dalton and Bevin, who were in close contact with the Russian Ambassador Maisky, that the Soviets were being ignored for ideological reasons. Unfortunately, but not surprisingly, the talks with the TUC representatives produced few results. Hoare described their response to the talks as "most unsympathetic,"[139] whereas Chamberlain felt that he had succeeded in keeping the door open to further representations.

In point of fact, labor's cooperation in the defense program had not been secured. It was a long way off. To abandon his policy would only provide the Labor Party with a platform upon which to rebuild its political fortunes and a possible return to power in 1940. Chamberlain was not about to jettison his appeasement policy just yet, only amend it. He was willing to consult with other countries, but he rejected out of hand any policy suggesting an alliance, for fear of dividing Europe into two warring camps and closing the door to appeasement for good.[140] Nor would he take the necessary steps to implement a command economy. For even if these measures proved successful in deterring Hitler from further aggressive moves, they would cause irreparable harm to the economy and the social order dependent on it.

The failure to gain TUC support for his policy was unfortunate, but not unexpected. Chamberlain now decided on a dramatic increase in the size of the TA in a bold move to forestall the growing demand for conscription. Hore-Belisha was asked by Wilson to come up with some forthright action increasing the size of the TA that could be taken as "immediate evidence that we mean business in resisting aggression." Chamberlain wanted to make the announcement to the 1922 Committee which he was scheduled to address on 28 March. Meeting with Wilson later on the afternoon of 23 March, Hore-Belisha complained that Wilson's (i.e., Chamberlain's) contemplated measures did not go far enough, and that "we would have to have conscription." Wilson said it was out of the question, laying the blame on the trade unions. Nevertheless, Hore-Belisha persisted in his recommendation for conscription, which Chamberlain angrily rejected as "impractical." Hore-Belisha then proposed to raise the level of the TA from 130,000 men to a wartime strength of 170,000 men, and then to double it to 340,000 men. He also proposed to raise the strength of the RA by 16,000, although 50,000 were needed. The total cost was estimated at £80 million and £100 million, [141] which did not seem to bother Chamberlain. He told Hore-Belisha that he "liked it," and the Cabinet readily approved the plan. In the context of Chamberlain's long-standing opposition to conscription, and given his obdurate personality, it is unlikely that his reluctance to introduce conscription stemmed from fear of the Labor Opposition, as he had alleged. Chamberlain's actions were consistent in pursuit of his double policy of limited rearmament and appeasement, and must be viewed from that perspective.

An interesting exchange of correspondence between Sir Edward Grigg, a Conservative MP, and Chamberlain helps to shed some light on Chamberlain's true position regarding conscription. Grigg reported on a speech that he had delivered at a town hall meeting on 30 March, in which he spoke in favor of conscription. With the exception of some trade union leaders, he believed that the people "were in favor of compulsory service."[142] Chamberlain wasted no time in replying. The next day he wrote back to Grigg, cautioning him against pushing the issue too hard: "Public meetings can be misleading indications of TU opinion, and in present circumstances, it is essential that we should not disturb the harmony which was having fruitful results on the output of munitions."[143] This was blatantly untrue. Munitions production continued to experience shortages of skilled labor and was still behind in meeting delivery dates. Chamberlain's response was a subtle attempt to influence public opinion away from a steadily growing demand for greater rearmament measures. Rather naively, or perhaps stubbornly, Grigg wrote back that he would continue in his efforts to rally support for expanding the TA: "I am afraid, lest the hidebound official Trade Union point of view should prevent us from making the full moral impression which is indispensable for that."[144] Chamberlain was becoming more entangled in his web of deception.

Incredibly, in spite of the growing pressure for conscription, Chamberlain repeated Baldwin's pledge against conscription in peacetime in the Commons on 29 March. If Chamberlain thought that his announcement to double the size of the TA, coupled with the Polish guarantee, would satisfy the foreign pressures affecting his double policy, and that his pledge against conscription would appease the Labor Opposition in the House, he was badly mistaken. In "another week of nightmares,"[145] as he described it, thirty Conservative MPs, including Eden, Cooper, and Churchill, tabled a motion for a truly National Government, and raised their demands for a Russian alliance.

Mussolini now sent a discouraging reply to Chamberlain's 20 March letter.[146] The formal conclusion of the Spanish Civil War on April 1 did not lead to the expected improvement in Anglo-Italian relations as Chamberlain had hoped. Instead, Mussolini cited Chamberlain's letter as proof of the "inertia of the democracies,"[147] and with a certain amount of perverse satisfaction, he ordered an invasion of Albania on Good Friday, 7 April. Mussolini's actions could not have come at a worse time for Chamberlain, who confessed to being "dispirited and lonely." He complained that, "The Albanian attack had exposed him to ridicule and weakened his authority in the country" just as the demands for conscription and a Ministry of Supply were gaining strength. No wonder he felt "profoundly depressed and unhappy" and "at the nadir all week."[148]

Then Lord Weir, a more accurate barometer of mainstream Conservative opinion, trying to be helpful, welcomed the invasion as an opportunity for Chamberlain to urge a greater rearmament effort on the nation, achieving "real acceleration, yielding rapid results," notwithstanding his recent decision to double the size of the TA. He wrote to Chamberlain, "Perhaps it is well that Mussolini has so promptly declared himself as a gangster;" he might have kept us guessing for some time. . . .The Albanian development leaves us in no reasonable doubt as to the gangster's game, and it would seem imperative to tell the country that it must readjust itself to new conditions. Nor did Weir anticipate difficulties with the trade unions as Chamberlain had consistently alleged. Weir thought that "Labor and [the] Unions would play up in a helpful way," adding, "As a matter of fact the Unions have played up well in the last few years."[149] Little did Weir, or any of his colleagues, understand the lengths to which Chamberlain was prepared to go in furtherance of his personal policy. And, if Weir, a staunch Conservative and a valued ally in the rearmament program, could not support his policy, on whom could Chamberlain rely for support in the country? How many more Conservatives were about to abandon his policy? If Chamberlain was merely carrying out the policies of the Conservative Party that he represented, could he not reverse his policy in accordance with the line laid out by Weir and supported by his Cabinet and most Conservative press lords? Some historians, while acknowledging Chamberlain's aversion to labor as symptomatic of the class division within British society, have gratuitously assumed that Chamberlain would never have placed his personal agenda ahead of the national interest, and that the policy he pursued in government was taken in accordance with the principles of the party that elected him.[150] Weir's position explodes that myth.

The Italian attack on Albania did not come as a total surprise to the British Government. Rumors of an Italian attack against Albania had been widely circulated in Government circles.[151] Nevertheless, the Government did not attempt to thwart the invasion by a timely warning or by a *démarche* with other countries, although Greece, Turkey, and the British position in the Eastern Mediterranean had been exposed to great risk. Chamberlain did not even bother to interrupt his fishing vacation in Scotland with Joseph Ball to deal with the crisis. He returned the next day, a Saturday, and called a Cabinet meeting for Monday.

The leisurely manner in which the government treated the Albanian Affair prompted Churchill to rise in the House of Commons on 13 April to wonder:

How was it that on the eve of the Bohemian outrage ministers were indulging in what was called "sunshine talk," and predicting the dawn of a golden age? How was it that last week's holiday routine was observed at a time when, quite clearly, something of a very exceptional character, the consequences of which could not be measured, was imminent? I do not know. I know very well the patriotism and sincere desire which animates the ministers of the Crown, but I wonder whether there is not some hand which intervenes, or filters down or withholds intelligence from ministers.[152]

It reminded him of a similar process of "sifting and coloring, and reducing information that had taken place with regard to the air program in 1934, when facts were not allowed to reach High Ministers of the Crown until they had been so modified that they did not present an alarming impression!" Most members thought Churchill was referring to Horace Wilson,[153] but it might well have applied to Joseph Ball or possibly Chamberlain himself.

On 10 April the Cabinet met in a state of confusion to contemplate its next moves in the Balkans. Greece was alarmed by the Italian threat and looked to Britain for assurances of support. Turkey was looking for support also, especially in conjunction with the Soviets.[154] Chamberlain's critics hoped that he at least would renounce the Anglo-Italian Agreement, but he did not. Instead, he drafted a rather "weak" reply, according to Cadogan. Halifax also disapproved of its tone.[155] Unable to agree on a policy, the Cabinet referred the question to the Foreign Policy Committee. Under French pressure it was decided to extend unilateral guarantees to Romania and Greece,[156] as had been done with Poland. To the French Ambassador, Chamberlain looked tired, and "gave the impression of moving forward only under the impulsion of the national will."[157] Reflecting latent sensitivity to the growing criticism of his defense policy, Chamberlain uncharacteristically solicited the views of Churchill, who favored the guarantee, and Dalton and Attlee, who were not impressed with it unless the Soviet Union was included in the scheme.[158] Chamberlain's subsequent announcement of the guarantees to Romania and Greece were favorably received in the House of Commons, but became the subject of renewed feuding with the leader of the Labor Party.

Having reluctantly taken Attlee and Dalton into his confidence concerning the situation in the Balkans, Chamberlain expected that Attlee would prevent the backbenchers from harassing him in the debate, and when he found they did not, he denounced Attlee to his sister: "Attlee behaved like the cowardly cur he is. . . . I have done with confidences to the Labor Party. They have shown themselves to be implacably partisan and they play a game in which they have all the advantages of a truce and none of the disadvantages. It is too one-sided for me to go on with it."[159] But, in fairness to Attlee and the Labor Party, the Prime Minister's words had been misleading in the past. They were now looking for deeds to match those words. While they supported the guarantees, they also wanted an alliance with the USSR to give effect to those words. Labor correctly understood Chamberlain's inveterate desire to appease the dictators, and they wanted none of it.

While Chamberlain intended the British guarantees to deter Hitler from aggression, it became abundantly clear that the deterrent factor would soon be lost without corresponding defensive preparations to render those guarantees effective and credible. Nevertheless, Chamberlain clung to the hope that part-time, voluntary measures would suffice to deal with the problem. Hore-Belisha's report to the Cabinet on 5 April put a damper on that idea when he revealed that the Army was still under-strength and that 100,000 TA personnel would be needed for the year.[160] Chamberlain appointed Simon and Chatfield to meet with Hore-Belisha to study the problem, especially in terms of its supply functions. But when the CID and the Panel of Industrial Advisers concluded, on the basis of doubling the TA and the new guarantees, that the defense requirements of the country could no longer be met through normal business channels and that a Ministry of Supply should be set up at the first opportunity,[161] Chamberlain retreated — ever so slowly. The rearmament program had taken on a life of its own, notwithstanding his own personal feelings. Further obstruction of the defense program bordered on criminal negligence, especially with news of German, Italian, and Hungarian troop movements in the Balkans. Under duress, Chamberlain wrote to Hore-Belisha on 11 April that he was now willing to consider a bill for a Ministry of Supply at the 19 April Cabinet meeting.[162]

Hore-Belisha was elated. He answered Chamberlain's note expressing the "fervent hope that we may be able to overcome any opposition to compulsion at this time."[163] Bolstered by the encouragement he had been receiving from Churchill and Colin Coote of *The Times*,[164] Hore-Belisha decided to press his advantage, and on 15 April he came out for conscription, at great risk to his political career. Hore-Belisha's transformation from a lightweight Cabinet flunky to a leading and forceful advocate for his department was nothing short of astonishing. Ever since Munich, and especially after the junior ministers' revolt in December, and through the intermittent international crises, he had shown more independence from the Prime Minister and more concern for his departmental responsibilities than any other Cabinet official.

The huge demands for manpower occasioned by his decision to double the TA triggered just the kind of problems that Chamberlain had sought to avoid when he originally opposed Hankey's proposal for a balanced defensive force in the early years of the rearmament program. More manpower translated into the need for more equipment, more industrial capacity, more skilled labor, higher wages, inflation, and loss of the export trade. As part of the baggage, Hore-Belisha's proposal inevitably included the eventual cooperation of the Trade Unions with their agenda for social programs and closer collaboration with France. Needless to say, Chamberlain was not pleased to receive this latest request for conscription on 15 April, following so closely on his belated decision to consider a Ministry of Supply. Although he forbade Hore-Belisha to circulate his paper on conscription to the Cabinet, the Secretary of War showed it to Halifax and Chatfield anyway, and they supported its recommendations.[165] Chamberlain was furious. Hore-Belisha described the interview with him on 18 April as "unpleasant:"

He [Chamberlain] said I was adding to his difficulties and that I had made up my mind; that I had a bee in my bonnet about conscription; that the War Office wanted it and that I therefore had a biased view; that I mentioned it in my speeches [most recently on 31 March] and so on. He referred to the repeated pledge Baldwin had given that conscription would not be introduced in the present Parliament, *but it seemed that what really influenced him was the attitude of the Labor Party and the Trade Unions.*[Italics added] From his inquiries he said, he felt it would be a very dangerous course to pursue.[166]

It was clear to Hore-Belisha that Chamberlain had not even read the paper, which carefully laid out the rationale for conscription, the impracticality of having a volunteer TA, and how it would be "open to ridicule."[167] At the conclusion of the stormy interview, Hore-Belisha asked Chamberlain "what he wanted [him] to do." Chamberlain told him to go back and reconsider his plan. Later that evening, Hore-Belisha called a meeting of the Army Council for that purpose; they unanimously agreed that there was no alternative to the War Office proposals.[168] Stanley agreed to initiate the discussion in the Cabinet on behalf of the War Office.

Apparently, Chamberlain was informed of their decision to stick with the proposal, and upon learning that even Hoare and Simon now supported conscription, he experienced a sudden change of heart. He could not discount the possibility of Hore-Belisha's forced resignation. Neither could he afford to lose yet another service minister at this critical moment, or exclude the possibility of a Cabinet revolt. The repercussions abroad, particularly in France and the United States, were too great to risk. Moreover, the aggressor states might be yet encouraged to exploit the situation and undertake new adventures. Slippage among his supporters in the House also added to Chamberlain's problems; forty-six members of Parliament, mostly Conservatives, had placed a resolution for conscription on the agenda on 15 April. Even the employers agreed on the necessity of conscription. Hore-Belisha noted that Chamberlain appeared to be a man "on the run."[169] Chamberlain's bastions of support were falling all around him.

Chamberlain called Hore-Belisha in to see him before the 19 April Cabinet meeting, in which the Ministry of Supply bill was to be considered. Chamberlain's manner had changed abruptly. Aware that the War Office paper on conscription had been circulated to some Cabinet members, he told Hore-Belisha that he could now present it verbally to the Cabinet, but he was not allowed to circulate it.[170] Hore-Belisha then made his case for conscription verbally. Volunteering had not been successful in meeting the defense needs of the country. Anti-aircraft defenses were the most difficult to maintain. Chamberlain's proposal to use Territorial Army personnel to man the searchlights at night on a volunteer basis for a three-to-six-month period was impractical. By law, they could be called up only in an emergency. Other problems of manning the anti-aircraft guns, observer corps, and balloon barrages were impossible to deal with on a voluntary basis. Often, volunteers were required to travel great distances to man their stations, only to find the necessary equipment lacking. It was essential, therefore, to have a fixed program assuring that all the stations were properly manned and equipped to carry out their duties on a steady and reliable basis. But Chamberlain was reluctant to resort to emergency measures because it would "alarm" the country and upset his plans to appease Hitler.

To these objections was added a Foreign Office concern that France was growing restive over the failure of the British Government to introduce conscription at this late hour.[171] President Roosevelt, too, was growing impatient. Ambassador Bullitt implied to Ambassador Phipps on 19 April that if Britain introduced conscription, the United States would be inclined to look favorably on Halifax's request that the U.S. fleet should be deployed in the Pacific to place a restraining hand on Japan.[172] As the danger of war drew closer, Chamberlain could not afford to alienate public opinion in the United States, and he needed to show some resolve to stand up to Hitler. The British strategy of deterrence rested on the concept of a long, drawn-out war, which of course depended on American financial and material resources to carry it through. American opinion, therefore, weighed heavily with London notwithstanding Chamberlain's personal anti-American feelings. Chamberlain, too, understood how psychologically important it was for Hitler to appreciate this special relationship.[173] The French talks and the keen interest expressed by the United States in getting Britain to stand up to Hitler apparently succeeded in moving Chamberlain forward where he had been reluctant to tread before.

Yet Chamberlain continued to resist conscription. Once again he reminded his colleagues of the likelihood of strong trade union opposition to any form of compulsory service, and he observed, somewhat petulantly, that the War Office was the only service likely to benefit from a scheme of compulsory service.[174] But the case for conscription was unimpeachable, as was the case for a Ministry of Supply. The Cabinet at last freed itself of Chamberlain's iron grip and voted to draft a Ministry of Supply bill, which was announced to the House of Commons the next day. Later in the day, Horace Wilson told Hore-Belisha that Chamberlain had decided to introduce conscription, as well, but to keep it a secret.[175]

The decision to create a Ministry of Supply was greeted with "loud and prolonged cheers"in the House of Commons that were muted by the announcement that Leslie Burgin, the Minister of Transport, would be appointed to head it. The disappointment was felt by those members of the House who hoped that Chamberlain, at last, would take this opportunity to broaden his Government and bring in Churchill at the very least. The cry for a more broadly based Government, heard repeatedly since the Munich crisis, was growing louder even in the Conservative Party. From the Opposition, the loudest voices raised against the Chamberlain Government were those of Lloyd George, Sinclair, Attlee, and Dalton. But, with the possible exception of Sinclair, they would not join in any Government headed by Chamberlain. So strong was their hostility toward Chamberlain that even after war broke out in September, Labor representatives refused to participate in Chamberlain's Government. Also joining in the chorus were the vast majority of newspapers. Those in favor of broadening the Government included *The Daily Mail, The Daily Herald, The Daily Mirror, The Evening News, The Daily Telegraph, The Yorkshire Post,* and *The News Chronicle.*[176]

Curiously, Chamberlain's decision to place Burgin at the head of the Ministry of Supply was intended to defuse some of the criticism that must surely follow the announcement, since Burgin was a National Liberal. But the critics were not reassured by his appointment. A more credible reason for Burgin's appointment was to keep Churchill out of the Government. If anyone deserved the position it was Churchill. After all, he was the first and foremost advocate for the Ministry of Supply, as early as the spring of 1936. He was also recognized as having some expertise in defense matters, as First Lord of the Admiralty in World War I and having served on the Air Council. But Chamberlain would have nothing to do with "Winston," whom he feared would steal his thunder in the Cabinet. Besides, Churchill would complicate the foreign situation. The German press had consistently singled Churchill out as a warmonger, and Chamberlain feared that if Churchill were invited to join in the Cabinet, it might permanently close the door to appeasement with Germany.[177] It would send the wrong signal to Hitler, from his point of view. And even if the inclusion of Churchill in the Cabinet sent the "right"message (i.e., of restraining Hitler), Great Britain would still be in for a long, drawn-out, and expensive rearmament program which Chamberlain had arbitrarily decided against. So Burgin was brought in and Churchill was kept out. Nicolson recorded: "There is a very widespread belief that he [Chamberlain] is running a dual policy, one the overt policy of rearming, and the other . . . appeasement."[178] He was right.

Chamberlain added yet another catch to the bill for a Ministry of Supply. It had to be drafted very carefully and it should apply only to the War Office at first.[179] Another feature of the bill was its flexibility; it could be expanded *or even reduced*. Following the ordeal over the Ministry of Supply, Chamberlain moved to the question of conscription. His proposed Military Training Bill was for a rather limited form of conscription. Though designed ostensibly to make it more palatable to Labor, it was also self-serving. It affected only 200,000 to 250,000 young men, for a six-month period of active duty to be followed by a period of inactive reserve duty. Furthermore, it was to be confined to home defense.[180] This latter stipulation caused some anguish in the Foreign Office because it would not be received very well in friendly countries, especially France, if these troops could not be sent abroad.[181] Hoare urged that the bill be expanded to give the Government exceptional powers to call up reservists and to requisition supplies and labor.[182] But Chamberlain did not wish to go that far. He argued that Labor would object strenuously to such wide discretionary powers. Unable to agree on the precise nature or the precise manner in which the highly controversial bill was to be presented, the Cabinet agreed to reconsider it the next day, when it was decided to drop the Exceptional Powers Bill at this time.[183] Chamberlain won another delaying action.

Meanwhile, Chamberlain agreed to meet with the leaders of the GCTUC "as a matter of courtesy," rather than with the leaders of the Parliamentary Labor Party. Citrine and Dalton of the GCTUC were strong supporters of rearmament and could be expected to receive the proposal with more understanding than the "cur" Attlee and the PLP. The meeting with the GCTUC leaders on 25 April proved disappointing, to say the least. Flanked by Halifax and three other ministers, Chamberlain failed to impress upon the representatives of the GCTUC the urgency that compelled the Government to depart from its pledge never to introduce conscription in peacetime. Citrine, who enjoyed unusually good relations with Chamberlain, complained that they had been led up the garden path.[184] Dalton felt "embarrassed" by the Government's action.[185] Hoare, who was present at the meeting, was shocked at the vituperative manner in which Bevin attacked the Prime Minister personally. "Until I listened to Bevin's attack, I had never realized the extent of personal bitterness felt by the Labor leaders against the Prime Minister."[186]

Matters did not improve when the bill was introduced into the House of Commons the next day. The galleries were packed , the benches were filled, and the excitement was unmatched since the days of Munich. Labor Party opposition to the bill was as strong as Chamberlain feared it would be. The Prime Minister tried to reconcile his pledge not to introduce conscription with his announced intention. Present circumstances, he explained, did not warrant the peace label. These were extraordinary times, and they required extraordinary measures. His appeal to patriotism and the cause of peace struck a hollow note. Even Leon Blum's appeal for unity failed to move the PLP. Attlee and Sinclair were furious at Chamberlain's deliberate snub. In the Commons they asked why they had not been consulted, as was the convention. Chamberlain offered the weak excuse that things were simply moving too fast.[187]

Bevin expressed his outrage at the betrayal by the Prime Minister, who, only weeks ago, had renewed his pledge not to introduce conscription in time of peace. He also reminded the Prime Minister of Labor's support for the voluntary National Service program launched in January 1939, relying on the promises of Ernest Brown and Sir John Anderson that voluntary recruitment would not be used as a prelude to conscription. Bevin also accused the Government of incompetence. Chamberlain, Hoare, Simon, and company were the same men who had orchestrated the steady retreat from Abyssinia to Prague. This was the same Government that dealt with Hitler and Mussolini, but refused to meet with the Soviet Union. And now that the Government was faced with foreign problems, it sought to resolve those problems at the expense of Labor because it was convenient to do so, notwithstanding its solemn pledge not to introduce conscription during peacetime. The Government, not conscription, was the answer to the country's problems, he argued. To Bevin, Chamberlain was "the embodiment of the narrow-minded, self-righteous middle-class attitude towards the working class, which had, at every stage, refused to take bold measures in attacking the problems of unemployment and the distressed areas."[188]

Chamberlain paid little attention to the views expressed by "men like Bevin and [Jack] Little, who have a more extreme view [and] are not exactly entitled to speak for the rank-and-file who are more concerned to do whatever will most impress the dictators."[189] Attlee bitterly denounced the Prime Minister in the House debate:

Is the Prime Minister aware that this decision will break the pledge solemnly given to this country and reaffirmed only four weeks ago, that compulsory service would not be introduced in peacetime, that it will increase the already widespread distrust of the Prime Minister, that so far from strengthening this country, it will be sowing divisions in the ranks of the country, and will greatly imperil the national effort, and that this departure from the voluntary principle will meet with strenuous opposition?[190]

Attlee's dire predictions were certainly exaggerated. The labor movement was already divided between loyalty to their country and loyalty to their leaders. In the end, patriotism proved stronger than class judging by the favorable public response to conscription.[191] The German absorption of the Czech state had sparked such an outburst of national indignation that the recruiting stations could not adequately handle the large turnout.[192] And, most of the press favored the decision.[193] The only negative opinions came predictably from the *The Daily Herald,* because of the shameless way in which the Government had broken its pledges; *The News Chronicle,* because of its break with traditional democratic values; and *The Manchester Guardian,* because it now made a true National Government impossible.[194]

Nevertheless, Labor's opposition to conscription had little measurable effect on the rearmament program, aside from the several-week delay in formulating the bill. The greatest obstacle to the program and the focal point of all the criticism continued to be the Prime Minister.[195] The PLP continued to resist the implementation of the bill "line by line." Every conceivable situation was debated long and arduously before being incorporated into the language of the bill. But Chamberlain was not unhappy with the time-consuming motions, and he let the debate drag on. Bevin questioned the effectiveness of the bill, since actual training would not take place for months. It was not until the end of May that the Military Training Bill and the Royal Auxiliary Forces Bill passed by a vote of 280 to 143. In an awkward attempt to sweeten the bitter pill of conscription, the Government also announced conscription of wealth and stiffened penalties on profiteering.[196] The Italian Government was rather pleased at the "modest proportions"of the Military Training Bill.[197] Two hundred thousand militiamen registered at the Ministry of Labor offices for processing, and on 15 July the first recruits reported for duty.

The determined opposition of the PLP to the Military Training Bill stood in stark contrast to the attitude taken by the GCTUC. But as the rearmament program began to pick up after the Holland scare, even the recalcitrant Amalgamated Engineers Union accepted dilution.[198] Chamberlain noticed the distinction, too: "The TUC are also uncertain and though resentful at having been taken unawares, I hear they are inclined to say that this is politics and that they leave politics to the Labor Party."[199] The sudden influx of 200,000 men into the Army in June created a demand for training facilities, equipment, and supplies that could not be met out of existing capacity. The immediacy of the problem demanded the closest cooperation between industry and the trade unions. Faced with a Ministry of Supply empowered to compel industrial behavior, the EEF and the GCTUC took a more pragmatic look at their adversarial relationship and decided to work out their problems in a more responsible and businesslike manner. Meetings between Sir Alexander Ramsay for the EEF, and Jack Little for the AEU, resumed in June 1939 after a year of feuding and posturing. By the end of the month the

AEU was at last prepared to talk about dilution.[200] The trade unions had come to the realization that further opposition to dilution was useless because their members, in fact, had succumbed to the blandishments of industry on a rather large scale.

Would Labor's support for the Military Training Bill have averted war by showing Hitler that the country meant business? Was Labor irresponsible in its attitude toward conscription? Attlee later felt bad about his position, and regretted having taken it because it was misunderstood by the public. To him, it was meant as a vote of no-confidence in the Government. Labor's alleged obstruction of the rearmament program has been vastly overstated. So much of the answer to these questions is locked up in the person of Adolf Hitler, who was given more to diplomacy by instinct than by logical analysis. If, as appears to be the case, Hitler was latched on to the fortunes of Neville Chamberlain and the latter's ability to control government policy, he could be reassured that whatever gestures the British Government might make, "Perfidious Albion" could be relied on to stop short of war.[201] Only a man of Chamberlain's strong character and unassailable political position could have provided Hitler with the assurances necessary to carry out his risky foreign policy. Under this scenario, nothing that Labor did was likely to affect the course of history as long as Chamberlain was in control of government policy. Of course, if Hitler was hell-bent on aggression, as many believe, then nothing could have prevented the catastrophe. At any rate, the full impact of the conscription bill was lost on Hitler as Henderson was instructed to alert Berlin to the defensive nature of the bill, designed not to provoke war but to prevent it.

The German response was swift. On 28 April, Hitler renounced the Anglo-German Naval Treaty and the German-Polish Non-Aggression Treaty of 1934. He also ridiculed Roosevelt's plea for German assurances of friendship toward neighboring countries while making no mention of the Soviet Union. In retrospect, it is clear that the latter's omission was intended as a signal to the Soviets for improving relations between the two countries. Moscow reciprocated the gesture a week later by announcing that Litvinov, a Jew, was leaving the Foreign Ministry and would be replaced by Vyacheslav Molotov.

The complicated and abortive Anglo-Soviet talks in the spring and summer of 1939 offer yet more evidence of Chamberlain's determination to resist Labor by appeasing Hitler, even after he had lost all support for his policy amongst his Conservative allies. While the floodgates of conscription and a Ministry of Supply had been partially opened, Chamberlain continued to seek ways to avoid war. He looked anxiously toward Germany for some sign that Hitler by now had fully appreciated the British resolve to resist aggression in Eastern Europe and was prepared to engage in meaningful discussions.[202] Chamberlain felt reasonably sure that British defenses had become strong enough to avoid the dreaded knockout blow, and that Hitler had "missed the bus" once again. To his way of thinking, Britain's rearmament program had grown significantly stronger since Munich, despite its many problems; and world opinion, especially in the

United States, was mobilizing solidly against Germany. Hitler would, therefore, be compelled to renounce the use of force and return to more traditional methods of resolving Germany's perceived grievances when faced with the prospects of fighting a long, drawn-out war on two fronts, a war he could not be expected to win. Economic assistance and colonial appeasement were expected to lure Hitler away from the German extremists. Consequently, Chamberlain did not feel it necessary to pay the price for a Russian alliance that all of his critics were insisting he must do.

When Britain and France announced their unilateral guarantees to Romania and Greece, the Soviets were invited to make a similar pledge on 14 April "in such manner as would be found most convenient for them." The Soviets responded on 18 April with a counter-proposal for a tripartite Mutual Assistance Pact guaranteeing any Eastern European country bordering on the Soviet Union against German aggression. This proposal was the logical extension of the system of guarantees already given by the British Government. The Soviets wanted support from Britain and France if Russia found itself at war against Germany as the result of Soviet assistance to her Eastern European neighbors. They were also willing to support the Allies if they (i.e., the West) found themselves at war with Germany. The Soviet proposal was not well received by Chamberlain. To accept the Soviet proposal might only add to the certainty of war by playing on Germany's fear of encirclement. Having made up his mind to appease Hitler, Chamberlain discounted the possibility of a war with Germany, thereby devaluing the necessity for a Soviet alliance. He felt that the disadvantages of associating openly with the USSR far outweighed any value of such a pact. He argued that it would antagonize not only Russia's border states but also countries like Italy, Portugal, and Spain. Suspicions of Soviet intentions loomed large in the thinking of the Foreign Office, the Foreign Policy Committee, the CID, and in the Cabinet as well[203] Conceivably, the Soviets might actually try to foment a European war in order to advance the cause of international socialism, just as World War I had brought the workers' movement to the forefront.

Paper guarantees were not worth much, as Hitler and Mussolini had demonstrated. And, of course, what assistance could Britain provide besides an ineffective naval blockade? Chamberlain's own mental reservations about the Polish guarantee are indicative of the climate of distrust in which the Soviet proposal was received. What if Germany attacked Poland? How could Russia honor its pledge if the Poles refused to allow the Russians into Poland? Would the Russians honor their pledge, or would they find a technicality to relieve them of their obligation? What military value could Russia possibly serve after the Stalinist purges had played havoc with their armed forces? The purges were thought to have weakened the Russian Army, but the resistance it put up in the Far East against Japan was conveniently ignored, as was Russia's ability to place a restraining hand on Japanese adventurism in the Far East.

On 19 April the COS were at last asked by the Foreign Policy Committee to study Russia's military value as an ally. They concluded that Russian military assistance would not be of any great value due to the country's internal problems, as well as its inability to manufacture weapons to supply Poland and Romania. Communication and transportation problems also reduced Russia's offensive capability. Only at sea might the Russian Navy provide significant military assistance by tying up a large part of the German fleet in the Baltic. However, Russia's cooperation would be invaluable in denying sources of raw material to Germany. The report closed on a rather ominous note, drawing attention to the very grave military dangers to the Allies inherent in the possibility of an agreement between Germany and Russia.[204] And although there had been rumors and warnings of a Nazi-Soviet *rapprochement*, Chamberlain was not inclined to place much credibility in the reports because they ran counter to his own scheme of things. The COS report only served to reinforce Chamberlain's predilections against a Soviet alliance. He confessed to being deeply suspicious of Russia. "I cannot believe that she has the same aims and objects that we have. . . .She is afraid of Germany and Japan and would be delighted to see other peoples fight them. She is suspected by everyone and it would be fatal to form a Balkan front against Germany. But we must not antagonize her."[205]

Only Hoare, Stanley, and Malcolm MacDonald spoke in favor of a Soviet alliance at this time. Halifax then summed up the sense of the Cabinet on the Soviet proposal. On the basis of the COS report, Russia's military value was not thought to be of great significance. But, he added, "We should endeavor to order our policy so that if war broke out, Russia would be either neutral or on our side."[206] Chamberlain agreed that "we must not antagonize her," although he continued to remain deeply suspicious of her.

The Russian proposal was formally rejected on 6 May. Two days later the British responded with a suggestion that the Soviets should make a unilateral declaration of support for only those countries which requested it, notwithstanding the fact that Poland and most of Russia's neighbors were unalterably opposed to associating openly with the Soviet Union. The British proposal was ludicrous on its face. It was not much different the 18 April draft. The tactic was merely a delaying action. Chamberlain was still seeking a tangible sign from Hitler to revive his dying hopes of appeasement. He sent a signal through *The Times* on 3 May. The editorial in *The Times* read, "Danzig is not worth a war." Chamberlain's alter ego, Horace Wilson, was thought to have instigated it.[207] At the same time, Cadogan confronted Wilson with a telephone intercept, "which look[ed] like No.10 were talking appeasement again."[208] Chamberlain had to tread the appeasement waters very carefully. That explains why Chamberlain was not so eager to grasp at Dirksen's proposal to improve Anglo-German relations, unless the proposals were published.[209]

Fears of continued appeasement were fueled by the failure to include men like Churchill and Eden in the Government. If British policy toward the dictators had changed, then why not bring into the Government those whose views had now been accepted as Government policy? The return of Nevile Henderson to Berlin to soften the announcement of conscription raised doubts as to whether Great Britain had actually changed its policy of appeasing Hitler. Under such circumstances, the Soviet Government had good reason to doubt Britain's resolve to resist aggression in Eastern Europe.

On 15 May the British Government was informed by the Soviets that its proposal of 8 May was unacceptable because it lacked "reciprocity." If Russia should find itself at war with Germany as a result of German aggression in the Baltic, for example, would Great Britain be obligated to defend Russia? The British offer to consult in such a situation did not meet Soviet requirements. The Soviet Union wanted nothing less than a triple alliance now. Meanwhile, the British Government had received information from the Vatican Minister, quoting a "highly reliable" source, that Italy was mediating between Germany and Russia, and that "agreement has practically been obtained."[210] Not enough information has yet been released yet from Soviet sources to untangle the web of Soviet machinations leading up to the Nazi-Soviet Non-Aggression Pact in August, but signs of a Russo-German *rapprochement* were becoming noticeably stronger in the spring.[211] Not-so-secret trade talks and diplomatic leaks hinted at the possibility of its realization.

While Chamberlain was willing to discount these reports, the CID and the military experts were not. Asked by the Foreign Office for its evaluation of Russia if it were not an ally, the COS pronounced in favor of a Soviet alliance for fear of the consequences of not allying.[212] It might throw Russia into Germany's arms, and even if it did not, it would leave Russia in a predominant position at the end of hostilities.[213] Suddenly faced with the stark reality of Russia's strong bargaining position, members of the Cabinet who were previously against the alliance now expressed support for it. Even Halifax, who was also suspicious of Soviet motives, carefully shifted his position. He now thought that an agreement with Russia should be reached at the earliest opportunity[214] because there was a serious danger that if Britain did not accept the Soviet proposals, negotiations would be broken off.[215] The Foreign Policy Committee was impressed by these three factors:

1. The undesirability of further delay, for fear of a Nazi-Soviet rapprochement
2. The difficulty in submitting another proposal in writing, only to have it rejected again
3. Fear that negotiations would break down.[216]

The French also were also pressing the British for closer relations with Russia, much to Chamberlain's distress.[217] He was visibly upset with the cascading tide of opinion against his Russian policy. He wanted to know "what effective help Russia could in fact give;" Chatfield referred him back to a previous memorandum (CP 108). Flustered, Chamberlain pulled out all the stops, but to no avail; he raised the question of what impact an Anglo-Soviet alliance might have on the Dominions. The Dominions, now becoming more anti-German,[218] were not strongly opposed to a Soviet alliance, and some even favored it.[219] For the first time in office, Chamberlain found himself openly in the minority on an important issue. Later, he complained that the only support he could get was from R.A. Butler, "and he was not a very influential ally."[220] Even Chatfield, a staunch anti-Communist, deserted him. Nor did Poland and Romania give him any grounds upon which to reject the alliance, as he had hoped.[221] They maintained a discreet silence on the latest proposal.

After a meeting between Vansittart and Maisky on 17 May had failed to elicit a favorable response from the Soviet side, Chamberlain reluctantly bowed to the overwhelming pressure favoring a Soviet alliance, and accepted the necessity of coming to terms with the hated Soviets.[222] But that did not prevent foot-dragging tactics. He now offered a mutual assistance pact to the Soviet Union under the auspices of the League of Nations, but Molotov quickly rejected that idea. Later, Chamberlain confessed that if he had had his way, he would have "closed matters with the Russians a long time ago,"[223] but he "could not carry [his] colleagues with [him]."[224] And so the Soviet talks went forward without his approval, just as conscription and the Ministry of Supply bill had gone forward without his support.

While the basis for his objections to a Soviet alliance appear to be ideological and prejudicial, Chamberlain was also afraid that "it would only create a bloc which would make negotiation with the totalitarians difficult, if not impossible."[225] In July, when military talks were about to begin, General Ironside told Hore-Belisha that Chamberlain's policy was one of "not hurrying on getting in Russia"[226] although British intelligence sources warned of a Nazi-Soviet *rapprochement*. Chamberlain placed little value on these reports. [227] There can be little doubt that the failure of Britain and the Soviet Union to reach an agreement on a mutual assistance treaty was the result of Neville Chamberlain's personal interference in the process. [228] But this is not to say that Soviet conduct was without fault. And although the talks had little impact on the rearmament program, they are significant for purposes of this discussion, because they shed light on Chamberlain's personal influence on the formulation and implementation of Government policy and demonstrate the lengths to which he would go in furtherance of "his" policy, notwithstanding the fact that it had no real basis for public support.

The military mission finally left for Moscow on 5 August, and discussions did not get under way until 12 August. The discussions nearly broke down when it was learned that the British representatives did not possess the proper authority to conclude an agreement. It was the last straw for the Russians, who, if they had not been convinced by now, were sure that the British had not been sincere in their desire to oppose Hitler. They now decided to make a deal with Hitler.

NOTES

1. Henderson, 180; CAB 23/97/2, 25 January 1939; CAB 27/624.

2. DBFP, series 3, vol 3, #505, 2 January 1939.

3. Ibid, #403, 8 December 1938; #434, 16 December 1938.

4. Ibid, #505, 2 January 1939.

5. *Inskip Diary 2,* 23 January 1939.

6. T. Taylor, *Munich,* 938.

7. CAB 23/97/1, 18 January 1939; CAB 23/97/2, 25 January 1939; *Cadogan Diaries,* 17–24 January 1939, 139–144; *Harvey Diaries,* 17 January 1939, 245.

8. CAB 23/97/2, 25 January 1939; COS 830.

9. *Cadogan Diaries,* 17 January 1939, Cadogan Memorandum, "Possibility of a German Attack on the West," 139–140.

10. CAB 23/97/1, 18 January 1939; Wilheim Deist, Manfred Messerschmidt, Hans-Erik Volkmann, and Wolfram Wette, *Germany and the Second World War: The Build-up of German Aggression,* vol. 1 (London: Oxford University Press, 1990), 675–677.

11. CAB 24/282/3; COS 830.

12. CAB 24/283/34.

13. COS 827; CP 28(39).

14. HB 1/5, 9 January 1939.

15. CAB 24/282/27.

16. HB 5, 19 January 1939.

17. Ibid., 24 January 1939.

18. Minney, 171.

19. CP 33(39).

20. *Inskip Diaries,* 2, 17 January 1939.

21. CAB 23/97/5, 2 February 1939.

22. *Inskip Diaries,* 2, 17 January 1939.

23. CAB 23/97/2, 25 January 1939.

24. HB 1/5, 26 January 1939.

25. *Harvey Diaries,* 19 January 1939, 246–247.

26. CAB 23/97/2, 25 January 1939.

27. Chamberlain, 249–257, speech to the Birmingham Jewelers' Association.

28. *Harvey Diaries,* 29 January 1939, 248.

29. *Cadogan Diaries,* 28 January 1939, 30 January 1939, 145.

30. *Nicolson Diaries,* 383.

31. *Harvey Diaries,* 12 February 1939, 251.

32. Ibid., 14 February 1939, 253.

33. *Cadogan Diaries,* 7 February 1939, 147.

34. *DBFP,* series 4, vol. 3, 592–593, 24 February 1939; Henderson, 192–198. On the other hand, Cadogan commented at the same time that Hitler would love nothing more than to smash the British Empire. *Cadogan Diaries,* 24 February 1939, 151–152.

35. CAB 23/97/7, 15 February 1939.

36. Ibid.

37. 18/1/1086, 19 February 1939.

38. CAB 23/97/10, 8 March 1939. The British Financial Attaché in Berlin, however, was not as optimistic and he advised against further ventures until the Germans gave something in return.

39. Lord Halifax, *In Fullness of Days* (London: Collins, 1957), 232; *Cadogan Diaries*, 11 March 1939, 155.
Harvey Diaries, 13 March 1939, 261.

41. Gilbert, *Churchill: A Life,* 610.

42. CAB 23/97/5, 2 February 1939. In point of fact, the cost of the proposal was only £11 million more than requested in the previous year's estimates that had been reduced by £70 million.

43. Ibid.

44. *Harvey Diaries*, 17 February 1939, 255.

45. CAB 23/97/5, 2 February 1939.

46. CAB 23/97/6, 8 February 1939; CAB 23/97/8, 22 February 1939.

47. CP 49(39).

48. *HB* 1/5, 19 January 1939 and 24 January 1939.

49. For example, a new factory had been started to manufacture 3.7-inch anti-aircraft guns, but production was not expected to begin until autumn. Minney, 175. It would take at least a year to ready the factories for a significant increase in production. Bond, *British Military Policy*, 328.

50. CAB 23/97/6, 9 February 1939.

51. NC 18/1/1089, 12 March 1939.

52. Ibid.

53. Cf. "Hossbach Memorandum," DGFP, series D, vol.1, #19, 10 November 1937 and #93, 2 January 1938.

54. *Ciano Diaries*, 19 March 1939, 48.

55. Frank Gannon, *The British Press and Germany, 1936–1939* (Oxford: Clarendon Press, 1971) 236, 260; Dennis,180–195.

56. Dennis, 180.

57. Ibid., 257.

58. Templewood, 339.

59. Dennis, 196.

60. Roskill, 397, Hankey to Burgon Beckersteth, 29 April 1939.

61. *Debates*, 345: 437ff., 15 March 1939.

62. *Nicolson Diaries*, 386.

63. *Debates*, 345: 461ff., 15 March 1939.

64. Ibid., 345: 535.

65. Chamberlain, 275.

66. CAB 23/98/2; 25 January 1939.

67. Aster, 40.

68. CAB 23/98/1 18 March 1939

69. NC 18/1/1090, 19 March 1939.

70. CAB 23/98/12, 18 March 1939.

71. Hungary had joined the Anti-Comintern Pact in February.

72. FO 371/22958, c3565/13/18, memorandum by Jebb, 18 March 1939.

73. CAB 23/98/11, 15 March 1939.

74. *Cadogan Diaries,* 20 March 1939, 161.

75. On 11 March, Halifax had informed Hore-Belisha that the French wanted to see some evidence of Britain's determination to make all of its resources available and effective in case a war should break out. HB 5/18, 11 March 1939.

76. CID 1659-B.

77. NC 18/1/1091, 26 March 1939.

78. *Cadogan Diaries*, 20 March 1939, 161.

79. CAB 23/98/12, 18 March 1939.

80. Ibid.

81. Ibid.

82. NC 18/1/1090, 19 March 1939.

83. Ibid. He wrote to his sister that he was "preparing another appeal to the same quarter as before, [i.e., Italy] . . . in the hope of putting on a brake."

84. *Cadogan Diaries*, 20 March 1939, 162.

85. The Foreign Office was right. Ciano cited the letter as proof of the "inertia of the democracies." *Ciano Diaries*, 23 March 1939, 51.

86. CAB 23/98/14, 22 March 1939; PREM 1/329, Joseph Ball to Horace Wilson; NC 18/1/1091, 26 March 1939.

87. *Ciano Diaries*, 19 March 1939, 48.

88. CAB 23/98/13, 20 March 1939.

89. CAB 23/98/14, 22 March 1939.

90. Max Belof, *The Foreign Policy of Soviet Russia*, (Oxford: Oxford University Press, 1949), vol. 2, 231.

91. Ibid., 219–220. [Italics added.]

92. *Cadogan Diaries*, 1 February 1939, 146.

93. Belof, 220–223.

94. Ivan Maisky, *Who Helped Hitler?* (London: Hutchinson, 1964), 119–121.

95. The "other quarters" were Finland, Yugoslavia, Italy, Spain, and Portugal, who also voiced strong opposition to a Soviet alliance. CAB 27/624, 27 March 1939.

96. NC 18/1/1091, 26 March 1939.

97. CP 74(39).

98. CAB 27/624, 27 March 1939.

99. CAB 23/98/15, 29 March 1939.

100. CAB 23/98/16, 30 March 1939.

101. Colvin, 194–195; Aster, 99–101.

102. NC 18/1/1092, 2 April 1939.

103. CAB 23/98/16, 30 March 1939; NC 18/1/1092, 2 April 1939.

104. CAB 23/98/16, 30 March 1939.

105. Ibid.

106. NC 18/1/1092, 2 April 1939.

107. CAB 23/98/16, 30 March 1939.

108. *Debates*, 345: 2415, 31 March 1939.

109. Aster, 158.

110. CAB 23/98/16, CP 74, 30 March 1939.

111. Aster, 115.

112. *Cadogan Diaries*, 30 March 1939, 165.

113. NC 18/1/1092, 2 April 1939.

114. Ibid.

115. Later Cadogan admitted it might seem to have been "cruel" to Poland, but added that the Poles should have been aware of Britain's military situation and of the imminence of the peril that threatened them. *Cadogan Diaries*, 167.

116. Templewood, 339.

117. NC 18/1/1075, 6 November 1938.

118. NC 18/1/1076, 13 November 1938.

119. NC 18/1/1079, 11 December 1938.

120. NC 18/1/1085, 12 February 1939.

121. On the previous night, Geoffrey Dawson, editor of the *Times,* had been seen outside the Prime Minister's room. Cf. Dalton, 244.

122. CAB 23/98/18, 5 April 1939.

123. Ibid.

124. Ibid.

125. NC 18/1/1091, 26 March 1939.

126. CAB 23/98/12, 18 March 1939.

127. Ibid.

128. Ibid.

129. NC 18/1/1091, 26 March 1939.

130. CAB 23/98/14, 22 March 1939.

131. NC 18/1/1091, 26 March 1939.

132. Ibid.

133. NC 7/11/31/285, Weir to Chamberlain, 25 October 1938. On 28 October 1938, Weir told Chamberlain that he was "standing by entirely at your disposal." NC 7/11/31/286.

134. NC 7/11/32/293, Weir to Chamberlain, 20 March 1939.

135. NC 7/11/32/294, Weir to Chamberlain, 11 April 1939.

136. After war had begun in September 1939, and Hankey had returned to the Cabinet, he made a cryptic reference to a meeting "of a very defeatist character" he was about to attend with the "fifth column," i.e., at the Duke of Westminster's home. Roskill, 431. Also cf. R. Griffiths, *Fellow Travelers of the Right* (London: Constable, 1980); Nicholas Bethell, *The War Hitler Won* (New York: Holt, 1972); DGFP, series D, vol. 8, #134, 25 September 1939; Cowling, 358.

137. NC 18/1/1116, 10 September 1939.

138. NC 18/1/1091, 26 March 1939.

139. Templewood, 337.

140. NC 18/1/1101, 28 May 1939.

141. HB 1/5, 28 March 1939.

142. NC 7/11/32/88, Grigg to Chamberlain, 30 March 1939.

143. NC 17/11/32/94, Chamberlain to Grigg, 31 March 1939.

144. NC 7/11/32/95, Grigg to Chamberlain, 3 April 1939.

145. NC 18/1/1092, 2 April 1939.

146. DBFP, Series 3, vol. 4, #573, 574, 1 April 1939.

147. *Ciano Diaries,* 23 March 1939, 51.

148. NC 18/1/1094, 15 April 1939.

149. Ibid.

150. This is Shay's contention. But in Shay's defense, it must be pointed out that he did not have access to the *Chamberlain Papers.*

151. *Harvey Diaries,* 4 April 1939, 272.

152. *Debates,* 346: 96, 13 April 1939.

153. Gilbert, *Churchill,* 612.

154. Irving, 60–61; 72.

155. *Cadogan Diaries,* 11 April 1939, 172.

156. Ibid., 173; CAB 23/98/20, 13 April 1939.

157. Parker, *Chamberlain and Appeasement,* 222.

158. CAB 23/98/20, 13 April 1939.

159. NC 18/1/1094, 15 April 1939.

160. CAB 23/98/18, 5 April 1939.

161. CAB 24/285/84.

162. HB 1/5, 11 April 1939.

163. PREM 1/336, 12 April 1939, Hore-Belisha to Chamberlain.

164. Ibid., 23 March 1939; HB 1/5, 11 April 1939.

165. Ibid., 17 April 1939.

166. Ibid., 19 April 1939.

167. Ibid., 18 April 1939.

168. Ibid.

169. Ibid., 19 April 1939.

170. Ibid.

171. CAB 23/98/21, 19 April 1939.

172. MacDonald, 152.

173. Rock, *Chamberlain and Roosevelt,* 175.

174. CAB 23/98/21, 19 April 1939.

175. HB 1/5, 20 April 1939.

176. Gannon, 198.

177. NC 18/1/1106, 1107, 8 July 1939 and 15 July 1939.

178. *Nicolson Diaries,* 21 April 1939, 292.

179. CAB 23/98/21, 19 April 1939.

180. CAB 23/99/22, CP 91(39), 24 April 1939.

181. Ibid.

182. Ibid.

183. CAB 23/99/23, 25 April 1939.

184. PREM 1/387.

185. Dalton, 250.

186. Templewood, 338.

187. *Debates,* 346: 1155 ff., 27 April 1939.

188. Bullock, *Bevin,* 638.

189. NC 18/1/1096, 29 April 1929.

190. *Debates,* 346: 1170, 27 April 1939.

191. NC 18/1/1097–1098, 29 April 1939 and 7 May 1939; *Harvey Diaries,* 29 April 1939, 285. A Gallup Poll showed that 58% of those polled favored conscription. *Gallup Polls,* 18.

192. Dennis, 190; Minney, 186.

193. Colin Coote of *The Times* to Hore-Belisha. Hore-Belisha noted that the "Sunday papers are practically unanimous." HB 1/5, 23 April 1939.

194. Dennis, 223.

195. *Harvey Diaries,* 27 April 1939, 284; 29 April 1939; 285.

196. *Debates,* 346:1153, 27 April 1939; CAB 23/99/29, CP 122, 23 May 1939.

197. *Ciano Diaries,* 26 April 1939, 172.

198. Parker, "British Rearmament", 340.

199. NC 18/1/1096, 29 April 1939.

200. Parker, "British Rearmament", 341.

201. To Lloyd George it was transparently clear that "the Government has no fight in them . . . .[The dictators] are quite convinced you won't fight. So am I. The Germans know it, and they are just looking at your record." Peter Rowland, *David Lloyd*

George (New York: Macmillan, 1975), 750. Dirksen reported that "Chamberlain's personality gives a certain guarantee that British policy will not be delivered into the hands of unscrupulous adventurers." *DGFP*, Series D, vol. 6, #645, 10 July 1939, Dirksen to Foreign Ministry. And on the eve of World War II, Ribbentrop asked Henderson whether he "could guarantee that the Prime Minister could carry the country with him in a policy of friendship with Germany." DGFP, series 3, vol. 7, #455, Henderson to Halifax, 29 August 1939.

202. NC 18/1/1095, 23 April and NC 18/1/1096, 29 April 1939. Chamberlain described Hitler's 28 April speech as "pacific." He also mentioned receiving German feelers for a relaxation of tension between the two countries, but without accompanying guarantees he did not see how he could entertain them. *Cadogan Diaries,* 5 May 1939, 178. Also, NC 18/1/1108, 23 July 1939.

203. Besides Chamberlain, strong doubts about Russian sincerity were expressed by Halifax, Inskip, Morrison, Cadogan, and Chatfield. CAB 27/624; *Cadogan Diaries,* 175.

204. CAB 24/285/95.

205. NC 18/1/1096, 29 April 1939.

206. CAB 23/99/24, 26 April 1939.

207. *Harvey Diaries*, 3 May 1939, 286.

208. *Cadogan Diaries*, 3 May 1939, 178.

209. NC 2/24A, 15 May 1939. Dirksen's proposal included (1) a renewal of the Anglo-German Naval Treaty; (2) reopening trade talks; and (3) the establishment of a large fund by the German Government for relocating refugees.

210. *Inskip Diaries, II*, 9 May 1939.

211. Francois-Poncet to Sir Percy Lorraine, DBFP, series 3, vol.4, #429, 5 May 1939; Ashtakov-Schnurre talks, #529. Also, cf., #469–471, 639–647. *Cadogan Diaries,* 18 May 1939, 181: "It is noticeable that during the last few months anti-Soviet propaganda in Germany has been almost completely damped down; we know that certain members of the German General Staff are in favor of an understanding with the Soviet Union, and we have some evidence that they have lately again been advocating it." Also, CAB 23/99/26, 3 May 1939; CAB 23/99/27, 10 May 1939; *Harvey Diaries,* 20–21 May 1939, 290.

212. CAB 23/99/28, 17 May 1939, CP108(39); COS 902. Also, the COS had learned that the German General Staff favored a Soviet alliance. *Cadogan Diaries,* 18 May 1939, 181.

213. CP108(39); CP116(39).

214. CAB 23/99/28, 17 May 1939.

215. CP 124(39).

216. CP 115(39).

217. Ibid., NC 18/1/1100, 20 May 1939.

218. CAB 23/98/16, 30 March 1939.

219. CP122(39).

220. NC 18/1/1101, 28 May 1939. Butler was Under-secretary of State and a Chamberlain loyalist.

221. Parker, *Chamberlain and Appeasement,* 230.

222. NC 18/1/1100, 20 May 1939.

223. NC 18/1/1108, 23 July 1939.

224. NC 18/1107, 15 July 1939. Also, cf. NC 18/1/1101, 28 May 1939; NC 18/1/1102, 10 June 1939; NC 18/1/1105, 2 July 1939.

225. NC 18/1/1100, 20 May 1939; NC 18/1/1101, 28 May 1939.

226. *Ironside Diaries*, 77. CAB 23/100/39, 26 July 1939.

227. CAB 23/100/39, 26 July 1939.

228. Hill, 61.

Chapter 8

Epilogue

For all practical purposes, the story of Britain's rearmament program culminated with the passage of the Ministry of Supply Bill in May 1939. The lid on the rearmament programs had been lifted. And, more important, the program began to take on a life of its own, despite Chamberlain's efforts to control it. Although Chamberlain's decisive interference in the program finally came to an inglorious end in the spring of 1939, that did not deter him from attempting to influence its development thereafter. Retrospectively, his conduct of the "Phony War" (September 1939 to May 1940) can be interpreted as an extension of his earlier efforts to avoid the terrible consequences of a command economy.

The additional cost of housing, training, and equipping the new conscripts thrust a seemingly intolerable burden on the Treasury. Alarmed, Simon circulated a highly sensitive document to the Cabinet on 23 May, trying to regain control over defense spending. He noted that rearmament was proceeding "nicely now, and could not some orderly priority be set up for future spending?"[1] The paper was obviously inspired by Chamberlain. It ran into stiff opposition from the service ministers and Chamberlain retreated tactfully behind yet another hand-picked committee consisting of Simon, Hoare, Inskip, Runciman, Morrison, Maugham, and Oliver Stanley. All of the defense ministers were excluded, including Chatfield, who had expressed skepticism about finances earlier when he had the temerity to ask where the additional funds were coming from, since he had been told a year ago that there was no more money to be found for defense purposes.

Their report was presented at the 5 July Cabinet meeting. To pay for the sharp rise in defense spending from £580 million in February to £750 million in July,[2] the committee recommended that indirect and excess profits taxes should be increased pushing the income tax to a record inter-war high of 7s. Also, the pound sterling was devalued, providing a short-term stimulus to the export trade, on which about 25 percent of the rearmament program depended. Simon again desperately sought to prevent a further escalation in defense spending by reimposing Treasury control over expenditures. He suggested that the service ministers should consult with him first if they had any problems.[3] Despite Chamberlain's backing for what Hore-Belisha called a "gloomy and half-baked" Treasury proposal to slow down rearmament,[4] Simon's attempt at re-establishing financial controls wilted under the combined pressure of the service ministers, concerned about the transparent weaknesses in the defense program, which were still considerable. In addition, Danzig was heating up. Only 72 of 240 heavy AA pieces were available; only 108 of 266 light AA guns; 144 of 240 anti-tank guns; and only 30 percent of approved ammunition stores were in supply. Tanks, small arms, gauges, and fuses also were in short supply.[5] Apparently the defense ministers took the Polish declaration much more seriously than the Prime Minister did.

Unable to do much about the constantly expanding defense programs except to delay their implementation, Chamberlain turned his attention to two major problems during the summer of 1939, both linked to the cause of appeasement: the Soviet alliance and Winston Churchill. He still retained sufficient negative influence in these areas to obstruct their fulfillment. If he could pull off another diplomatic triumph in Poland, as he had at Munich, he might yet save the British Empire and salvage his own sagging political fortunes, due to expire within a year.[6] Parliamentary elections were on the horizon, and if he could defuse the Polish problem and avoid war, he could go to the electorate confidently for another five-year mandate.

As defense costs continued to rise, Chamberlain was driven more than ever to seek an accommodation with Germany, hoping to avoid further large-scale programs in the future and perhaps eliminate them altogether. During the final summer months of peace, numerous unofficial contacts were maintained with German sources in Chamberlain's obsessive quest for peace.[7] Hitler was enticed with offers of huge loans, colonial adjustments, trade, and treaty revision if he could somehow reestablish his credibility, not only with Chamberlain but with the British people as well. It was a tall order to fill, but was not ruled out by Chamberlain.[8] In July, secret meetings were held between Wilson-Hudson and Dr. Helmuth Wohlthat of the German Ministry for Economic Affairs, to discuss economic and colonial appeasement. The British Government was rumored to have offered Germany a £1 billion loan. Chamberlain disclaimed any responsibility for the talks. He told his sisters that Hudson was merely trying to advance his own career. He also admitted that Wilson did talk with Wohlthat but, incredibly, "none of these issues came up."[9] Despite Chamberlain's disclaimer, Wohlthat was given to understand that these talks had Chamberlain's approval.[10] Wohlthat met with Joseph Ball after these discussions. Why Ball should have been involved is another "unexplained mystery." He had no official standing in the Government. The only reason, of course, is that he was enlisted for his special and close relationship with Chamberlain.

Had Chamberlain been left undisturbed in the exercise of his powers in office, he might well have pursued the peace initiatives on his own, behind the back of the Foreign Office, as he had done on many occasions before. He wrote to his sister that "a way could be found of meeting German claims while safeguarding Poland's independence."[11] Presumably, Chamberlain was willing to concede German hegemony in Eastern Europe, where the Russians would be forced to deal with Hitler's aggression. But since Prague his authority and prestige had diminished substantially, and his ability to control foreign policy had been severely compromised. Nevertheless, it did not prevent him from trying to work around these difficulties. Unfortunately, but not surprisingly, these moves were interpreted in Berlin as a sign of British weakness, and encouraged Hitler to push his advantage to the limits. And, of course, as these initiatives were learned in Moscow, it spelled disaster for the faltering Anglo-Soviet talks.

An important corollary to the success of the latest appeasement initiatives was the exclusion of Churchill from the Cabinet. Count Schwerin, head of the English section of the Abwehr and known as one of Britain's best sources of information in Germany, advised British authorities to take Churchill into the Government because he is the "only Englishman Hitler is afraid of. He does not take the Prime Minister and Lord Halifax seriously."[12] Yet Chamberlain disregarded this very important piece of information because he felt that Churchill's presence in the Cabinet would be "uncommonly difficult to deal with,"[13] and would increase the chances for war. "If Winston got back into Government," he wrote, "it would not be long before we were at war."[14] Eden had been kept out as well, because Chamberlain "was not prepared, for the sake of. . .sham unity, to take as partners, men who would sooner or later wreck the thing with which [he was] identified."[15] Consequently, Eden's offer to go to Moscow in furtherance of the Anglo-Soviet talks in June was rejected by Chamberlain, and a low-level official, William Strang, was sent to replace the ailing Ambassador Seeds. Eden would have guaranteed the integrity of the talks, though not necessarily their success. But Chamberlain was determined to abort the talks, anyway, because they cut across his attempts to appease Hitler, and he did not need any more complications.

In July, Chamberlain tried to head off the groundswell of opinion developing against his policy. He called Lord Camrose of *The Telegraph* to explain why he could not take Churchill into the Cabinet, but was unsuccessful in convincing his one-time supporter, whom he now described as a "changed man" influenced by Randolph (Churchill).[16] But if Camrose was not convinced by Chamberlain's specious reasoning, neither was Chamberlain moved by the press, nor by the urgings of Hore-Belisha, Halifax, and other junior members to take Churchill into the Cabinet. Nor was he moved by public opinion polls, which showed an overwhelming preference for taking Churchill into the Government. Only Lord Kemsley's newspapers, *The Sunday Times* and *The Daily Sketch,* continued to support his policy. Approvingly, the German Ambassador, Dirksen, reported that "Chamberlain's personality gives a certain guarantee that British policy will not be delivered into the hands of unscrupulous adventurers," despite the efforts being made to reverse his policy.[17]

Under increasing fire from press and Parliamentary critics, and embarrassed by the disclosure of the Hudson-Wilson-Wohlthat talks in July, Chamberlain welcomed the August recess. But when he proposed to recess Parliament for two months, he was assailed by Attlee and Churchill in the strongest terms for fear of a second Munich. Their fears were not ungrounded. As the situation in Danzig appeared to be heading toward a *dénouement,* Chamberlain expressed confidence to his sisters that "a way could be found of meeting German claims while safeguarding Poland's independence." He also indicated that he would like to have another meeting with Hitler. But after Munich, he realized it just would not be possible.[18] He would have to have some tangible, good-faith evidence from Hitler to embark on that road again. Nevertheless, Chamberlain's optimism was fueled in part by a conversation with the League of Nations Commissioner for Danzig, who reported that Hitler would do nothing to provoke a conflict over Danzig.[19] Chamberlain focused on the forlorn hope that "Hitler had concluded that we mean business and that the time is not ripe for a major war. Therein he is fulfilling my expectations."[20] Therefore, the disagreeable business of negotiating a treaty with the Soviets need not be taken too seriously. It was tactically feasible now to accept the Soviet definition of indirect aggression and to proceed with military talks, knowing they would be inconclusive. Instructions were given to the military mission to "proceed with caution."[21]

These reckless decisions were taken in the full knowledge that Nazi-Soviet relations were warming up, and that the possibility of a *rapprochement* could not be ignored. Yet, Chamberlain continued to discount it,[22] and the military discussions floundered until they were suddenly broken off when the signing of the Nazi-Soviet Non-Aggression Pact was announced on 23 August. The encirclement of Poland was now complete. Britain could not possibly render military assistance to her beleaguered ally. Hitler felt that perhaps Britain (and France) would stand aside now.[23] He was obviously well informed of Britain's military preparations. He told his generals that England and France had undertaken obligations that neither was in a position to fulfill: "The construction program for the navy has not been fulfilled. . . .Little has been done on land. England will only be able to send a maximum of three divisions to the Continent. A little has been done for the air force, but it is only a beginning. At the moment, England has only one hundred and fifty anti-aircraft guns. . . .England does not want a conflict to break out for two or three years."[24]

If Hitler had counted on Chamberlain's dominance over the Government to cause Britain to abandon Poland, he was badly mistaken. The attitude of the Cabinet had changed dramatically since Prague, and moved more in step with public opinion than the strong-willed Prime Minister was willing to admit. Whatever reservations Chamberlain might have entertained about Britain's obligation to defend Poland, were severely compromised by the public outrage sparked by the unholy alliance between the two dictator states. On 25 August the Cabinet agreed to ratify the Mutual Assistance Pact with Poland, and the lines of battle were irrevocably drawn. Hitler was "shocked."[25] Britain was more committed than ever to defend Poland. A frantic last-ditch effort seeking a repetition of Munich failed, and a broken-hearted, dispirited Prime Minister took to the airwaves on 3 September to announce that his "long struggle to win peace had failed." To the House of Commons, mustering what little self-respect remained, he acknowledged that "Everything that I have worked for, everything that I hoped for, everything that I have believed in during my public life, has crashed into ruins."[26]

1. "Control of Expenditures," CP 118(39). The Cabinet has been warned of this problem earlier. Now it was too late [ed. note].

2. CP 149(39).

3. HB 1/5, 3 July 1939. Hore-Belisha must have seen or learned about CP 118 ahead of time, because it was not considered by the Cabinet until 5 July.

4. Ibid.

5. Bond, *British Military Policy*, 328.

6. NC 18/1/1111, 5 August 1939. Chamberlain expressed his confidence in winning re-election.

7. See Parker, *Chamberlain and Appeasement*, 260–271. Also, Aster, 244–258; E.W.D. Tennant. *True Account* (London: Parish, 1957).

8. NC 18/1/1096, 29 April 1939; NC 18/1/1107, 15 July 1939.

9. NC 18/1/1108, 23 July 1939. Later, after war had begun, Chamberlain tried to appoint Hudson as Minister of Economic Warfare, but Cadogan blocked the appointment. *Cadogan Diaries*, 4 September 1939, 213.

10. "Wohlthat Memorandum," DGFP, series D, vol. 6, #716, 24 July 1939.

11. NC 18/1/1107, 15 July 1939; Lamb, 119.

12. Gilbert, *Churchill*, 616.

13. NC 18/1/1111, 5 August 1939.

14. NC 18/1/1106, 8 July 1939.

15. NC 18/1/1072, 15 October 1938.

16. NC 18/1/1106, 8 July 1939.

17. DGFP, series D, vol.6, #645, 10 July 1939.

18. NC 18/1/1107, 15 July 1939.

19. CAB 23/100/39, 26 July 1939.

20. NC 18/1/1108, 23 July 1939.

21. CAB 23/100/39, 26 July 1939; *Ironside Diaries*, 77; also cf., Aster, ch. 11.

22. CAB 23/100/39, 26 July 1939.

23. CAB 23/100/43, 26 August 1939.

24. DGFP, series D, vol.7, #192, 22 August 1939, Hitler to the German Commanders-in-Chief.

25. CAB 23/100/45, 28 August 1939.

26. *Debates*, vol.351: 291-292, 3 September 1939.

Chapter 9

Conclusion

Britain's rearmament policy was shaped by two factors in the 1930s: the economic crisis of 1931 and the political challenge of Labor. The economic crisis was the immediate context in which that policy was formulated, but it was the challenge of Labor that sustained it. That Britain failed to rearm in a manner consistent with its international obligations in the 1930s was due largely to the baneful influence of Neville Chamberlain on the defense program. Without his commanding presence in the National Government, British defense (and hence foreign) policy would have taken a vastly different turn. Virtually every major figure in the defense establishment, except Chamberlain, advocated stronger defense measures. Articulate, well-prepared, but most of all persistent, he single-handedly confronted the Opposition with a brilliant display of bureaucratic legerdemain and political sophistry that enabled him to prevail over programs that contradicted his own.

Hiding behind a policy of non-interference with trade, Chamberlain was able to maintain a reasonably dispassionate, but principled, appearance of responsibility, collegiality, and statesmanship. He could claim to represent the national interest while continuing to limit the rearmament program. He could, for example, agree with Lord Swinton on the need to accelerate the air program, but in the same breath deny its feasibility because of its adverse impact on trade, without which it would be impossible to finance more rearmament, the fourth arm of defense. But this was a specious argument. As we have seen throughout this narrative, Chamberlain never really accepted the urgency of a timely and credible rearmament program,[1] preferring instead to rely on his furtive policy of appeasement to protect Britain's interests, however humiliating it might prove to be, under the mistaken assumption that it would only be temporary. But the Holland war scare unnerved the defense ministers (but not Chamberlain) and brought a halt to limited liability. And even if his appeasement efforts failed, Hitler's *Drang nach Osten* policy would divert the Nazi threat toward the Soviet

Union, giving Britain ample time to rearm.

The Polish declaration was a face-saving device for Chamberlain's personal policy, not an irrevocable line drawn in blood. He did not intend to go to war over Poland; nor was it just a bluff to persuade Hitler not to use force in furtherance of his policy. It was a part of a prejudicial anti-Soviet policy. We know that he was prepared to hand over colonial mandates, concede Germany's revisionist demands in Eastern Europe, and offer generous economic concessions in furtherance of his policy. We also know that he was in favor of a Japanese alliance, and under certain conditions, an alliance with Germany — but not with the Allies, because it would force him into a position of dependence on the United States.[2] Unwilling to pay the price of an alternative policy of vigorous rearmament, Chamberlain's defense policy emerges as a desirable goal, but not a critical one.

The most effective means by which Chamberlain assured acceptance of his program of limited liability was through the Treasury. More financial support could have been raised to accelerate Britain's defenses, but was not,[3] due to Chamberlain's personal preference. Had Chamberlain decided to use his talent and his office to rearm the country to the level necessary to protect Britain's vital interests, certain economic hardships would have to have been endured. More defense spending meant higher taxes, government controls over wages and prices, and a lower standard of living, but it also would have resulted in more employment opportunities for the 12 percent unemployed. However, no meaningful assessment of the labor requirements was ever considered.[4] Nor was it ever determined what impact more defense spending would have had on the economy; it was simply assumed to be detrimental. Peden has concluded that it would have been advantageous to do so during the 1937–1938 recession.[5] Hore-Belisha pointed out the potential benefits of an economic stimulus provided by the export of arms, which he calculated would last "a long time,"[6] but he was ignored by the obstinate Prime Minister, who showed no interest in programs or ideas that went against his own. P.K. Debenham, an official of the Economic Advisory Council, submitted a report in October 1938 that proposed to raise £400–500 million annually by:

a. putting the unemployed back to work in the export trades,
b. reducing consumer spending,
c. establishing exchange controls,
d. setting up export monopolies and export boards,
e. controlling domestic investments,
f. limiting dividends,
g. controlling new stock issues, and
h. setting price controls. [7]

Chamberlain dismissed the idea because it meant the legitimization of Labor's political agenda and more government controls over the economy, thereby turning Great Britain into a different kind of nation.[8] Instead, he chose to subordinate such ideas to his own formula for security, based on the logical but misguided assumption that war was a senseless enterprise in which there were no winners except international socialism which could be avoided by making timely concessions to Britain's enemies.

While it is true that the Exchequer was strapped for funds, it is equally true that the Government did not seriously address the financial question until 1937, three years into the rearmament program, and it was not until 1938 that talks with Labor were initiated; and even then, they were only superficial and cosmetic. Once again, it was Chamberlain's powerful voice that prevailed. When Sir Warren Fisher and Baldwin suggested borrowing for defense in 1935 and 1936, Chamberlain successfully refuted them with alarmist arguments supplied by Hopkins, Phillips, and Bridges at the Treasury. Borrowing was discouraged because of its purported inflationary impact on the economy, forcing up interest rates and prices, which in turn weakened Britain's ability to compete for world trade, thus hampering the Government's ability to meet the defense bill. Ultimately, taxes were considered to be the best method of raising money for the defense program by Chamberlain because they would not be inflationary, nor would they cause serious damage to the export trade. The argument was theoretically sound but belated and flawed in terms of the national interest. How much loss of trade, for example, would result if arms were increased by £10 million or £20 million or £100 million? Or might a five – or ten – or even twenty-year loan accomplish the purpose? No attempt was made to ascertain the tolerance level for such incremental and strategic borrowing practices, until Keynes, an adviser to the Treasury, made a case for more borrowing in 1939 — too late to materially affect the rearmament program.

The domestic economy would be affected most, but the effect could be offset by providing greater employment opportunities in the defense industries for the millions of the chronically unemployed. Yet, income tax rates increased only gradually until 1938, so as not to disturb public opinion. There may have been justifiable political reasons for holding the line on taxes up to 1935, but after the general election taxes were increased by only a modest 3d in 1936, another 3d in 1937, and 6d in 1938, at a time when considerable progress could have been made in financing increased productive capacity and in training the skilled labor known to be essential in the coming perilous years. The financial aspects of rearmament should not be minimized. The problem was formidable, but not insurmountable, given the sincere will to rearm. As Duff Cooper pointed out, financial problems can only lead to severe embarrassment and inconvenience, but the failure to rearm might result in the loss of the Empire.

Chamberlain's most serious attempt at rearmament financing, his £1.5 billion five-year program was far short of the mark, considering that Germany was believed to be spending almost £1 billion a year in 1937.[9] In the first place, the five-year plan was framed in terms of not interfering with trade, and not by what was considered to be adequate by the defense experts. And, second, it was predicated on the specious assumption that it was the maximum amount available for defense. But when the financial restraints imposed by Inskip's famous memorandum proved impossible to achieve after the Anschluss, the cap was lifted to £1.8 billion. And in 1939, after conscription passed, another £400 million for defense was found, causing Lord Chatfield to wonder where it came from, since he had been told that the Treasury was empty. Chamberlain's failure to provide the same kind of creative financial schemes that enabled him to meet the severe economic crisis of 1931 raises serious doubts about his motives. Many historians now believe the Treasury argument to be weak.[10]

Time and time again, as Government officials wrestled with defense problems, their ideas suffocated in the many committees where Treasury influence, invariably proved decisive in setting the rearmament agenda. These Treasury officials received their instructions from Chamberlain's hand-picked officials. Fisher, once one of the most influential men in the Government, found out, as did Vansittart and others, that failure to provide enthusiastic support for Chamberlain's programs led to isolation and a loss of influence. Fisher, much like the Economic Advisory Council, would have taxed the rich and luxuries more heavily, and would have cracked down on profiteers.[11] If Fisher would not "devil" for Chamberlain, then Chamberlain would look for others to do so. Bridges, Hopkins, and Phillips readily filled that role at the Treasury, and Simon eagerly grasped it as Chamberlain's successor at the Exchequer. Later in 1938, Bridges was rewarded for his loyalty by replacing Sir Maurice Hankey as Cabinet Secretary when Hankey, who had often disagreed with Chamberlain over the need for a larger Continental army, was forced into a short-lived retirement.

To avoid giving the impression that he was skimping on defense, Chamberlain frequently adduced other reasons for not rearming the country in a timely manner. Manpower, industrial capacity, skilled labor, and politics were alternately cited, often allowing him to override the advice of the military and technical experts in the defense program. These arguments should not be taken at face value. Postan claimed that industrial capacity, not finance, became the major obstacle to air rearmament by early 1938.[12] And the Government's official historian, Paul Inman, concluded that the labor supply position was "relatively satisfactory" up to the outbreak of war.[13] As has been noted, manpower studies indicated the existence of an adequate supply. Industrial capacity was there but was not being utilized. More shadow factories could have been designated and more shifts could have been added without impinging on the existing physical facilities too severely between 1936 and 1938. Skilled labor presented a problem, to be sure, but it could have been secured with the cooperation of the trade unions. Union support was needed for training more apprentices (but the unions first wanted to find employment for thousands of their members still out of work), for relaxation of rules in the workshop defining skilled labor (dilution), and for acceptance of women into union programs. But the political ramifications of including labor in the defense program precluded the outsourcing of skilled labor. And in that sense, skilled labor continued to be a limiting factor in the defense program sense, not its procurement.[14]

Hankey, a strong opponent of socialism, and the Minister of Labor, Brown, urged that timely steps be taken to address the industrial question in preference to "late-in-the-day measures," but were ignored. When weighed against the perceived danger from abroad, it is difficult to defend Chamberlain's half-hearted attempts to secure this important component of the defense program, especially since many other prominent Conservatives, including Weir, Halifax, and Baldwin, were willing to place the social question in its proper context.

Invariably, as the service ministers beginning with Swinton, challenged these assumptions, Chamberlain fell back on the Treasury argument, for which Simon proved to be his most loyal and consistent supporter in the Cabinet. Only after Munich, when the realization of war hit home with such force, did Chamberlain's hold on the Government begin to relax as one minister after another began to doubt the wisdom of the Prime Minister's policy. Spurred on by an angry and vociferous public opinion, Halifax, an inveterate appeaser, balked at the Godesberg terms. Inskip followed several months later, abandoning his objections to a Ministry of Supply during the Holland war scare, and had to be replaced. Hoare reversed field and became a proponent of an Anglo-Soviet alliance in 1939, while Hore-Belisha pushed on for conscription.

Undeterred by the Holland war scare, Prague, or even Albania, Chamberlain persisted in his double policy. Reluctantly he accepted conscription and a Ministry of Supply, but he was careful to limit and delay their implementation, hoping to obviate those measures by continuing his efforts to reach a *modus vivendi* with Germany.[15] As Chamberlain's ability to control the Government by the sheer force of his personality waned, he resorted to more subterfuge and secretive diplomacy, going outside the normal government channels. Wilson, Henderson, Ball, and others were used as Chamberlain stepped up his efforts to appease Hitler. For that reason the Soviet alliance had to be resisted, Churchill and Eden and the United States kept on sidelines, and the Parliamentary Opposition silenced.

To say, as many historians have said, that Chamberlain was somehow responding to Treasury concerns, or to Conservative Party pressure, is to ignore a significant body of evidence to the contrary. Chamberlain defined the Conservative Party in the 1930s, not the other way around. He reorganized the Conservative Party Central Office into a comprehensive, coherent bureau for the development, distribution, and discussion of party goals. Conservative ministers sought guidance from the Research Bureau for new programs and debating points. Abandonment of his NDC tax on businesses in 1937, often cited as an example of Chamberlain's subservience to the Conservative Party, demonstrates his dominance over the party. That Chamberlain, an astute politician, felt confident enough to ignore the Bank of England's warning to drop the tax and go against the employers in what he termed "the bravest thing he had ever done in politics," speaks volumes about his character and *modus operandi*. He would not be deterred from a course of action once he decided on its merits. The same consideration applied to his defense and appeasement policy. Once he had embarked on that course, he would not be deterred unless compelled by circumstances beyond his control to do so. Even then, he would pursue his objective by other means if he thought he could manage it. He wrote to his sister, "The only thing I care about is to be able to carry out the policy I believe, indeed, know to be right, and the only distress that criticism or obstruction can cause me is if it prevents my purpose."[16]

Had Chamberlain been intimidated or influenced by his Conservative Party constituency, he would not have been able to deny the widespread demand for greater rearmament measures, or for an end to appeasement after the Munich crisis. But neither the back-bench members of Parliament, the Parliamentary Opposition, nor the press ever made any significant impression on Chamberlain's Government. This is not to say that Chamberlain was immune to outside pressure, whether it came from party, press, Treasury, or abroad. The only effect of such pressure was to alter his style, not his policy. One cannot ignore the consistent and strenuous efforts made by Chamberlain to accomplish *his* purpose of resisting the Labor Party, which he perceived to be founded on the narrow grounds of selfish class interest and not on the national interest.

Chamberlain carefully weighed the costs of increasing armaments and forming alliances against his own double policy of gradual rearmament and appeasement. He ultimately decided against those measures because the consequences of adopting such measures, as conscription and a Ministry of Supply, were considered to be much more detrimental to the national interest than appeasement and limited liability, since they were more fundamental and more far-reaching than the temporary threat of German revisionism. Therefore, the urgency of rearming did not assume the critical importance for Chamberlain that it did for other members of the Government. And, just as World War I had resulted in the establishment of socialism in one country, so World War II must inevitably lead to the socialization of all of Europe. Consequently, active war, as well as a prolonged cold war, had to be avoided at all costs. It was a risk worth taking in his scheme of things.[17] Even if Germany was able to establish hegemony in Eastern Europe, it was not altogether certain that she would then use that leverage against Western Europe. She would first have to contend with the Soviet Union, giving Britain more time to rearm. Nor did the prospect of a Nazi-Soviet *rapprochement* cause Chamberlain to shed his bias against the Soviet Union. He believed that Hitler's hatred for Bolshevism was at least as strong as his own, and that an alliance between the two countries would never materialize. Given the choice between Hitler and Labor, Chamberlain chose the former. Schmidt was indeed correct in portraying appeasement "as a crisis strategy essentially determined by domestic policy."[18]

Without Chamberlain, then, there would have been no Munich. Without Chamberlain, more guns, tanks, planes, and factories would suddenly have appeared, and considerable moral and diplomatic support might have been received from potential allies, such as the Soviet Union and the United States. Whether these measures would have restrained Hitler's revisionist demands is outside the parameters of this study, and can only be surmised. But, given the opposition of the German generals to Hitler's risky foreign policy,[19] the likelihood of a coup cannot be discounted. At any rate, the outcome could not have been worse than Chamberlain's ill-fated double policy of gradual rearmament and appeasement.[20] At best, World War II might have been averted.[21]

NOTES

1. Feiling, 387; Cross, *Swinton*, 600.

2. Kennedy, "British Net Assessment and the Coming of the Second World War," in Murray and Millett, *Calculations,* 41.

3. Peden, *British Rearmament and the Treasury*, 104–105 and 129; 180–184; Middlemas, *Diplomacy*, 124–127.

4. Parker, *Manpower*, 39.

5. Peden, *British Rearmament*, 179–180.

6. CAB 23/93/24, 18 May 1938.

7. CAB 24/270/165

8. CAB 23/93/18, 6 April 1938. Shay, 287–288.

9. NC 2/23, 2 August 1935.

10. Cf. Bond, 249; Middlemas, 124–127; Peden, 180–184; Reader, 246; and Parker, *Chamberlain and Appeasement*, 274.

11. Shay, 246.

12. Postan, 21.

13. Inman, *Labor in the Munitions Industries*, 35.

14. Parker, *Chamberlain and Appeasement*, 283–284.

15. NC 18/1/1116, 10 September 1939.

16. NC 18/1/1078, 4 December 1938.

17. Newton, 86.

18. Schmidt, 388.

19. Lukes, 209; Esmonde Robertson, *Hitler's Pre-War Policy and Military Plans, 1933–1939* (New York: Longmans, 1963), 79 and 108.

20. Murray, *The Change in the European Balance of Power*, 181.

21. Parker, *Chamberlain and Appeasement*, 347.

Bibliography

OFFICIAL DOCUMENTS AND UNPUBLISHED COLLECTIONS

House of Commons Debates, 5th series, London: HMSO.

Documents on British Foreign Policy, 1919-1939, E. L. Woodward and Rohan Butler, eds. 2nd and 3rd series, London: HMSO.

Documents on German Foreign Policy, Raymond Sontag and James Beddie, eds. Series C and D, Washington, D.C.: U.S. Government Printing Office.

Public Records Office, London: HMSO.

    CAB 23 – Cabinet minutes

    CAB 24 – Cabinet memoranda

    CAB 27 – Foreign Policy Committee

    CAB 57 – Ministry of Labor memoranda

    PREM – Prime Minister's correspondence

Neville Chamberlain Papers (Birmingham University)

    NC 2/23–24 Diary

    NC7/ – Chamberlain's correspondence

    NC 17/ – letters to Chamberlain

    NC 18/1/ – Chamberlain to his sisters Hilda and Ida

    NC 18/2/ – Hilda and Ida to Chamberlain

Lord Weir Papers (Churchill College, Cambridge)

Hore-Belisha Papers HB (Churchill College, Cambridge)

Sir Thomas Inskip Diary (Churchill College, Cambridge)

Sir Maurice Hankey Papers (Churchill College, Cambridge)

David Margesson Papers (Churchill College, Cambridge)

PUBLISHED MEMOIRS AND DIARIES

Amery, Leo. *My Political Life.* Vol. 3. London: Hutchinson, 1953.

Attlee, Clement. *As It Happened.* London: Heinemann, 1954.

Avon, Earl of (Anthony Eden). *Facing the Dictators.* Boston: Houghton-Mifflin, 1962.

Bond, Brian, ed. *Lt. General Henry Pownall Diaries.* Vol.1, 1933–1940, London: L. Cooper, 1972.

Chamberlain, Neville. *In Search of Peace.* New York: Putnam, 1939.

Chatfield, Lord. *It Might Happen Again*. London: Heinemann, 1947.

Citrine, Walter. *Men and Work*. London: Hutchinson, 1964.

Cooper, Alfred Duff. *Old Men Forget*. New York: Dutton, 1954.

Dalton, Hugh. *The Fateful Years*. London: Muller, 1957.

Dilks, David, ed. *The Diaries of Sir Alexander Cadogan, 1938–1945*. New York: Putnam, 1972.

Gibson, Hugh, ed. *The Ciano Diaries*, 1939–1943. New York: Doubleday, 1946.

Grigg, P.J. *Prejudice and Judgement*. London: Jonathan Cape, 1948.

Halifax, Lord. *In Fullness of Days*. London: Collins, 1957.

Harvey, John, ed. *The Diplomatic Diaries of Oliver Harvey, 1937–1940*. London: Collins, 1970.

Henderson, Nevile. *Failure of a Mission*. New York: Putnam, 1940.

Home, Alec Douglas. *The Way the Wind Blows*. New York: Quadrangle, 1976.

James, Robert Rhodes. *Winston S. Churchill: His Complete Speeches*. London: Chelsea House, 1974.

James, Robert Rhodes, ed. *Chips: The Diaries of Sir Henry Channon*. London: Weidenfeld and Nicolson, 1967.

Jones, Thomas. *A Diary with Letters, 1931–1950*. Oxford: Oxford University Press, 1954.

Kirkpatrick, Ivone. *The Inner Circle*. London: Macmillan, 1959.

Liddell-Hart, Basil. *Memoirs*. London: Cassell, 1965.

MacLeod, Roderick and Kelly, Dennis, eds. *The Ironside Diaries, 1937–1940*. London: Constable, 1962.

Macmillan, Harold. *Winds of Change, 1914–1939*. London: Macmillan,1961.

Nicolson, Nigel, ed. *Diaries and Letters of Sir Harold Nicolson*. London: Collins, 1966.

Percy, Eustace. *Some Memories*. London: Eyre and Spotswood, 1958

Reith J. W. *Into the Wind*. London: Hodder and Stoughton, 1949.

Self, Robert, ed. *The Austen Chamberlain Diary Letters, 1916–1937*. London: Cambridge University Press, 1995.

Simon, Viscount John. *Retrospect*. London: Hutchinson, 1952.

Strang, William. *At Home and Abroad*. London: Andre Deutsche, 1956.

Swinton, Earl of. *I Remember*. London: Hutchinson, 1952.

Templewood, Viscount (Sir Samuel Hoare). *Nine Troubled Years*. London: Collins, 1954.

Tennant, E.W.D. *True Account*. London: Parish, 1957.

Vansittart, Lord Robert. *The Mist Procession*. London: Hutchinson, 1958.

Wilson, Sir Arnold. *Walks and Talks Abroad*. London: Oxford University Press, 1936.

SECONDARY WORKS

Adams, R.J.Q., and Poirier, Phillip. *The Conscription Controversy in Great Britain, 1900–1918*. Columbus: Ohio State University Press, 1987.

Addison, Paul. *The Road to 1945*. London: Jonathan Cape, 1975.

Adorno, Theodore W., et al. *The Authoritarian Personality*. New York: Harper, 1950.

Andrews, Christopher. *Secret Service: The Making of the British Intelligence Community*. New York: Viking Press, 1985.

Ashworth, William. *An Economic History of England, 1870–1939*. London: Methuen, 1960.

Aster, Sidney. *1939: The Making of the Second World War*. New York: Simon and Schuster, 1973.

Barnett, Corelli. *The Audit of War*. London: Macmillan, 1986.

Bell, Peter. *Chamberlain, Germany and Japan, 1933–1934*. London: Macmillan, 1996.

Bell, P.M.H., ed. *The Origins of the Second World War in Europe*. New York: Longmans, 2nd ed., 1997.

Belof, Max. *The Foreign Policy of Soviet Russia, 1929–1941*. Vol. 2. Oxford: Oxford University Press, 1947.

Bethell, Nicholas. *The War Hitler Won*. New York: Holt, 1972.

Bialor, Uri. *The Shadow of the Bomber: Fear of Air Attack and British Politics, 1932–1939*. London: Royal Historical Society, 1980.

Birkenhead, Lord. *The Life of Lord Halifax*. London: Hamish Hamilton, 1965.

Bond, Brian. *British Military Policy Between the Wars*. Oxford: Clarendon Press, 1980.

Boyce, Robert, and Robertson, Esmonde, eds. *Paths to War*. New York: St. Martin's Press, 1989.

Bullock, Alan. *The Life and Times of Ernest Bevin*. Vol.1. London: Heinemann, 1960.

Burridge, Trevor. *Clement Attlee*. London: Jonathan Cape, 1985.

Cato. *Guilty Men*. New York: Frederick Stokes, 1940.

Charmley, John. *Chamberlain and the Lost Peace*. London: Hodder and Stoughton, 1989.

Charmley, John. *Churchill: The End of Glory*. New York: Harcourt, Brace, 1993.

Churchill, Randolph. *The Rise and Fall of Sir Anthony Eden*. New York: Putnam, 1959.

Churchill, Winston. *The Gathering Storm*. Boston: Houghton-Mifflin, 1948.

Cockett, Richard. *Twilight of Truth: Chamberlain, Appeasement and the Manipulation of the Press*. New York: St. Martin's Press, 1989.

Colville, John. *The Fringes of Power*. New York: Norton, 1985.

Colvin, Ian. *The Chamberlain Cabinet*. New York: Taplinger, 1971.

Cowling, Maurice. *The Impact of Hitler*. Cambridge: Cambridge University Press, 1975.

Cowling, Maurice. *The Impact of Labour, 1920–1924*. London: Cambridge University Press, 1971.

Cowman, Ian. *Dominion or Decline: Anglo-American Relations, 1937–1941*. Oxford: Berg, 1996.

Cross, J. A. *Lord Swinton*. Oxford: Oxford University Press, 1982.

Cross, J. A. *Sir Samuel Hoare*. London: Jonathan Cape, 1977.

Daalder, Hans. *Cabinet Reform in Britain, 1914–1963*. Stanford, Ca: Stanford University Press, 1963.

Dahlerus, Birger. *The Last Attempt*. Trans. Alexandra Dick, London: Hutchinson, 1947.

Deist, Wilhelm, et al. *Germany and the Second World War: The Build-up of German Aggression*. Trans. P.S. Falla, et al. Research Institute for Military History, London: Oxford University Press, 1990.

Dennis, Peter. *Decision by Default*. Durham: Duke University Press, 1972.

Dilks, David. *Neville Chamberlain, 1869–1929*. Cambridge: Cambridge University Press, 1984.

Dutton, D. *Simon*. London: Aurum Press, 1992.

Eubank, Keith. *Munich*. Norman: University of Oklahoma Press, 1963.

Eubank, Keith. *World War II: Roots and Causes*. Lexington: D. C. Heath, 1992.

Farr, Barbara. *The Development and Impact of Right Wing Politics in Britain, 1903–33*. New York: Garland, 1987.

Feiling, Keith. *The Life of Neville Chamberlain*. London: Macmillan, 1946.

Fuscher, Larry. *Neville Chamberlain and Appeasement: A Study in the Politics of History*. New York: Harper, 1982.

Gallup, G.H., ed. *Gallup International Public Opinion Polls. Great Britain, 1937–1975*. Vol.1, New York: Random House, 1976.

Gannon, Frank. *The British Press and Nazi Germany*. Oxford: Clarendon, 1971.

George, Margaret. *The Warped Vision*. Pittsburgh: University of Pittsburgh Press, 1965.

Gibbs, Norman. *Rearmament*. London: HMSO, 1976.

Gilbert, Martin. *Churchill: A Life*. New York: Holt, 1991.

Gilbert, Martin. *Roots of Appeasement*. London: Weidenfeld and Nicolson, 1966.

Gilbert, Martin. *Winston S. Churchill*. Vol. 5, Boston: Houghton-Mifflin, 1976.

Gilbert, Martin and Gott, Richard. *The Appeasers*. Boston: Houghton-Mifflin, 1963.

Glynn, Sean and Oxborrow, John. *Inter-war Britain: A Social and Economic History*. New York: Harper and Row, 1976.

Gordon, G.A.H. *British Seapower and Procurement Between the Wars: A Reappraisal of Rearmament*. Annapolis: Naval Institute, 1988.

Graebner, Norman. *America as a World Power*. Wilmington: Scholarly Resources, 1984.

Graves, Robert and Hodge, Alan. *The Long Week-end: A Social History of Great Britain, 1918–1939*. London: Faber, 1940.

Griffiths, Richard. *Fellow Travelers of the Right*. London: Constable, 1980.

Gulley, Elsie. *Joseph Chamberlain and English Social Politics*. New York: Octagon Books, 1974.

Harris, Kenneth. *Attlee*. London: Weidenfeld and Nicolson, 1982.

Havigurst, Alfred. *Britain in Transition*. Chicago: University of Chicago Press, 1985.

Haxey, Simon. *England's Money Lords*. New York: Harrison-Hilton, 1939.

Herman, John. *The Paris Embassy of Sir Eric Phipps: Anglo-French Relations and the Foreign Office, 1937–1939*. Brighton: Sussex Academic Press, 1998.

Hill, Christopher. *Cabinet Decisions on Foreign Policy: The British Experience, October 1938–June 1941*. Cambridge: Cambridge University Press, 1991.

Hinsley, F.H. *British Intelligence in the Second World War*. Vol.1, London: H.M.S.O., 1979.

Howard, Michael. *The Continental Commitment*. London: Temple Smith, 1972.

Hyde, H. Montgomery. *Neville Chamberlain*. London: Weidenfeld and Nicolson, 1976.

Inman, Paul. *Labour in the Munitions Industries*. London: HMSO, 1952.

Irving, David, ed. *Breach of Security*. London: Kimber, 1968.

James, Robert Rhodes. *Churchill: A Study in Failure*. London: Weidenfeld and

Nicolson, 1970.

James, Robert Rhodes. *Anthony Eden.* London: Weidenfeld and Nicolson, 1986.

Johnson, Franklyn. *Defence by Committee: The British Committee of Imperial Defence, 1885–1959.* Oxford: Oxford University Press, 1960.

Jones, Neville. *The Beginnings of Strategic Air Power.* London: Frank Cass, 1987.

Kaiser, David. *Economic Diplomacy and the Origin of the Second World War.* Princeton: Princeton University Press, 1980.

Kennedy, John. *Why England Slept.* New York: Wilfred Funk, 1940.

Koss, Stephen. *The Rise and Fall of the Political Press in Britain.* Vol. 2, Chapel Hill: University of North Carolina Press, 1984.

Kyba, Patrick. *Covenants Without the Sword: Public Opinion and British Defence Policy, 1931–1935.* Waterloo, Canada: Wilfred Laurier University Press,1983.

Lamb, Richard. *The Ghosts of Peace.* London: Michael Russell, 1987.

Laybourn, Keith. *The Rise of Labour.* Huddersfield: The Polytechnic, 1988.

Lenman, Bruce. *The Eclipse of Parliament: Appearance and Reality in British Politics Since 1914.* London: Edward Arnold, 1992.

Liddell-Hart, Basil. *The Defence of Britain.* New York: Random House, 1939.

Liddell-Hart, Basil. *The German Generals Talk.* New York: Morrow, 1948.

Lukes, Igor. *Czechoslovakia Between Hitler and Stalin: The Diplomacy of Edward Benes in the 1930s.* New York: Oxford University Press, 1996.

MacDonald, C.A. *The United States, Britain and Appeasement.* New York: St. Martin's Press, 1981.

MacLeod, Ian. *Neville Chamberlain.* London: Muller, 1961.

Maisky, Ivan. *Who Helped Hitler?* Trans. Andrew Rothstein. London: Hutchinson 1964.

Margach, James. *The Abuse of Power.* London: W. H. Allen, 1978.

Martel, Gordon, ed. *The Origins of the Second World War Reconsidered.* London: Unwin Hyman, 1986.

Marwick, Arthur. *Britain in the Century of Total War.* Boston: Little, Brown and Co.,1968.

McKercher, B.J.C. *Transition of Power: Britain's Loss of Global Pre-eminence to the United States,1930–1945.* Cambridge: Cambridge University Press, 1999.

Middlemas, Keith. *Diplomacy of Illusion.* London: Weidenfeld and Nicolson, 1972.

Middlemas, Keith. *Politics in Industrial Society.* London: Deutsche, 1979.

Middlemas, Keith and Barnes, John. *Baldwin.* London: Weidenfeld and Nicolson 1969.

Minney, R.J. *The Private Papers of Hore-Belisha.* London: Collins, 1960.

Mommsen, Wolfgang and Kittenacker, Lothar, eds. *The Fascist Challenge and the Policy of Appeasement.* London: Allen and Unwin, 1983.

Morris, Benny. *The Roots of Appeasement: The British Weekly Press and Nazi Germany During the 1930s.* Portland, Oregon: Frank Cass, 1991.

Mowat, Charles. *Britain Between the Wars.* Chicago: University of Chicago Press, 1955.

Murray, Williamson. *The Change in the European Balance of Power, 1938–1939.* Princeton: Princeton University Press, 1984.

Murray, Williamson and Millett, Allan, eds. *Calculations: Net Assessment and the*

Coming of World War II. New York: Free Press, 1992.

Namier, Sir Lewis. *Europe in Decay: A Study in Disintegration, 1936–1940*. London: Macmillan, 1950.

Naylor, John. *Labour's International Policy: The Labour Party in the 1930s*. London: Weidenfeld and Nicolson, 1969.

Naylor, John. *Hankey: A Man and an Institution*. Cambridge: Cambridge University Press, 1984.

Newton, Scott. *Profits of Peace: The Political Economy of Anglo-German Appeasement*. Oxford: Clarendon Press, 1996.

Offner, Arnold. *American Appeasement: United States Foreign Policy and Germany, 1933–1938*. Boston: Harvard University Press, 1969.

Parker, H.M.D. *Manpower*. London: H.M.S.O., 1957.

Parker, R.A.C. *Chamberlain and Appeasement*. New York: St. Martin's Press, 1993.

Parkinson, Roger. *Peace for Our Time*. London: Rupert Hart-Davis, 1971.

Peden, George. *British Rearmament and the Treasury* . Edinburgh: Scottish Academic Press, 1980.

Peden, George. *British Economic and Social Policy*. Oxford: Philip Alan, 1985.

Pimlott, Ben. *Labour and the Left in the 1930s*. Cambridge: Cambridge University Press, 1977.

Pimlott, Ben. *Hugh Dalton*. London: Jonathan Cape, 1985.

Ponting, Clive. *1940: Myth and Reality*. Chicago: Ivan Dee, 1990.

Post, Gaines. *Dilemmas of Appeasement: British Deterrence and Defence, 1934-1937*. Ithaca: Cornell University Press, 1993.

Postan, M. M. *British War Production*. London: H.M.S.O., 1952.

Price, Richard. *Labour in British Policy*. London: Routledge, 1986.

Pyper, C.B. *Chamberlain and His Critics*. Toronto: The Pyerson Press, 1962.

Radzinzky, Edward. *Stalin*. New York: Doubleday, 1996.

Ramsden, John. *The Making of Conservative Party Policy*. New York: Longmans, 1980.

Reader, William J. *Lord Weir: Architect of Air Power*. London: Collins, 1968.

Richardson, H. W. *The Economic Recovery of Britain*. London: Weidenfeld and Nicolson, 1967.

Robbins, Keith. *Munich 1938*. London: Cassell, 1968.

Robbins, Keith. *Appeasement*. 2nd edition, Oxford: Blackwell, 1997.

Roberts, Andrew. *The Holy Fox: A Biography of Lord Halifax*. London: Weidenfeld and Nicolson, 1991.

Robertson, E.M. *Hitler's Pre-War Policy and Military Plans*. New York: Citadel Press, 1963.

Robertson, Scot. *The Development of RAF Strategic Bombing Doctrine, 1919-1939*. Westport, Connecticut: Praeger, 1995.

Rock, William. *British Appeasement in the 1930s*. New York: Norton, 1977.

Rock, William. *Chamberlain and Roosevelt, 1937–1940*. Columbus: Ohio State University Press, 1988.

Rose, Norman. *Vansittart: Study of a Diplomat*. New York: Holmes and Meier, 1978.

Roskill, Stephen. *Hankey: Man of Secrets*. Vol. 3, London: Collins, 1974.

Rowland, Peter. *David Lloyd George*. New York: Macmillan, 1975.

Rowse, Alfred L. *Appeasement: A Study in Political Decline*. New York: Norton, 1961.

Salter, Arthur. *Personality in Politics: Studies of Contemporary Statesmen.* London: Faber and Faber, 1947.

Schmidt, Gustav. *The Politics and Economics of Appeasement: British Foreign Policy in the 1930s.* Trans. by Jackie Bennet-Rirete. New York: St. Martin's Press, 1986.

Shay, Robert. *British Rearmament in the Thirties.* Princeton: Princeton University Press, 1977.

Shepherd, Robert. *A Class Divided.* London: Macmillan, 1988.

Stannage, Tom. *Baldwin Thwarts the Opposition.* London: Croom Helm, 1980.

Taylor, A.J.P. *The Origins of the Second World War.* New York: Atheneum, 1962.

Taylor, A.J.P. *English History, 1914-1945.* Oxford: Oxford University Press, 1965.

Taylor, A.J.P. *Lloyd George: Twelve Essays.* London: Hamish Hamilton, 1971.

Taylor, Telford. *Munich: The Price of Peace.* New York: Vintage Books, 1980.

Thane, Pat, ed. *The Origins of British Social Policy.* New Jersey: Rowan and Littlefield, 1978.

Thomas, Martin. *Britain, France, and Appeasement: Anglo-French Relations in the Popular Front Era.* New York: Oxford, 1996.

Thompson, Neville. *The Anti-Appeasers.* Oxford: Clarendon, 1971.

Thorne, Christopher. *The Approach of War, 1938-1939.* London: Macmillan,1968.

Thorpe, Andrew. *Britain in the 1930s.* Oxford: Blackwell, 1992.

Trotter, Ann. *Britain and East Asia, 1933-1937.* London: Cambridge University Press, 1975.

Waley, D. *British Public Opinion and the Abyssinian War.* London: Maurice Temple Smith, 1975.

Wark, Wesley. *The Ultimate Enemy: British Intelligence and Nazi Germany, 1933-1939.* London: Tauris, 1985.

Watkins, K. W. *Britain Divided: The Effect of the Spanish Civil War on British Public Opinion.* London: Thomas Nelson, 1963.

Watt, D.C. *Personalities and Policy: Studies in the Formulation of British Foreign Policy in the Twentieth Century.* London: Longmans, 1965.

Watt, D.C. *How the War Came: The Immediate Origins of the Second World War, 1933-1938.* London: Heinemann, 1989.

Watt, D. C. *Too Serious a Business.* New York: Norton, 1975.

Webber, G. C. *The Ideology of the British Right, 1918-1939.* New York: St. Martin's Press, 1986.

West, W. J. *Truth Betrayed.* London: Duckworth, 1987.

Wheeler-Bennett, John. *Munich: Prologue to Tragedy.* New York: Duell, Sloane and Pearce, 1948.

Wicks, Ben. *No Time to Wave Goodbye.* New York: St. Martin's Press, 1988.

Wicks, Ben. *The Day They Took the Children.* Toronto: Stoddart, 1989.

Wrench, John Evelyn. *Geoffrey Dawson and Our Times.* London: Hutchinson, 1955.

Young, G. M. *Baldwin.* London: Rupert Hart-Davis, 1952.

ARTICLES

Booth, Alan. "Britain in the 1930s: A Managed Economy?" *Economic History Review* 2nd series. 40 no.4, (1987): 499–522.

Cockett, Richard. "Communication: Ball, Chamberlain and Truth,"*The*

Historical Journal 33, no. 1, (1990): 131–142.

Coghlan, F. "Armaments, Economic Policy and Appeasement: Background to British Foreign Policy, 1931–37." *History* 57, (1972): 171–180.

Dilks, David. "Appeasement Revisited." *University of Leeds Review* 15 (1972): 28–56.

Dunbabin, J.P.D. "British Rearmament in the 1930s: A Chronology and Review." *Historical Journal* 18 (1975): 587–609.

Eatwell, Roger. "Munich, Public Opinion, and Popular Front." *Journal of Contemporary History* 6 (1971): 122–139.

Kennedy, Paul. "Appeasement and British Defence Policy in the Interwar Years." *British Journal of International Studies* 4 (1978): 161–177.

Manne, Robert. "The British Decision for Alliance with Russia, May, 1939." *Journal of Contemporary History* 16 (1981): 501–512.

Parker, R.A.C. "British Rearmament, 1936–1939: Treasury, Trade Unions and Skilled Labour." *English Historical Review* 96 (1981): 306–343.

Parker, R.A.C. "The Pound Sterling, the American Treasury and British Preparations for War, 1938–1939." *English Historical Review* 98 (1983): 261–279.

Peden, G. C. "Sir Warren Fisher and British Rearmament Against Germany." *English Historical Review* 94 (1979): 29–47.

Peden, G. C. "Sir Richard Hopkins and the Keynesian Revolution in Employment Policy, 1929–1945." *Economic History Review* 2nd series, 36 (1983):281–296.

Prazmowska, Anita. "The Eastern Front and the British Guarantee to Poland of March 1939." *European History Quarterly* 14 (1984): 183–209.

Thomas, M. "Rearmament and Economic Recovery in the Late 1930s." *Economic History Review*, 2nd Series, 36 (1983): 552–579.

Trevor-Roper, Hugh. "Neville Chamberlain Remembered." *New York Times Magazine* August 1948.

Watt, D.C. "Appeasement: The Rise of a Revisionist School?" *Political Quarterly* 36 (1965): 191–213.

Watt, D.C. "Was the Committee of Imperial Defence a Failure?" *Political Quarterly*, 46 (1975): 83–87.

Watt, D.C. "Misinformation, Misconception, Mistrust: Episodes in British Policy and the Approach of War, 1938–39." In Bentley and Stevenson, eds. *High and Low Politics in Modern Britain*. Oxford: Oxford University Press, 1983.

Index

About the Author

JOHN RUGGIERO is Associate Professor of History at St. Francis College in Loretto, Pennsylvania.

ISBN 0-313-31050-5

90000>

9 780313 310508

EAN

HARDCOVER BAR CODE